Ask Me Now

Ask
Me
Now

CONVERSATIONS ON JAZZ & LITERATURE

Edited
by
Sascha
Feinstein

INDIANA

UNIVERSITY

PRESS

Bloomington & Indianapolis

This book is a publication of

Indiana University Press
601 North Morton Street
Bloomington, IN 47404-3797 USA

http://iupress.indiana.edu

Telephone orders   800-842-6796
Fax orders   812-855-7931
Orders by e-mail   iuporder@indiana.edu

Library of Congress Cataloging-in-Publication
Data

Ask me now : conversations on jazz & literature /
edited by Sascha Feinstein.
    p.   cm.
  Includes index.
  ISBN 978-0-253-34951-4 (cl) — ISBN
978-0-253-21876-6 (pbk) 1. Jazz—Interviews.
2. Jazz in literature—Interviews. I. Feinstein,
Sascha, date
  ML3506.A76 2007
  781.65—dc22
                              2007002128

1 2 3 4 5   12 11 10 09 08 07

for Jon Bogle & Deb Caulkins

I would trade everything I've written if I
could play the saxophone the way I want to.
ROBERT PINSKY

"Howl" is all "Lester Leaps In."
ALLEN GINSBERG

Contents

Introduction xi

1. *Amiri Baraka* / Better You Say It First — 1
2. *Hayden Carruth* / Those Upward Leaps — 25
3. *Jayne Cortez* / Returning to Go Someplace Else — 43
4. *Bill Crow* / Just a Matter of Time — 59
5. *Cornelius Eady* / Did Your Mama Hear Those Poems? — 81
6. *Gary Giddins* / Legwork — 101
7. *Lee Meitzen Grue* / The House as Open Ground — 129
8. *Fred Hersch* / Respiration and Inspiration — 151
9. *David Jauss* / Stolen Moments — 171
10. *Yusef Komunyakaa* / Survival Masks — 191
11. *Philip Levine* / Detroit Jazz in the Late Forties and Early Fifties — 213
12. *Haki R. Madhubuti* / Where the Call Needs to Be Heard — 231
13. *William Matthews* / Mingus at the Showplace — 253
14. *Dan Morgenstern* / Consideration — 269
15. *Hank O'Neal* / The Greatest Equalizer in the World — 295
16. *Eugene B. Redmond* / Levels of the Blues — 317
17. *Sonia Sanchez* / Cante Jondo — 339
18. *John Sinclair* / Ask Me Now — 371
19. *Al Young* / Makes Me Feel Like I Got Some Money — 401
20. *Paul Zimmer* / Something to Believe In — 417

Acknowledgments 433
Index 437

INTRODUCTION

The conversations in this collection first appeared in *Brilliant Corners: A Journal of Jazz & Literature,* which I founded in 1996. Prior to the first issue, I had relatively little experience running a national literary journal, but I knew two important things: first, that the world certainly did not need another generic magazine, and second, that a journal of jazz-related literature—poetry, fiction, and nonfiction—could not only be of service but of value. I had spent several years focusing my attention on literature that had been informed by jazz, and was intrigued, as I still am today, by the inherent challenges and possibilities of manipulating the concrete nature of language in response to an invisible art. At the same time, I had to recognize the unfortunate truth that most jazz-inspired literature—from poems with self-conscious phrasing where the speaker sounds hipperthan-thou to essays with sloppy research and wooden prose—fails. Filling *Brilliant Corners* with second-rate material would be easy; presenting ninety pages of substantive writing would not. But lengthy discussions with people passionate and knowledgeable about both literature and jazz could anchor each issue as well as highlight one of the more important similarities between language and music: the oral tradition.

That's how these interviews began.

Obviously, this collection is not meant to represent a comprehensive discussion of jazz-related literature, any more than a series of twenty interviews on jazz would be considered a comprehensive evaluation of the music. I see this series more as events from a jazz festival, with one performance following the next, united not by homogeneity but by the compelling language of music. The challenge for a poet responding to music is not the same as a musician trying to integrate poetry into a composition; one person's experience watching a theatrical production that incorporates jazz hardly compares with the act of reading liner notes while listening to the corresponding CD. And within genres, writers and their work differ as widely as musical styles from Dixieland to free jazz. As these varied conversations suggest, the engaging complexities of synesthesia defy restrictive summaries.

Like most interviews, these discussions provide an increased understanding of the creative process and the artist's craft. (As a teacher of
writing, I continually remind students, especially those in my literature
courses, that published texts—even "classics" printed on tissue-paper-
thin anthology pages—were generated by passion, philosophy, history,
and desire.) While interviews do not necessarily expose the secrets of
a magic act, they can nevertheless explore the inspiration behind wondrous performances. For both artists and scholars, such moments can be
genuinely revelatory. As Wilfrid Sheed proposes, albeit tentatively, in his
introduction to *Writers at Work: The* Paris Review *Interviews:* "Can the
interview as a form pass beyond the realm of necessary small talk into
art itself? Perhaps."

As an interviewer, I have tried to act as an unobtrusive conduit. Occasionally I have told my own stories and stretched out questions in order
to set a mood and evoke more from the writer or musician, but during
the transcription of those taped discussions, my reflections disappear
and my questions shrink to what is required. Similarly, these interviews
are not live recordings; they're studio sessions that have been balanced
and remixed. Before running a tape recorder, I make a point of saying
that the text should be seen as a work in progress, and that any correc-
tions can be made before publication. There's plenty to be said for pure
spontaneity, but I believe it's far more beneficial to record an artist's exact
intention.

Although the collection acts as a ten-year marker for *Brilliant Corners,* each interview marks history in other, more important ways, somewhat like a band playing stop-time, for interviews almost inevitably concentrate on the past. Like jazz recordings, documented conversations
counteract the evanescence of music, locations, and people. All writers
whose careers have focused on jazz express profound gratitude, sometimes even a sense of salvation; they can almost chart their lives with recordings and club dates.

Perhaps that's why, in thinking about conversations and jazz, I drifted
back to 1984, when my college spring break coincided with my twenty-
first birthday. I had gone home to Manhattan and checked the club list-
ings in *The New Yorker.* Bradley's, an ideal venue for jazz piano, had sched-
uled my favorite pianist, Tommy Flanagan. I didn't question whether I'd
hear Flanagan at Bradley's that week; I just didn't know how many times
I'd be able to attend.

Can one articulate why Flanagan's artistry has such a strong pull?

Thinking of his dynamic range as a performer—as extreme, say, as the subtle palette coloring a canyon in Arizona and the muscularity of the rock itself—the ineffability of music seems to defeat language almost immediately. Still, a writer can try. In the liner notes for Flanagan's *Jazz Poet*, for example, Dan Morgenstern describes the music as "sheer musical poetry, sounds and thoughts that, insofar as they can be translated into words, require such superlatives as pure and sublime." Morgenstern adds: "But let the reader of such words not fall into the trap of equating poetic sensibility with the ethereal and the introspective. . . . There is strength and sinew in his music, as well as gentleness and grace." Stanley Crouch, discussing the "grace" and "grandeur" of Flanagan's *Nights at the Village Vanguard*, writes: "That sense of purpose dominates a poetic sensibility far from meek or maudlin; at the center of his sound is the power of a large talent so perfectly disciplined that every gesture has the weight and the mystery of the inevitable." Gary Giddins once described his solos as "spare and sculpted, hammered like fine silver." William Matthews called him "the Mozart of jazz piano."

In the notes for Flanagan's *Sunset and the Mockingbird*, Peter Straub complains about the misuse of language to describe this "passionate, tremendously muscular piano player":

> Adjectives like "elegant," "civilized," "poetic," "modest," and "discreet" recur so often as to suggest that the charming Mr. Flanagan offers harmless salon vapors based upon the poems of Mr. Mallarmé. Any such notion is, let us say, laughable. . . . The clarity of his articulation and the resolute unflappability of his progression from one inspiration to the next can be called elegant and is nothing if not civilized in the best, widest possible sense, but most of the time this music is about as delicate as Mohammed [*sic*] Ali's left hand.

Straub's criticism perhaps specifically targets Whitney Balliett, whose *New Yorker* profile on Flanagan was titled "Poet," although that essay in no way diminishes the pianist's rhythmic propulsion and complexity: "There are also interior movements within these lines: double-time runs; clusters of flatted notes, like pretend stumbles; backward-leaning half-time passages; dancing runs; and rests, which are both pauses and chambers for the preceding phrase to echo in." Balliett concludes:

> Flanagan is never less than first-rate. But once in a while—when the weather is calm, the audience attentive, the piano good, the vibes right—

he becomes impassioned. Then he will play throughout the evening with inspiration and great heat, turning out stunning solo after stunning solo, making the listeners feel they have been at a godly event.

And that's why, if one really wanted to focus on Tommy Flanagan's artistry, there was no better venue than Bradley's. An excellent grand piano, which had been donated by Paul Desmond, marked the elongated club's center (positioned at the end of a long bar that greeted customers and just in front of the marginally obscured dining area). Whether there for drinks or a meal, people in attendance tended to be classy and extremely attentive. Yes, at the very worst, the experience would be first-rate.

I rode the subway to the Village and met up with a buddy of mine. We sat at the bar—the closest available seats to the piano—and ordered beers. Flanagan hadn't come out yet, so we had time to catch up. He asked about college, and I replied enthusiastically, adding that I was studying a lot of jazz. The bartender placed our beers on the counter and said, with surprising edge to his tone, "How do you *study* jazz?"

Even at twenty-one, I sensed the forthcoming lecture of superiority: how jazz has to be experienced, not studied; how books intellectualize passion; how academe sterilizes art.

"Hey," I said, looking him in the eyes, "I'm *here*, right?"

He gave a nod, and left us alone. We laughed, clinked glasses to my birthday, and then settled in for serious listening.

Had we not been interrupted, I might have explained what I meant by studying jazz. I was listening to every live gig possible, from coffeehouses to university events, and playing jazz, too (saxophone—tenor, mainly—both in the college ensemble and in a quintet that performed on campus and around town). Although an English major, I had taken some elective classes in jazz, as well as African and African American music, all of them taught by working musicians. And the literature on jazz that supplemented my listening and playing—liner notes, general histories, biographies—began to enrich both what I heard live and on record. I began to appreciate more completely how the history of jazz should be considered like grooves on an LP: connected and fluid. Books that I had purchased or received in high school—especially the oral histories compiled in *Hear Me Talkin' to Ya* and *Bird: The Legend of Charlie Parker*, as well as some jazz autobiographies, such as Charles Mingus's *Beneath the Underdog* and Art Pepper's *Straight Life*—became increasingly important as my gratitude for jazz swelled. I enjoyed learning more about the history of famous recordings—Parker on "Lover Man," Coltrane's *A*

Love Supreme, the Monk and Miles argument on "The Man I Love"—but, much more important, literature provided a new appreciation for the *humanity* of these artists, many of whom had died by the early '80s.

I also became more aware of the music's centrality to the history of twentieth-century poetry, and how some poets, or even whole movements, could not be discussed without addressing the influence of jazz. Anthologies such as Stephen Henderson's *Understanding the New Black Poetry* allowed me to consider the politics of jazz in ways that the music itself, given its abstract nature, could only suggest. And I tried to become a more discerning reader, dismissing vacuous hipster jargon for the values of deep listening and brilliant articulation. Even early on, I knew jazz-related literature would forever aspire to the qualities of music, and I began to question, if not dismiss, overly eager scholars who manipulated descriptions of literature and music in order to suggest ridiculous parallels—that poetry, for example, is *exactly* the same as music.

Literature is largely an art of isolation, written in private, sometimes never to be performed. In contrast, jazz is inextricably linked to performance (musician to audience) and communication (musician to musician). Reading a tribute to Thelonious Monk, no matter how evocative the poetry or poetic the prose, can't possibly provide the same aesthetic experience of hearing Monk's music. But that does not diminish what *can* be achieved through language: memorable works that not only provide different aesthetic experiences but that retain their own identities quite apart from the music. If one cannot define Tommy Flanagan's improvisations in exact terms, should music criticism be dismissed like reels of unused takes? And if a poet's greatest strength has to do with articulating ambiguity, why diminish the abstraction of jazz—or its complex, nearly mythic history—as an irresistible and unfailing source?

Twenty-one years after my twenty-first birthday, I can still hear that bartender's challenge—a mere scrap he would have forgotten almost immediately. Sometimes, language can be as ephemeral as music; if unrecorded, words and notes evaporate with the temporality of the body. Maybe that explains why most of the literature on jazz focuses on triumphant musicians whose artistic contributions have largely disappeared from the consciousness of America. Writing stops time, the way taped conversations and recorded sessions stop time.

If this collection had been organized chronologically, as opposed to alphabetically, the first piece would have been my discussion with William Matthews in which he talks about his poems for Charles Mingus. Of the four tributes, my favorite remains the last, "Mingus in Shadow," an elegy that concludes with references to a black-and-white portrait of the dying bassist:

> It was human nature,
> tiny nature, to take the photograph,
>
> to fuss with the aperture and speed, to let
> in the right blare of light just long enough
> to etch pale Mingus to the negative.
> In the small, memorial world of that
> negative, he's all the light there is.

Less than two years after our interview, Bill himself was gone, leaving behind his books, of course, as well as book-collections-worth of stories to be shared by those who knew him. The only hour of his voice that I have on tape appeared in print in *Brilliant Corners,* and then in Bill's posthumously published *The Poetry Blues,* and now in this book. I suppose one could say "It was human nature, / tiny nature" to set that cassette in motion, to etch his voice onto the tape and then ink it into this "small, memorial world."

No transcription fully replaces the totality of an artist's presence, but, if nothing else, there's something to be said for our "tiny nature" that desires and celebrates what has been recorded. So much in our world, after all, disappears quickly. Bradley's closed in the '90s, and Tommy Flanagan died in 2001. Did anyone record him at that club? I don't believe so. Still, as vividly as I can recall this morning's coffee, I remember leaving Bradley's and walking along University Place in Manhattan's bruised, after-hours light with the evening in my ears, Flanagan's long lines keeping rhythm with the uptown IRT, his music lavish and generous enough to stay with me my whole life.

Ask Me Now

Amiri Baraka. *Photo by Sascha Feinstein.*

1

Better You Say It First
Amiri Baraka

For fifteen heavy minutes, I knocked on the front door and buzzed, but no one answered. Then I peered through the first-floor windows and rapped against the panes. Nothing. A few minutes later, I took out a piece of paper and prepared to write a tough note about being disappointed. I'd traveled three hours (and gotten lost in the heart of Newark) only to be blown off, '60s style, by Amiri Baraka.

Then the door swung open to loud conversation (some fellow, I don't know who, departed) and Baraka greeted me with enthusiasm.

"You been out here long?"

"About twenty minutes."

"Oh, I'm sorry, I'm sorry. Couldn't hear a thing." Then: "You like wine? Let's get some wine."

It was early afternoon and bright. As we walked, half the people on the street waved or nodded. At a corner smoke shop, he had a brief, animated exchange with the clerk about a boxing match the night before, and then he bought a gallon of burgundy. Back outside, he glanced at a small gathering of young men and said out loud but to himself, "They shouldn't be there." He seemed one with the neighborhood, and I felt lucky to be in his company. In a matter of minutes, I'd gone from someone locked out to someone in the inner circle. Given the remarkable transitions in Baraka's career, that kind of turn seemed appropriate.

We sat in front of a sunny bay window, and although family members and friends periodically interrupted our discussion, he never lost his focus. Throughout the afternoon, he spoke with great energy and honesty—sometimes singing, sometimes shouting, and sometimes making us both laugh loud enough to overwhelm the tape's memory.

Born in Newark, New Jersey, Amiri Baraka (LeRoi Jones) moved to New York's Greenwich Village in the 1950s and became a seminal figure in the Beat movement, editing the avant-garde journals *Yugen* and *Floating Bear*, and publishing his first collection of poems, *Preface to a Twenty Volume Suicide Note*. His play *Dutchman* was produced in 1964 and won an Obie. Since 1965, Baraka has recommitted his life and work to the African American community through the Black Arts Repertory Theater School and other cultural and political activities. His many books include *Transbluesency: The Selected Poems of Amiri Baraka / LeRoi Jones (1961–1995)*, *Blues People*, *Eulogies*, and *The Music*.

The following poem and prose excerpts correspond to works mentioned and themes raised in our conversation. The interview took place at his home in Newark, New Jersey, on September 19, 1999.

Dutchman
(excerpt)
Amiri Baraka

CLAY: Charlie Parker? Charlie Parker. All the hip white boys scream for Bird. And Bird saying, "Up your ass, feeble-minded ofay! Up your ass." And they sit there talking about the tortured genius of Charlie Parker. Bird would've played not a note of music if he just walked up to East Sixty-seventh Street and killed the first ten white people he saw. Not a note! And I'm the great would-be poet. Yes. That's right! Poet. Some kind of bastard literature . . . all it needs is a simple knife thrust. Just let me bleed you, you loud whore, and one poem vanished. A whole people of neurotics, struggling to keep from being sane. And the only thing that would cure the neurosis would be your murder. Simple as that. I mean if I murdered you, then other white people would begin to understand me.

You understand? No. I guess not. If Bessie Smith had killed some white people she wouldn't have needed that music. She could have talked very straight and plain about the world. No metaphors. No grunts. No wiggles in the dark of her soul. Just straight two and two are four. Money. Power. Luxury. Like that. All of them. Crazy niggers turning their backs on sanity. When all it needs is that simple act. Murder. Just murder! Would make us all sane.

Black Art
Amiri Baraka

Poems are bullshit unless they are
teeth or trees or lemons piled
on a step. Or black ladies dying
of men leaving nickel hearts
beating them down. Fuck poems
and they are useful, wd they shoot
come at you, love what you are,
breathe like wrestlers, or shudder
strangely after pissing. We want live
words of the hip world live flesh &
coursing blood. Hearts Brains
Souls splintering fire. We want poems
like fists beating niggers out of Jocks
or dagger poems in the slimy bellies
of the owner-jews. Black poems to
smear on girlemamma mulatto bitches
whose brains are red jelly stuck
between 'lizabeth taylor's toes. Stinking
Whores! We want "poems that kill."
Assassin poems, Poems that shoot
guns. Poems that wrestle cops into alleys
and take their weapons leaving them dead
with tongues pulled out and sent to Ireland. Knockoff
poems for dope selling wops or slick halfwhite
politicians Airplane poems, rrrrrrrrrrrrrrrr
rrrrrrrrrrrrrrr . . . tuhtuhtuhtuhtuhtuhtuhtuhtuh
. . . rrrrrrrrrrrrrrr . . . Setting fire and death to
whities ass. Look at the Liberal

Spokesman for the jews clutch his throat
& puke himself into eternity . . . rrrrrrrr
There's a negroleader pinned to
a bar stool in Sardi's eyeballs melting
in hot flame Another negroleader
on the steps of the white house one
kneeling between the sheriff's thighs
negotiating coolly for his people.
Agggh . . . stumbles across the room . . .
Put it on him, poem. Strip him naked
to the world! Another bad poem cracking
steel knuckles in a jewlady's mouth
Poem scream poison gas on beasts in green berets
Clean out the world for virtue and love,
Let there be no love poems written
until love can exist freely and
cleanly. Let Black People understand
that they are the lovers and the sons
of lovers and warriors and sons
of warriors Are poems & poets &
all the loveliness here in the world

We want a black poem. And a
Black World.
Let the world be a Black Poem
And Let All Black People Speak This Poem
Silently
or LOUD

Jazz Writing: Survival in the Eighties
(excerpt)
Amiri Baraka

When I began to publish writing about the music it was the late
'50s moving into the '60s, and there was an explosive trend at work and
perceptible in the society. What would be obvious as the civil rights
movement began to lose its nonviolent black bourgeois trappings and
erupt into the more popularly oriented Black Liberation movement. . . .
    One of the first major articles I wrote, in the defunct *Metronome,* was

called "Jazz and the White Critic," in which I tried to come to terms with why there were so many white critics of an essentially black music. One thing that was important to me in discussing this phenomenon was that many of these white critics, since they came from a different class life in America than the musicians and the essence of their music, all too often imposed a critical standard on the music that was opposed to the standards the music itself carried with it and described.

Years have passed, decades filled with struggle and some transformation; but after the high-water marks of mass insurgency against this exploitive and oppressive white racist monopoly capitalist society, the cooling out of that mass movement, by means of murder, imprisonment, behavior modification, exile, bribery, has meant that there has been a cooling out, decline, retreat in many other areas, such as the arts and critical writing, that take their impetus, like it or not, from the flow and motion of social movement. . . .

[T]he "survival" of quality writing on the music must be linked up to the survival of the highest levels of expression of the music itself. And both these must be connected to the survival of a general *liberating intelligence,* which must be about working and struggling to see that civilization itself survives. We must not forget that most of the lost and vanished civilizations died by their own hand or were destroyed by other human beings. Not by Martians, Gods, or Devils.

Duke Ellington: The Music's "Great Spirit"
(excerpt)
Amiri Baraka

Duke's collective work sings and "speaks" as a reflection of the social and political economic character of the historic African American culture. Its aesthetic character is itself artistic expression as the most evocative summation of that people, contexted by their mean experience of the "Whole" world encyclopedic African presence as development, journey, summation. . . .

Ellington's Blues is his breathing life inside the works. The Blues is always a presence, form, content, spiritual essence and reach. Blues as the Being wherefrom the Being re-being as Music (Thought seen—Sonic Light).

But Blues for Ellington is a life and life force—from the "favorite color" it was in West Africa (see Equiano) stretched twisted tortured.

Soaked with a deadly abstraction of invisibility soaked in Blood. There-fore across the whole spectrum of color, sounds, speed, direction, Ultra Violet (invisible as it emerges from Blackness, Indigo as it appears as the twilight diameter of touching worlds, history now memory now Mood—The Doom of the Slave trade and Middle Passage, is thrown dialectically to its origins as Mood (Doom!).

So Blue (Beauty) post-passage is Loss, Sadness, Memory as Recherché, Redux, yet afire as it remains. Laughter, Joy is often the ironic contempla-tion of sadness. Happy Blues. Crazy Blues. Billie's Blues, Blue Monk, Po-tato Head Blues.

You Blue
You Blew!!
Yeh, Blow!!! (Express)
He really Blew (Like Trane)

SASCHA FEINSTEIN: Why do you think there isn't stronger jazz criticism being written?

AMIRI BARAKA: I know fine writers on the music, but they've been dis-couraged in the last couple of decades because now most of the maga-zines that deal with the music are commercial and don't have really thoughtful kinds of presentations. That's why *Brilliant Corners* should have some impact, because the serious discussion of music has not been happening anymore. You get these reviews, and these glosses, and they review everything. It would be like if you were talking about Eu-ropean classical music, and you're covering an imitation of Brahms with Spike Jones. I mean, they would rather review that than some se-rious discussions of the development of the music in the nineteenth century, you know what I'm saying? And with jazz—American classi-cal music—there's been no summation, really, of the last thirty years.

When I first came into New York in the '50s, back from the ser-vice, [I realized] the Europeans had done a lot more analytical studies of music than most Americans. And then I fell into a group of young American writers—Martin Williams, Larry Gushee, Dick Hadlock, Dan Morgenstern—around a magazine called *The Record Changer*. I was a stock clerk; I packed the boxes and stuff like that. And a lot of guys walking around at that time were "moldy figs," saying that the music died with Duke Ellington. (Some of them have since up-dated their views.) Hadlock ran the magazine, and Dick was a bit of a "moldy fig" too. I don't think he was completely locked into New Orleans, but all those guys were great New Orleans types. And, to be frank, I didn't know a great deal about that. When I applied for the job I said, "Well, I don't know much about the music before Louis Armstrong," and Dick said, "Nobody else does, either." [Laughs.] But it was good training because I learned that there were people who took the music very seriously.

That confirmed what I had learned in college, because I had a great professor: Sterling Brown the poet—who I didn't know from Adam's cat. But I happened to be a student there with A. B. Spellman. I was a sophomore (I had gone to Rutgers first), he was a freshman, and Brown taught us Shakespeare, for which I am forever grateful, because of his insights. A lot of people read Shakespeare and still don't know what it's about, that all of that stuff is talking about the ills of capitalism—a new class getting ready to overthrow those old aristocrats. You just look at those kings and queens, those ugly portraits. Richard III, MacBeth. They're gruesome, the bourgeoisie, because Shakespeare's getting ready to dump them!

But Brown took A. B. Spellman and me to his house, and that certainly wasn't the beginning of my love for the music, but he amplified it into history—that the music was actually the history of the Afro-American people right there. If you understood that clearly, how one thing turned into another—what the social context of each kind of music is, and why it changed, and what the influences were, and how those influences changed—if you were conscious of what that was, then you would have a good understanding not only of Afro-American history but American history, as it was played out to that particular group.

FEINSTEIN: By the time you went to Howard, you must have known about [Brown's] *Southern Road*.

BARAKA: No. I literally did not know who he was.

FEINSTEIN: And yet he was the primary one who helped guide you in your appreciation for music and literature?

BARAKA: Yeah, it was Brown. The whole summation that he made: This is history, this is your history.

The first poetry in music, that I liked, was blues. (You could talk about spirituals in a sense because they used to speak with the music playing, too: "May the Lord watch between me and thee, while we're absent, one from another," and so on.) But the words and the music to me had something to do with the blues and the gospel and then, when I became a teenager, with bebop. I had come into contact with bebop before I went to college, and I think that's why Brown saw us in a little different light—because we were so aggressively haughty with our knowledge of, you know, *Charlie Parker*. Like we *knew* what was happening. [Laughs.] Charlie Parker, Dizzy Gillespie. We knew. But there was no depth to it. We loved what we loved, but we didn't know enough. So the blues and the gospel, the placement of words and music together, they meant the most to me.

And a bit of bebop—someone like Babs Gonzalez. Babs came up in Newark—me and his brother used to be tight—and the music that he was involved in creating (*ooh bop shabam a-koo-koo mop,* all that kind of stuff) had a very indelible influence on me as a kid. Dizzy Gillespie. Slim Gaillard. A real heavy influence.

Later, about '57, I heard Langston Hughes. He was working with Mingus at the Five Spot. By that time, I had been reading with the music. I had a job in Long Island, reading once a week with a little band. And there were a couple of people around New York doing that. Jack Micheline and I used to hang out at a joint where they had started to do that.

FEINSTEIN: You've written so much—including liner notes—and I see you're now writing some reviews for *JazzTimes*. In the most recent issue, you make something of a finger-pointing gesture, that musicians need to listen to Duke Ellington, and Monk, and other mainstream figures. Is that a general commentary?

BARAKA: Absolutely. See, take Wynton Marsalis, who—whatever the pros and cons are—I appreciate [for] his presenting the classics of music. I don't know how anyone can put that down. You can nitpick, when he does Duke, about whether or not that's the ultimate reproduction of the work. It might not be, in a lot of ways. But that idea is important to me. I think a lot of people complain about Wynton because they can't play in Lincoln Center. I mean, Lincoln Center's slick. A lot of the avant-garde, they can't play at Lincoln Center—but the point is, you play somewhere else. Don't stand around and complain. The point of Wynton doing the music of Monk, the music of Bud Powell, the music of Duke—that's very important, and I don't think anything should get in the way of that.

I work with musicians all the time, and what I don't like is a lot of times musicians, who think themselves very advanced, do not know the music. It's like a lot of poets: They don't know past one or two names. The point is [for serious musicians]: Have you really listened to that [classical jazz] music? And I can say that about myself. I was running around talking about the music long before I sat down and really listened to, say, the music of Duke Ellington. I mean, I knew Duke's music since I was a baby (which is on one hand good and one hand bad, because you start taking things for granted). But when you sit down, you start saying, "My *God,*" you start to see what that is, and that's a whole other thing. I think a lot of these young musicians don't do that. I'm not saying whether this is the majority; I'm not making that kind of accusation. I'm just saying that too often, of people that I've met, they do not know the music. They'll release an album with all their tunes—which is cool—but there's got to be some kind of attention to the great works that have been created.

Take a guy like David Murray. Last year, David did a whole concert of Duke Ellington's music, the little recorded works of Duke and Strayhorn. That was, to me, a marvelous thing, 'cause here's one of the leading new music people, and he was playing the difficult stuff, like Strayhorn's "Blood Count" and "Lotus Blossom." Those are estimable works, but a lot of people don't even know about them.

With my own groups, I'm always making them sit down and listen to that music. We're doing a concert, an Ellington tribute, next week in the park out here—

FEINSTEIN: You and the group Blue Ark?

BARAKA: Yeah. Me and my wife [Amina Baraka], Herbie Morgan is the tenor saxophone player, Wilber Morris is the bass player, Pheeroan akLaff is the drummer, and D. D. Jackson is the piano player. My brother-in-law, Dwight West, who's a marvelous singer, sings [Ellington standards such as] "In a Sentimental Mood," "I Got It Bad and That Ain't Good," "Don't Get Around Much Anymore." Those are fantastically beautiful songs.

FEINSTEIN: And how do you work them into your own poetry?

BARAKA: We do it together. On this particular thing, I open with a prose intro on Duke, and then I read a poem called "Ellingtonia" that's accompanied by "Mood Indigo." Then, when the poem's finished, Dwight comes in and sings "Mood Indigo." Then we go right into "Night Train," which gives a historical underpinning to the thing—now we're talking about getting out of the South, the Underground Railroad and the overground railroad. We do a piece of Wilber's called "Chazz," and my wife reads a piece, "Being Colored," and then we go into "I Got It Bad." We do a group of poems that go with Powell's "Un Poco Loco."

I always try to use the great, classic works with the poetry. If you were doing a European thing where you were doing Stravinsky and Beethoven, you're using the heaviest works and that gives dimension to the poetry in a whole other way. So we're doing something (a lot of people don't know this work) of Duke's called "Air-Conditioned Jungle," and then we're doing Strayhorn's "Blood Count" with a two-part poem on Malcolm X. The music is so grand that it's actually like you're getting a free ride. The music raises the poetry to another level, if it can be raised.

FEINSTEIN: One of my favorite recordings of yours is ["Black Art" on the long out-of-print LP] *Sunny's Time Now!* with the great drummer Sunny Murray. Is it true that you have the tapes for that?

BARAKA: Oh, sure. In fact, the first album should be out next week—the one we're doing with Sun Ra with my play *Black Mass.* We're re-releasing that, and we're rereleasing *Sunny's Time Now!* and all those records, because I recorded those myself in the late '60s. Albert Ayler, Sunny Murray, Don Ayler.

In the last ten years I've recorded a lot of stuff—not always good recordings, but one day they'll be very valuable. Somebody'll say, "Oh, we can barely hear this, but this is Sun Ra with Pharoah Sanders"—which I have. "This is Albert Ayler and Pharoah Sanders"—which I have. And nobody'll ever hear that in any way except that way.

FEINSTEIN: When you were reading [your poem] "Black Art" with Sunny Murray, what was that like?

BARAKA: We did it in the Spirit House. We had been working together. But it was a concession, 'cause we'd just go straight through it. There wouldn't be a lot of technical stuff; we'd just go down and do it. Our view was that to get it down was the point. Whatever the imperfections—the coulda been, coulda been, coulda been—that's another thing. We were trying to get it down, and as it turned out it was right, because in another couple of years Albert was out of here. [Albert Ayler died in 1970.] Don was out of his mind, and Sunny's over in Paris.

At one point, Sunny was driving a cab [in the States] and he drove all the way [to Newark] from Philadelphia. So he says, "Hey, Baraka, I gotta get the master of that gig. I gotta make some money, man," and I said, "Okay, man, here, I'll give it to you." But I gave him a copy of the master. [Chuckles.] And he sold it to the Japanese, immediately, for whatever that was—chump change plus a dollar? And they issued it, but they don't have the rights. It don't bother me. It's good; let them issue it. But we still have the master, and we're getting ready to re-issue it.

FEINSTEIN: I first heard *Sunny's Time Now!* in the apartment of a fine jazz drummer, Stan Gage. He's no longer alive, but he used to play *loud*, and he'd lost a lot of his hearing, so when he played that record, the walls shook. And I think—because the music's so powerful, so aggressive—that's probably the way it should be heard.

BARAKA: Yeah. The band was at the top of their stuff. And records are *near* it, but that ain't it. Albert's sound and presence were entirely out to lunch. That's why you say you need to hear it loud, because you just can't hear what he sounded like. Maybe if they recorded it today it would sound a little more [true], but Albert's sound, like you say, was intimidating, and unlike anything I'd ever heard. There was a ferocious kind of weight to it, you know what I mean? It *wasn't* passive. [Laughs.]

Albert was in my house when I lived in Cooper Square, and we were bullshitting about something, and then he said, "There's a concert up in Lincoln Center." This concert had John Coltrane, Cecil Taylor, Pharoah Sanders, Eric Dolphy—it was a monster. Anyway, we went backstage while they were out there playing, and Albert took his horn out, put it together, and suddenly, man, in the middle of that thing he came out. He had the horn held over his head like this. [Baraka raises his hands over and behind his head.] Way up there, and he starts: *Ah-hhhhhhhhhhhhhhhhhhhhh*. It's the wildest thing I've ever heard in my life. He just walked out on the stage: *Ahhhhhhhhhhhhhhhhhh*. Everybody had to look at that, hear that. And it was fantastic. It threw the stage into an uproar, and the music business itself, because that was totally out, new.

Afterwards—it was very funny—Trane came off the stage and he said one thing: "What kind of reed you usin'?" [Both laugh.]

FEINSTEIN: That's pretty good!

BARAKA: You know what I mean? In other words, "What the fuck was that?" [Both laugh.] That was unbelievable. But on the records, the sound is contained by that device, no matter how loud it is. When it was live it was like something that could grab you. You know what I'm saying? It was a live thing and it didn't depend on you at all.

FEINSTEIN: In fact, you *can't* control it.

BARAKA: That's what it is. And it's so loud, so brassy, so aggressive, so self-declaring. It's *mean*. Albert was like that in a lot of ways.

FEINSTEIN: Someone said to me recently that you were annoyed because critics keep falling back to *Dutchman* [1964], as if that's the only play you've ever written.

BARAKA: It's true. That's what they do. That play was done then, and has that [spirit of the time] with it. Later on, when I got more obnoxious in terms of Black Nationalism, they didn't want to see that too tough. And then—[laughs]—the communism was even worse. I had a better chance when I said, "White people ain't shit" than the fucking communist shit. "Everybody get together and kill these bastards." That's *really* a no-no. It's bad enough when you say this black/white shit, but this red shit—no! [Both laugh.] And I can appreciate that. I know exactly what it is. And so they salvage what they can from that period.

They're doing *Dutchman* in Hartford right now, and the guy [directing] called me for a companion piece. So I sent him two things. Since *Dutchman* is a white woman and a black man, I sent him one play that I just wrote called *Skin Trouble* that features a light-skinned black woman—who could be the same woman. (She calls herself black, but that's America. I mean, you got black people who are whiter lookin' than white people. They could be from the same family. You know the shit that went on behind closed doors in this country. How anybody can be sure that they're *this* is beyond me. [Laughs.]) The other play—this happened in my family—is about these brothers with a different father (one of whom was my grandfather), and the brother who is the "black sheep" brings home a young girl he's just got from the field. She's very dark skinned, so you get that whole caste thing operating. The little boy, who later turns out to be Clay [from *Dutchman*], is standing and watching all this shit going on—how the girl is being mistreated and talked bad about—not really understanding what it is, but being influenced, not in a positive way. So to have this before *Dutchman* is a dimensioning of it that might be interesting.

I do get tired of that [focus on *Dutchman*], because I've written a lot of plays. The first full-length play I wrote was in [Edward] Albee's workshop, where *Dutchman* got performed first [at the Cherry Lane Theatre]. His *Zoo Story* ... which I have not seen and never will see, because people said it influenced *Dutchman*, so I said, "I'll *never* see it. Fuck that." [Both laugh.] I'm *never* going to see that play. Fuck it. So if anybody asks me I'll say, "I've never even seen the fucking thing.

I don't know why you're saying *that*. I don't know nothing about that play." [Both laugh.]

But Albee could get money for that workshop. (I was in his house one time and I said, "That's a beautiful reproduction of Picasso," and he said, "That's not a reproduction." That's the kind of guy that he is, know what I mean?) So the producers [of *Dutchman*] asked me to write another play. I wrote a long play [*A Recent Killing*], and then Edward gives his opinion about it that he doesn't like it. And I wanted to know, "What do you have to do with it? I might not understand the world completely, but what do you have to do with it?" Remember, he had gotten himself known, with *Zoo Story,* only a month or two before I did, so I was wondering how he could walk around and tell me to—whatever. And the producers didn't produce the play—I was really pissed off—because he was their consciousness. I give Edward credit; he does what he does. But I know he doesn't have anything to do with what I do, and I know that he ain't got no way of telling what I *was* doing, either.

The play *A Recent Killing* was done years later. It's about a boy in the air force, which I was in, in Puerto Rico. All the books and things that he's ever read begin to be dimensionalized by his own needs. So you see the characters out of *Ulysses*—for instance, Leopold Bloom—or you see from *Brideshead Revisited* Sebastian Flyte. They come into the room and they're discussing things with him. And finally, it's a tragic ending: this city black boy, this country black boy, and this Jewish kid from the Lower East Side—who I actually knew, who never wanted to hang out with anybody else because it was corny in the air force. And here was a little group that knew about the music.

In real life, I was the librarian. I mean, I was a gunner and all of that shit, but I had a regular job as a night librarian. This elderly white woman found out that I could deal with the book thing, and so she said, "If you need me, call me at this number." She was in the civil service, went on vacation, and left it in my hands. Now, this was the '50s, and to put this little black kid in charge of the library . . . [Laughs.] "Gimme the keys. You got it." And then I stocked that library, boy, and that was our hangout. We'd get a bottle of rum that you could buy for a dollar, and we taught each other the history of Western music and Western literature. For a year, every night, we would read and discuss. That was really college for me. I started with the motets and Gregorian chants. I was in charge of buying, and every week I would buy more stuff. We bought the history of the music all the way through, and then the same thing with the literature. So when people would say, like, "Hey, Jonesy—what's a Kafka?" I'd say, "What the fuck is a Kafka? I don't know." So I'd order all the Kafkas. [Both laugh.] We'd get them, read them, and discuss them. We all wanted to learn. We all had pretentions of being intellectuals. Blacks, whites, a Mexican kid. We had pretentions, and we applied ourselves. The library would have to close when we got too bombed, stagger out of there. But we'd be there until just about midnight. We'd play music, loud. Close all the windows and play Stravinsky, loud. We played Beethoven so *loud*. That's real education.

FEINSTEIN: Many of your plays have been infused with jazz. What do you think of other playwrights who have tried to incorporate jazz into their work—people like August Wilson?

BARAKA: I've known August a long, long time. I always look at August as a kind of student of mine—not in any kind of formal way but in an associative sense, 'cause I knew him when he was a young poet out in Pittsburgh. That was when we were in the Beat thing, and when I became a nationalist he used to ask me for years, "Why you doin' that, Roi? Why you doin' that?" And then in the last part of his evolution, before he became a well-known playwright, he became a Muslim, which is incredible—these people who became Muslims after Malcolm got wasted. But I think his stuff's good.

Ron Milner did a play called *Jazz Set,* where the whole structure of the play is like a jazz orchestra. I think it's a good thing. Langston [Hughes]'s got quite a few plays people don't know about—one called *The Organizer* [1938] that he did with James P. Johnson's music. (It's just been reprinted in *Lost Plays of the Harlem Renaissance.*) That is a fine play. It's an opera. I'd love to get hold of that music.

I support everyone who uses the music with language—plays, poetry. I think it's a positive thing. We're trying now to get a twelve-part series on public radio dealing with nothing but poetry and music. To me, that's something that's just being retouched. There's been a lot of it going on, even Langston's *Ask Your Mama*—people are starting to do that a little more. I have a couple of versions. You had the stuff that Mingus did, and then there was the stuff that Kenneth Patchen did (which I don't know if people know too much about). Kenneth Rexroth. There's a lot of stuff.

FEINSTEIN: What's your take on those late '50s sessions? So much of it was terrible.

BARAKA: I think you have to winnow it out. For instance, a guy like Kenneth Patchen—his stuff is cute, but you have to select exactly what you think is most interesting. I'm not going to make a case for, even, Rexroth's thing about Dylan Thomas—

FEINSTEIN: "Thou Shalt Not Kill."

BARAKA: Right. But it needs to be heard. And then there are people like Amus Mor from Chicago who's never been heard, not likely to be heard, who's had an extensive influence on my generation that people are not even aware of. By the time the Last Poets started picking up on what we were doing, we had been picking up on other people—people like Larry Neal and Askia Touré, who are my contemporaries, but they influenced me a great deal. Amus Mor is my contemporary, but he influenced me a great deal. Just hearing him read once or twice was enough. On the record that Woodie King put out [*Black Spirits*], you can hear the exclamations of us sitting around when he read. You can hear my voice, Larry Neal's voice, [Stanley] Crouch's voice—because Crouch was there before he turned into Crouch. And you can hear all of us saying, "Jeez, what the fuck was that?" It was real stunning. Amus used the music, without music playing, as an organic part of what he was doing, which I think some of us have learned to do now. You can be the music yourself. You don't have to have a band. It's good to have a band when you can, but when I don't I still do the same tunes I would do only *I* do them. And that's what he was doing then.

FEINSTEIN: Mor has that great poem "The Coming of John."

BARAKA: Yeah. Hell, isn't that something? I remember when that came out. And I heard him read that. What it is, is you hear somebody as if he's walking down the street, and you say, "Hey, how you doing?" and the guy suddenly scats—like it's part of the milieu rather than some literary imposition on it.

Another guy who's really good is Gylan Kain, who was with the original Last Poets, when it was Felipe Luciano, Gylan Kain, and David Nelson. That's before the second group—who are better known, have certainly been very influential, and are good. But the first group was doing something a little different. Felipe's a great poet, and people sleep on that. David Nelson's a very fine poet. Gylan Kain is fantastic; few people can read like Kain. He's got a group now with a bass drum, and it sounds like a Holy Roller group—you know, Daddy Grace, 125th and 7th Avenue style, that *boomty boomty boomty boomty boom.* That's an amazing kind of sound, just that bass drum.

Sekou Sundiata is another guy who I think is good. Not only is his poetry good, but he knows how to deal with the question of music. It's not altogether my taste as far as the music is concerned, but he certainly knows what he's doing and writes great poetry. Jayne Cortez is another person, she and the Firespitters group that she's got. There are quite a few people out there, and quite a few new people who are coming around. A guy named Kamau Daáood in Los Angeles is very good; he's got a CD out. There are a lot of folks who are beginning to see what this thing can be. For a while, people looked at this as a novelty, but it's not a novelty. If you understand the history of what we are talking about, [you realize] that's the way it originated. Poetry's a form of musical presentation.

FEINSTEIN: When you were talking about Amus Mor, you said that "Crouch was there before he turned into Crouch." [Baraka chuckles.] Now, you've written about jazz criticism—especially the imbalance of white critics, how few black writers there are—

BARAKA: Yeah—

FEINSTEIN: And in one essay you refer to Crouch as a very knowledgeable listener.

BARAKA: He is. But Stanley's problem—and we argue fiercely (I've known him since the beginning of the world)—is that he doesn't know anything about politics, or at least, in my view, he's got a backwards view politically. But he knows more about the music than he knows about, say, the political development of the United States. *I* think. For instance, he's been talking about coming out with a book on Charlie Parker for years and years, and I told him in an open forum, with Martin Williams, [Dan] Morgenstern, Gary Giddins: "Hey, the *Village Voice* is going to make Gary Giddins the chief jazz writer. They're gonna let you write that little funny stuff that you write, the little prose pieces, the little arty stuff, and then you're gonna disappear quietly out there. Because they don't want you. Because that's too important. Why? Because there's not one major newspaper in the United States with a black featured critic on jazz. Not one." (Briefly, during the '60s, when they thought that these black people gonna burn the world down, there were two or three. There was a guy with the *Philadelphia Enquirer,* the *Washington Post* had a guy, the *Voice*—and then they all became sports writers. It's incredible.) So I said, "I don't think they're going to do this, Stanley. I don't think you're gonna come out with the Charlie Parker book." Publishers don't want to do his books on the music, because the books on the music—and this is wholly conjecture—are more progressive. Because he *knows* more about the music.

Why aren't the music books out? Ask him. He's got a dumb book out called *The Hanging Judge.* He's got another dumb book out called *The Skin Game,* for which all kinds of people denounce him. At least I talk to him and tell him face to face, "I think this stuff is full of shit." But his musical criticism has never been that out to lunch. Stanley always knew quite a bit. As a matter of fact, of people that talk about the music, Stanley is one of the most engaging.

I don't agree with him all the time—for example, this revisionist shit that he wrote recently, how black musicians don't like Gershwin. I'm trying to figure that out. Black musicians don't like Gershwin? They play him all the fucking time! Tell me who don't play him? [Laughs.] He said the reason they don't like him is because he's a better composer than any of them except Duke. I said, "That's gratuitous ignorance, Stanley. That's gratuitous ignorance." First of all, to make that kind of juxtaposition is dumb. Name somebody that don't play Gershwin. That's bizarre to say that.

I put Gershwin in a play of mine called *The Life of Willie "The Lion" Smith,* a musical. It's only been done at NYU, [as] part of the Lost Jazz Shrines project, which is trying to rebuild the jazz neighborhoods. I had some quotes out of Willie "The Lion"'s book, *Music on My Mind,* where he says that Gershwin used to come up to Harlem in the '20s, and when he premiered *Rhapsody in Blue* he invited James P. Johnson, Fats Waller, and Willie "The Lion" down to this party on Park Avenue. So The Lion says, "He [Gershwin] was hogging up the piano, and me and James P. and Fats was at the bar getting drunker and drunker, and finally, when I got *so* drunk, I got enough nerve to say, 'Get up from the piano, you tomato, and let a real tickler sit down!'" Now, I quoted that in this play, and a month later everybody got this huge Gershwin Gershwin Gershwin . . . I wasn't putting Gershwin down. First of all, I was quoting Willie "The Lion" Smith about what that was. And here comes, from outer space, some defense which was not a defense. Gershwin don't need to be defended.

And this stuff about the black musicians—who's he talking about? Miles Davis played him every other tune. Sarah Vaughan. Billie Holiday. Even Art Blakey. Trane. That's just trying to find something that's not there. So I asked Stanley, "Do you really believe that?" and he says, "Well, the songs, the songs." But how can you say that with the songs?

It's crazy. You don't need Gershwin carrying the mark of Cain on him. His shit stands for itself. You don't have to do anything with it. You don't have to do "The Man I Love." "Summertime." I heard John Coltrane do it, I heard Charlie Parker do it, so obviously it wasn't anathema to them.

FEINSTEIN: You will not remember this, but my father met you once in about 1961, at a party on Park Avenue, where they had an all-black band, except for Larry Rivers, who kept trying to sit in but kept getting cut.

BARAKA: That was up at [the apartment owned by] the woman who published *Kulchur* magazine, Lita Hornick. I got the band for her.

FEINSTEIN: Really? Who played?

BARAKA: I can't remember. But I was one of the editors for *Kulchur*. Lita's husband, Morty, was a great asshole, but he was a nice guy. [Feinstein laughs.] Morty was the kind of guy who'd say, "Liberals are the people that'll tell you what to do with your money." That's the kind of guy he was. "I was a vice president at twenty-one." But he was a guy you could always get on. I'd say, "Man, Morty. You so full of shit." [Laughs, then, in a very nasal voice:] "Well, look, Roi . . ." Morty went along with whatever "Lee-tah" wanted—one of those guys. And Lita was all over the fuckin' place. I don't think she was an adulteress, but she was, like—*whew!*—out of her fuckin' mind. One day she would want to, you know, paint poodles green or some sort of shit, and Morty would say, "Whatever Lee-tah wants."

I guess Lita had introduced him to dyed-blond hair and culture. But she gave money for this magazine, and she bought these people's paintings. Larry was always a good friend of mine, but . . . [Laughs.] Larry always wanted to be Charlie Parker but, alas, he was Larry Rivers. And that ain't such a terrible compromise. [Both laugh.] But the point is, Larry, bless him, his heart was always in the right place. He wanted to play. His early days, on the edges of society—that's what he's playing.

Kulchur was a funny magazine. There was myself. Frank O'Hara. And if it was Park Avenue, that party had to have been there with Lita and Morty.

FEINSTEIN: My father said you must've also hated the party, because my parents and you all left really early, and in the elevator down there was total silence—not a word—until the doors opened on the ground floor. And just before you went your different ways, my dad said to you, "Well, I've enjoyed our little chat."

BARAKA: [Laughs.] That was me. At the time, I was going through a lot of changes. I was getting ready to get out of the Village, and to see what that meant. And it was just such things as that [party] that made me think, "What am I doing? What's the point of this? I mean, it's not that I hate everybody, but there's nothing that I want to do with *this*. It's got nothing to do with me." And that was the kind of quantitative build up—a whole lot of bullshit that had nothing to do with anything. And as serious as I can be about things, at that time I was probably more serious. And I just didn't see the relevance.

FEINSTEIN: Isn't that true, though, for decade after decade?

BARAKA: Sure. I think so. The Village and Lower East Side—they're really like Coney Island. It's a superfluous kind of mode. They're becoming a lot more "up top," but there are a lot of people there who are poseurs and various kinds of attractions. It's a lot of bullshit. Now, you can find that anywhere. Over here in Newark there's a lot of bullshit. But the point is, I don't need to be bombarded with shit presuming or proposing itself to be something that it ain't. At least most of the shit around here isn't presuming to be nothing but what it literally is. The politicians are full of shit, but once you find that out, it's no mystery. [Laughs.]

New York is the marketplace. The great supermarket. But though you can get over more easily in terms of doing art, it's not about that. What it gives you back is no longer satisfying. Jesus God. If you can be satisfied with the returns of that milieu in life, well, good—then you deserve to be there. [Laughs.] But it's nothing that I can use. I'd rather be here, in this little town, which is my birthplace, where I can't walk down the street without talking to four or five people because they know me. It's a sense, then, of actually being part of something real. This is where I live. This is my community. This is where I was born. My father lives down the street. My kids—you see them—in and out of here. I'm a real person. It's not like the fictitious life of the Village, where half of the people aren't telling the truth about their lives. They come from someplace *there,* so you don't know anything about them. It's different here because this is something that I am literally in real life trying to change and deal with. That makes a difference. That's the real thing.

And God knows there's a whole lot of opposition and resentment, and I'm sure the name Baraka does not elicit applause, even in this town. People want to know why I've changed so much. Hey, I'm alive. That's all. "Well, you said this yesterday"—yeah, but that was yesterday. That's Du Bois. Look at Du Bois. A great man. Lived to be ninety-five years old, and he changed every few minutes. Every time he thought the shit that he said was wrong, he'd say, "Hey, that shit I said was fucked up." If you can say that, it seems to me, that's healthier than having people say, "That shit you said last year was fucked up." Better you say it first.

· · · ·

FEINSTEIN: It seems to me that one of the challenges you have at this point in your career is trying to celebrate the voices that aren't heard often—maintaining that kind of integrity—but also understanding that the best way to do it is in a larger forum. In other words, knowing that the group downstairs is probably going to have the most heat, but you're also doing the Dodge Festival, PBS, even Hollywood. [Baraka had a part in the movie *Bullworth*.] How do you strike that balance?

BARAKA: The way *I* feel about it is if you're doing what you can see as useful—or necessary, important, whatever you want to call it—then the point is to do it wherever you can do it. As for Warren Beatty's thing, *Bullworth:* He called me one night and said, "Do you know me?" I said, "Do I know you? Yeah, I get out of the house every few years." [Both laugh.] And I said I'd do it, if he let me write my own words. That was my approach to it.

FEINSTEIN: What was his response?

BARAKA: "I'll call you back."

FEINSTEIN: Pretty guarded.

BARAKA: Oh yeah.

FEINSTEIN: And, in the end, did you write your own words?

BARAKA: Yeah. Some of the stuff that he gave me to do I did, but I, at least, held onto a core of what I wanted to do. See, he sat in front of my wife and I one night and told me the whole story, and I wrote it all down, copying the whole script in my notebook. I said, "Okay, I got it. I'm gonna go home and read it." So you have some influence on this; it's not just one-way. I could rap with him: "Hey, this is not going to work like this. We need to see some real black folks in this movie. You can't be Warren and out. We need to know where you got these great opinions from."

I think this is ultimately where it's at: "Have no fear" is the line. Because even if you make a mistake, as long as you try to do your best—and you might not do it, you might fuck up, you might get tricked, you might do anything—but I don't have that guilt. I just say, "No, I went in there to win. So he hit me in the head with an iron pipe. Well, next time I'll remember that." But it's the question of the guilt that people get, and I don't have that because I don't mean to do anything funny. If I go into the Hollywood world, I'm going to go in there saying, "Well, fuck you. Whatever you're gonna do, I've got something for you." I'm gonna say what I'm gonna say.

And Warren's mad at me. He wanted me to fly out there on a Sunday and give eight hours of interviews to television people, then go to the premiere, and then fly back. Now, this was in the middle of my son's political campaign, which he lost. (He won the general election, and then the mayor double-crossed him in the run-off.) I said, "I can't do it, Warren. I can't do it," and he insisted. "I can't do it." So he took my name off the credits—not in the movie, but in the advertising. He was pissed off, though he denied it, 'cause I asked him. I said, "I didn't know you were that fuckin' small minded, Warren." He said, "What?! What?!" I said, "Look. If I was getting the social remuneration that thou is getting, I might've come, dropped everything—if I was the wholly owner, wholly director, wholly producer, wholly star. I got a royalty check the other day that was completely surprising, and that's great. But I know if I was getting the royalty check you're getting I would be more hyped up about running down."

He was going to send a car over here, get me, drive to LaGuardia, fly me to goddamn Hollywood, stay there ten/twelve hours, and fly back. Now I've done that. I've flown out there and done nothing but sit in the hotel room, sit in the trailer. (Everybody's got a trailer—TV, stove, shower, bed. I mean, it's a groove: you sit in there getting paid. I'm listening to music and reading.) But I didn't do anything, and he flew me back. They got per diem money, and people get seduced by that: pick up the money—three or four hundred dollars—walk around, look at stuff. But they pick you up, you sit from 2:00 in the afternoon until 2:00 in the morning, doing absolutely nothing. "Well, we're not going to get to that today. We'll call you in four days." They give you the airplane ticket, you go back to the airport, and come back home.

They made me up so much . . . I was the only one who couldn't leave the set, 'cause when I left the set I couldn't get back on. I'd come back and they'd say, "What do you want?" [Laughs.] I'd say, "I'm an actor." "What are you talking about?" [Laughs.] 'Cause you look like a bum, a black bum walking around those expensive hotels and shit. They want to know what you're doing in there. The first thing I do is hold my hands up: "I ain't got no cutters on me!"

FEINSTEIN: Same thing happened today just about four blocks from here.

BARAKA: Really?

FEINSTEIN: I missed a turn, asked for directions, and as soon as I rolled down the window, a fellow on the street said, "I didn't steal nothin'!"

BARAKA: Well, you know what that is. They figure if they see a white face here, it's either (a) the police, or (b) someone coming from the suburbs to cop some dope. That's true. And that's the nature of segregation, particularly in Newark. This is a very segregated town. But it's not as bad as people say. This is an old, old city. These are the settlers, pre–Revolutionary War. There are roots in it that go back to that. My family's been here since the '20s. There are old, old people in this town, and at the same time there's a sort of transition in the last fifty years.

This is a hard little town, there's no doubt about that, but at the same time there's a kind of will to humanity that's never been crushed, from all sections of the population. This is a very diverse city—which, again, people don't know. There [are] a lot of Italians. This is the largest settlement of Portuguese in the country. Then there's Haitians, and Dominicans, and Puerto Ricans, and Jesus-God-knows-what.

FEINSTEIN: When you are quoted about Newark—in all sorts of publications—they always choose the negative statements—criticizing the Arts Center, and so on. And that's true, too, for your statements about public figures.

BARAKA: I think this is what they see as a continuum of the Black Nationalism and the height of negativity of the communism. They're determined to put you in a box that makes you seem like Mr. Nobody. It's a good strategy as far as the powers that be are concerned, so you have to do some other things to get outside of that. It's very, very difficult sometimes.

You're not hungry, are you?

Hayden Carruth

2

Those Upward Leaps
Hayden Carruth

When I first contacted Hayden Carruth to request an interview, he declined. "I've done so many interviews over the years," he said, "that, frankly, I just don't see the point. I've said pretty much everything I want to say."

Without much thinking, I played what seemed to be my only card:

"I appreciate what you're saying. But let me ask you this: Has anyone ever talked to you about Vic Dickenson?"

Carruth paused. "No. Not that I can recall."

"I had hoped to focus the interview on Dickenson and his influence on your work."

He paused again. "Yes," he said. And then, with still more enthusiasm, "Yes—let's do it."

What inspired my suggested focus on Vic Dickenson? Initially, it was Carruth's tribute, "What a Wonder Among the Instruments Is the Walloping Tramboone!" which had surprised me, since I knew Carruth's horn was the clarinet. The poem made me pay more attention to his other trombone-related pieces, particularly those inspired by Dickenson.

We agreed to meet at his home in Munnsville, New York. (According to a census reading the year of my visit, the village of Munnsville has a square footage of less than one mile and a population of 437 people— roughly 400 more than I would have guessed.) In his home, built-in bookshelves lined the walls and wrapped around corners. Carruth sat in the center near a wood stove. With sweeping white hair and an expansive beard, he looked like one of Tolkien's wisest characters.

His wife, Jo-Anne, had made a fabulous carrot cake and a pot of coffee, and we sat across from each other in their small kitchen. At first, Carruth seemed a bit guarded—the way, I suspect, he feels around any stranger—but as the afternoon progressed, he seemed to enjoy the conversation more and more. Before I left, I asked him to inscribe some of his books, and in my copy of *Sitting In,* he wrote: "This was a damn fine session."

Hayden Carruth has published more than forty books, chiefly of poetry but also including a novel, four books of criticism, and two anthologies. His recent books include *The Collected Shorter Poems, 1946–1991* (winner of the National Book Critics Circle Award), *Scrambled Eggs & Whiskey* (winner of the National Book Award for poetry), and *Toward the Distant Islands: New and Selected Poems.* He has had fellowships from the Bollingen Foundation, the Guggenheim Foundation (two), the National Endowment for the Arts (four), and others. He has also been honored with numerous awards, including the Lenore Marshall Award, the Vermont Governor's Medal, and the Ruth Lilly Prize.

The following poems reflect Carruth's admiration for Dickenson and jazz. The interview took place on September 16, 1998.

* * *

Paragraphs
(excerpts)
Hayden Carruth

26
A day   very solid   February 12th, 1944
cheerless in New York City

                              (while I kneedeep
elsewhere in historical war
was wrecking Beauty's sleep
and her long dream)

                        a day (blank, gray) at four
in the afternoon, overheated in the W. O. R.
Recording Studios. Gum wrappers *and* dust
and a stale smell. A day. The cast
was Albert Ammons, Lips Page, Vic Dickenson,
Don Byas, Israel
Crosby, and Big Sid Catlett. (*And* it was Abe Linkhorn's
birthday.) And Milt Gabler
presided over the glass with a nod, a sign. Ammons
counted off
                    a-waaaaan,,,   *tu*!

                and went feeling
his way on the keys gently,
                        while Catlett summoned

27
the exact beat from—
                say from the sounding depths, the universe . . .
When Dickenson came on it was all established,
no guessing, and he started with a blur
as usual, smears, brays—Christ
the dirtiest noise imaginable
                        belches, farts
                                curses
but it was music
                music now
                    with Ammons trilling in counterpoise.
Byas next, meditative, soft/
                    then Page
with that tone like the torn edge
of reality:
                and so the climax, long dying riffs—
groans, wild with pain—
and Crosby throbbing *and* Catlett riding stiff
yet it was music   music.
                        (Man, doan
fall in that bag,
                you caint describe it.)
                        Piano & drum,

Ammons & Catlett drove the others. *And* it was done
and they listened *and* heard themselves
        better than they were, for they had come

28
high above themselves. Above everything, flux, ooze,
loss, need, shame, improbability/   the awfulness
of gut-wrong,   sex-wrack,   horse & booze,
the whole goddam mess,
And Gabler said "We'll press it"   *and* it was
    "Bottom Blues"
BOTTOM BLUES   five men knowing it well   blacks
    & jews
yet music, music   high
in the celebration of fear, strange joy
of pain: blown out, beaten out
                                a moment ecstatic
in the history
of creative mind *and* heart/   not singular, not the rarity
we think, but real and a glory
our human shining, shekinah . . .   Ah,
                    holy spirit, ninefold
I druther've bin a-settin there, supernumerary
cockroach i' th' corner, a-listenin, a-listenin,,,,,,,
        than be the Prazedint ov the Wuurld.

In That Session
Hayden Carruth

In the mind's house of heaven the great night never
Ends.
    All the brothers are there: Berigan, Bechet,
Russell, Hawkins, Dickenson, Hodges,
And Mary Lou and Lady Day
And so many others.
                    And oh they play, they
    jam forever,
Shades of strange souls nevertheless caught together
In eternity and the blues.

No need
To cut anyone any more, no fatigue
From the straights out front or the repetitive changes,
But only expressiveness,   warmth,
Each invention a purity, new without strangeness
In that session.
                    Always they strained on earth
For this thing, skin and soul to merge, to disappear
In howling sound.
                        God, but it would be worth
Dying, if it could be done,
            to be there with them and to hear,   to *hear.*

Mort aux Belges!
Hayden Carruth

Consider the administration of
        justice in what was called the Belgian
Congo. If one man was convicted
        of thievery or irreligion

the soldiers went into his village
        and amputated the right hands
of all the inhabitants, men, women,
        and children, so that on the weekend

if you visited you'd find a circle
        of empty huts and in the center
on the beaten earth right hands heaped
        in a little pile for you to encounter

on your journey and think of those who
        lost them, helpless in the forest, children
probably bled to death—a village
        in every possible way abandoned.

Who'd be a Belgian? In '59
        for their Exposition they hired a band,
Bechet, Clayton, Dickenson to play the low-down blues,
        and still they didn't understand.

What a Wonder Among the Instruments Is the Walloping Tramboone!
Hayden Carruth

That elephantine bray in the upper register, that sagacious
    rumbling down below, that glissing whoop,
A human glory, a nobility—but ach, the good words for
    goodness have been bollixed in our degradation.
Recall then from the darkness of your adolescence, my still
    empowering spirit, the names of gladness,
J. C. Higgenbotham, Jim Harrison, Wilbur de Paris, Kid Ory,
    George Lugg, Dickie Wells, Trummy Young, Honore Dutry,
    Jimmy Archey,
And although in retrospection Teagarden was overrated, the
    white names too, Miff Mole, Floyd O'Brien, Brad Gowans,
    Lou McGarity, Vernon Brown,
May all their persons be never forgotten and their music
    continue in the ears of the chosen forever!
When the ancients first raised up the ram's horn to the heavens,
    it was in this loud register.
When mountaineers in their isolation laid down an alpenhorn
    to sound across the chasms, it was also the same.
And when the medieval genius of orchestra found itself in the
    voice of the sackbut, it discovered resonance, which is to say,
    sensuality unlimited.
Let me, spirit, assert no equalness beyond the insanity that is the
    built-in tragedy of homo sapiens,
But let me nevertheless, a pipping pallid clarinetist, say to the
    darker masters that although
The tenor sax has seemed the proper instrument for your
    sensibility, and much sound has come from it,
It is at best a facile machine lately devised by the engineering
    and anti-musical European intelligence,
Whereas the trombone, known fitly and affectionately as the
    sliphorn, is truly more near your *virtu.*
Spirit, let me revere and celebrate in poetry the life of Vic
    Dickenson, and let me mourn his death.
As for you, pipsqueak literati, for whom all writing is a
    conspiracy of rhetoric, draw yourselves far off yonder, for
    here is none of such intention.

Dickenson, no other could sing as you, your blasts, burbles, and
bellowing, those upward leaps, those staccato descensions,
Your smears, blurs, coughs, your tone veering from muted to
stentorian, your confidences, your insults,
All made in music, musically. Never was such range of feeling so
integrated in one man or instrument.
How you made farts in the white mob's face at the Belgian
International Exposition and Mr. Bechet laughed out loud.
You were the Wagner of tonal comedy, you were the all-time
King of the Zulus, you were jazz.
Thanks be to St. Harmonie for the others, yet next to you they
are extraneous to the essence, a throng milling outside.
I learned it all from you (and from a few dozen others), evinced
so incompletely in these poems, yet in my mind
A bliss for fifty years, my resource, my constancy in loneliness or
loving. Now you are dead.
You grew old, you lost your teeth, you who had seemed
indestructible have been destroyed, and somehow I survive.
Not long, however. Hence from aged humility I dare to speak.
May these words point to you and your recorded masterwork
forever,
Which means as long as our kind can endure. Longer than that,
who cares? Thereafter will be only noise and silence.

SASCHA FEINSTEIN: I want to talk about the trombonist Vic Dickenson
and his influence on your work, but perhaps we can lay some groundwork. Who introduced you to jazz—or did you do that on your own?

HAYDEN CARRUTH: Almost on my own. The first jazz record I heard was
in 1933, I think—somewhere around then. At that time I lived in a
very small agricultural town in New England and never heard any
jazz. But there was a rich kid in town (the only rich kid in town) and
he went to a private school and came back with a couple of early records by the Goodman band. I used to think that the first jazz record I
heard was *Stompin' at the Savoy,* but Goodman didn't record that until
'36. Maybe I heard the Chick Webb version somewhere. It doesn't matter: From that point on I was hooked.

We moved, fortunately (for my interest in jazz anyway), to the suburbs in Westchester County, and I was able to hear more jazz on the
radio. As I got a little older, I was able to go down to the city [New York

City] and visit the Commodore shop, and, eventually, go to Nick's and places like that on 52nd Street. And it went on from there.

Ever since I was a little kid I've played a tin whistle, what we used to call a ten cent Woolworth tin whistle. Six hole upright flageolet. [Laughs.] I still play it. And I studied the violin when I was a kid but I was not a good violinist. I was too tense and couldn't relax enough to play it. But I learned to read music, and after the [Second World] War—I was in my twenties—a friend of mine in Chicago loaned me an old Albert system clarinet, and I started messing around with that.

FEINSTEIN: Albert system clarinet—that's a tough horn.

CARRUTH: Well, if you start on it it's not tough. The tough part is when you start on an Albert and switch to a Boehm—[laughs]—as I did. Most of the old timers played the Albert system. Sidney Bechet—

FEINSTEIN: George Lewis—

CARRUTH: All those guys. I loved the clarinet, and I became a pretty good clarinetist, although I was ill, and living in seclusion I hardly ever played with other people. Of course, I never even thought about performing professionally.

FEINSTEIN: I find it interesting that you've written more about trombonists than clarinetists.

CARRUTH: I just love the trombone. If I had the right teeth and the right temperament and the right everything else, I'd have rather been a trombonist than anything else in the world. I love the sound, I love the range, I love all the textures and tones you can get on the damn thing. As I wrote in a poem at one time, I think it's a proper instrument. It's not a machine, like a tenor saxophone, or something like that. It's a basic tube which you slide on. I love that! [Laughs.] But I'd have been glad to play anything.

FEINSTEIN: Unlike most poets who address jazz, you tend to focus on earlier players.

CARRUTH: That's because I'm seventy-seven years old, and that's what I heard when I was growing up. I suppose the early music you hear in your life is the one that sticks with you the most. I was listening to jazz very actively from, say, 1935 to 1980. The period since then I have not listened so much. I'm not sufficiently trained to appreciate the work that's being done by the workshop musicians and all those guys, and frankly it doesn't appeal to me so much. I'm an old-time jazz guy. I like jazz that swings. I like jazz that's raucous and ripe.

FEINSTEIN: That reminds me of those great lines in your poem "Freedom and Discipline" [from *Nothing for Tigers*, 1965]: "Freedom and discipline concur / only in ecstasy, all else / is shoveling out the muck. / Give me my old hot horn." [Carruth chuckles.] Could you talk a bit more about the difference in freedom between music and poetry? It sounds as though jazz has the edge.

CARRUTH: Jazz has the edge over poetry for me. It's more expressive, it's what I would have liked to do if I had been able to, but I don't remember if that's what I had in mind when I wrote those lines—which was a helluva long time ago. I think the combination of discipline and freedom in the arts is very well exemplified by a jazz musician who's playing a twelve-bar blues. The form is absolutely fixed—as fixed as a triolet in poetry, or any other artificial form—and yet it provides him or her with almost limitless freedom to do what he or she wants to do in the way of harmonic and rhythmic invention. In my writing of poetry, I have always tried to emulate the improvisation that occurs within a fixed and sure and recognizable form. I like that. I think the analogy between music and poetry can be pushed only so far—but it can be pushed that far.

FEINSTEIN: Is that the central influence that jazz has had on your poetry?

CARRUTH: Well, jazz is the sexiest music there ever was, and I hope some of my poetry is the sexiest poetry there ever was. [Both laugh.]

FEINSTEIN: One of my favorite books of yours remains *Brothers, I Loved You All*, which concludes with the long poem "Paragraphs"—twenty-eight sections, each with fifteen lines—

CARRUTH: I invented that form, called it a "paragraph" (for no very good reason). Yes, fifteen lines, with a set rhyme scheme and a set metrical scheme. I use it loosely in different places. It occurs first in a poem called "Asylum," then in "Contra Mortem," then in those paragraphs, and then in *The Sleeping Beauty*, and I've written a few since then.

FEINSTEIN: It seems in keeping with what you were saying about blues musicians—improvisation within a set structure.

CARRUTH: Oh yeah. I think so.

FEINSTEIN: The last three sections in "Paragraphs" address jazz most directly. Do you remember writing them, or just the lines, "I druther've bin a-settin there, supernumerary / cockroach i' th' corner, a-listenin, a-listenin,,,,,,, / than be the Prazedint ov the Wuurld"?

CARRUTH: [Laughs.] I love that—if I say so myself. I can *vaguely* remember writing them. It was a long time ago. The record I was writing about [*Albert Ammons and the Rhythm Kings*, Commodore 1516] is one that I still play from time to time. I think it's a great record, with Dickenson on there doing his thing. I don't know what exactly I had in mind with those final lines, except that I was imagining a voice—I think a woman's voice, maybe Billie Holiday's voice—saying those lines.

FEINSTEIN: It seems to me a jam session is the perfect close when you've taken on as much as you have in "Paragraphs." It brings it all together.

CARRUTH: The sequence of poems in those paragraphs is pretty rough and ready. I did put those three paragraphs at the end because that's where I wanted them to be. Originally the sequence was longer—quite a bit longer. There were about eighty of them. But various people didn't like them, and I started cutting them out, which may have been a mistake. It's the kind of thing I've done in my life, a number of times. So it got reduced to what's there. I think they do draw things together. The themes in the paragraphs are about suffering and war and deprivation and the defoliation of the world.

I made a mistake in those last three paragraphs, which I've always regretted but never have found a way to change.

FEINSTEIN: Change it now.

CARRUTH: Can't. [Laughs.] It's built in. There's someplace in there where I say that this is a music of "blacks & jews," but there isn't any Jew on that record. I thought that bass player [Israel Crosby] was a Jew, but he's not. He's a black man. [Laughs.]

FEINSTEIN: Let me ask you about a different ending. Your poem "Mort aux Belges!" originally concluded with references to Bechet and Dickenson and Clayton. This is a poem about crime and punishment, or perhaps criminal punishments. What made you close with jazz?

CARRUTH: I've always loved the recording that was made in Belgium [Sidney Bechet, *Recorded in Concert at the Brussels Fair, 1958*, Columbia 1410]. Do you know this record?

FEINSTEIN: No, I don't think so.

CARRUTH: I'll play it for you.

[Carruth finds the LP and tracks it to "Society Blues." After several other solos, Dickenson enters, and soon he infuses his solo with loud, prolonged growls so fart-like in their translation that we both laugh throughout the rest of the tune.]

FEINSTEIN: Man, that was great.

CARRUTH: It was. And you have to imagine the scene. There are these wonderful exponents of a vital culture on the stage in Brussels, facing a huge audience of affluent Belgians and tourists, and you can bet there wasn't a black person in the whole damn crowd. Then Dickenson did what he did—right at them. In fact, that's what the phrase "in your face" means, isn't it? Moreover, he got paid to do it, which I'm sure delighted him. But the real point is that he did it musically, within the context of the music. Dickenson was a joker and a wry philosopher, but he was never a mugger; he never played Uncle Tom for the white audience the way Armstrong did. Dickenson and the others—Bechet, Clayton, et cetera—were always aware of their dignity as artists and human beings. That's why Armstrong got rich and they were always poor. Give Armstrong all the credit he deserves—he was a fine musician, a great leader, an important influence—but he played the fool, too. He did it over and over, like Stepin Fetchit. Dickenson never, never did that.

FEINSTEIN: Do you think Dickenson, then, was a greater figure than Armstrong?

CARRUTH: No. Anyway, who knows? Let's leave the final judgments to St. Peter. But I do think that Dickenson and musicians like him did more than Armstrong to sustain the artistic integrity of jazz in the long run. They are the ones who made jazz the most important cultural achievement of the twentieth century—which is what some of us predicted would happen fifty or sixty years ago.

FEINSTEIN: Dickenson's having so much fun on that date. What commentary! Perhaps that's why you closed the poem ["Mort aux Belges!"] with that concert—as commentary. But when you reprinted the poem in *Scrambled Eggs & Whiskey,* why did you cut that final stanza?

CARRUTH: [Looks down, then up again.] That's news to me. [Feinstein laughs.] I don't think I took it out.

FEINSTEIN: It's not there.

CARRUTH: Huh. I'll have to take it up with those guys out there. [Laughs.] Somebody dropped it, I guess—on proof it just got lost—and I never paid any attention to it. You know, I don't read my own books much. But I have no recollection of deleting those lines, and I don't think I would have.

FEINSTEIN: In your poem "In That Session," you say it would be worth dying just to hear that group play. Did you ever hear Vic Dickenson live?

CARRUTH: I never heard him live. That's true, in my case, of a great many musicians. As I've said, I have been ill and secluded much of my life, and I feel very uncomfortable in public places. So my listening is mostly on records. You know, there are aspects of technology that all of us deplore, but recording technology has been a lifesaver for me, and for music in general. There are some unfortunate aspects to it: I do think that jazz—taken as a whole span from 1910 to the present—has evolved too fast, and I think in part that's because of recordings. Musicians can listen to what they've done, and listen to what other people have done, too easily. And then the urge for novelty overtakes them.

FEINSTEIN: I never thought of it that way.

CARRUTH: If you listen to the history of European music from, say, Monteverdi to early Beethoven, it's a nice, slow progression over 150 or 200 years. If that had happened in jazz, I think there would have been more small developments and more filling out of the different modes and styles and movements than there has been.

FEINSTEIN: Let me ask you about a more recent poem, "What a Wonder Among the Instruments Is the Walloping Tramboone!" [Carruth laughs.] Did you make those lines so long so that they would wrap around like trombone slides?

CARRUTH: I don't know. My practice in writing poems has always been to say things in my mind, to establish a rhythm and a kind of tone or texture. Certainly I was writing about trombones, and maybe I was trying to do something [with the form]—but I don't think [it was done] consciously.

FEINSTEIN: Among the many trombonists in this poem, Dickenson stands out as the most celebrated figure. Here's one line that refers to him: "May these words point to you and your recorded masterwork forever." Is that one function of jazz poetry—to bring more attention to great jazz musicians?

CARRUTH: It is *a* function, why not? Any kind of writing is a drawing of attention to the topic, whatever that may be. If the topic is jazz, and you can attract some readers to enjoy and appreciate jazz, well, I think that would be great. There is that built-in propagandistic element in any art, and if it becomes too prominent or conspicuous then the art is spoiled. But to deny that it exists would be foolish.

FEINSTEIN: I felt that there was an impulse in this poem to say to the world, "You need to check out Vic Dickenson."

CARRUTH: I did have that motive. I wanted to draw attention to Dickenson, to jazz—I've tried to do that in all of my jazz poems—though I don't know how successful it was. That poem was published in a very small publication. I doubt if many people read it.

FEINSTEIN: But it also appeared in your *Collected* [*Shorter Poems*], which has been appropriately celebrated and honored.

CARRUTH: Yeah. It's in that book. Dickenson had just died when I wrote that poem, and partly I just wanted to write an elegy.

FEINSTEIN: Your praise for him seems limitless. Here's another line from that poem: "Never was such range of feeling so integrated in one man or instrument."

CARRUTH: Well, that's a very sweeping statement, and who knows if it can be supported.

FEINSTEIN: No, but there's real passion. Why does Dickenson do it for you?

CARRUTH: In the first place, he's a marvelous musician. I don't know anything about his life. I don't know anything about his training. I doubt if he was classically trained on the trombone, but maybe he was. In any case, he taught himself how to exploit the instrument fully, and with great technical virtuosity. He could play very difficult passages, and play them perfectly. But at the same time, he was a man of enormous exuberance and vitality and had the kind of sweetness of emotional fabric that gets into the music, and he was intense about it. And the rest of those guys of his generation were, if they were any good. That's one of the reasons why I like that music—it's fully expressive. It isn't showing off. It isn't simply virtuosity. These guys were playing because they had feelings and wanted to say something.

Music is an integrative force in the human sensibility—much more than poetry. Poetry's always distracted by ideas and abstractions, but music is as concrete as you can get. If you have feelings, it's going to come out in the music as an integrated piece of work. It's one of the things about music that's so wonderful.

FEINSTEIN: In your recent collection of autobiographical essays, *Reluctantly*, I was surprised that Miff Mole was discussed more than Dickenson. In fact, I don't think Dickenson is even mentioned.

CARRUTH: I don't think he is. That's a book I won't even read . . . [Chuckles.] It is a book about personal reminiscence, and so I write about people I knew, and I knew Miff Mole, a little bit, when I was in Chicago, so I stuck him in there.

One of the things about jazz that makes me so sorrowful is the ending of most musicians' lives. So many of them who did brilliant work ended up in poverty, alone, and suffering in one way or another.

And certainly Mole did. I don't think he was a great musician. I think he was a good, capable musician of his time. He was influential, certainly, in white jazz of the '20s and '30s. But when I knew him, he was down and out: old, wandering around the South Side of Chicago like a lost soul.

FEINSTEIN: That's very sad.

CARRUTH: Yeah.

FEINSTEIN: I agree, too, with what you say about his musicianship. To be fair, Dickenson was a vastly superior player, and he could play in all sorts of settings. He was even on that Langston Hughes record, *Weary Blues.*

CARRUTH: I've heard that, but I've never owned it, never listened to it properly.

FEINSTEIN: Dickenson primarily plays ensemble work—

CARRUTH: I think he was a very much admired musician, and he was often used as a sideman. Last night I was listening to that record that Odetta made [*Odetta Sings the Blues*], where she sings with a little band that Panama Francis put together, and Dickenson was on that. He really is a wonderful complement to her. He was a good accompanist as well as a good soloist.

FEINSTEIN: Oh absolutely. The Hughes gig, of course, is a mixed bag of stuff. What's your opinion of jazz and poetry collaborations?

CARRUTH: Most of them are not successful, and I've always resisted doing it myself. People have wanted me to do it, but I don't know how to do it. The best one I ever heard was Michael Harper playing with Julius Hemphill and the guy on cello was—

FEINSTEIN: Abdul Wadud—

CARRUTH: Yeah. I heard them down in Wilkes-Barre [Pennsylvania], a number of years ago, and they had worked out a program ahead of time, which was pretty well rehearsed and pretty well integrated. Of course, Michael is the kind of a guy who could do that, who could fit in well. And Baraka has done a couple of good things, too. But the things that [Kenneth] Rexroth did and people like that I thought were pretty awful. [Laughs.] You know, somebody stands up and reads a poem, and then they play some music—and there's no connection, no thread running through the program.

FEINSTEIN: Your book *Sitting In* [*Selected Writings on Jazz, Blues, and Related Topics*] remains a favorite of mine, and there aren't many like it— that offer both poetry and prose. What inspired that kind of project?

CARRUTH: It was a miscellaneous book. The essays were written over a period of time. I was living in Pennsylvania at the time, teaching at Bucknell in Lewisburg, and had a lot of time on my hands. I didn't know very many people, but one of the persons I did know down there was Bill Duckworth, a classical composer—quite a good one. (I've written some lyrics in collaboration with him.) He knows jazz, appreciates it a lot, and we used to listen together. So I was thinking about jazz, and a lot of the essays in there were written quickly, spontaneously, but on ideas and feelings and moods and themes that I had been brooding about for years. So it was easy to write about them. But I don't know what I had in mind—I had no audience, and I had no reputation as a jazz writer. I published almost always in literary magazines where I felt, sometimes, they seemed out of place. Some of the essays appeared in *APR* [*American Poetry Review*] and places like that. But the book as a whole was not thought of as a book until later on.

FEINSTEIN: In a few essays, you hit some poets pretty hard, such as William Carlos Williams, for not being able to hear jazz, to understand jazz. Which poets do you admire for their appreciation of the music?

CARRUTH: None of the older ones. None of them. I don't think there was anyone in Williams's generation, or even the generation following him, that knew how to listen to jazz or had any appreciation of it at all, as far as I know. I never ran into one. It wasn't only Williams who was deaf to jazz; all of them were. Even the guys like [Carl] Van Vechten, who made an effort to understand African American culture in the '20s and '30s, didn't understand the music. I don't know why.

It was like my mother, who hated jazz. She was very musical, she had perfect pitch, she liked opera, she loved to listen to symphonic music. But the idea that jazz came out of the whorehouse and that's where it belonged was so deeply ingrained in her that she literally could not hear what was happening in musical terms. And that was true all through the generation of World War Two. Delmore Schwartz couldn't understand jazz. Randall Jarrell couldn't understand jazz. None of those guys could. I think—if I may say so immodestly— I'm just about the oldest poet in the country who does understand jazz. Most of the poets who have written intelligently about jazz are younger than I am—people like yourself, or Yusef [Komunyakaa], or my friend Paul Zimmer. Stephen Dobyns knows jazz and has written about it a little bit. But the older poets, no.

FEINSTEIN: What do you think, in general, about contemporary poetry? Do you think it's too safe?

CARRUTH: I think it's awful. It's conformist. It's workshoppish. It's governed pretty largely by the politics of literature. The poets themselves have been mistrained and misguided. It's dead. I mean the known, official poets. Some young poets writing in obscurity are doing fine original work.

FEINSTEIN: Do you think the dead ones need to listen to Dickenson?

CARRUTH: That would be *great*. [Laughs.]

Jayne Cortez

3

Returning to Go Someplace Else
Jayne Cortez

"Boy, we sure are out there," said Jayne Cortez, responding to the Pennsylvania landscape. In fact, we were less than three hours outside of Manhattan, and I didn't fully catch on until she asked about Klan activity. I tried to suggest that these towns weren't quite as bleak as they looked (my only lie during her visit) and changed the topic: I had recently been in touch with a poet she knew who had also been associated with the Black Arts Movement of the '60s. In a recent exchange, he claimed that various Black Arts writers had conspired to box him out of the limelight, making sure, for example, that his work was not frequently anthologized. Cortez shook her head. "He left New York," she said, coldly. "When you leave New York, you lose."

Jayne came to my college in Williamsport to give a reading, so interviewing her in Pennsylvania seemed convenient and smart. In retrospect, though, I should have conducted the interview in Manhattan; it was tough for her to find her stride in these woods. (When she finally got hungry, it was four in the afternoon and we had difficulty finding a restaurant that served food between lunch and dinner hours; you can imagine her astonishment.) Strangest of all was our conversation just prior to the interview as we walked to her guest suite. She mentioned a poem by William Matthews, and I assumed she brought him up because Bill had died eight days earlier. But she hadn't heard the news, and when I told her, I could tell she felt stricken.

I mention this because the interview is among the shortest and seems comprised of bursts as opposed to lengthy meditations. Perhaps someone else could have inspired more fluid responses; perhaps, in the spirit of someone like Thelonious Monk, she preferred pithy statements to hang in the air without greater explanation.

At that evening's performance, I might add, her whole demeanor changed: She charged up the crowd like a great tenor player blowing chorus after chorus on a swinging blues. She read and chanted and sang. She drove her lines harder and harder. And the audience clapped and cheered and whistled after every single poem.

Jayne Cortez is the author of many books of poetry, most recently *Somewhere in Advance of Nowhere* and *Jazz Fan Looks Back*. She has also recorded nine CDs of her poetry, including *Find Your Own Voice: Poetry and Music 1982–2003*. Her poems have been translated into twenty-eight languages and have been widely anthologized. Her many honors include the American Book Award, the International African Festival Award, and two National Endowment for the Arts fellowships. She lives in New York City and performs her work around the world in a great variety of settings, from the Museum of Modern Art to the Arts Alive International Festival in Johannesburg, South Africa.

This conversation focused on the following jazz poems: "About Flyin' Home," "States of Motion," and "Bumblebee, You Saw Big Mama." The interview took place in the Admissions House Guest Suite at Lycoming College in Williamsport, Pennsylvania, on November 20, 1997.

About Flyin' Home
Jayne Cortez

What would you say to yourself
if you had to lay on your back
hold up the horn
& play 99 courses of
a tune called Flyin' Home
exactly as you recorded it

55 years ago
& what would you think
if you woke up in the afternoon
& your head was still spinning with
voices shouting
Flyin' Home blow Flyin' Home
& what would you do
if someone whispered in your ear
hug me kiss me anything
but please don't play Flyin' Home
& what if a customer said:
tonight I'm having sex with
a person who has been up
in a flying saucer
so please funk me down good with Flyin' Home
& what would you think
if someone started singing
Yankee Doodle Dandy
in the middle of your solo on Flyin' Home
& what if you had to enter
all the contaminated areas in the world
just to perform your infectious version of
Flyin' Home
& what if you saw yourself
looking like a madman
with a smashed horn
walking backward on a subway platform
after 50 years of blowing Flyin' Home
& what would you think to yourself
if you had to play Flyin' Home
when you didn't have
a home to fly to
& what if Flyin' Home became
your boogie-woogie social security check
your oldie-but-goodie way out of retirement
& was more valuable than you
I mean somewhere
in advance of nowhere
you are in here
after being out there
Flyin' Home

States of Motion
Jayne Cortez

Sun Ra left the planet traveling in a pyramid made of metal keys
Willie Mae Thornton sailed away in an extra large moisture-
    proof harmonica
Pauline Johnson flew off to the meeting in her brass trimmed
    telephone
Thelonious Monk withdrew seated in a space ship shaped like a
    piano
Art Blakey departed in a great wood & stainless steel bass drum
Esther Phillips bowed out in a nasal sounding chrome
    microphone
Charles Tyler, George Adams & Clifford Jordan reached another
    realm riding in receptacles constructed like saxophones
Okot p'Bitek shoved off in an attaché case full of songs, books &
    whiskey
Leon Damas hit the road in a big black banjo
Audre Lorde departed while wrapped in her book jackets
Dizzy Gillespie zoomed off in a sweet chariot shaped like a
    trumpet
Miles Davis left in a magnificent copper mute
Marietta Damas vacated the terrain in one beautiful house filled
    with folkloric & electronic gadgets
Romare Bearden crossed over the rainbow in a blimp made of
    his collages & etchings
Norman Lewis pushed away from the shore in a vault shaped
    like a bicycle
Ed Blackwell concealed in an assortment of cymbals marched
    off to the Mardi Gras
Tchikaya U'Tamsi floated away in a big heart-shaped tuba
Vivian Browne departed draped in her painted forest canvases
Larry Neal went to the bush enclosed in two bookcases of
    poetry & Bebop tapes
Kimako Baraka evacuated the surface in a stone temple marked
    with Egyptian hieroglyphics
Wilfred Cartey got away from the hurricane in an ocean liner
    made of rum bottles
Johnny Makatini took off in a black, green & yellow rocket
Kathy Collins departed in a container made of unedited film clips

John Carter left in a fabulous silver clarinet
Evan Walker split in his boat that was shaped like a bird
Dumile Feni hurried to South Africa in one of his muscle-
    bound wooden sculptures
Peter Tosh reached the intersection in a bus filled with herbs &
    political newspapers
Bob Marley retreated away in a booming amplifier draped in
    African flags tied with dreadlocks
Ana Mendieta made her exit as a bronze Silueta
Michael Smith left for the forest in one huge audio cassette case
Elena & Jawa Apronti traveled from Accra in compartments
    made of ceremonial umbrellas
Bill Majors rode off into the sunset in a highly polished brass
    mercedes benz
Coco Anderson went to the festival in a fixture shaped like a
    yam wrapped with eight patchwork quilts
Franco L. Makiadi rolled off in a king-size purple guitar
Nicolás Guillén went to the rendezvous in a grand rumba cow
    bell
Tamu Bess traveled home in a queen-size computer plastered
    with eyeglasses
Flora Nwapa crossed the horizon concealed in pages of her new
    novel
Sarah Vaughan ascended in a misty glass recording booth
Gilberto de La Nuez disappeared into one of his paintings in
    Havana

Bumblebee, You Saw Big Mama

Jayne Cortez

You saw Big Mama Thornton
in her cocktail dresses
& cut off boots
& in her cowboy hat
& man's suit
as she drummed &
hollered out
the happy hour of her negritude
                    Bumblebee

You saw Big Mama
trance dancing her chant
into cut body of
a running rooster
scream shouting her talk
into flaming path of
a solar eclipse
cry laughing her eyes into
circumcision red sunsets
                        at midnight
                        Bumblebee

You saw Big Mama
bouncing straight up like a Masai
then falling back spinning her
salty bone drying kisser of music
into a Texas hop for you to
lap up her sweat
                        Bumblebee

You saw Big Mama
moaning between ritual saxes
& carrying the black water of Alabama blood
through burnt weeds & rainy ditches
to reach the waxy surface of your spectrum
                        Bumblebee

You didn't have to wonder
why Big Mama sounded
so expressively free
so aggressively great
once you climbed
into valley roar
of her vocal spleen
& tasted sweet grapes
in cool desert
of her twilight
                        Bumblebee

You saw Big Mama
glowing like
a full charcoal moon

riding down
Chocolate Bayou Road
& making her entrance
into rock-city-bar lounge
& swallowing that
show-me-no-love supermarket exit sign
in her club ebony gut
you saw her
get tamped on by the hell hounds
& you knew when she was happy
you knew when she was agitated
you knew what would make her thirsty
you knew why Big Mama
heated up the blues for Big Mama
to have the blues with you

after you stung her
& she chewed off your stinger
Bumblebee
You saw Big Mama

SASCHA FEINSTEIN: We reprinted "A Miles Davis Trumpet" in the first issue of *Brilliant Corners,* so perhaps we could talk about others from
Somewhere in Advance of Nowhere. This afternoon you discussed the
dangers of simply echoing what other people have played, or even
your own playing. Is that what inspired "About Flyin' Home"?

JAYNE CORTEZ: There was a celebration of the tune "Flyin' Home," and
for tenor saxophonist Illinois Jacquet who had recorded the tune with
the Lionel Hampton band almost fifty years ago. When I was about
ten years old, I heard the Hampton band at an afternoon concert in a
baseball stadium in Los Angeles. The band played "Flyin' Home" over
and over. It was a crowd pleaser. The people were especially excited by
Illinois' solo and big honking Texas sound. My poem "About Flyin'
Home" is about repeating something exactly as it had been recorded
and how that something is no longer a release. I admire Illinois very
much. He definitely has that big time black Texas sound and energy.

FEINSTEIN: Several jazz musicians have been saddled with a famous
tune—

CORTEZ: There are signature poems, signature tunes, theme songs, et cetera, but that has nothing to do with depth or art or spontaneity. A signature is a signal before an intermission or it means the gig is over and goodbye. It's nice to have famous tunes, especially if you get residuals or royalties. But if I had to read the same poem over and over, night after night, I would get no satisfaction.

FEINSTEIN: Your book is framed by "About Flyin' Home" and—I guess it's actually the penultimate poem—"States of Motion," which reads like a series of brief elegies.

CORTEZ: The poem "States of Motion" was written for the book *Fragments*, a collaboration with sculptor Melvin Edwards. Actually, I was responding to some of his sculpture when in walked "States of Motion" like a dream. A great surprise that created its own sculpture: "Sun Ra left the planet traveling in a pyramid made of metal keys."

FEINSTEIN: Other poems of yours seem to be built in similar ways. Do you see poems as sculpture?

CORTEZ: No. I don't see poems as sculpture.

FEINSTEIN: There are a great many jazz musicians mentioned in the poem. They might dominate—

CORTEZ: I knew the musicians mentioned in the poem—

FEINSTEIN: Is that simply because there have been so many losses?

CORTEZ: There have been many losses. This project gave me an opportunity to respond to those losses, to creativity, creation, and creative people.

FEINSTEIN: There is a strong sense of cadence in "States of Motion," but it's not the same kind of cadence that you have, say, in "About Flyin' Home," where you return to a refrain. I can't think of anyone who uses the refrain as effectively as you do.

CORTEZ: The refrain might be expected but what the refrain is relating to is unexpected.

FEINSTEIN: It's so hard to do that well.

CORTEZ: There are always comings and goings. You go, you return, and in between there are internal and external changes, environmental changes, changes based on personal experience, based on information. There are no exact ocean waves. The refrain is a device to add the next layer of sound, next metaphor, next transformation.

FEINSTEIN: You've done that as far as I can remember, starting with *Pissstained Stairs* [from 1969]. Do you see substantial changes in your poetry in terms of the use of repetition or otherwise?

CORTEZ: I see changes. I use more repetition. I make use of more material from the subconscious, from dreams. I try to go to the other shore, or to let go of the other shore, and let whatever's in the deep water come up to the surface. I use those hidden elements, those impulses to develop poems and surprise myself, and to keep on wanting to write poetry. The work has changed because I've changed.

FEINSTEIN: Of course. But you've always worked from the subconscious, as all good artists *have* to—

CORTEZ: I would like to have no known references, let references pop up from the out-of-nowhere place in me. Just let it happen and write, or write and let it happen.

FEINSTEIN: Do you find that the majority of your poems come in one burst like that? Do you do a great deal of revision?

CORTEZ: A number of poems come like that. Sometimes I do revision. For example, the guitar poem ["The Guitars I Used to Know"] took me about three years to complete. I kept starting and stopping, revising and revising. I couldn't find the shape, the launch pad, the point of departure. When I started working on my CD *Taking the Blues Back Home,* I felt that I had to have the guitar poem as a part of the project. There were two great guitar players [Bern Nix and Carl Weathersby] set for the session, so I rewrote the poem and finalized it during the rehearsal period. Maybe I needed that kind of pressure. Maybe it was the right time. But it took three years of tearing up a lot of paper for it to be what it is.

FEINSTEIN: Did "About Flyin' Home" and "States of Motion" come faster?

CORTEZ: "Flyin' Home" came flyin' out. I had an early relationship with "Flyin' Home." I knew the tune. I heard the Lionel Hampton band.

FEINSTEIN: Perhaps the poem was brewing for a long time without your consciously thinking about it.

CORTEZ: Maybe it was stored in the storage space of my mind. But I wasn't even thinking about "Flyin' Home" until the day that they were celebrating the fiftieth anniversary of the tune. I started thinking about routine, and what it leads to.

FEINSTEIN: You recently recorded "Bumblebee, You Saw Big Mama," a poem for Big Mama Thornton. Did you have a relationship with her, too?

CORTEZ: I knew the music of Big Mama Thornton because I attended teenage dances where she would be singing with the Johnny Otis band in L.A. Later, I heard her at clubs, blues and jazz festivals, and once at the Cookery. In the 1970s and early '80s, the Cookery was a spot in New York City where you could hear great women musicians like Mary Lou Williams, Nellie Lutcher, and Rose Murphy. When the owner of the Cookery rediscovered Alberta Hunter and she made her singing re-entry, she became the only attraction. The Cookery was her home base in New York City. So hearing Big Mama there with pianist Sammy Price was a rare occasion. It was really nice for me because I had a chance to talk to her.

I liked Big Mama's sound. The way she produced her music, her deep spiritual feeling. She was so dynamic and unpredictable. I was very impressed. She was an aggressive singer, and obviously an aggressive person. She could play the drums, she could play the harmonica, she could sing, she had a band, she looked the way she wanted to look, she dressed how she wanted to dress. She was a person who seemed very free.

FEINSTEIN: Your description of her reminds me of Robert Hayden's poem for Bessie Smith, "The Empress of the Blues."

CORTEZ: Oh, yes. I always remember his poem about Bessie, and Sterling Brown's about Ma Rainey.

FEINSTEIN: What did you talk about with Big Mama Thornton?

CORTEZ: We talked about the past, about certain people and clubs in Houston, Texas. And I reminded her of the teenage dances in L.A., how she sang in the band that also featured Little Esther Phillips.

FEINSTEIN: Big Mama Thornton isn't nearly as well known as she should be.

CORTEZ: No. She's not well known. And Big Maybelle is not well known. They didn't have the opportunity to express half of the music in their souls on record.

FEINSTEIN: Obviously individual poems don't create legacy.

CORTEZ: Right.

FEINSTEIN: But did you write and perform the poem in part to tell the world about this magical singer?

CORTEZ: I wanted to remember her, to retrieve something from my memory about her. The poem is about a creative person and the creativity in my community. It's about stinging and being stung. I wrote it because I was inspired by her and she was a magical singer. I don't know if the poem will make Big Mama famous. I don't know how many people will read the book or hear the CD or search for more information on Big Mama Willie Mae Thornton.

≈ ≈ ≈ ≈

FEINSTEIN: Earlier today I mentioned how much I admired Ed Blackwell, someone you knew very well. Can you talk a bit about the relationship between, say, a brilliant drummer and a very musical poet?

CORTEZ: Blackwell was like a brother. I met him in Los Angeles around 1953 or '54. I heard him play in many different spaces. He wrote a tune for my son called "Denardo's Dribbles." He would babysit and put those rattles in Denardo's hands and shake out some rhythm patterns. Maybe that's why Denardo became a drummer.

I read my work with Blackwell in the 1970s in concert with Wilbur Ware, Clifford Thornton, and Sam Rivers at a gig organized by Bill Cole at Amherst College. Blackwell sounded like a one-man African drum ensemble. My poem "Everywhere Drums" is dedicated to Blackwell and we recorded that piece together with Denardo and Ghanaian drummer Abraham Adzinya in 1990. Blackwell was such a powerful inventor of sound, rhythm, and time. He sure could charge up the atmosphere. I can't think of Blackwell without thinking cymbals, drums, and drumsticks.

FEINSTEIN: In the same way, perhaps, that I cannot think of your work without thinking of percussion.

CORTEZ: Is that right? Well, that's a compliment.

FEINSTEIN: I was asking about drums and poetry because your work is so propulsive.

CORTEZ: I think all experiences and memories carry different rhythms, different conflicts, and are conflictive rhythms. Drumbeats accent and support various pitches, phrases. Denardo can follow me, converse with me, and play what I say on his drums. That makes the encounter rhythmically exciting. I like reading my work with an assortment of drums. Several of my poems about drums and drummers have been published—"I See Chano Pozo," "Everywhere Drums," "If the Drum Is a Woman."

FEINSTEIN: With your band The Firespitters, you've recorded eight CDs. What are some of the struggles inherent in creating a solid union between poetry and music?

CORTEZ: The definition and implication of words. The definition and implication of harmony and rhythm. The effort to combine speech and music. Finding the key set of words, the pitch, the direction, the tempo. At rehearsals, we talk about the subject, about what the images suggest in musical terms. I read, they play. We make up things. We listen to each other. We try to make connections. Getting the gig is a struggle. Never having enough money to pay for the space and time needed to experiment is a struggle. I started reading my poetry with music in 1964. I organized the Firespitter band with Denardo in 1980. Now the poetry is the focus. The musicians respond to the poetry.

FEINSTEIN: There must be times when things aren't going well.

CORTEZ: Anything can happen in a recording session. I'm usually in an isolated booth, and each instrument is usually isolated. Sometimes we can't see each other. We are depending on the engineer and on the headsets. The sound in the headset always needs adjusting. We usually do a recording session in one day. We are wired up. It's very intense.

In 1982, when we recorded the album *There It Is,* the setup in the studio was negative. There were no isolation spaces. I had to scream my lungs out in the middle of the room so the musicians could hear the words and respond.

FEINSTEIN: But now you have Harmolodic [a record company—a subdivision of Verve] in place—

CORTEZ: Denardo and his father [Ornette Coleman] have Harmolodic in place.

FEINSTEIN: And you have outstanding musicians.

CORTEZ: Yes, and good engineers. And I'm learning about that whole process.

FEINSTEIN: What connections do you see between your poems and spoken blues?

CORTEZ: My CD *Taking the Blues Back Home* had to do with investigating the blues from a different point of view, to focus in on the deeper levels of the blues, the political aspects of the blues. The blues has so many codes I wanted to investigate them. The musicians may be playing a twelve-bar blues, but I'm talking about the blues before it became those twelve bars.

FEINSTEIN: There's the suggestion in your title and in the poems themselves that the blues have been abused.

CORTEZ: The blues have been abused. The black people who produce the blues have been abused.

FEINSTEIN: Are you also criticizing contemporary blues, saying that it's watered down?

CORTEZ: In some cases it has been watered down. In some cases it's used by people who have no understanding of the language of the blues and of the blues people. They have no notion about where the blues come from or what they say. They're just mimicking, imitating, and minstrelizing. It sounds good to them in their voice, and they can get over, and that's all it is. Others are using the cornier lyrics of the blues, and they're just corny.

FEINSTEIN: Langston Hughes had clear distinctions in his mind between blues poetry to be read and blues lyrics to be sung. He tells that wonderful anecdote about singing his poems and some stranger coming up to him to see if he's ill. [Cortez laughs.] But there seems to be more crossover for you.

CORTEZ: Well, you know, I really can't sing. So I don't sing, but I may chant a little bit. There may be something that comes with the music that makes me do that.

FEINSTEIN: And you have a splendid sense of inflection and the musicality of phrases.

CORTEZ: Thanks.

FEINSTEIN: Are there poets writing about the blues whom you admire?

CORTEZ: I like the blues poetry of Sterling Plumpp and Raymond Patterson, and the poetry and jazz fusions of Amiri Baraka.

FEINSTEIN: I'm not surprised that you focus on Baraka. I think the two of you have done a great deal in terms of blurring the distinctions between music and the musicality of language.

CORTEZ: I have many opportunities to read my work at music festivals around the world, and so does Baraka. We are very lucky.

FEINSTEIN: Al Young also works frequently with musicians.

CORTEZ: I haven't heard Al. I have heard other jazz poems by poets like Ted Joans, who is a jazz poet. I think that Bill Matthews did a nice job with the piece that he wrote about Bud Powell ["Bud Powell, Paris, 1959"]. There have been good jazz poems. But a number of poets today write about jazz musicians and jazz music because it's the hip thing to do. They know nothing about the music, the struggle or the contribution, or why some musicians are against calling their music "jazz."

FEINSTEIN: That's been true for decades—ever since Vachel Lindsay, who didn't know anything about the music.

CORTEZ: He didn't know anything about it.

FEINSTEIN: A lot of poets just latch on to the term.

CORTEZ: And the media is good at latching on to something like that and pushing it forward. [Laughs.]

FEINSTEIN: You've mentioned the difficulty of finding contemporary trumpet players who take risks, who play, as you put it, "out there." Now, your poems take a lot of risks, but that's not true of many if not most of the poets writing today.

CORTEZ: That's true. That's because people are very repressed. The whole reason to create is so that you are free. In art you have to be absolutely free. If you're not, then you shouldn't be in it.

FEINSTEIN: It's pretty stunning when you think of all the poets from, say, the dozens of black poetry anthologies from the '60s—how so few of them are anthologized today, how we don't see their work, hear their voices.

CORTEZ: That's right. There was really a move to blot out the '60s.

FEINSTEIN: Out of fear?

CORTEZ: The poems were militant. They reflected the desire for more freedom and liberation. They questioned the American dream. The poems explored African roots. The poems called for an end to exploitation, domination, and oppression. Now, thirty-two years later, we have rappers who give us watered down versions of those messages backed by drum machines and made available as part of the pop music scene. I have nothing against rappers. If they can communicate and survive by rapping, cool. However, I do think they lack understanding about what went on before they arrived to rap. In the '60s, people were protesting. They were opening doors, burning down cities, calling for justice. People were serious. The censorship that came as a result of the '60s caused a lot of folks to hide their true feelings and caused some poets to give up writing poetry.

FEINSTEIN: Your poems often dip into the music of the 1960s.

CORTEZ: It was a rich time. There were definite breakthroughs—politically and artistically.

FEINSTEIN: Do you miss that energy of the '60s?

CORTEZ: No, because I think I'm still breaking through. [Laughs.] You know, you just continue to deepen and develop. That was a very electrifying time. A great moment in history. More people became politically aware and we took that awareness to another level in the '70s and the '80s and '90s. We are in a better position to confront contradiction, and keep creativity alive. Evolution may be slow, but we do keep evolving.

Right now I'm having fun reading my work with music and creating art with other artists. It's great.

FEINSTEIN: It is great. And we're very grateful.

Bill Crow

4

Just a Matter of Time
Bill Crow

A few years after I founded *Brilliant Corners,* I received a subscription request from Bill Crow—or at least *a* Bill Crow—and the name alone brought to my ears reels of music: sessions with Stan Getz and Zoot Sims, and all those wonderful recordings with Gerry Mulligan, especially *What Is There to Say?* I *had* to know if this was the bassist I had admired for so many years, so when I mailed the current issue of *Brilliant Corners,* I included a gushing note. He wrote back promptly and said that, yes, he was indeed the fellow about whom I had said such nice things. I was knocked out. In addition to knowing his music fairly well, I had read both his books, *Jazz Anecdotes* and *From Birdland to Broadway,* two wonderful contributions to jazz literature. Now I had to meet him.

Because I already had plans to visit Manhattan with my family, and since he lives about an hour outside of the city, we arranged to meet at his home. While Bill and I chatted inside, his wife, Aileen, took my wife and children around the house and showed them gardens that perfectly reflected the people who planted them: informal, woodland settings—mainly shade gardens—that seemed to extend the natural landscape rather than organize it artificially.

Bill was the first musician interviewed for *Brilliant Corners,* and my only difficulty in speaking with him had to do with focus: I wanted to talk about his experiences as a musician, but, for the sake of the journal, I forced myself to concentrate on the relationship between jazz and literature. Most of the time, at least.

Because I had a family waiting, we wrapped things up a little swiftly, but not before I asked him to sign his books. In *From Birdland to Broadway,* he wrote, "With the anticipation of a continuing friendship," and in *Jazz Anecdotes,* he penned what might be my favorite book inscription from anyone: "(See other book)."

As a bass player, Bill Crow has made numerous recordings for more than fifty years. The session leaders for those recordings include Benny Goodman, Marian McPartland, Stan Getz, Al Cohn, and Zoot Sims. He is probably best known, however, for the 1950s LPs made with Gerry Mulligan. Crow has also published widely. His many articles have appeared in publications such as *Down Beat, The Jazz Review,* and *Jazzletter. Jazz Anecdotes,* which won the 1991 *JazzTimes* Readers' Poll for best book of the year, has been expanded and reprinted. For more than twenty years, he has written a monthly column for *Allegro,* the newspaper of Local 802.

The following excerpts from his essays reflect topics from our discussion. The interview took place at Crow's home in New City, New York, on March 25, 2001.

The Bass in Jazz
(excerpt)
Bill Crow

The string bass has been called the "heartbeat of jazz" for good reason. It provides a deep pulse, sometimes felt as much as it is heard, giving the music both a harmonic and a rhythmic foundation. As in many other forms of music, the role of the bass in jazz is mainly supportive. Bass players certainly have developed marvelous techniques for soloing, especially in recent years. But a bassist doesn't have to be a great soloist to be in demand. The main thing other jazz musicians want from a bass player is "good notes," bass notes that thread through the harmony in an interesting way, and "good time," a steady rhythmic feeling that helps bring the music to life.

Bass notes are stepping-stones for the rest of the band. They form a path that provides support and direction. To be able to consistently select good notes and drop them into exactly the right places in the music, a bass player needs a strong sense of harmony and rhythm and an empathetic connection with the other members of the rhythm section. In small groups, the bassist chooses his line as the music goes along. Even when playing written music in larger ensembles, jazz bass players usually recompose their lines, using what the arranger has written as a guide but relying on their experience and their "sixth sense" to choose the particular notes and figures to be played.

Charlie's
(excerpt)
Bill Crow

Charlie's Tavern became a clubhouse for musicians during the big band era. If you gave up your room while you were on the road, your mail could be sent to Charlie's. When you were out of work, Charlie would run a tab for you, and he'd cash your checks when you got paid. A musician could park his wife or girlfriend in a booth at Charlie's before a job and know that nobody would bother her until he got back.

Charlie Jacobs, the owner and chief bartender, bore a resemblance to Wimpy, the character in the Popeye comic strip, but he was no wimp. Once a circus strongman, Charlie was nobody to fool with. He knew his customers and encouraged outsiders to find another bar. He took care of the cops who dropped in, but he didn't like them to hang around. They made his customers uncomfortable. He'd pour a drink or make a sandwich for a bluecoat if he came in when it was quiet, but if one arrived when the place was busy, Charlie would meet him at the door and walk him back out to the sidewalk, slipping him the obligatory gratuity as he ushered him out.

I hung around Charlie's as much during the day as I did at Birdland at night. I couldn't afford to drink at Charlie's, but since I didn't enjoy alcohol, I didn't mind as long as Charlie didn't. He just ignored anyone who failed to order something. I stood around talking with other musicians as long as I wasn't in the way. Any time I felt I was taking up space that could be occupied by a paying customer, I moved on.

Stan the Man
(excerpt)
Bill Crow

Stan Getz . . . had driven me to the job with my bass, and on the way home he asked if I'd mind waiting while he stopped to visit some friends. He drove to a private house where a party was going on. Stan introduced me to a lot of people, including Blackie, an old schoolmate of his. The lady of the house made me a sandwich and a cup of coffee, and I chatted with her for a while in the kitchen.

Eventually I began to wonder where Stan was, and when he was going to drive me home. I found him in the basement rec room with four or five other guys. He was leaning on the pool table, tying up his arm and getting ready to shoot up some heroin. I said, "Come on, Stan, don't do that. It's time to go home."

"I'll be right with you," he frowned. "I just want to do up one more little taste."

He injected the drug, loosened the tie on his arm, turned pale, and collapsed on the floor. Blackie quickly rolled him over on his back.

"He isn't breathing!"

"Oh, my God!" yelled the host. "Get him out of here! I don't want no stiff in my house!"

"Push on his ribs!" I shouted. "Artificial respiration! He's turning blue!"

Blackie pumped his chest while I pried his mouth open and pulled his tongue forward. After a few tense moments, Stan made a strangling noise and sucked in some air. His color returned, and he began breathing on his own again.

When he opened his eyes, he scowled at Blackie and said, "Man, get off me! You're getting my suit all dirty!"

"Motherfucker! You were dead!" yelled Blackie, jumping to his feet. "I've been pumping air into you! You were blue, man! You were dead!"

Stan got up and brushed himself off. He gave everyone a surly look and said, "Well, I bet I'm higher than any of you."

The Gerry Mulligan Quartet
(excerpt)
Bill Crow

In late 1958, we began recording an album for Columbia Records. Gerry complained that he couldn't write anything at home because the telephone and the doorbell were always ringing. I gave him the key to my Cornelia Street apartment and told him, "There's a piano there, and nobody will bother you. I'll be over at Aileen's place tonight. Go write something."

He did, and came to the last session with a lovely treatment of "What Is There to Say?" which became the title song of the album. Gerry had asked the rest of us to bring in tunes, so Art [Farmer] and I each wrote one. Art's was an untitled blues. Since Newport had been our first job together, Gerry suggested the title "Blueport."

Art had told me that "Buckethead" had been his childhood nickname, so I wrote that at the top of my tune, another blues, in three-quarter time. When Art looked at the trumpet part I handed him, he laughed and said, "Oh, no, please don't call it that!"

"How about 'News from Blueport'?" Gerry offered—a spoonerism on "Blues from Newport." That became the title. The liner notes erroneously listed Gerry as the composer of both tunes, but Art and I receive the royalties.

SASCHA FEINSTEIN: Did your interest in writing begin at roughly the same time as your love of music?

BILL CROW: I was lucky. My mother taught me to read before I started school, so I came to the first grade as a reader, and they put me right into the second grade—which was a dumb move, because my math has suffered ever since. [Laughs.] But they put me with a lively group, and by the time I got into the sixth grade, I ran into a teacher who was an omnivorous reader. I think she was the one who introduced me to *The New Yorker* writers.

She was interesting. She traveled; she took her vacations in Hawaii and Japan and places like that. I was living in Washington state then, so New York seemed far away, and the intellectual world seemed far away. But [*New Yorker* contributors James] Thurber and [E. B.] White—I could understand them right away, and I admired their writing style.

We had a tiny library in Kirkland, Washington. It was in a house smaller than this one. And I read everything in that library by the time I graduated from high school. There were some books where I needed to get a note from my mother, because they were so big that they thought I might be using them to press flowers or something. [Laughs.] That was my Greek mythology period. So reading was really hot for me. I had a strong imagination, and I began to appreciate writing style at a very early age.

FEINSTEIN: And then you went to college on the G.I. Bill.

CROW: For a little while. I started at the University of Washington for just a semester before I went into the army, and then when I came out I didn't last more than two quarters before a drummer said, "Look, if you want to be a musician, you better go where the music is." So I got on the bus and came to New York. That was the end of my formal training.

FEINSTEIN: And while you were in school you focused on radio, right?

CROW: When I went into the University of Washington, I was looking for a major, and they didn't have anything that looked like what I wanted to do. I had never considered being a professional musician because I didn't know any; the musicians that I knew were teachers, and I knew I didn't want to do that. I wanted to be an actor for a while. I was involved in school plays a lot, and I got a scholarship when I graduated for the Priscilla Beach Theater in Plymouth, Massachusetts, one summer—summer of '45, I guess that was. We put on plays—a different one every week—and we learned them in the traditional, road company, Thespian style: They would give you sides, which were just *your* lines and your cues (you never got to read the whole play), and it was fast. You'd rehearse a play all week and be playing a different play that night. It was wonderful. They just threw us right in the water.

FEINSTEIN: Do you think this helped you with your prose style—your sense of cadence, delivery?

CROW: Whatever of that exists in my writing is in the editing. I edit forever, and what I'm looking for is to really say what I mean, to eliminate ambiguities and vagaries. I used to love to be read to, and I used to love to read to my son when he was little, and I *hear* the words. I'm very conscious of the music of language.

FEINSTEIN: Among the hundreds of musicians whom you've met over the decades, who were the most articulate, or well read?

CROW: Let's see. Bob Brookmeyer. He's got a stream-of-consciousness way of writing that has always appealed to me, and he's a rare one because he's really not afraid to say what he thinks. He doesn't reconsider. [Laughs.] He's got a lot of wit, and the ability to invent interesting tropes.

Jimmy Raney was interesting. I don't know if he ever wrote anything, but he was an intellectual, and that appealed to me. We liked to go to museums and liked the same artists a lot.

FEINSTEIN: Such as?

CROW: Klee, and Picasso, of course. Jimmy was more into Cubism than I was. He tried to paint that way for a while. In my early days in New York, in the '50s, all of those free forms of entertainment were great, because I was broke—scuffling along on very little income—so to be able to go to the Met was a wonderful, wonderful resource of stimulation and education.

FEINSTEIN: [Paul] Desmond was also, apparently, very witty and bright.

CROW: Yeah. Unfortunately, I never got close to Paul. I knew him a little bit, but he was more on the West Coast than I was, and by the time he got to New York, our circle of friends, somehow, didn't bring us close together. But I certainly admire the things that I've read that he said.

I was a little put off from Paul, I think, because I admired a heartier, more robust type of jazz than Paul represented to me—the whole Brubeck group—and I didn't come to really appreciate Dave until he wrote "In Your Own Sweet Way." I said, "Wait a minute. There's a real musician here." [Chuckles.] And I went back and listened to his playing. My feeling about Dave's playing was always that he gave himself too much rope, somehow—that he went on and on and on and on. It was probably what he needed to do, but it just wasn't what I wanted to listen to at that time. I wanted to hear Zoot [Sims] and Lester Young, you know?

So I was a latecomer to appreciating that group and those people. Paul always seemed like a wonderfully inventive player, but I always felt that he held himself in a physical way that made his tone a little too precious for my taste. I could follow his ideas and appreciate them, but I didn't want to listen to that sound a lot.

FEINSTEIN: I'm a little surprised. I would have expected—judging from your recordings, and some of the things you've said in print—that you would have had greater reservations about musicians who had edgier sounds.

CROW: I've always appreciated tone, and I've always felt that Paul would have had a better tone if he just blew into the horn a little more. It was pretty—crystal, beautiful sound—and there was a lot of that in Stan Getz, too, who I had a lot more to do with.

FEINSTEIN: You saved his life!

CROW: Yeah, at one time. [Chuckles.] He made a very pure tone for a long time. The year when I was playing with him [1952] was probably the year when he made a sound I appreciated the most. Though . . . I don't know how to express it. There was a false juvenility [in the tone] that I didn't really believe. It was a lot like Stan's character: When he was sober, he was the good little boy, and as soon as he'd get high, the horns came out. [Laughs.] He was one of the few non-passive junkies I ever met. Most of those guys would get quiet and space out, but Stan would really get evil. I was lucky that he didn't do anything really mean to me, but I saw him do some rotten things to a lot of other people who cared for him, and I didn't understand that. It seemed pathological to me. And I thought a lot of that split in him was expressed in the sound of his instrument. In later years, he kept the boyish tone, but he put a little nagging edge on it, which I didn't like and which I thought also was expressive of his character. A little knife in there.

He was a rare bird. Aside from all that personal stuff, he was one of the most talented musicians I ever met in my life. He was just amazing. He told me one time, "I never have any trouble playing anything I can think of. The hard thing is thinking of stuff that I think is really worthwhile playing."

FEINSTEIN: Wow. [Crow laughs.] What did you think of that biography on him [*Stan Getz: A Life in Jazz* by Donald Maggin]?

CROW: I thought it was pretty good. The guy researched it pretty well.

FEINSTEIN: Do you think it's true to Getz's spirit? Research is one thing—

CROW: Yeah. But I think he got a feeling of Stan.

FEINSTEIN: I thought it was one of the better jazz biographies, and we both know that most are pretty weak.

CROW: Oh yeah.

FEINSTEIN: How about the critics? [Crow grins.] Are there any who you admire?

CROW: I've done some criticism myself, and I really didn't like it, although I had some fun with it. But it's really hard for someone outside of an art to say things about what the artist's doing in a way that's meaningful to the artist and to his peers. It may be meaningful to those who are outside of the actual creative process, but it left me with a bad feeling. The critic is in the position of having too much influence on the livelihood of the artist, and that part of it disturbed me. I've stopped really reading criticism because I don't value it very much. Who's a good critic? I'm not sure anybody is.

FEINSTEIN: And yet you still review books.

CROW: Yes. I won't review anything by Oxford University Press because they're my publisher (and it also gets me out of doing a lot of work I don't want to do!) [Laughs.] But I do write reviews for *Allegro,* the musicians' newspaper for the Local 802, and I very seldom have given anyone a real pan. I just tell them that I don't want to review that book.

Once I was so offended by the book that I did complain in print. But most of the time I just try to describe it, and to explain what interested me. That's a different kind of reviewing than critiquing the writing. I mean, I don't feel smart enough to be able to analyze somebody else's work and understand what they're doing.

FEINSTEIN: That's nonsense! [Crow laughs.] If anybody should do it, it should be you.

CROW: Well, I'm intelligent, you know, and I can make an intelligent statement about things, but to really understand what somebody else has in their mind, and what their project was, and what they went through, and all of that—you're clear outside of it. You look at the result and you can say, "This is how it hits *me*," but I can't really say that I understand what a musician or a writer is trying to do, and whether they've achieved it or not, you know?

FEINSTEIN: But you can say substantive things. I mean, you can explain to someone why a Mulligan recording, say, is stronger than a Kenny G recording.

CROW: [Laughs.] Yeah, well . . .

FEINSTEIN: So can no one write solid prose in response to jazz? Should we have no literature on the subject?

CROW: No, no. I'm just saying where *I* am.

FEINSTEIN: How about someone like Gary Giddins?

CROW: I've seen some good things that Gary's written. Once in a while you get the feeling that, for some of the young writers in the *[New York] Times*, for example, it must be hard to come up with stuff at that rate, and to make deadlines. You're looking for something to say that's going to be worth having said and at the same time get it out that fast. Or covering someone that you wouldn't normally have covered if you weren't in that position. So I feel for them. It's interesting to read what they have to say, but I don't give it a whole lot of weight.

FEINSTEIN: I think the longer articles in the *Times* are far more interesting than the reviews.

CROW: Yeah. I remember when I was involved with *The Jazz Review* with Nat Hentoff and Martin Williams. Their idea was to enlist players to say what they had to say. There was no money in it; we got free copies of the records. But it was an interesting project because I had to sit down and see if I could say what I thought.

It was a discovery process. I think I wrote a decent review of a Wilbur Ware album. And I did a terrible review of Tony Scott. I took my hatchet to him. Tony was riding high in those days: the center of attention at Newport, his records were selling, he was at Birdland all the time. But there was a kind of jive quality about Tony's work that irked me, and this particular record they gave me was juxtaposed to one by Pee Wee Russell. And it seemed to me that the battle that Pee Wee had always engaged the music in was such a different focus and seriousness than what Tony was kind of jiving his way through on this album. I really took after him, and the upshot of it was horrible. It almost drove him out of New York. [Laughs.] It was a terrible thing. So that brought me up short as a critic, I must say.

I wrote a few other things for that magazine (I think it only lasted two years [1959–1961]). Some of them were more perfunctory; some were more thoughtful. Sometimes you don't have anything to say about a record, or what you have to say has already been said so many times.

Once Nat called me up and said, "George Wettling sent us something, and it's really not in condition to print. Do you think you could do an interview with him and get this stuff that he should have put in here out of him?" I said, "Sure, I love George." We made a date and George came over with his wife—but he was smashed. And I couldn't get a coherent sentence *out* of him. He was sitting there, smiling with good will, but—oh. [Laughs.] I just had to junk it. Couldn't do a thing with it.

Some of the writing for that magazine that I enjoyed reading: Cannonball [Adderley] did a couple of reviews, and Bill Evans did some really nice, thoughtful writing.

I used to love Eddie Condon's writing. He knew how to turn a phrase, and he had a respect for the reader: You were going to *get* what he said. He really took you into his confidence. Bud Freeman was not as enjoyable a writer because Bud had all of that front to keep up.

FEINSTEIN: What do you mean?

CROW: He was an Anglophile. He wanted to be an Englishman so badly that he almost became one. [Chuckles.] He was always carrying that image of himself around, and he couldn't drop it enough to just be direct with you as a writer, which is too bad, because he had a lot of interesting things to say.

FEINSTEIN: He wrote a couple of books [*Crazeology* and *You Don't Look Like a Musician*].

CROW: Yeah, little ones. Wonderful.

Somebody told me a great story about him. He'd been invited to visit England by a big jazz fan who had one of those stately homes. This was Bud's first trip to England, and he's taken to this baronial fantasy-of-a-house: Rolls Royces and all of this. Bud gets out and looks around and says, "Ah! This is just the way I knew England would be!" [Both laugh.] Fulfilled his fantasy completely.

FEINSTEIN: I see you have that wonderful Mingus set over there [*The Complete 1959 Columbia Recordings of Charles Mingus,* featuring *Ah Um, Mingus Dynasty,* and, on the third CD, unreleased takes from those sessions].

CROW: I just ordered that. Haven't gotten through it yet.

FEINSTEIN: Two of the discs you'll know by heart, but the alternate takes are really thrilling to have.

You wrote that most of your experiences with Mingus were edgy, because of race issues.

CROW: I was *around* him a lot more than I would say I was with him. One time, I was in Teddy Charles's apartment—we lived in the Prescott Hotel on Columbus Circle—and Mingus and Oscar Pettiford came by. They'd both been drinking and were in a mellow but effusive mood: "This is my *man,*" and so on. Somehow, in the middle of all this over-demonstrative wrestling around, Mingus pulled a button off the leather overcoat that Oscar was wearing, and Oscar was furious. Mingus was trying to act like he's making too much of it—rather than just saying, "I'm sorry"—and they end up trying to kill each other. Teddy throws them out because they're knocking over lamps and stuff. [Chuckles.] The last we saw them, they were standing out in the street, taking haymakers at each other, and neither was reaching the other! They were just swinging as hard as they could and missing. [Laughs.]

Charlie was that way: He was so prickly, always on the lookout for any kind of a draft or bad scene. He would do such self-damaging things. Some lady's noisy in the club, so he breaks his bass. Really counter-productive activity. [Chuckles.]

I remember sitting in the [Village] Vanguard one afternoon listening to Jimmy Giuffre when Brookmeyer had just joined them, and [the owner] Max Gordon comes up and says, "Charlie Mingus has got this new group, so they're going to sit in for one set." Now, half of the audience had come to hear this quiet jazz [by Giuffre] and the other half were the usual talkers, socializers. And Mingus—I don't know what he had in mind—started out with such hostile vibes. They're playing this *Raaaar* kind of music, and a lot of us listened; we weren't too thrilled in having this laid on us, but we were being an audience. But there happened to be a table full of people, right in front, who, as the music got loud, started talking louder. Mingus gets up to the microphone and says, "Alright. On this next number, as long as you all wanna talk, we gonna play four bars, and then you *talk* four bars." [Both laugh.] Most of us fell out laughing, but this table didn't pay any attention to the announcement.

So they kicked off this tune, and they played the head, and then they religiously went through this routine of playing four bars, then counting out four bars while these people talked. [Laughs.]

FEINSTEIN: Outrageous.

CROW: Wonderful. I remember when Dick Katz, Jim Hall, and I walked in to hear Mingus's new group. As soon as Mingus sees Dick Katz he says, "Hey man! My piano player didn't show up. You gotta come up and play with us." Dick says, "Oh no, Charlie. I can't do this thing; I don't know this music." But Mingus says, "No, no, man. You gotta save my life," and he practically carries him up to the stand. Dick is looking at the music, they start, and, inside of eight bars, Charlie's over his shoulder: "*No,* man! What the fuck are you *doin'*?! *That's* not the way it goes!" [Both laugh.]

The first five or six times I heard him, he was playing with other people. I heard him sitting in with Bird once at Birdland, and later with Sonny Stitt's group. And when I was with Marian McPartland—

FEINSTEIN: At the Hickory House?

CROW: Yes, with Joe Morello. There was a club in Columbus where she liked to play, and we heard that Bud Powell had a trio downtown, so we took a long intermission, and the club owner and our trio ran in to hear a set. Bud Powell's trio was Mingus and Elvin [Jones].

I had only heard Elvin a couple of times up until then, and he was a much louder drummer than I really liked. In those days, the only loud drummer that I knew was Buddy Rich. Elvin just played *all* the time. Mind boggling, when you're used to the drummer being mainly support for the piano player. [Chuckles.] I mean, my ideals for drummers in those days were Roy Haynes and those from the Jo Jones school. The drummers that I learned to play with had a light touch and heavy swing: Kenny Clarke and people like that. So Elvin was a bit much for me, but I could see that he was good. It was just a matter of fitting that goodness into the realities of the group, and a lot of times he simply overwhelmed everybody.

With this trio, with Mingus, it seemed when we walked in that there were three different time centers—all strong, and all simultaneous, but never together. (At one point, Mingus and Elvin sounded like they'd really locked in tight together, and right away Mingus stopped playing, got out his rag, started wiping off his bass strings, and then he jumped in. And it was just an instant away from Elvin's center.) Bud's got this crazy grimace. And I thought, "Boy, as soon as these guys stop playing they're going to start beating each other up. There seemed to be such tension up there. But as soon as they stopped playing and the set was over, they were over in the booth with their arms all around and saying how much they love each other. I thought, "This is really strange."

So I had chalked Mingus up as a good technician and somebody who came on strong, but not a rhythm section player—which is odd for a bass player. Some years later, I heard him with the first band he put together (with George Barrow, I think, and Dannie Richmond on drums) at the Half Note, and Mingus sounded *wonderful* in the rhythm section. He just was carrying the whole band. He had such a powerful swing going. And I thought, "Well, you sonuvabitch—you can play that way when you want to, can't you?"

He had so many things going on in his mind; I didn't really know what he had in mind a lot of the time.

FEINSTEIN: What do you think of his autobiography [*Beneath the Underdog*]?

CROW: Oh, I thought it was wonderful fantasy. [Laughs.]

I thought it was interesting, when I was researching for *Jazz Anecdotes,* to find that story about how Mingus left Duke, and later, when I was going through oral histories, I found an interview with [Juan] Tizol, with an entirely different story [of the same event]. So I put them both in!

FEINSTEIN: What about other jazz autobiographies? Any that you admire?

CROW: I like Dizzy's book [*To Be or Not to Bop*] a lot. Basie's autobiography [*Good Morning Blues*] was nice. I was disappointed by Duke's [*Music Is My Mistress*].

FEINSTEIN: Too safe?

CROW: He never was going to tip his hand. He walked that line his whole life. It was a marvel to watch happen, but there were large parts of him where you thought, "Oh Jesus, Duke. You don't have to lay it on quite that thick." [Chuckles.]

But I guess he did. When I got to reading more about him, I realized there was so much superstition and ritual that was a necessary part of his life.

FEINSTEIN: Also, the absolute politeness of his nature that carried into his autobiography: I'll write a piece on everyone so no one will feel offended. There's a great generosity about that act.

CROW: Yes. I thought Rex Stewart's stuff [in *Jazz Masters of the Thirties*, a collection of brief portraits,] was wonderful.

FEINSTEIN: How about Art Pepper's [autobiography] *Straight Life*?

CROW: It was interesting. It's not the kind of book that I would recommend to someone for a good read—[chuckles]—because there's that junkie quality that makes junk life's great tragedy. I used to say to my junkie friends, "Come on. This is something that you're doing to yourself. The hand of God did not come down and select you to suffer, you know?"

I asked one junkie friend, Freddie Greenwell, who had a pretty good sense of humor, "What is it about this stuff? It's obviously poison, and it's obviously a life-wrecker, and it can kill you." So I asked what was so wonderful about it—because I tried it a couple of times just to see, and I felt like I'd been severely poisoned, didn't have any fun. And he said, "Well, it's just nice to know that there's something in your life that you'd give everything else for." Now, he said that kind of as a joke, but there was a lot of kidding on the square.

I liked the idea of getting high and having fun, but what I disliked about it was that it *wasn't* a high, it wasn't fun, it was not a pleasure. So the only thing I could think of was that people who are tremendously anxious use heroin to free themselves from anxiety, and that anaesthetizing of the central nervous system is experienced as pleasure. If you don't have that combination, you're not going to be a junkie, I don't think. It's just not any fun.

FEINSTEIN: Was Mulligan addicted when you were playing with him?

CROW: No. I knew him early in New York—the first year I was here [1950]—because I wasn't even a bass player when I went to a concert that he did in the park. Then I was at a few gigs where he sat in. I remember [Mulligan's girlfriend] Gail Madden was kind of his mentor at that time; she was trying to be the mentor of all of the jazz junkies, starting with Bird. She ended up going to the [West] Coast with Gerry, and on that trip he kicked his habit, and that was the end of it,

I think—although he ended up doing some time later, because he was at the wrong party . . .

It was a social thing at that time. Everybody in Woody [Herman]'s band was fooling around with it. And although everybody got hooked to a certain extent, because that's what the drug does, the psychological hold that it had on some guys was much stronger than on others. Some guys messed around for a year or so and that was it. Some guys didn't last a year; they messed around *wrong* and died. And then other guys, like Al [Cohn] and Zoot [Sims], kicked their habit by becoming alcoholics, and years later ended up paying those dues with a destroyed liver.

FEINSTEIN: You've mentioned several times in your writing how, for the most part, you weren't interested in that kind of self-destructive behavior.

CROW: I was introduced to pot in the army, and it was great fun. The first six months of being a pot smoker is probably something that everybody can look back on with great affection—[Feinstein laughs]—because it *does* turn your head in a different way. I listened to music and looked at paintings in a way that I'd never done before, and that was just a personal trip. By the time I came back to New York—all the time that I was really scuffling—there was always somebody willing to turn me on. So I smoked a lot of pot. And then when I started working with Stan Getz, that was where the big change came, because everybody was looking at him, and I said, "I have no eyes to go to *jail*." It's not worth it. So I just stopped doing that.

Of course, my life was changing for the better at that time. I had better work, I fell in love, and a number of things happened that made life very happy for me. And I've never gone looking for that again. Alcohol I gave up on when I was in the army. I tried to drink like all the other guys, and I was never any good at it. Terrible. I'd either get sick, or get silly, or fall asleep. I certainly couldn't function that way.

FEINSTEIN: What did you think of the Mulligan biography [*Listen: Gerry Mulligan* by Jerome Klinkowitz]?

CROW: That seemed okay. I didn't really think that he came up with any great insights about Gerry. It was an okay history of his life, but I think someday somebody will probably get interested enough to redo that.

FEINSTEIN: I'm interested in the separation between player and writer, because the musician's life is so complex.

CROW: Yeah.

FEINSTEIN: And to do justice to that life—

CROW: Also, it happens in such a different way. The thing that I love about music is that you jump on that time warp. You deal with what comes by you and what comes out of your own head, and you don't have any chance to go back. Even in the record studio if you say, "I don't like that take—let's do it again," you're doing it again the same way, maybe trying to avoid the mistake. But you're still on that time continuum. That is what the game is about: dealing with it in time and on time.

Writing is completely the other way. I'll sit down and write something, and then—unless I've got a deadline that's really hanging over me—I can play it over again in my head and think of all kinds of other things and go off in other tangents. It's all rethinking.

I thought I could teach myself how to write short stories. I started with a couple of stories that were too hot to handle about real people, but the story idea was something I could deal with fictionally. Then I got into a form I liked, and borrowed a couple of things from Damon Runyon, and a couple of things from here and there—just to see how that would work. And a couple of them are finished; I'm not really sure. Three or four definitely are not, and another two or three are just ideas.

FEINSTEIN: Are these stories jazz-related?

CROW: Oh yeah. I started out with a premise of an idealized Charlie's Tavern, which is the place where I spent so much time when I was first in New York, and I took as a narrator a piano player who's just kind of on the scene, does all kinds of work. People he talks to, and the stories that come up about them. His life, his career.

The thing is, it's just like that alto saxophone that's sitting in the other room. I played an alto when I was a kid and never really got it right before my life took me some place else, and I thought, "That would be a nice hobby." I had some time on my hands, but as soon as I got the alto, a whole lot of other stuff turned up, and I've hardly had a chance to pick it up and fool with it. It's just a matter of time.

It's the same with the writing. I had some time at my disposal. I was writing every day. But I'm home so little now, doing so many things . . . But it's there, and I'm certainly interested in it, so I'll get back to it one of these days.

⬥ ⬥ ⬥

FEINSTEIN: One of my favorite jazz recordings is Gerry Mulligan's *What Is There to Say?* [recorded in late 1958 and early '59, with Mulligan and Crow, as well as Art Farmer on trumpet and Dave Bailey on drums].

CROW: That quartet was very special. Art was at a place in his own development that was very exciting. He had just—within the previous year, I think—shaken out all of the Dizzy Gillespie-isms that he had grown up with, and had found his own voice. I would attribute part of that to the fact that he was one of the few people who took George Russell's Lydian/tonal organization and used it. That was his practice book for about a year, and he was finding new melodic intervals that appealed to his ear out of those scales and modes. It turned his melodic sensibility loose and freed him from the love of Dizzy. It's very much like what you hear in Dizzy's early recordings where you hear a lot of Roy [Eldridge], and then all of a sudden that's gone, and he's into this other place. That's what happened to Art, and he never looked back. He went through such a long, beautiful career of melodic inventiveness. It was a thrill to be there with him.

And I think it was good for Art to be with Gerry at that time because Gerry was a form organizer, and Art had such a strong musical dedication that being put into that little box of Gerry's somehow made him find things that he might not have found so quickly. He said years later that people didn't realize what that quartet could do. Something special.

It's interesting to hear that same material that's on the *What Is There to Say?* album on some of the CDs that've come out from the concert tour that we did [four months later, in the spring of 1959]. We took more choruses in the live performances than in the studio, and you can hear us really stretching out on that material.

FEINSTEIN: As the bassist, how much pressure did you feel in that quartet setting—and other piano-less quartets with Mulligan?

CROW: I never really thought much about it.

FEINSTEIN: Did you feel you had to play more?

CROW: No. It would be like saying, "What's it like to be the piano player with Count Basie?" [Chuckles.] The form is there, and you just deal with it. I always heard bass lines as a melodic continuum, so it seemed like something I would know how to do, to get into a group like that. You know, a lot of times when I'm playing with a piano player, I wish that he would play less. There's a lot to be said for the tonal memory of the ear; you don't have to keep stepping on the starter all the time to relate to the music that's inherent in the form.

That's why I loved to play with Jimmy Rowles. He had wonderful voicings, and he would throw his hands down and listen to see what that was, and then he would start developing things that came out of that. He loved to surprise himself; he loved to surprise the rest of the musicians. If you rehearsed something at one tempo, you could guarantee that the next time he would take it at an entirely different tempo, or a different key. His whole interest was in listening to what was out there and seeing what you could do to make it even more interesting, and that didn't involve hammering at it. He would wait. He had patience.

FEINSTEIN: When people ask me to recommend Zoot Sims CDs, I tell them to buy anything that he recorded with Jimmy Rowles. You can buy them blindly.

CROW: Yeah. And that album Rowles made with Al Cohn is beautiful, too—*Heavy Love.*

FEINSTEIN: You still write a regular column for the musicians' union publication [*Allegro*], right?

CROW: Yes, a column that's been running for eighteen or nineteen years now.

FEINSTEIN: Do you have any writing projects that you're working on or eager to create? Have you pretty much done what you wanted to do with these two books?

CROW: These two projects kind of evolved without me. [Feinstein laughs.] *Jazz Anecdotes* was Sheldon Meyer's idea at Oxford [University Press]. Oxford had done a number of other anecdote collections—I think they'd done one for opera, one for the military, and so on. Sheldon, being a jazz fan, thought that somebody should do one for jazz and asked his writers for the right person, and they all pointed at me. So I sent him my columns, and he said, "Oh yes. Let's do this." And while I was doing that, my own stories seemed to not fit in here somehow—they had a different tone to them—so I figured, "Well, maybe that's another book." I saved them, and when this [*Jazz Anecdotes*] did well, I called Sheldon up and said, "I think I've got another one." Now having done that, I don't want to do a "son of" either one, and I haven't really thought of a book-sized project to get involved in.

I did a chapter for Bill Kirchner's *Oxford Companion to Jazz* ["The Bass in Jazz"]. That was interesting—and not nearly as big a project as these were.

FEINSTEIN: That's a curious collection, but I won't ask you about it because you're part of it *and* it came out from Oxford.

CROW: I haven't read the whole thing. I've read the first third of it now.

FEINSTEIN: I wonder about the audience for such a book. I don't fully understand who they're targeting.

CROW: I don't really understand, either, but I'm glad it's there for research purposes.

FEINSTEIN: Are there young bassists whom you admire?

CROW: I've never been very good at judging bass players because the experience of playing is so different than listening to them. But I hear guys who can do things on basses, and I can't even begin to think of how they do that, in terms of technique. The guy who I really admire that has that kind of technique and still plays the way I like to hear a bass player play is George Mraz. He's a good section player, and he seems to do the right thing, and still he can play anything that he wants to play.

FEINSTEIN: He's exceptional—although not, at this point, a young player.

CROW: I'm not really sure who the young players are. Haven't been around the clubs—

FEINSTEIN: Christian McBride's certainly one of the more popular ones.

CROW: Christian is wonderful. I got a chance to play on some concerts where there were several bass players, and I remember hearing him. He's out of that old Ray Brown school—which I consider the Oscar Pettiford school. [Laughs.] Getting a big sound.

FEINSTEIN: You were not on the *Mulligan Meets Monk* album, but you rehearsed with Mulligan and Monk.

CROW: Gerry had said, "Look, we're playing the same material, and going to concerts"—meaning, not even night clubs, where you can stretch out and try new stuff—"and it would be really fun to have Monk come to one of our rehearsals and open up our heads to another set of possibilities." We must have rehearsed in the Village, because I remember going to a bar in between.

FEINSTEIN: You said you talked about "mundane stuff" during that break. I can't imagine Monk chit-chatting.

CROW: Oh, he was talking about baseball, and brands of beers, and stuff like that. But he was in a much more communicative phase at that time. When I saw him later on, he would get that fixed look on his face and he wouldn't talk to anybody. I didn't know whether his mind was slipping a little bit, or if he had just taken on another public persona. He was very good at that!

FEINSTEIN: You made a very beautiful statement—quoting Monk—about finding the right note.

CROW: It was a strong idea. I would go to a Monk record and hear an interval and think, "What the hell is that?" and I'd go find it: "It's a *sixth*! How come it sounds different when Monk plays it?" [Laughs.] But Monk himself said, "Can't be no new notes. They're all the same notes there on the keyboard. But you've got to *mean* that note. You've got to *mean* that note. Then it'll sound new."

Cornelius Eady. *Photo by Tom Ellis.*

5

Did Your Mama Hear Those Poems?
Cornelius Eady

In September 1999, during my interview with Amiri Baraka, I asked about jazz-related plays and we had a brief discussion about his own play, *Dutchman*, as well as Langston Hughes's *The Organizer*, but it made me eager to conduct an interview that focused more completely on jazz-related theater. I tried and failed to coordinate a meeting with August Wilson. Then I read a review in the *New York Times* of Cornelius Eady's play, *Running Man*, which had been set to jazz by the composer Diedre Murray. I knew and admired Eady's poetry, and I had enjoyed our previous meetings, but, at that time, I was ignorant of his work in the theater. If nothing else, I felt confident our discussion would extend my appreciation for his artistry.

Running Man was actually Eady's second theatrical collaboration with Murray. The first, *You Don't Miss the Water*, had been adapted from his poetry collection *You Don't Miss Your Water*. (The producers of the opera wanted a similar but not exact title and came up with *You Don't Miss the Water*, but throughout our interview Eady used the original title for both the poetry book and the libretto.) Since then, Eady has become increasingly involved with the stage, and this conversation might be considered a marker for his early theatrical projects.

For reasons I can't recall, we met at my father's home on the Upper West Side rather than Cornelius's apartment or office, but this worked out well for us both: I appreciated knowing ahead of time that the room would be quiet and comfortable—not always the case—and he enjoyed seeing my parents' art work, as well as the panoply of objects in the living room where we spoke, from African baskets to Indonesian fishing traps. Talking there set a mood, and Cornelius answered all questions with enthusiasm, sometimes genuine delight. In some respects, we began where we would end, with his discussion of loving the backstage, having "access to places that only the artists are supposed see."

In addition to the librettos mentioned above, Cornelius Eady has published several other books of poetry, including *Victims of the Latest Dance Craze* (winner of the 1985 Lamont Prize from the Academy of American Poets), *You Don't Miss Your Water,* and *The Autobiography of a Jukebox. Brutal Imagination,* a finalist for the National Book Award, became the foundation for another theatrical production with Diedre Murray. His many honors include fellowships from the National Endowment for the Arts, the Guggenheim Foundation, and the Rockefeller Foundation. With Toi Derricote, he co-founded Cave Canem.

Our conversation focused on Eady's work for theater, especially *Running Man,* from which we have excerpted "Episode 2." The interview took place on the Upper West Side of Manhattan on February 5, 2000.

* * * * * * * * * * * * * * * * * * *

Running Man
A Roots Opera in One Act
(excerpt)
Cornelius Eady

CAST
TOMMY (RUNNING MAN)
MISS LOOK (SISTER)
DUKE (FATHER)
MOTHER
SEVEN (ROOT WOMAN)

Episode 2
Slave cemetery in Virginia on the Chesapeake. Miss Look has returned to her favorite place from childhood. She dreams of her brother.

(Next two lines are in unison)
RUNNING MAN: Can I offer a bit of advice?
SEVEN: Can I offer a bit of advice?
MISS LOOK:
    I am walking with my brother.
    We are walking in our dream.
    Tommy
RUNNING MAN: Yes, girl?
MISS LOOK: Is it really you I see?
MISS LOOK, RUNNING MAN: We are in our favorite
MISS LOOK: Place—in the slave cemetery

(Next two lines are in unison)
MISS LOOK, RUNNING MAN: This is our quiet
MISS LOOK: Africa lies here
RUNNING MAN, MISS LOOK: It is buried 'neath our

(Next four lines are in unison)
MISS LOOK: feet, walking
RUNNING MAN: feet, we've been walking
MISS LOOK:
    talking the
    in our favorite place the
RUNNING MAN, MISS LOOK: Moss itches our nose our nose
MISS LOOK:
    I know this not from school
    I know this from my brother,
    Who forms the word in his mouth
    Like the pastor says God—

    —or a cracker says Nigger.

        (Next line spoken)
    —like he owns it.

    How can a head hold so much?
    He has given me the names of things.
MISS LOOK, MOTHER, SEVEN:—Ah—

RUNNING MAN:
   All the flowers in this plot feed on the dust of Kings and Queens.

   I laugh
   And nod my head.
   She agrees with my smile.
MISS LOOK: What clever music he speaks!
MISS LOOK, MOTHER, DUKE: Oh what clever music he speaks
   (repeat)
MISS LOOK:
   Is it only the wind?
   Are you real?
   Are you staying?
RUNNING MAN: Why did you make me go?
MISS LOOK: I had to show you my back.
RUNNING MAN:
   You never understood me!
   Why do what I do
   Sometimes for money
   Sometimes for kicks
   Sometimes to see the sweat on their brows
   Sometimes I believe
   I can smell their fear.
   Sometimes it's knowing
   That they'll wake up in a sweat
   And wonder if I'll return
   The flesh wants what it wants,
   My knuckles against a cheek
   Sometimes it's because they run
   Sometimes it's because I know I'm faster
   Or they try to fight
   But I know I'm stronger.
   I know all the angles before they thought
   Of them.
   I am Running Man
   —Yes, I'm Running Man—
   Why not is my blood
   My story
   My middle name

Running Man disappears. Miss Look's daydream is broken.

SASCHA FEINSTEIN: How did you make the transition from a book of poems, *You Don't Miss Your Water,* to a play production?

CORNELIUS EADY: I was approached in '94 or '95 by a musician who had read my work, wanted to do an opera on Yusef Hawkins [killed by racists in Brooklyn, 1989], and thought that I'd be the appropriate librettist. I'd never written a libretto before, but I liked the idea and said we could talk about it. Now, he knew some producers—at the Music-Theater Group, Lyn Austin and Diane Wondisford—and we pitched the idea to them, leaving samples of our work: He left a tape, and I left the manuscript from *You Don't Miss Your Water.* Lyn and Diane didn't like the music—

FEINSTEIN: Which is why you've not mentioned the musician by name?

EADY: [Chuckles.] Exactly. But they loved the poetry and said they wanted to work with the prose poems from that book. I thought about it, agreed, and then they hooked me up with Diedre [Murray]. We got along immediately, and that's when we started to re-imagine the book as a theater piece.

FEINSTEIN: What kind of rewriting did you have to do?

EADY: That was a wild process. Lyn and Diane got a director—a friend of Diane's—and she was left alone. She had a wonderful sense of my poetry, and we pieced together all the family poems that I'd written over the years—prose poems from *You Don't Miss Your Water,* as well as work from other books—and created a narrative. Then Diedre started to create music underneath. It was a musical, basically. And for a while, naïvely, I thought we were doing quite well. [Laughs.]

At some point during the rehearsal process, Lyn and Diane re-emerged, took a look at it, and went berserk. Ballistic. They thought it was horrible. [Laughs.] They couldn't believe that they'd kept their hands off of this. We started to cut and rework things, but basically this was a workshop, and we were finding out how to do it as we went along. And at the last evening's performance, Doug Abel, the creative director at the Vineyard Theater, saw it, and he thought it was messy but had a lot of potential. Not long after, Lyn and Diane co-produced it at the Vineyard Theater, where our new director decided we should cut out everything except the prose poems in *You Don't Miss Your Water.*

FEINSTEIN: Did you leave the poems as they appear in the book, or did you mess with the lines and phrases?

EADY: I messed with a few of the lines, but not much. She changed the order of the poems so that they had more of a [chronological] narrative to them, and Diedre wrote a beautiful score to underpin the words.

FEINSTEIN: You had already published many poems inspired by the blues and jazz, but this was your first time working with a musician, no?

EADY: Oh, yes. Absolutely.

FEINSTEIN: That can be exciting, but also, sometimes, maddening.

EADY: It *is* maddening, but it's also very challenging. And with our first project it was more frustrating for Diedre than it was for me. We were going to keep the integrity of the poems as much as we could, so musically she had to support the text, and for her that sometimes got very frustrating—to find music that had vitality without overpowering the poems. But the poems were in place.

With the second piece [*Running Man*], we got closer to the idea of real collaboration. As we were working on *You Don't Miss Your Water* [which focuses on Eady's father], Diedre got the idea to write a piece about her family, and she had this story about her brother that she really wanted to do. She approached me with the idea of trying to write the text to this, I told her I was interested, and we started to wrestle over an outline.

We work like this: She'll have an idea and send me an outline. I'll try to interpret the outline—map out the possibilities for stories to open it up, et cetera. Then I write what I can and fax it over to her. She tries to write music for it. And then the negotiations begin: how much needs to be altered, trimmed, reworked, rethought.

FEINSTEIN: Were there moments when you thought, "I just can't hear the poems this way"?

EADY: That happened quite a bit. There were a number of complications. *You Don't Miss Your Water* was my story, and she really respected that and kept her hands off as much as she could. And I tried to do the same with *Running Man,* because this was her story, her brother, and therefore it was her call. So I was trying to write poems that would be the most useful for her. There were times when I couldn't hear the music—poetically—and I'd say [after she'd explain what she wanted to compose], "You can't possibly have this," or, "You've just cut the gut out of this poem." And then she'd play the piece, and suddenly I'd realize that she'd added emotion, musically, to the center of the poem. I started to withhold my opinions until I actually heard the piece.

Sometimes she probably couldn't understand why I was insisting on a certain point of view, and then she would see it dramatically acted out and she'd understand immediately why it had to be that way. I think the great thing about our collaboration process is that we're advocates for our side but we also have a lot of respect for the other person's talent—a real simpatico relationship—and because of that we'll listen very carefully. We can't always agree, but we have a lot of respect.

FEINSTEIN: She also had some musical cues in the text. I mean, *You Don't Miss Your Water* may not be written in blues form, but emotionally— in terms of tone—it seems steeped in the blues.

EADY: I'm glad you saw it like that. That's what I was trying to get at: blues songs. I was experimenting with the idea of getting the emotional weight of the blues without having to use the form of the blues. So I was trying to weave in a lot of different blues elements— sometimes references to certain songs, or lyrics—but I was trying to generate that feeling without presenting it [in form] the way Langston Hughes might have done it. So I'm glad to hear you say that.

It was a difficult book to write because it was so personal. I didn't even begin to write those poems until a year after my dad was dead. In the end, I was only able to get twenty-one poems that worked. (There wasn't much more. A couple of other poems were too personal, and some didn't turn the way I wanted them to turn.) So I had the problem of having this really slim book of poems, and that bent a few people out of shape because, you know, these days, poets aren't supposed to write small books, and you're not supposed to write prose poems. [Laughs.] But it was a very difficult book to write.

One day I was in Jackson, Mississippi, giving a reading from *You Don't Miss Your Water,* and there was a silence in the room. It wasn't a "listening hard" kind of silence or a bored kind of silence. It was a kind of weird silence. And finally somebody put up his hand and said, "Did your mama hear those poems? Did you read those poems to your mama?" It was like, "Can you *say* that stuff?"

And I think Diedre and I hold that in common: We had no idea how difficult a journey it was going to be to write these two pieces. We both didn't understand that when you write about family—supposedly about somebody else—you're really exposing more about yourself than you ever will about the subject. And I think that was more of a shock for Diedre [when she started thinking about *Running Man*]. She thought she was going to tell a couple of stories about her brother, and maybe her mother, but at a certain point she realized that every-

body was going to come in and look at this. There it was. So she realized there would be some people in the audience saying, "Look what
you're saying about your family. *Mmmm-mmm.*" [Laughs.]

FEINSTEIN: Blues and jazz musicians, of course, do that every night—but
not necessarily in such a straight-ahead narrative.

EADY: Right. In fact, Diedre had written and recorded some wonderful
instrumental pieces about her brother. Beautiful elegies. But to actually put words to it . . . You take a stand, and that's what writing is
about. "This is what I really mean."

FEINSTEIN: There was a bit of emotional distance, of course, since you
wrote the actual words [about Diedre's family].

EADY: Exactly. And that kind of distance helps make it fictional instead
of sheer biography, but it definitely has some deep truths about her
brother. I mean, part of *Running Man* has to do with the realization
that you can love somebody without knowing them fully. And I think
she wanted to respond to her brother that way.

FEINSTEIN: The way, perhaps, you wanted to respond to your father in
You Don't Miss Your Water.

EADY: Exactly. In both those pieces, there are a lot of cross agendas.

All this was complicated further by the whole process of working in
theater. There's a director who wants answers to big questions—from
you. Actors who want motivation—from you. The producers are com-
plaining 'cause all this money is burning up. Other people are pushing you, whether you want to be pushed or not. There's no such thing
as time in the theater; you have to do it now—or yesterday. [Laughs.]
But we got through it.

FEINSTEIN: Not only "got through it" but succeeded in all ways. I mean,
the reviews for *Running Man* were smashing.

EADY: People really responded. And we were nervous about it because the
form was so unusual. People keep playing with terms: "Is it an opera?
Is it an operetta?" I think it *is* an opera, but Diedre enacted a kind of
scene change in the way musical theater can be approached.

I was listening to NPR this morning, a piece about the career of
Aaron Copland and how he decided to put jazz elements into his work.
(I started thinking about Gershwin, too, of course.) But instead of
bringing jazz *elements* to the work, Diedre actually brings jazz to the
theater, and that's different. She's not just a fan, like I am; Diedre's
really what you'd call "a dyed-in-the-wool jazzbo." [Laughs.] The pit
musicians don't dabble in jazz; they're actually jazz players—many
from Henry Threadgill's band. So a lot of changes had to happen to
make this piece work. Even the players had to think about this differ-

ently than if they were doing a [more standard] gig. The playing was really open and free, but for theater you have to find a way to contain that each evening, for as long as the run lasts.

That's a new element that she brought to theater, but because of that, we didn't know how people would respond. It's not the standard narrative and, as the [*New York*] *Times* pointed out [on March 5, 1999], there are no "big songs." (There are big moments musically, but they aren't songs in that sense—you know, hummable songs.) So we were really pleased that they could get that.

FEINSTEIN: The *Times* doesn't always "get it," but the reviewer [Peter Marks] really explained that this was a hybrid of styles, and a hybrid that works.

EADY: God bless Peter Marks! [Laughs.]

FEINSTEIN: How strange was it to hear these poems with pitches assigned to the words?

EADY: I found it very exciting. Perhaps it's because I write music myself (I claim that, though I don't do it professionally). But I found it exciting to hear enough musicality in the line to know that it could be adapted. I like to think of myself as a lyric poet on some level.

One of the great moments for [the theater version of] *You Don't Miss Your Water* was when the musicians were together—first rehearsal, all of us on stage in a semicircle—and Diedre said, "Okay, here's the opening." The musicians started playing it, and everyone looked at each other and knew it was going to work. Up until that moment, nobody was sure. But it was like, "Oh, yeah. Listen to that."

It's also been a pleasure watching Diedre mature as a composer. She got the Obie for *Running Man* but she should've gotten the Pulitzer as well. Nothing that year was even close, musically. *W;t* was a beautiful piece, but it wasn't a musical, and *Side Man* was okay . . . All those other shows were on the periphery of jazz, and *Running Man* really opened up the possibilities of jazz. To me, she's like Charles Mingus. She's really in that league.

FEINSTEIN: There's been some criticism about *Side Man* and other recent projects—that they glorify white musicians without fully crediting the black innovators.

EADY: You have to consider if there are really legitimate cases being made for white jazz musicians. In terms of theater, I could make the argument that each play's a story about something you wouldn't normally pay attention to, and so you put the emphasis where you least expect it. But in the larger context, a play like *Side Man* just becomes a story about white guys—[laughs]—and it makes the case that this is the epitome, the apex—and you can't believe it. You simply can't believe it. I know it's a good piece on a written level, but what's it actually saying, and do you really want to buy that?

I felt the same way about Michael John LeChiusa's *Marie Christine,* performed at Lincoln Center. It was written for Audra McDonald, who is a fantastic singer, and she's at that point in her career where she really needs large roles. The play's based on *Medea,* but it's interracial: She's mulatto—upper class, mannered, cultured, and moneyed—and she meets this white sea captain. And they have a little affair. But the piece was really disappointing because, ultimately, it insinuates that her African blood is what makes her wild. And she pays a price for her wild blood. There's this one scene where they actually copulate on stage. They flirt, then they run off to the bushes: They go down the hill, up goes the dress, down goes the actor on top of her—and I'm thinking, "This is a white boy fantasy." [Laughs.] This is a white boy fantasy about black women. Yes, you can argue that a black artist of McDonald's stature needs large roles, but this is the best they can do for her?

FEINSTEIN: Who do you think is writing well—really infusing jazz and drama?

EADY: I'll take the easy way out and choose the obvious: August Wilson—not so much in a musical sense but in terms of language. I thought *Seven Guitars* wasn't a fabulous plot, but the language was superb! It was like a feast, listening to those actors read those lines. Nobody does that as well as he does. He has the vernacular, and it doesn't surprise me to know that he started off being a poet.

FEINSTEIN: Baraka thinks of him as something of a protégé.

EADY: Well, sure. You know, one of the tragedies about Amiri Baraka is that, ironically, he's like the Flying Dutchman now. They treat him like he's a ghost, so he can't get productions up, and major presses won't publish his work. It's ridiculous. I don't get it. I don't know what the fear is at this point. He's not only one of the most exciting poets of the twentieth century, but he's also a major voice in theater, and people tend to forget those plays that he wrote. They're out of the repertoire. That's why I thought of August Wilson and not Amiri Baraka.

Not enough people, for example, know the stuff that he's been doing with jazz musicians. It's fabulous.

FEINSTEIN: His group, Blue Ark, has great musicians: D. D. Jackson on piano—

EADY: Yeah, and nobody's paying enough attention to all that stuff. It's almost like an underground knowledge, and that's a real tragedy.

FEINSTEIN: What do you think of Langston Hughes's play *The Organizer?*

EADY: It made me think of all the different levels that Langston would write on. He could write really high up. He could write really down to the middle. And for this [play] about a political organizer, he knew his audience; it was totally accessible—even to someone who, if you walked up to him on the street and said, "Let's go hear an opera," would run as fast as he could. [Laughs.] This is about torture, and who wants to hear that? But the language is direct: "This is your life. I know what your life is. I'm going to let you recognize yourself in this piece." He had that ability to talk in a way that wasn't condescending, but, rather, compassionate and understanding.

I recently taught a literature course at The New School, and this was one of the things [about Hughes] that I was bringing up: A lot of poets find their voice and stay in that one voice, but Langston had the ability to speak in different voices—to shift and move, different voices at different times. Brilliant, and not a lot of poets can do that.

It can be irritating, too, because, number one, you'd like to think you have the ability to do that and you often don't. But also, when you read *The Collected* [*Poems of Langston Hughes*] and find the "occasional" poems, or doggerel poems, you start thinking, "My God, he can do better than that." But no: There's a reason why he's writing at that level, a logic. It isn't just doggerel. Some critics have found this work condescending, but I think he was more of a social poet than the rest of us are these days. He had a sense of a social poet, the duty of a social poet. And we have our concerns—but not in the same way that he was thinking of.

FEINSTEIN: It's terrible, isn't it, that no one can find James P. Johnson's score for *The Organizer?*

EADY: It is terrible. If there was a score, you could produce it right now. And there's not a *lot* of Johnson's work around, so anything you lose is a double tragedy. I wish someone could find it—and if they can't, I wish someone would find another composer to approximate the music, because the libretto [by Hughes] is really vivid. Without the music, people won't hear it, at all; there just won't be the same kind of interest in reviving it.

Hughes uses the blues cadence seamlessly. It's the kind of work you'd want to give someone who has a problem with blues poetry, who thinks it's limited: "See? This is what you get when it's in the hands of a true master."

FEINSTEIN: The refrains are so strong—church-like, I guess—that you do get a *sense* of the music.

EADY: Oh, absolutely. I can hear it, and you can begin to imagine what that would've been like. But . . . there's regret.

FEINSTEIN: "The Sheets of Sound" [a poem about John Coltrane that appeared in *The Gathering of My Name*] is probably your most ambitious jazz-related poem.

EADY: Yes. In a career, there are jumps, and then there are little epiphanies. I remember the day I finished "Gratitude" from *The Gathering of My Name*, and I just knew I had finished a big poem, that personally I had made a big jump from what I had been doing before. And when I finished the ten-part John Coltrane poem, I also knew I had made a big jump, poetically. A lot of times, these changes simply have to do with going where you need to go without trying to censor yourself. In this case, it was a little weird for me because I'm not usually comfortable with the long form; I've always been more comfortable with the short form. I felt both those poems needed to be expansive, and that was a risk for me.

FEINSTEIN: Your work does tend to focus on shorter poems, and it seems to me that theater offers one way for you to weave pieces together in order to make a still-larger statement.

EADY: That's right. Also, working with someone else's story [*Running Man*] forced me to use muscles I had never used before. That's one of the things that keeps pushing me as a writer. But sometimes I've been resistant to taking risks. I resisted, for example, doing a cycle of dance poems [*Victims of the Latest Dance Craze*]. It took a long time for me to get to the point where I realized what the book was about. My friend Shreela Ray, who was my mentor in college and who died recently, told me she had an earlier copy of the manuscript where only half the book were dance poems, and they were pushing the others out of the way. But it took a long time for me to admit that the entire book needed to be dance poems. I really felt people would think it was a gimmick.

After the book was published, I read a book—I believe it was by Al Young . . .

FEINSTEIN: *Dancing*?

EADY: Yeah—thank God I didn't read that book before mine got published! [Laughs.] I would've stopped. I would've said to myself, "Well, it's been done. He did it. Great book. We don't need two [poetry] books about dancing." [Laughs.] That's the anxiety. You can give yourself all sorts of reasons not to do things.

The same is true for *You Don't Miss Your Water.* I was trying to write poems the way I usually write poems, and it just wasn't working. I knew there was something else going on that I had to get at, and when I started doing the prose poems I knew that they were the way in. I try to keep anxiety enough at bay so that I can explore and make a book what *it* needs to be—not what I need it to be, but what the book needs to be. To make it true to itself.

FEINSTEIN: Among your many shorter jazz poems, do you have some favorites?

EADY: The ones I read. The Miles Davis poem is one of my favorites, and I love reading the Dexter Gordon poem. Word got back to me that Max Roach got a copy of his poem and loved it, and that always makes you feel good. [Laughs.] [These three poems—"Photo of Miles Davis at Lennies-on-the-Turnpike, 1968," "Photo of Dexter Gordon, About to Solo, 1965," and "Photo of a Max Roach Solo, 1964"—are part of a series in *The Autobiography of a Jukebox.*]

FEINSTEIN: Visually, your most dramatic jazz poem might be your elegy to Hank Mobley ["Hank Mobley's" from *The Gathering of My Name*], where the text of the poem is pushed unusually far to the right. I like it very much.

EADY: I'm glad. It's one of my favorites, too. It's a true story: I was in Richmond [Virginia] in a used record store, and there was this long tirade in the [liner] notes about how Mobley died totally busted. I mean, I love Hank Mobley's work, and I still read books and encyclopedias that say he isn't this or he isn't that, that he's workman-like . . . There's a lot of pleasure in his work. I mean, he's meat and potatoes.

FEINSTEIN: There's been an effort in the last few years to celebrate his achievements, but for a long time, critics did little more than compare him unfavorably to John Coltrane, and some still do.

EADY: And it's kind of pointless and silly to compare the two. It really is. There's so much pleasure in his work. One of my favorite records is *Workout.* It's a brilliant piece, and it really gives you an idea of what was happening then.

FEINSTEIN: And what was at the heart of the Blue Note label.

EADY: Exactly. And he wasn't a bad composer: "Slice of the Top"—

FEINSTEIN: "A Caddy for Daddy"—

EADY: I really enjoy his work. So when I wrote that poem, that's what was going through my head: What an awful end.

FEINSTEIN: There's also a directive to the reader—"I want to tell you about a wonderful musician, and you should hear him."

EADY: That's right: "I want to tell you." That's a large reason why we write poetry, and I felt *somebody* had to write that poem.

FEINSTEIN: There have been very few poems written in honor of Mobley, before or since yours, so I'm glad you wrote it, too.

EADY: Thanks. I also like my Thelonious Monk poem ["Thelonious," also from *The Gathering of My Name*]. I wrote it with an odd line structure—intentionally. I was trying to write an homage to the way Thelonious's music sounded to me: the way he takes meter and makes it very strange. He'll take an everyday melody and make you *really* listen to it. "Tea for Two," "April in Paris"—

FEINSTEIN: "These Foolish Things"—

EADY: Things you've heard a zillion times, and suddenly he cracks them open in such a way that you have to re-hear it. And a really good poem does the same thing: It takes the absolutely ordinary and makes you reassess it. That's the parallel for me. There's a poetry in the way that he plays.

FEINSTEIN: You said earlier that you played music.

EADY: I started out as a drummer. When I was growing up in Rochester, New York, one of the great things about the school system was that the Eastman [School of Music] students would teach Saturday music lessons at different high schools. You paid a quarter, I think, or maybe fifty cents. I studied percussion with a guy named Dick Moore, and I got sort of adopted by Moore and his drumming buddies. I'd be the last lesson of the day, and then a bunch of us would go out to lunch at the White Swan—we called it the Dirty Duck. Then we'd hang out. I *loved* drumming, and I think, to a certain extent, that's part of the information I get as a poet.

FEINSTEIN: What about literary "information." For example, when you were writing the libretto for *Running Man,* did you sense the influence of [Ralph] Ellison?

EADY: No. I wish I could say I did because he's one of my favorite writers. But he wasn't in my head. Now, subconsciously, who knows? A lot of times I'll be writing something and months later I'll realize, "Of course, that came from there, and that came from there. What was I thinking?" Well, I wasn't thinking at all; it just seeps in.

The writer who was probably at the top of my brain was Hughes. One of the concerns I had with *Running Man* was making sure the vernacular was working, but I didn't want it to be straight vernacular. I was concerned that a lot of the shows with African Americans are basically revues—things like *Ain't Nothin' but the Blues,* which is running like gangbusters now. There's nothing wrong with them, but they keep presenting a certain face in African American theater. I realize, of course, that on some levels there's a need to feel familiar. But I wanted something else.

The main thing I got from Diedre's stories is that her family was highly educated, smart, and articulate. (In my life, for example, I talk differently when I'm speaking to you than when I'm talking at home and fall into cadences—but I don't talk down when I'm talking in either place.) I wanted to get a sense of that in the play. I was thinking vernacular—that's Hughes to me—but I wanted to be clear. I wanted a tension in the voices.

FEINSTEIN: Hughes often talked about the blues fusing opposite emotions.

EADY: That's what I was trying to get at and deal with.

FEINSTEIN: I was reminded of [Ellison's] *Invisible Man* not so much in terms of voice but of theme—identity and place—and because Ellison really did hear the music.

EADY: That's all true, but you can also think of the voice and the idea of double consciousness. That was another aspect of *Running Man:* the private family as opposed to the public. And of course, though there aren't any white people in *Running Man,* they're out there! [Laughs.] The characters act the way they do because, invisibly, there's this attitude going on.

FEINSTEIN: Running Man says, "God made me smart / God made me black" and Seven responds, "Which only proves / God's infinite sense of humor." Those lines only work because of an invisible white presence.

EADY: Exactly. They're present. Again, we were trying to set up a universe where you get the sense of the outside pressuring in: Why is the mother so adamant about him making it? Why is the father so afraid of him making it? Because basically, it's the same thing: how to survive.

FEINSTEIN: Have you often been slotted as a Jazz Poet, where you have to perform work with a live band?

EADY: No. Diedre and I occasionally perform together (she calls it Po-Music) and we've done a few gigs, but what often happens is that people don't show up! It mystifies me why the audiences are so sparse.

FEINSTEIN: Al Young said he used to be a little annoyed when he'd get billed as a Jazz Poet—and for that matter, I don't care for it, either; I'd rather be known as a poet who happens to love jazz—but then, he said, he got hip to the money and it didn't bother him so much.

EADY: [Laughs.] Yeah, isn't that what it comes down to in the end? "Give me that check! 'Pork and Bean Poet'? Fine!" [Laughs.] But people don't think of me as a performance poet. Actually, I think my reputation is much more staid than that. I think people think of me as an academic poet.

FEINSTEIN: Really?

EADY: I get that feedback every so often. It's basically because I spent a long time teaching, and once I got tenured at Stony Brook, people would say, "He's really an intellectual poet." I've heard that in different ways.

FEINSTEIN: Are you still there [at Stony Brook]?

EADY: No, I resigned—for a lot of political, complicated, boring reasons. But it also had to do with theater. I was in the middle of *Running Man,* and I dreaded going back [to teaching full-time]. I suddenly realized that I was spending a lot of energy and time on things that I didn't think were necessary, and I wasn't writing enough. I still teach part-time at The New School and, occasionally, at NYU. This spring I'm doing a workshop at City College. I have to make a living—and with these jobs, plus judging contests and stuff like that, I make a decent salary. It's riskier than having a full-time job, but I make enough to get along, and it gives me the time to do theater.

I do love teaching (without the stuff that goes with it), and one of the things I tell my workshops is that you can't teach experience. Basically, I try to teach creative writing students how to have some sort of handle on what happens to the rest of their lives. They need to have some sort of method for transforming experiences into writing. I'm not really teaching writing; I'm teaching them to be prepared for what happens to them after they leave class.

FEINSTEIN: At the schools you just mentioned, there is a tremendous range in their personalities among the poets, but most of them have, to a greater or lesser extent, written about jazz. What is it about this music that keeps filtering through the lives of such disparate people?

EADY: I think it is a truly human art. And because of that, we gravitate towards it. I think people are also attracted to the nature of possibility. Of course, some people also like the lifestyle and like to think of themselves as hip and cool. [Laughs.] They'll gravitate towards that, too. But there's a real language about jazz that challenges or delights us as writers. As I said before, one of the reasons why I wrote about Thelonious was because I wanted to translate what I heard.

FEINSTEIN: Did you ever hear Monk live?

EADY: No.

FEINSTEIN: What do you think about Michael Harper's statement that people should only write about jazz musicians whom they've actually heard?

EADY: Well, he can say that, and he's old enough to say that. [Laughs.] Unfortunately, I never heard Miles live, or Thelonious, but the music means a lot to me. It's part of my chemical makeup, and because of that I feel I have the right to try to capture that. The nonverbal stories that musicians tell you are deep.

It's interesting that you mention Harper. I first met him years ago, when he was teaching a summer workshop in Rochester. That week, he did a reading from *Dear John, Dear Coltrane* while playing a tape of [John Coltrane's] *A Love Supreme.* That was the first time I heard poetry and jazz together, and, on a subconscious level, I *got* it. It wasn't just poetry he was talking about; he was also talking about our lives. "This is the sound of our lives. All the stuff that goes on in your neighborhood—that's the essence of that sound." Sound as story.

Years later, writing my own Coltrane poem ["The Sheets of Sound"], I thought I was so clever to break into "A Love Supreme": close to song, close to song, and then suddenly it breaks open into song. How 'bout that?! Oh, how clever! But my wife made me realize that this was me remembering Michael Harper reading. That's what the section was really about: remembering Harper reading to Coltrane.

FEINSTEIN: Harper also once claimed that jazz is so indigenous to American culture that you have to be informed about it if you want to be informed about American culture.

EADY: I agree with that, and I think that's one of the reasons why jazz is so compelling to a number of people. There's also the underground nature of it. Jazz and poetry are very similar in that way: It's about telling the story that's not really the official story.

FEINSTEIN: What do you think about Edward Albee writing a whole play [*The Death of Bessie Smith*, 1960] based on the misinformation about Bessie Smith's death? I mean, she didn't die because she was denied entry to a white hospital.

EADY: Really? I didn't know that.

FEINSTEIN: Of course, she dealt with so much racism during her lifetime that it might as well be true.

EADY: You're right: It might as well be true. And jazz is also about mythology. For example, before I read my Thelonious Monk poem, I usually tell this story: I'm reading at a prison, and a prisoner comes up to me and claims that Thelonious used to walk down the street in Harlem, put his head to a lamp post, hear the hum, and then go home to try to play the hum. People will ask me, "Is that a true story?" Who cares?

FEINSTEIN: You choose to believe it.

EADY: Right, I choose believe it. That *could* be Thelonious. It doesn't matter so much if it's a true story or not, and I think that's the same thing with Albee's play. It's about the pressures that totally crush this woman. If it's a factual story or not—doesn't really matter. We all know what goes on around us.

Toi Derricote once challenged members of a workshop to see the way racism works in this country: that people always think it comes from one direction. That is, if you're Caucasian, you think you have no connection to this story, and you hurt yourself when you think it's only black people whining about what happens to them. If you don't examine that, you're really damaging yourself. That might be another way of thinking about jazz. Jazz allows you to enter in this discussion and acts as a bridge.

FEINSTEIN: A couple of years ago, I was invited to speak at the maximum security prison in Lewisburg [Pennsylvania] by the NAACP branch of that prison. Immediately, there were all sorts of class and race issues. I mean, when I walked in, 10 percent of the guys left. [Eady laughs.] But as soon as we started talking about jazz, we had a real exchange. The love of this music cut through so much.

EADY: That's it. That's the bridge. Jazz can be common ground. When I was a kid, playing drums, the high school band was a great equalizer. No one played really well, but we had this context to talk to one another, and that had a big influence on me. You could see people for who they were, not who you thought they might be.

Through music, I also got a sense of being in a world that the audience doesn't see: backstage—you know, access to places that only the artists are supposed to see. That's probably why I like theater. Backstage, there's this little universe.

Gary Giddins

6

Legwork
Gary Giddins

At the time of this interview, Gary Giddins was still on staff at the *Village Voice,* and when he suggested we meet at his downtown office, I anticipated a sterile cubicle. But this office—an apartment, actually—had nothing to do with the *Voice* and was certainly not sterile. Lined with tightly packed bookshelves and racks of records and CDs, the rooms emanated warmth and intelligence. We sat on a sofa, I started the tape recorder, and soon the formalities often associated with interviews dissipated.

In a number of crucial ways, Giddins speaks the way he writes: with directness, deep consideration, and narrative clarity. Some taped conversations have been a nightmare to transcribe; this one was a pleasure. His rhetorical gifts might not surprise those familiar with his books and reviews, but prolific and prodigious essay writing does not always equate with fluid speech. (Prior to this meeting, I conducted an interview with a jazz critic known for his poetic prose, and it remains my only unpublished effort—a failure due to a relentless string of single-sentence answers.) Gary never sounded impatient or distracted, and what he had to say about his own research, and the efforts of others, should act as a challenge for future biographers.

On my way out, I mentioned that I hadn't imagined him clean-shaven, since I had most recently seen him bearded on the Ken Burns *Jazz* series. Gary laughed and said that, during his taped interviews for that series, he needed lead time in order to grow the beard back; he also kept the same outfit pressed and hung in his closet. I suppose that kind of interviewing necessitates artifice, and like many of his musical heroes, he has learned to play some games—but when he needs to perform, for television or *Brilliant Corners*, artifice gives way to what is genuine, instructive, and memorable.

Gary Giddins wrote on jazz for the *Village Voice* for more than thirty years. His books include *Celebrating Bird, Satchmo, Weather Bird, Bing Crosby,* and *Visions of Jazz,* which won the National Book Critics Circle Award. His other awards include several ASCAP-Deems Taylor Awards for music criticism, two Ralph J. Gleason music book awards, a Guggenheim Fellowship, a Peabody Broadcasting Award, and an American Book Award. For seven years, he was artistic director of the American Jazz Orchestra, which he founded in 1985. He currently writes a monthly column for *JazzTimes.*

The following excerpts from his writings on Louis Armstrong, Charlie Parker, Duke Ellington, and Bing Crosby demonstrate his gifts as a prose stylist and correspond to key figures in our discussion. The interview took place in his office in downtown Manhattan on October 4, 2003.

Satchmo
(excerpt)
Gary Giddins

In 1968, as an undergraduate in charge of college concerts, I arranged for Armstrong to play at a convocation at Grinnell College in Iowa. He never knew about two incidents that marred the occasion for me and seem now to delineate the bastard place jazz occupies in America's cultural life: Nearly two dozen intellectuals and artists were on campus to participate in a series of discussions and to receive honorary degrees, yet the college refused to award one to Armstrong; outside the gymnasium where he performed, a handful of students picketed because they wanted a rock group. . . .

Between the locker room and the steps leading up to the stage was the space of a few feet cast in shadow by stark lighting. Each musician disappeared into it before attaining the stage. As Armstrong emerged into the light, arms slightly raised, palms out, he appeared transfigured. The ashen color was gone, the eyes blazed, the smile blinded. When he sang, he engaged the crowd eyeball to eyeball. When he blew trumpet, he kept his eyes open, but the pupils rolled upward as though he were no longer in the room. His huge tone was as gold and unspotted as ever. Each musician had a feature number, at which time Armstrong walked into the shadows to rest. He would return glowing with energy.

I've often thought that had I been a critic then, I might have disdained the same old same old: the inevitable "Indiana" opener, the excessive drum solo, the chick singer, "Hello Dolly." But maybe not. The set worked. And when Armstrong was onstage, nothing else mattered. He carried the weight of his own myth in all its grandeur, but it was the myth made human—made possible.

Celebrating Bird
(excerpt)
Gary Giddins

One wonders if it is even possible to peel away the Charlie Parker created in death by family and disciples, hagiographers and voyeurs, and if so to what purpose? Would a Charlie Parker reduced to life size be more easily apprehended, understood, and admired, or even closer to the truth, than the one of legend? The one irreducible fact of his existence is his genius, which will not cater to the routine explanations of psychologists, sociologists, anthropologists, or musicologists. But a basic ordering of facts, as best they can be adduced with limited resources in the face of conflicting claims (most of them plenary), may complement the music of Charlie Parker and engage the imagination of listeners who know the ravishing pleasure of his art.

Visions of Jazz
(excerpt)
Gary Giddins

The posthumous works of no major contemporary artist have excited greater interest than Ellington's, except perhaps for Hemingway's.

The critical estimation of his music was revised upward throughout the '70s and '80s as previously unknown pieces were discovered and old ones reevaluated. . . .

On the eve of Ellington's centennial, it can safely be said that he is held in higher esteem the world over than ever before and that his music has been absorbed into the very nervous system of American life. Jazz, of course, is unimaginable without him, however restricting he found the category. Ellington's music is Shakespearian in its reach, wisdom, and generosity, and we return to it because its mysteries are inexhaustible.

Bing Crosby
(excerpt)
Gary Giddins

Here he is: swinging with such poise that he lifts the whole band, but with that choirboy voice that speaks right to you even as it suggests a sleepy-eyed nonchalance. This is not a singer to commune self-consciously with his muse or to emote for the hipster musicians. His approach is disarmingly, almost nakedly, artless, yet so artful that he never shows his hand, never shows off his phrasing or his easy way of rushing or retarding a phrase, never does any of the things singers do to show you how hard they are working. He is so smooth, you may not notice the flawless diction of the rhymes *startin'* and *kindergarten* in a phrase that ends with a model mordant on the last word (*wild*); the impeccably timed cadences of the phrase "I can see the judges' eyes as they handed you the prize"; and the neat embellishment on the reprise of "judges' eyes." [Bob] Haggart's excellent arrangement puts the verse in the middle for a change of pace and shows off the ensemble and tenor saxophonist Eddie Miller in an interlude that begins with a hint of "Muskrat Ramble." The sustained chords at Bing's return have the effect of suspending the rhythm. A number one hit, "You Must Have Been a Beautiful Baby" was reckoned as one of the top sellers in a year dominated by big bands. Bing won the *Down Beat* poll as best jazz singer of 1938.

SASCHA FEINSTEIN: Before we talk about jazz biographies, I'd like to know which arrived first: your passion for writing or your passion for music?

GARY GIDDINS: That's an interesting question. They came pretty much on the heels of each other. But music was first, no question about it. When I was a kid—a really tiny kid, three or four, before I could really read—I was somehow able to memorize which label on the 78 went with which song, and my aunt would spread the 78s around, and I would say, "This is Tony Bennett," "This is Sinatra," and they were all like "How—?" Because somehow I had just memorized the lettering, and also I had the ability to hear a song and then know it. So my parents thought, "Ah, Mozart revividus." I studied every kind of instrument, but I knew instantly that I had absolutely no aptitude for playing music. I was reading precociously at an early age, and yet, after years of studying [piano], I could barely read the left hand. It was as though I were mentally retarded. My real aptitude was for playing records.

At the same time, writing for me was always a creative act, whereas the idea of me being a musician—all I wanted to do was replay the Sonny Rollins solo, or be able to play Art Tatum. I never thought of myself as having original ideas, musically. Writing also started early. I think when I was eight I had read a children's biography of Louis Pasteur and decided I wanted to be a chemist or scientist. My older cousin gave me a copy of *Microbe Hunters* by de Kruif, so I read that, which was a little more difficult, and then I read a couple of other biographies and I realized very quickly that I didn't want to be a backwoodsman or explorer or scientist; I wanted to be the guy who wrote all the books. And I wrote a short story in fourth grade and all that kind of stuff, but it wasn't really until I got out of college that I finally confronted what for me was the hateful realization that music was going to be my subject and that I was a critic, because up until shortly before, I had other ambitions: I wanted to be the Hawthorne of my generation. When I discovered Hemingway and Fitzgerald, that's what I was going to do. And then when I was in college, I really didn't confront the fact that I didn't have that kind of talent. I think reading [Thomas Pynchon's] *V* suddenly made me realize, "This is way beyond what I can even *imagine* doing right now."

I had a professor, Mike Lieberman—M. M. Lieberman was his byline. He had written a number of short stories and won two O. Henry Awards and he was the head of the English department at Grinnell. Crusty little guy. My kind of teacher. Most of the kids were just terrified of him. I took a number of classes from him; one was Creative Writing, and I wrote a story for him and he said, "Rewrite it." So I rewrote it, and he never said a word about it, never gave it back to me. And then Kent State happened, and Grinnell, out of solidarity, closed down the campus. Everybody was given forty-eight hours to leave the campus, with the exception of those of us who lived off campus and faculty. Suddenly faculty members and seniors were drinking together and hanging out, which in those days was still unusual. So one day I met Lieberman in the Student Union and he said to me, "You know, you still have to do your oral comprehensives." (I was an English major. My subjects were Edmund Wilson, T. S. Eliot, and Hemingway.) We talked for six or seven minutes, and he said, "Oh, you know this stuff well enough. Let's talk about something else." I said, "You know, you never got back to me about that story," and he said, "Well, Mr. Giddins, there really wasn't very much to say. It was completely worthless." It was that kind of thing. [Both laugh.] "If I was you, I would never try to write another piece of fiction. However, if you're really serious you won't listen to anything I have to say." But then he went on, and I blush to remember this: He said of all the students he had taught, I had a peculiar gift for criticism. I was blushing like a prom queen. I didn't give a shit about what he had said about the story. This was the first time anyone had ever given me real, positive feedback. He remembered the essays I had written.

For a long time, I experienced a certain guilt, because as a critic you spend your adult life indulging the passions of your adolescence, and you get paid for it. There were days when I had to overcome the question, "Am I really allowed to spend every day listening to music to write this piece?"

FEINSTEIN: What's the connector between Lieberman's endorsement and your career as a critic?

GIDDINS: I found jazz when I was fifteen and became totally enamored of it. It was my religious experience. Hearing Armstrong's '20s recordings changed everything that I knew about everything. I had loved jazz for a few months before that. Before that I loved rock. I grew up on classical music. I loved the B minor Mass [Bach]—and that's what really did it: the fact that Armstrong's was the first music that seemed to me as glorious as the B minor Mass. And I wasn't expecting that from him. He was a clown, as far as I knew—the guy on *The Ed Sullivan Show* with the handkerchiefs and the sweat. The music simply wasn't in the culture to any serious degree then, but hearing Armstrong completely changed my life. I think I said this in the Ken Burns film: It took me six months to listen to the entire album, this album. [Gid-

dins pulls from the shelf *Louis Armstrong and Earl Hines,* 1928.] Just
to look at it humbles me every once in a while. And I would only play it
when there was nobody in the house; I was embarrassed to have even
bought a Louis Armstrong record, it was so "uncool." [The first time
I played it] I heard this little celeste tinkling along and my heart fell
into my stomach: "Oh God! This is even worse than I thought." And
then suddenly Armstrong enters. [Giddins hums the trumpet line.]
Oh, God ... At the end of the track, I ran to the turntable to take the
needle off. I played it over and over again—until I knew it by heart—
before I went to track two.

I started listening to it in the fall of '63. My birthday's in March, so
in March of '64, I thought, "I'd better do something for myself. What
should I do? Oh yeah! I should play Side Two." [Both laugh.] I'd been
putting it off because when you get to the end of Side One, it's "Tight
Like That," and I thought there was nothing that could get beyond
that. Absolutely nothing. First I thought "Muggles," nothing could go
beyond that. "St. James Infirmary" is light compared to that, but it's
a magnificent recording, and then you get to "Tight Like That," and
I thought, "Holy Christ. What kind of a man *is* this?" And then you
turn it over, and the first track is "West End Blues."

FEINSTEIN: Oh yes.

GIDDINS: But of course, the rest of the album is not as good [as "West
End Blues"]. It's a real falling off, so I thought, "Well, he *is* mortal,"
which came as a great relief to me. Anyway, that was it. And I became
obsessed. I was reading everything. I used to read the *Evergreen Review,* because I was a [Samuel] Beckett fanatic, and that's where I discovered Martin Williams. I read his essays, and anything he wrote
about I would buy the record and listen to it with his essay in front
of me. In *Down Beat,* I loved Dan Morgenstern's writing. He had a
tremendous impact on my writing. I knew his prose after two sentences, like a blindfold test: Before I turned the page, I knew it would
say "D. M."

Even though I was a complete ignoramus—knew nothing about
the subject—there were a few writers that I instinctively trusted right
from the get-go. If they told me to buy the record, I bought the record,
whereas there were others who raved just as loudly, and perhaps eloquently, and I never took them seriously. Hard to explain those kinds
of things. But I became more and more impassioned about the music,
and I felt I could write about it, but I didn't think it was something
I was going to do to earn a living. I also felt that I really had some-

thing to say because I was arrogant enough to think that all these critics who were putting down George Coleman and Paul Gonsalves just didn't know what they were talking about. So when I got out of school [in 1970], I tried to function as a literary critic. I got rejected from every magazine. I tried film criticism. I sent some short stories out. For a year I just collected rejection slips. And then I started doing some liner notes and Dan Morgenstern gave me a couple of assignments for *Down Beat.* A woman I interviewed—Nel King, who edited Charles Mingus's *Beneath the Underdog*—got me a job as a film critic at the *Hollywood Reporter.* I did that and jazz pieces for about a year, and then I decided I had to choose one. I don't know why but I got it into my mind that you couldn't do both without being a dilettante. And there was really no choice because I felt there were a lot of good movie critics around, and I had my opinions, but the world wouldn't necessarily be a lesser place without them, whereas, when it came to jazz, I felt that it would be! [Laughs.] I wanted to say some stuff, and I had a Messianic complex: I thought I could bring the music to my generation, because I had spent years and years at odds with my friends. *Sgt. Pepper* came out and it was a big deal, and I'd say, "Wait a minute. Listen to this Miles Davis record." You know? I couldn't get people to go with me to the [Village] Vanguard to hear Coltrane, and then, after he died [in 1967], they'd say, "Oh, Coltrane. He was really cool, right? We should have gone." All that kind of crap. So I really believed that I could write about jazz and make it appealing to people my age and get rid of the stigma, because there *was* a stigma about jazz in the late '60s and early '70s. Miles Davis made the famous statement, "Calling me a jazz musician is like calling me a nigger." It was considered *Playboy Magazine*-type jive. People didn't know the difference between Dizzy Gillespie and Herb Alpert. It was an awful period. Shortly after that, I started writing for the *Voice,* and never stopped.

FEINSTEIN: What year was that?

GIDDINS: My first piece in the *Voice* was April '73. I had met an executive at the *New York Times.* He liked me and he said, "Why don't you write a piece for me? It would have to be on spec, but I'll bring it over to Arts & Leisure." So I wrote this piece, and he said that he liked it and thought it was going to be published. Weeks went by. He kept saying, "Get back to me." Finally we spoke, and he said that John Wilson, the *Times* critic, wanted to review the same two records. I said, "You know what, I don't care about that. I just need to know *would* you have published this? Is it good enough for the *Times*?" and he said, "Yeah, absolutely. I loved it." So I said, "Could you send it back to me?" because I didn't have a copy. (I was working as a copy boy for the *Post* at the time.) I took it out of the *Times* envelope and put it in an envelope addressed to the *Voice* with a note: "I didn't write this for the *Voice*. It's in the *Times*'s style: everybody's referred to as 'Mr.,' but it's an example of my work. Can I write for you?" And a week later, I'm walking through the city desk, and Sylvianne Gold, a copy girl, says, "Congratulations! I just saw your piece in the *Voice*." [Feinstein laughs.] So I ran downstairs. I was really pissed off. It had all the "Mr."s. There wasn't one word changed. So I called up Diane Fisher, the music editor, and this time she took my call, which she had never done before. I was a little truculent, and she said, "Well, I liked it a lot and put it in." I said, "Am I getting paid?" She said, "Yes, certainly." I said, "So, can I write for you?" and she said, "Well, I think we should meet." I went up there. This was still the tail-end of the hippie period; she's wearing one of these long, granny dresses, and there are candles and incense burning, and throw pillows all over the place. [Feinstein laughs.] And I said I wanted to write a column. I *knew* what I wanted to do. I did *not* want to be one of those guys who goes out five nights a week and writes little 200-word reviews. I wanted to write essays. She said, "You don't ask for a column. You have to pay *Voice* dues."

So I wrote riffs. I wrote and wrote and wrote. Sometimes I wrote two or three a week and she'd run most of them, though I didn't see her again for a year. I'd write the pieces, put them through a mail slot every Sunday evening, and then buy the *Voice* on Wednesday to see if my stuff was used, which it almost always was. Then the *Voice* was bought, and Diane knew that her job was up (a lot of people did), and she called me and said, "You once asked me for a column and I said, 'You have to pay *Voice* dues.' Well, you have, and if I keep my job, I'll give you the column." I thought, "Oh, great . . . wonderful." [Feinstein laughs.] Two days later, I heard that she was fired. Bob Christgau was hired. All I knew about him was that he had published a rock column in *Esquire* talking about how Miles Davis's music hadn't changed in years, and how much he hated Bill Evans. But then Bob called me and said, "I want you to write a column," and we hit it off instantly—best editor I've ever worked with in my life—and we've been working together on and off for thirty years now.

FEINSTEIN: Do you find yourself constantly learning about jazz?

GIDDINS: When I worked with the American Jazz Orchestra, which I co-founded in 1985 with John Lewis and the poet Roberta Swann, I

learned more about bands than I ever would have known. I never realized the degree to which drummers work out different patterns for
different soloists in different sections. Mel Lewis used to teach me
about this. You know, I just heard them keeping time, because I don't
have any musical background, really; I never studied music seriously. I
took a class in music when I was a junior [at Grinnell] and the professor, who was first violinist with the Lenox String Quartet, a wonderful
guy named Peter Marsh, paid me off: I didn't have to write the paper
if I would teach two classes on jazz history. So I'm teaching in college because I was known as a jazz nut. But in terms of studying it in a
formal way, no; I did it all autodidactically. I had *tons* of sheet music.
Every time somebody published a volume of [transcribed] solos, I
would study the solo while listening to the record. That's where I really
learned. Sometimes when you see it visually, it affects your ears. I
mean, the first time I went over a transcription of Louis Armstrong's
"Muggles" was the first time I realized that the ping-pong of two notes
was a C and a C an octave higher. My ear wasn't sophisticated enough
to tell that.

FEINSTEIN: And there's such beauty in his simplicity. I'm thinking of the
note he holds at the end of "West End Blues."

GIDDINS: And not only that he holds it, but that it doesn't shake.

FEINSTEIN: It's like a moon.

GIDDINS: Like a moon hanging in the sky.

◦ ◦ ◦ ◦

FEINSTEIN: In your Bing Crosby biography, you delve into biography with
so much more detail than your previous books—even the monographs
on Louis Armstrong and Charlie Parker. Why did you choose Crosby
for this kind of endeavor?

GIDDINS: The Armstrong and Parker books were basically commissions.
They were conceived by a packager as picture books. I had a limit
on words. In fact, because I went up to the limit of my words, they
wouldn't give me an extra page for an index in the original editions.

FEINSTEIN: That's outrageous.

GIDDINS: Those books were conceived as long critical essays. One of my
favorite biographical essays was Sartre's "Tintoretto," which is in [*Un
Théâtre de*] *Situations.* It's so brilliant. It's about the same length as
Celebrating Bird, I imagine. Maybe a little shorter. And I used that as
my prototype. In fact, there were moments that I was so inspired by
it that I thought anyone who reads this Parker book is going to think

right away, "Oh, it's Sartre's 'Tintoretto.'" Of course, there are probably only two people on earth who have read both. [Laughs.] Sartre told the story, the biographical information, but it was primarily a critical essay. I did some research, got the story. There are a lot of things that nobody knew. Except for Stanley Crouch, nobody else had spoken to [Parker's first wife] Rebecca Parker [Davis]. I did a lot of legwork to put Parker into the context of the period. I thought I got quite a lot done in a few words.

FEINSTEIN: Very much so, and my question about length and depth is in no way a criticism of those projects.

GIDDINS: No, I understand.

FEINSTEIN: I think they're wonderful books.

GIDDINS: Thanks. The Armstrong book I did in the same way. The packager turned out to be a lying bastard. I was involved with legal wrangling for two years until I finally got some money. It was an appalling thing and the worst professional mistake I ever made, though I like the books.

FEINSTEIN: Did you have any desire to expand these biographies?

GIDDINS: I wanted to write a serious biography, and I had no doubt about whom it was going to be: It was going to be Ellington. I thought this would be my life work. I had a publisher who was interested. My agent was up for it. And then [Ellington's son] Mercer gave all the Ellington papers to the Smithsonian, and they were embargoed for two years for an inventory. So I was really crushed. Then it turns out that the guy who was doing the inventory, John Hasse, was writing an Ellington biography. We wrote an angry letter; they wrote back, "There's no way Mr. Hasse will be writing an Ellington biography." [Chuckles.] Well, of course his book came out [*Beyond Category: The Life and Genius of Duke Ellington*], and I was stuck without a subject.

After I finished the Armstrong book, Paul Bresnick, who was my editor at Doubleday, asked me if I would do a book on Crosby. I said, "No. I like his earlier stuff, the jazz records. But, no. I have no interest whatsoever." And Paul kept on me for over a year. Every once in a while he'd call and say, "Well, I think I have a writer for my Bing book," like he could persuade me with this. [Feinstein chuckles.] I'd say, "Great! Good luck with it." But it always fell through and he'd keep coming back. Finally, when the Ellington [book] fell through, my agent said, "Why don't you think about Crosby because I think I can get a good advance on that." So I went to the Strand [bookstore] and I bought everything [on Crosby], and I was stunned, I have to tell you. I just assumed that because he was *so* famous that there must have been a shelf of books. There was nada. There were two hatchet jobs. There were fan books. The last serious book, a musicological study of Crosby, was from 1946 or '47 by a professor in Chicago named Dr. [J. T. H.] Mize. He did a privately published analysis of Crosby [*Bing*], 120 pages or something. And then Barry Ulanov had done what for that period (1948, I believe) was a serious Crosby biography [*The Incredible Crosby*]. *Very* little after that.

I assumed the hatchet jobs were accurate, that he was a total son of a bitch but that he was a marvelous artist. And the reason I finally decided I wanted to do this book was because I loved the idea of somebody who privately is cold, remote, unknowable—borderline evil—but, in terms of what he creates in public, he's not only the soul of warmth, but he's an absolutely necessary figure for the country, which embraces him as it has never embraced a popular artist before or since.

That was the book I thought I was writing. That was the book I wrote a proposal on. Then I started researching. Everybody I talked to said, "Oh, greatest leading man I ever worked with," "Smartest man in Hollywood," "Nicest," "Most generous," "Bankrolled all these bands," "Got all these people out of trouble." So one day I'm in California— I've interviewed twenty or thirty people—and I'd met Brian Johnson, a film maker doing a documentary on Crosby, and since we were sharing information, I called him up one night, completely confused: "Brian, am I talking to the wrong people? I don't have one thing that supports anything that I have assumed is true of Crosby. I mean, I get some philandering but not the lifelong alcoholism or the alleged child and wife beating. I'm finding the opposite, to some degree." And he said, "I've been thinking the same thing." Well, as you know, as a biographer you have to go with what you have. So then I started to really look for the dirt. He certainly wasn't a saint. He played around, especially during the war and after. But he had two families—one family, the kids all adored him; the other family was mixed and we all know what Gary wrote [in his book *Going My Own Way*]. I interviewed Gary for many hours, and Gary was very defensive about his father and retracted a lot of things in the book. As I started getting deeper and deeper into the subject, I realized Bing is really a man of parts.

And then I started finding out things that nobody remembered: that the man financed the invention of tape! He was the first person to record on it, to create the first tape-based studio. First guy to use the microphone as an instrument—all these technological things he had done. I had no idea of how deeply involved in jazz he was; I just thought he was a pop guy who had great time. But, you know, the relationship he had with Armstrong had never been written about, never explored. The letters between them were a revelation to me. So as I'm digging deeper and deeper, I'm thinking, "Not only is this the perfect subject for me"—because it gets me to write about movies, Hollywood, jazz, vaudeville, all of my major obsessions—"but I could try and do the biography that I've always wanted to see written about a pop figure." Really delve into where he comes from. I mean, here's a guy from the wrong side of the tracks—blue collar, Irish Catholic (Shanty Irish, as they used to say)—and he becomes one of the wealthiest and most beloved men in the world. I wanted to track, inch by inch, how you get from here to there. I knew a lot of people didn't need all of it, but that's the book I wanted to write, and Bresnick was behind me: "The narrative is great. Keep on doing what you're doing." I said, "Is it okay that there are twenty pages [covering the time] before he was born?" and he said, "Yes, it's interesting stuff."

So years go by. I'm having all sorts of difficulties getting it done, partly because it is such a long work and I'd never written anything like that without the safety net of an editor looking over my shoulder. And I had to make a living, so I'm buying time to write the book, and then I've got to work full time at the *Voice,* and I'm taking freelances on—it's just a mess. Finally, I bit the bullet, took off from the *Voice* for a couple of years. I had written 500 or 600 pages; I was pretty close to what I thought would be the end of the first volume. So I said to Bresnick, "The good news is, I have a book for you. The bad news is, I want to do it in two volumes." It took all the wind out of him. He said, "I can't even give you permission on my own. I have to go to the publisher." So he went to the publisher, and just at that point, [Rupert] Murdoch's Harper Collins bought Morrow, and they wouldn't consider it. Bresnick quit (he's now a literary agent) and one of the new editors said to my agent, "Who's Bing Crosby? Isn't he just someone our parents know?"

FEINSTEIN: Oh no . . .

GIDDINS: They were glad to get their advance back. That's all they cared about. So I was in a state, but somebody had told me about Sarah Crichton at Little Brown. Sarah came over here, she read a few chapters, she loved it, she wanted the book. I said, "There's one thing I need to tell you: It's two volumes." "I'll get back to you." A few days later, she called my agent: "I want the book any way Gary wants to do it." So I finished it. The whole process was great; she kept telling me it was going to be a bestseller, that they loved it. The day the book was published, she was fired. (That's another interesting thing that people don't understand about writing today: You never know who you're working for anymore. I'm signed by Little Brown and I think, "Wow. That's the legendary publishing company—published *The Catcher in the Rye* and goes back into the nineteenth century." Then I realize, "No, it's actually Time Warner." Well, by the time the book was finished, it was actually AOL.) So AOL comes in, and they fired people, and Sarah was let go, and I was sort of orphaned: I was on a book tour, which I continued, but there were places where there were no books. When I came back, and it got tremendous press, they said, "Oh, you know, we missed the boat . . ." Great. [Feinstein chuckles.] The book was on the *New York Times*'s extended bestseller list, for seven weeks, but they [AOL] didn't do anything to push it up, and it was extremely irritating. They kept mentioning a second volume—like Peter Guralnick's books, which made money on the second volume. So I'd say, "Yes, but I need the money now so I can *write* the second volume."

FEINSTEIN: Of course.

GIDDINS: So I'm back in the situation of trying to stockpile some money from freelancing and the *Voice*. I'm now on half-time at the *Voice*, buying time to write the book.

FEINSTEIN: Why do you think no one has taken the kind of time and attention that you have with Bing Crosby to cover Coltrane and Monk and Parker and so many others?

GIDDINS: I think it's *beginning* to happen. I think that a lot of white writers, who were the most visible jazz writers for a long time, felt a little bit apprehensive about dealing with a black subject. I know I did. That was the thing that scared me about Ellington. (Parker and Armstrong were essentially warm-ups for me.) I did feel that there was a world out there that I didn't know, but the older I got, the more experienced I got, I realized people are people and they're going to tell you what they're going to tell you. But I think there was some of that apprehensiveness.

As more black writers start to write about jazz, we're beginning to get more detailed and serious work. There's a guy in Europe, [Frank Büchmann-]Møller, who I thought did a respectable job on Lester Young [*You Just Fight for Your Life*]. Stanley Crouch's Charlie Parker book, when he finishes it, will be an important book. But I don't know—I can't explain it. I mean, it amazes me that at this stage there has not been a definitive Ellington or Armstrong biography like, say, David Lewis's *W. E. B. Du Bois,* which is a magnificent biography.

When people ask me if I would consider writing another biography, I find myself quoting Jeanie Strouse who, after she got her MacArthur [fellowship] (she had just finished *Morgan*), said, "Biography is like marriage: You only do it once or twice in a lifetime." It's exhausting, and it's hugely expensive. I mean, I got a big advance [for writing *Bing Crosby*] and it was gone in two years. Planes, hotels—mostly transcribing interviews. I'll *never* make back the money I put into this book. Never. But it's an obsession, like writing a novel, writing a play. A lot of people don't understand that because there are professional biographers who can turn out a book every two years. I can't. I don't have that kind of chops.

I said earlier that people often ask me if I'd do another biography. The only figure I can think of who I might want to tackle—only because I've already done so much of the legwork, and because he remains my North Star—is Armstrong. But I just don't know. This Crosby book is going to be around my neck for a couple of years. I'm considering another project because it has a decent advance, and if it's a hit there might be enough royalties to help me get through this.

Also, research never ends. At some point, you just have to end it. I should tell you this story, because this is a cautionary tale that would-be biographers and readers should give some thought to: The [Crosby] book was finished. It was in page proofs. And publishers don't like you to make a lot of changes once it gets to that point because they pay to re-do the typesetting. So I'm listening to my phone messages, and a very cheerful voice tells me, "Hello! My name is Howard Crosby. I'm Bing Crosby's nephew, and I used to play golf with Uncle Bing when I was a teenager. I heard you were writing this book and thought I might share some stories of Uncle Bing." So I called him right back and said, "It's great to hear from you, and I really want to talk with you, but I'm doing the book in two volumes, and you're talking about the '60s and '70s so I'll get back to you." We talked for a bit, and I said, "I feel I should be straight and tell you that [in the current volume] I'm dealing with a feud between Bing and your father." And he said, "Yes, well, nobody really understands that. It wasn't like a lot of people say." I told him what I'd heard, and he replied, "No, no, no—it wasn't like that, and I know it wasn't like that because I've got letters." [Giddins pauses, opens his eyes wide.] I said, "Excuse me?" "Oh yes. I've got dozens of letters between Bing and my dad." I said, "Can I *see* the letters? I don't want anything to be out of your pocket—photocopying, postage—send the cost of the Fed Ex, or whatever it is." He said, "Yes, I think I can do that." Two weeks later, I get a huge package with a note saying that he didn't have time to photocopy the letters so here were the originals.

FEINSTEIN: Oh my God . . .

GIDDINS: He was going to be doing business in New York; he'd pick them up then. (I couldn't believe he trusted these to the mail.) Well, talk about a biographer's dream! It's like being in the room with these people, because letters don't lie. That's the one thing that you learn: Letters never lie. Even if the person writes a lie in a letter, the fact that he *wrote* that lie in a letter is the truth. So here is all this arcane business stuff from Bing's accountant. I mean, I had heard rumors that he didn't have a lot of money when the war started, and here were the facts and figures showing how nearly in debt he was; how much money he had thrown away on the race track; all of these arguments going back and forth between the family, of how badly Dixie was drinking and all of that stuff. Sixty to seventy percent of this material belonged to volume 2, but some of it required rewriting volume 1.

The funny thing is, that was the most researched chapter in the book. I had interviewed everybody—but it was all secondhand. I had them all quoted and I thought I had the story. But, first of all, I was premised on one huge mistake, a wrong date—as proved by the letters. So I called up [my editor] Sarah [Crichton] and said, "Sarah, I have to completely rewrite a chapter." And Sarah was great about it: "Well, if you have to." So I rewrote the chapter.

But here's the thing: What if Howard hadn't called me? Or what if Howard had called me two months later? The book would have gone out, and this chapter would have *easily* been attacked as being a total crock of shit, which would have created a question of credibility for the entire book.

FEINSTEIN: That's right.

GIDDINS: And as I told [the book's first editor] Paul [Bresnick], "You know, when I originally signed the contract, it was to be done in three years—a 300-page book—but if I had done that, it would have been absolutely worthless, because I would have depended on all the research that was out there, which was wrong!" [Laughs.]

Someone told me a story, a really ugly story that I discounted. Then someone else told me the same story, so I thought, "Well, okay. Where did you get this story?" They both trace back to the same guy in California. I was going out there for some interviews; I made an appointment with him. I said, "A number of people have told me this story they got from you." He said, "Oh yes, it's absolutely true." I said, "How do you know? Where did you get it from?" He said, "Well, I don't remember where I heard it, but I know it's true." "How do you know it's true?" "Because I was at a party one night, and Gary Crosby was there, and I mentioned it to him and he didn't say anything. He just grimaced and nodded his head." So I said, "Great. I'm having lunch with Gary tomorrow."

I told this story to Gary, and he almost fell off his chair. He called to the maître d': "Bring me a telephone! Dial that sonuvabitch's number! I *dare* him to tell me to my face—" All of that. [Feinstein laughs.] I said, "I don't think that'll be necessary."

FEINSTEIN: What was the story?

GIDDINS: It was about Bing killing a hunting dog. Gary said, "Jeez, my dad *loved* animals. Where do they come up with this stuff?" But you know, a hateful story like that has its own life. That's why you read books about Hollywood stars that say Errol Flynn was a Nazi spy. I have a book about Cary Grant, and there's nothing in the book about what a charming, extraordinary figure he was or why people loved his work; it's all about this penny-pinching, semi-homosexual, nasty, acid-taking, wife-beating, crabby guy. That's not Cary Grant. That's only the Cary Grant in his *house.* The other Cary Grant is just as fucking important. So even if Crosby had been a total asshole, that was okay with me; I didn't have anything vested in it one way or the other. The music is what it is. And the persona was his greatest achievement, really. Artie Shaw said to me, "Bing was no more Bing than Bogart was Bogart." That's a profound statement. They created these images, and Crosby's was the one that helped get this country through the Depression and World War Two. That has to be remembered no matter *what* he was like once he closed his front door. But as it turned out, I found him admirable, unpretentious, and altogether decent, though I wouldn't have wanted to be a son in that first family.

FEINSTEIN: Most jazz biographies, it seems to me, are poorly written, and I'd like to hear you discuss possible reasons for this.

GIDDINS: Albert Murray said to me a long time ago, when I was first writing and he was mentoring me in a way, "You can tell the ambitions of a writer, what he wants to do and how good he is and serious, by the writers he reads." If you just read tabloid crap, you'll write tabloid crap. If you read Richard Ellmann on [James] Joyce, it means that's the kind of book you'd want to write; whether you have the talent or not, that's where you're looking. And I think there's a lot of truth to that. I'm always amazed to realize, for example, how many jazz critics and also film critics have never read classical criticism: Coleridge or Johnson or Arnold, let alone Eliot or Wilson or Trilling. They just don't know what has been done in the field. They're just opinion mongers.

I used to teach criticism at Columbia [University], and I'd say, "Your opinion about something, whether it's good or bad, is no more useful to me than if you flipped a quarter and said, 'Heads it's good, tails it's bad.' The whole issue is articulation." The kids would get pissed, because opinions were all they *had*. I'd say, "Look. There's nobody in this class who hasn't gone to a movie with a friend, and one of you hated the movie, the other one liked it. It was the *same* movie. It doesn't mean that one of you is an idiot and the other one got it. So what value is there in either of your opinions? It's going to be the *way* you express it to me. If you loved it, then your enthusiasm has to touch me in some way. If you hated it, you have to give me some thematic texture and background and show me why. Otherwise, it's just TV shit where they do thumbs up and thumbs down. Worthless." Doctor Johnson said, "He who professes love ought to feel its power."

FEINSTEIN: Have there been any jazz biographies that you've liked?

GIDDINS: A major jazz biography?

FEINSTEIN: Yeah—any figure.

GIDDINS [Pauses]: None that I would put on the top shelf with Michael Holroyd and David Lewis and biographers I really admire like Geoffrey Ward. I wish Geoffrey Ward would do a jazz book. He talks about that once in a while.

FEINSTEIN: Don't you find that astonishing?

GIDDINS: I find it astonishing and disappointing.

FEINSTEIN: I mean, I'm only asking for *one*—one great jazz biography on any figure.

GIDDINS: No, there isn't one.

One of the better jazz biographers, in terms of doing legwork and getting valuable information, is John Chilton. He's not a great writer, and his books have limitations. But he's done Roy Eldridge, Red Allen, Coleman Hawkins—he's done books that other people wouldn't consider doing. He gathers information and he's a trustworthy researcher. But one of the problems is that Chilton is an Englishman and lives in London. He or the publisher doesn't have the money to send him to New York and put him up in a hotel for six months, and if you're going to write about an American subject, you need to be here. (If an American writes a biography on Victor Hugo, you can goddamn bet that he went and looked at the archives in France . . .)

FEINSTEIN: I've read Chilton's books, but his prose sure doesn't sing.

GIDDINS: His prose doesn't sing. As I said, he's not a first-rate writer. I'm just grateful for his industry, that he does what he does. [Glances at the bookshelf.] R. W. B. Lewis—I'm just looking at his biography on Edith Wharton—now there's a great biographer. There's a guy whose prose sings! My God. And no: For some reason, jazz hasn't attracted that kind of writer yet.

To do a serious biography on Ellington, for example, you'd have to go about it the way David Lewis covered Du Bois. Someday, you'll be able to do a biography on Ellington in one volume, but only after someone's done the multiple volumes! To do him now would require a Michael Holroyd–type job.

FEINSTEIN: I found the most recent book on Miles Davis—*So What* by John Szwed—quite disappointing in terms of extended narratives and biographical exploration, even though I was grateful for a lot of the information. In fact, Szwed told me before the book was published that *he* was disappointed in it because he knew he could not get fully around, or into, his subject, that Miles Davis was too elusive. Do you think it's possible to write a great biography on someone like Miles Davis, or Lester Young, or Thelonious Monk?

GIDDINS: I have a lot more trust in a biographer who acknowledges that all human beings, at some level, are unknowable, as opposed to those amateur psychologist biographers who write the vast majority of biographies—virtually all the movie biographies, for example. These idiots not only tell you what their subjects did but what they *thought.* I just read a forthcoming biography on Sammy Davis, Jr., and the guy's constantly in his mind; I wrote all over the galleys, "Source? Source? Source?" [Feinstein laughs.] I kept going back, and there were no sources. It should have been published as a novel. But this is commonplace because once you're dead, you can't be libeled. With Crosby, I made a concerted effort not to explain what I'm not qualified to explain. I wanted to tell the story as honestly and as factually as possible, and trust the reader's imagination to help fill out his character.

So, yes: Miles Davis, at some level, is unknowable. Lester Young, at some level, is unknowable. You can't get into his brain, nor would you want to. But there *is* the story. There *is* the information that's available. There's so much more information. People, all of us, leave incredible paper trails that we don't know about. There are court records and census reports, and if you're in the public view at all, you can bet there are newspaper stories all the hell over the place, and archives filled with them. So it is possible, if you do the legwork—if you get on the planes and go to the places, read through all the stuff. The material is there and the material is all the biographer can offer.

You know, one of my favorite film directors of the last century was [Ernst] Lubitsch. And what I love about Lubitsch (what they used to call "the Lubitsch touch") is that, basically, the camera stops at the bedroom door. He made the sexiest damn movies, but they're all about courtship, because every courtship is different, but fucking is the same for everybody. [Feinstein laughs.] So there's no point in going into the bedroom. He gives you the whole courtship, the whole seduction, then they walk into the bedroom, close the door, and the camera stops on the doorknob and cuts. To me, that's *adult* film making. I don't need to see them with their legs wrapped around each other; I *know* what that's about! And I feel the same way about biography: You can only go so far.

To a certain degree, biography is really autobiography, anyway, because you're often thinking, "Well, why would he do that? What if it was me? How would I have handled that?" But as soon as you start thinking about yourself, you realize how unknowable *you* are.

FEINSTEIN: Or you realize your own limitations, whether or not they're self-imposed. For example, Duke Ellington's autobiography, *Music Is My Mistress,* is a remarkably polite book.

GIDDINS: *Music Is My Mistress* is a magical text, I think, because if you read it too quickly, it seems extremely superficial, and sometimes it is. But there is so much there—in between the lines, and sometimes in the lines. You have to take Ellington *very* literally. When he says something, he may say it in a frou-frou sort of way that makes you disbelieve him, but he's almost always saying what he believes. I think that's the way to read that book. When he praises one person, he doesn't *forget* to praise the other person. There's a reason why someone's in the book or why someone's not in the book. And all of that has to be taken into account.

It's a crime that so many people have died and they haven't been interviewed. When I think of all the questions I would ask Armstrong that nobody ever asked him . . . It's unbelievable how superficial 90 percent of his interviews are because they were done by white guys who were either in awe of him or had no clue. He went on [the] *Dick Cavett* [*Show*] one night. (Cavett, I think, is a narcissist. Everyone else is his straightman.) But he has Louis Armstrong there, towards the end of his life, one of the few people in the history of Western civilization who can be described as the fount of his art, the man who invented an art and then took it to its highest place in the early years—a Shakespearean figure. Armstrong always gave candid answers. So Cavett asks a question, and Armstrong is about to give a serious answer, but television people cannot allow silence, so he breaks in with, "Well, you've been married a lot, right? Four times!" "Oh yeah." The audience starts laughing, and Armstrong realizes, "Okay, they want comic relief, we'll give them comic relief."

Ralph Gleason says, "Is it true about what happened with 'Heebie Jeebies'?" Armstrong says, "Oh, the paper falling." He doesn't say, "Yes." He laughs because it's a joke, and if everybody wants that old story he's not going to deny them. But you don't have people ask, "Pops, what *really* happened?" He would have told. I have no doubt in my mind, because when you look at the serious interviews he did (mostly on European television), he's completely forthcoming and brilliant.

People didn't ask him the questions that should have been asked. Basic things: Where'd you first hear the blues? Why the blues instead of these chord changes? What did you get from [King] Oliver besides phrases? How do you develop a sound—is it something deliberate, or simply a reflection of who you are? Did you hear other sounds and say, "That's the sound I want"? Basic stuff that we need to know.

FEINSTEIN: What about jazz autobiographies?

GIDDINS: Now there *is* an area where I think there are some great achievements, and I think it doesn't exist in any other field but jazz: the almost-always justifiably despised "As Told To" genre. Most "As Told To"s are done with Hollywood stars or politicians, and they're crap. But in jazz, you have Don Asher's Hampton Hawes book [*Raise Up Off Me*], which is poetic. I think it's a spectacular book. Every chapter is beautifully done. You totally believe it. It's never overwritten. You believe it's Hampton Hawes's voice, even though you know that no one talks quite that eloquently at that length. Asher is a novelist, and he brought to bear all his talents on this subject, which certainly wasn't going to make him a rich man, but he did a superb job. I think that the book the Peppers did—Laurie and Art Pepper [*Straight Life*]—is one of the greatest prison memoirs ever published. There are also some bad ones. The Dizzy Gillespie one [*To Be or Not to Bop*, with Al Fraser] doesn't work because it isn't edited. Everything was just thrown into it and glued together. But it's an interesting genre.

Other jazz autobiographies? You tell me.

FEINSTEIN: How about Charles Mingus's autobiography [*Beneath the Underdog*]?

GIDDINS: Mingus's book is very interesting. Before that book came out, for about ten or twelve years, he published what he said were excerpts, in liner notes and so on, but not one of those excerpts is in the book. I mentioned earlier that I got a job reviewing films for the *Hollywood Reporter*. How I got that job is that when I first met Dan Morgenstern, the Mingus book had just come out, and after the title page, there's a page that says, "Edited by Nel King." [The next page includes this dedication: "I would like to express my deep thanks to Nel King, who worked long and hard editing this book, and who is probably the only white person who could have done it."] And I thought, "What does that mean? Who is Nel King? Everybody who saw the manuscript said it was 1,000 pages; this is a fifth of that. The excerpts aren't here; why not, and what exactly did this editor, who got a full-page credit, do?" So I said [to Morgenstern], "I'd like to interview her," and he said, "Great." I found her. She was living in an apartment in New York City. She was just about to move to L.A.; the place was barren except for a little record player (she was playing Brubeck and Mingus records), and a sofa and a couple of chairs. A very nice lady, but every time I asked her a very pointed question, she'd ask me to turn the tape recorder off. Finally, I said, "Nel, you're giving me nothing that I can go with here, so to hell with the story, just tell me what happened." Then she called me two days later after she got to California and said a friend of hers had become executive editor of the *Hollywood Reporter* and wanted her to be the film reviewer and she wasn't interested, but was I?

FEINSTEIN: So what *was* the story behind the manuscript?

GIDDINS: I can't even remember what she told me about it. But I like that book. It's a silly book at times—all that sex stuff—but there were some passages in it . . . The scene in which he flicks somebody in the Ellington band's ass with a knife, and some of the stuff about Fats Navarro, and some anecdotal passages in there are just wonderful.

FEINSTEIN: You say that there has not been a great Ellington biography, but there have been several very lengthy studies on him. It's almost an industry. And I do like *The [Duke] Ellington Reader.*

GIDDINS: *The Ellington Reader* is a great book. Mark Tucker did a magnificent job, and that's the best jazz companion that's ever been done; all the imitations don't come up to it. He really did legwork, and that book is a revelation because I don't think anybody knew Ellington had published *that* much *that* early. So, yes—that book is a real contribution.

FEINSTEIN: What about Thelonious Monk? There are a number of people who played with him who are still alive. You have his son—

GIDDINS: Well, Peter Keepnews has worked for years on a biography. I think he fell into the trap that we all do of being overwhelmed by your research, and he walked away from it for a few years, which he needed to do, and now he's feeling restored to the subject. I believe he's writing it again and will eventually finish it. He recently wrote some liner notes for Monk reissues, and they're terrific. So I think Peter will do a very good book.

There was a very interesting book by a French pianist, Laurent . . .

FEINSTEIN: de Wilde [*Monk*].

GIDDINS: Yes. I like that book a lot; it's not a biography, but it's written with great feeling. Unfortunately, most of the stuff that's done about these performers is hack work. The writer goes into one library morgue and then just cuts and pastes.

FEINSTEIN: Who would you say are the great jazz writers?

GIDDINS: Okay: I have to begin with Dan Morgenstern. Everybody always knows what other writers should be doing, you know? [Grins.] But I know in my heart that if there was anyone alive who could have written *the* Armstrong book, it's Morgenstern. He has a feeling for the music and a knowledge of it that's incomparable. Sometimes Dan's writing is, I don't know, a bit glib. But when he's cooking, he achieves things I've always striven for and don't know if I'll ever get—for one, a contagious warmth, where you totally believe him because he's so inside the music and so sympathetic with the goal of the artist. Dan will do a track by track rundown in a liner note and say this is so-and-so's best sixteen bars, and he's always on the money.

He's *finally* going to come out with a book next year [*Living with*

Jazz], an anthology of his writings from some forty-five years, and, I think, especially for young writers who don't recall when Dan was a ubiquitous force as critic and editor, it will restore his stature. I've often said that the ideal jazz writer would be a combination of Dan, for his warmth, humanity, and knowledge, and Martin Williams, for his technical insights, focus on ideas, and his ability to structure formal essays that sum up in few words a body of work. One thing I learned from Martin is you don't have to write about every track or solo. You can pick a few that represent what the artist does, and the reader can extrapolate from the rest. Those are two writers who've held my attention a long time. But I've learned from many—Al Murray, Ira Gitler, [Whitney] Balliett, [Ralph] Ellison, [Gunther] Schuller of course, Baraka, Max Harrison.

My contemporaries? I'm really treading on dangerous ground here. [Both laugh.] Bob Blumenthal is a wonderful writer, very underrated, chiefly by himself. I do not understand why Bob hasn't done a book. I *really* look forward to his liner notes. He does his homework—he's been doing Blue Note reissues, clearly his favorite jazz, and he never imposes himself on the material. Stanley Crouch is on another level, a very exciting critic in the '70s who for a long time has been on the other side of the footlights, which is where Blumenthal now is. Stanley's financial and personal involvement with Wynton, as his official spokesman, and with Lincoln Center, has been a major loss for jazz criticism. He also became more conservative in his tastes, which is no reason to discount his work. On the contrary, his independence makes him more valuable. He's extraordinarily intelligent and absolutely fearless. When Julius Hemphill died, I wrote an appreciation and pulled out the old LPs, which Stanley annotated, and I told him, "Man, this stuff is great. You were so inside this music." He was pleased, but then he said, "But you know I can't listen to that anymore." He's still a remarkable critic, and it's a shame he isn't doing more of it, but he's enjoying a successful career as a newspaper pundit and establishing himself as a novelist—he has just finished his second novel. His Charlie Parker biography will be very, very important. When we were first starting out, I greatly admired J. R. Taylor's writing, and still do when I come across his old pieces, but he dropped out—another loss.

I don't read much jazz crit anymore, but there are writers of my generation and younger whom I enjoy when I see their stuff—Steve Futterman, Will Friedwald, whose writing on singers ploughs a lot of new ground, Gene Santoro, Gene Seymour, Kelvyn Williams, Ben

Ratliff, Don Heckman, whose '60s essays were very influential, Bill Milkowski, Eugene Holley, John Litweiler. Francis Davis is writing a Coltrane biography I'll read. Academics like Scott DeVeaux, David Brackett, and Lewis Porter, among others, do fascinating work. So as a discipline, it's still a wide-open, exciting field. Alfred Appel's *Jazz Modernism* is a book anyone who cares about jazz and modern culture needs to read.

FEINSTEIN: I'll certainly read Davis's Coltrane biography, too. Do you think, though, there's some kind of public way to point out the desperate need for serious biographers on serious jazz musicians? Again, think how you paused when I asked for a great jazz biography on *anybody*.

GIDDINS: And not just biography. You know—[Giddins points to the bookshelf across the room]—this wall is almost entirely literary criticism. That wall is mostly biography. The wall this size in the other room is all jazz. People look at that and say, "Well, what's left to be done?" but there is *so* much work that hasn't been done. Biography is certainly one major field.

I have to assume, now that so many people are coming out of the academy having studied jazz, that there will be more cross-currents between the English departments and history departments, and that writers will come out wanting to do it. But you know, it took this long for someone to do Du Bois right. Look how long it took for the definitive [George Bernard] Shaw—he'd been dead for, what, forty years?

FEINSTEIN: Among the jazz musicians you've known, which ones seemed most interested in literature?

GIDDINS: Well, Gerry [Mulligan], certainly.

FEINSTEIN: What kind of books did Mulligan enjoy?

GIDDINS: He liked nonfiction a lot. I specifically remember he had just read this book about the conspiracy on the death of the Pope [David Yallop's *In God's Name: An Investigation into the Murder of Pope John Paul I*]. He was completely wired on this. We talked about it for nearly two hours. (Afterwards, I immediately went to a bookstore to buy the book.) He loved Barbara Tuchman's stuff. He read a lot of books about World War One. I think mostly history; I don't remember talking to him a lot about fiction. From childhood, he loved trains and knew everything about trains and he had a lot of books about that. He read magazines, and he really *read* them; they weren't just for the coffeetable.

FEINSTEIN: And then he'd come up to you and say, "Did you see this article in—?"

GIDDINS: Absolutely, and I was the listener, because, you know, I wasn't trying to teach him something; I wanted to learn from him.

FEINSTEIN: Did he ever discuss [Jerome] Klinkowitz's biography [*Listen: Gerry Mulligan*]?

GIDDINS: Not that I can recall.

I'll tell you one thing I do remember: I came up there one day, the afternoon he had received a Mosaic box, *The Complete Quartets,* or something [*The Complete Pacific Jazz and Capitol Recordings of the Original Gerry Mulligan Quartet and Tentette with Chet Baker*]—one of the early Mosaic box sets. (I'm currently reviewing the new Mosaic box of the Mulligan concert jazz band, which is desert island stuff. They could not have done a better job. They did it right: each album with its own original sequence. I was kvelling like a son of a bitch for hours listening to this music.) But for the first one, they didn't do it that way: It was, like, eight takes, and every false start. He was *furious,* but he also kept his humor: "Do you know how *hard* it is to sequence an album? Do you know how many hours we spend? These records are supposed to be *fun.* They're not doctoral theses." He just hated having six tracks [of the same tune]. He said, "What was that about? How would you like it if somebody went through your garbage and published your false starts?" He changed my whole perspective on it.

FEINSTEIN: Were there other musicians with whom you discussed books?

GIDDINS: Cecil Taylor. He was the first person I knew who read Peter Gay and Breyten Breytenbach.

But Gerry was just really curious. He was interested in everything. We were listening one day to an album he picked up of radio remotes of the Claude Thornhill band, and it had really cornball singers [The Snowflakes]. I think we were listening to "On Moonlight Bay," and he said, "Oh, man. I remember how hard it was to play that stuff," and I said, "What?!" because I'm listening to these terrible singers. He said, "Oh, Gil [Evans, who arranged many of the charts] would write these notes that you had to hold until you were blue in the face, and then somebody else would have to come in so you couldn't tell. It's like one big cloud bank." So suddenly I'm listening to the record past the singers to what's going on in the ensemble. And fucking Gil Evans, man! [Both laugh.] He just had something going on in every measure, but I don't think I ever would have tuned in to it if Gerry hadn't said, "Oh, God, that was so hard to play."

You know, that's really the best part of this whole business of being a jazz critic: meeting these people, knowing these fantastic people. When I think of the hours I spent backstage with Sarah Vaughan, or dining with John Lewis or Benny Carter or Mel Lewis, or sharing a joint with Dizzy Gillespie, all of the craziness of the world subsides. I continue to shake my head in wonder that I shook the hands of Armstrong and Ellington. They are my gods—the modern Olympians.

Lee Meitzen Grue. *Photo by Kichea Burt.*

7

The House as Open Ground
Lee Meitzen Grue

My interview with Lee Grue took place during my first trip to New Orleans, and she made sure I experienced the city beyond the kitsch of Bourbon Street: the surreal series of shops displaying porcelain Mardi Gras dolls, clumps of colored beads, and baby alligator heads. She drove us along the river to see a home her son had recently built, and then to a restaurant she frequents for fresh fish and crab. When we arrived at her home, she showed me various performance areas, from the outdoor theater to the indoor studio used for readings and small art shows, before we settled in the center of her house.

We spoke for a couple of hours—what's documented here, as well as more casual conversation about mutual friends—and then Lee drove me to meet a jazz musician who she thought I'd appreciate. His wife let us in, and then we walked to a dark part of the house where he sat very much alone and almost lost in a big chair. He looked dazzlingly stoned, and I felt intrusive. We left pretty quickly. "Sometimes he's quiet," Lee said, without having to wink. She knew this part of the visit hadn't worked out terribly well, but she also knew it didn't matter. Sometimes success is secondary to effort; in the long run, what's important is the desire to bring people together.

On the ride back to my hotel, she pointed out restaurants ("That place is all right, and it's not too expensive"; "Eat at the bar, otherwise the wait's much too long") and recommended some of the hipper jazz clubs. She spoke of musicians who had been over-praised and others worthy of more attention. But what struck me most was how she spoke with equal detail and energy about venues that were now defunct: clubs and cafés she used to frequent but that hadn't survived. She described the environments and the music, even the characters who ran the establishments. All afternoon, in fact, she made it clear that the history of New Orleans was like a jazz musician: forever playing the changes.

Lee Meitzen Grue, a Louisiana poet and fiction writer who often writes about New Orleans culture and music, has published several books: *Trains and Other Intrusions: Poems; French Quarter Poems; In the Sweet Balance of the Flesh;* and *Goodbye, Silver, Silver Cloud,* a collection of New Orleans stories. She has performed at the Tennessee Williams Festival, the New Orleans Jazz & Heritage Festival, and Snug Harbor, as well as The Knitting Factory in New York and many other places across the country. Her recent jazz-related work can be heard on the CD titled *Live! On Frenchmen Street.* She is also editor of *The New Laurel Review.*

The following poems were mentioned during the conversation. The interview took place in her home in New Orleans on March 31, 2001.

Babe Stoval on a Bare Stage
at the Quorum Club: 1963
Lee Meitzen Grue

in a blue bebop hat
C.C. Rider . . .
Oh, see what you done done
You made me love you now your man done come.

Face, irregular and reseamed
like a pair of old jeans,
eyes yellow to the core,
repeats of sneaky pete . . . thunderbird and muscatel.

On the Square, Babe the street musician
says,
pass the bottle
to a shaky guitar man,
drinks out of a brown paper bag
in the city of the go cup.
Babe keens where he comes from, Mississippi,
his band, two guitars and a washtub
at a no pay party
for friendship . . . drinks,
sings about Brown so she's a color and a woman,
picks steel guitar dirt farm
for a bunch of dropouts
who sop up brotherhood like it's gravy
with No War like it's cornbread,

twenty year olds on the floor, parents
of a new born . . .
spoons, beer cans and don't
wake the baby in the next room, plays
as if they—we—can learn where he's been,
see what he's seen,
his raspy voice
strains cords in his neck like
hemp at a lynching, but that wasn't
what his music was,
it was a spread table,
all we had to do was eat.

Tuesday Night on Frenchmen Street
Lee Meitzen Grue

between
cool tiles
and the simmering ceiling
the band sets up,

street side I sit at a green table
eating fried chicken livers and pepper jelly
out of a styrofoam box. Curious

some late part of my brain
is trying to put face to name, voice
to face—Ready Teddy
of Ready Teddy's Blues Show on WWOZ
somewhere on Frenchmen Street tonight.

The band plays
some offbeat slow drag. Goes

on and on. A friend pumps me once
and forever around the floor
like a winded foot organ
in a church with siding.

Across the street—outside
Café Istanbul, I see somebody—maybe
Ready Teddy. Looks
hungry, hung over,
on a lookout for customers.

I'm one of three. Dolores
takes my three bucks, doesn't
stamp my hand. Says,
I'll remember you.
Beyond restless I wander the street.

At Check Point Charlie's
nobody knows
the name of the band,
at Brasil it's the dark search for Kurtz,

at Café Istanbul I'm now one of six.
Teddy's on stage talking blues, turns flips,
stands on his head.
Sings
Meet Me with Your Black Drawers On.

Teddy, Teddy, Teddy,
there's no body
I want,
no wild sex before he leaves:
He left,
gone to shoot somebody's dirty little war
for *Life.*

Teach me, he said.
We can play it like a movie we both like.
Oh, I said, *You be Harold. I'll be Maud.*
He's so conversant with death
he thinks I'm on his plane

going down.

I have a request, Teddy
sing,
I'm Through with Love.

You don't know it!
What do you mean
you don't know it? Fake it.
I do.

In the Garden

> *in memory of the poet Tom Dent*

Lee Meitzen Grue

New Orleans
has too much water
most of the time.
It snakes around us, boils
and thrashes the willows,
breaches the levee,

pours in April, muddies dancers, seeks
cracks in slates, broken shingles, runs
down walls,
through gutters overflowing
seeks its level, in May
drowns us in underpasses.

It rains and rains and rains.
It's pouring.
              But shh—shh.
It's quit.

In June we thirst,
hot pink crepe myrtles bloom,

marigolds burn up,
the garden needs watering.

How precious. How rare
Tom's words now
burning tears down
our dry faces.

Just a few words on a dry street.
Oh, gentle, gentle rain, his
slow cadences collect in slow drains.
Force us to think.

The source is not the mouth,
the source is the source,
part of the big river.

Lundi Gras

Little People's Place: 1992
Lee Meitzen Grue

It's any Monday night.
Red beans and rice on the stove.
About nine o-clock the uptown boys
come with their black instrument cases
filling up the floor.
A young man in a sweat suit slides
to the juke box   sings along.

Davis sets up his keyboard. Somebody
checks out Kermit's photograph on the wall.
Davis plays over the juke box—loud.
The bassist picks up.

These boys
are ready. Some woman makes a selection.
Elliot fronts
some quarters. Half-a-song. *Unplug it.*
What'd you say?
Unplug it.

Kermit's got his horn.
Mouth screwed up sings
some sour tart.

Things warm up when
Marva's Mama starts to second line.
She does a bump with a man
about twenty-five.
Does a hump with a man about thirty-five.
Sashays to the bar for her beer, says,
My daughter don't like me to do that,
but I got life.

Kermit sings *Big Fat Woman*
and everybody sings *Little Liza Jane.*
Kermit blows cutting the rest of the band.
His Mama says, *That's my son.*
The keyboard thumps. Davis
shakes his scrappy chin whiskers
like punting on the Thames.

The blues *ragazzi* from Bologna sweat
black leather jackets,
New York Judy sips berry wine coolers
jumps to what
she didn't know before.
The rest share quart Bud.
Nobody cares for nothing
but red beans and brass.

Walter Payton slips in after his gig,
pulls bass until a couple of buddy cops
come in like earache at 1 a.m.
and shut us down.

It's the first careful Lundi Gras
of anybody's lifetime.
We all shuffle over
to Copastetic Bookstore

where somebody has just read a poem
with *nigger* in it.
Folks are walking around stiff-legged,
although the poet says, *I got a right to say it.*
                    I got stabbed in the eye.

Ahmos the owner says, *That word don't bother me.*
                    You got a right to tell it.

> Nobody's happy with what's happening
> on the street or the man trying to be governor
> who wore a sheet, and what's this jive about
> the music being too loud?
>
> So everybody moves over to Sidney's on St. Bernard Avenue
> where the Rebirth Brass Band sets up and starts over
> because nothing's going
> to kill this jazz.

SASCHA FEINSTEIN: You recently released a CD [with flute player Eluard Burt] of poetry and jazz: *Live! On Frenchmen Street.* At what point in your career did your interest in the two arts fuse?

LEE MEITZEN GRUE: I've always loved music, and one of the things about being born in Louisiana is that you get taken along to places where music is played from your very beginning. They don't leave babies at home. My grandchild was out with us last night at a club. It was fine; nobody complained. He had a very good time, and everybody was very nice to him. And that's always been the way I remember it. So I heard music—a lot of jazz—from the time I was very young. (I spent summers in Texas as a child, lived there a while, and that was very, very different.) When I first came here to New Orleans—I was about fourteen; I probably had been in New Orleans before, but I was born in Plaquemine, Louisiana—and when I first heard jazz on the street, I knew that this was my home.

When I was about eighteen years old, I moved into the French Quarter, and I consider myself a witness. I think writers are witnesses. I think we're supposed to write about what we see and what we understand, or try to understand. So I would sit at the bars (I never drank very much) and talk to people all night long; if there was music, I'd be even happier. And then in the 1960s, I got involved with two coffeehouses: first the Ryder coffeehouse, and then the Quorum [Club] coffeehouse—and there I met Eluard Burt. He had been in San Francisco, where they had been doing a lot of poetry and jazz, and the Quorum was the first non-segregated club in New Orleans. There were black and white people performing onstage and creating friendships, and all of us began working together. I would read my poetry at that point, though I was very shy, and I began doing poetry with

Burt and other musicians. I started writing more, and the music was always part of it.

The first book that I wrote [*Trains and Other Intrusions*] had a very small printing and I don't even know if there's a jazz poem in it. But the second book, *French Quarter Poems* from 1979, included some of the poems I had begun earlier in the '60s. I think I'll eventually put all of those on a CD, because they really are aural poems. (You and I talked over lunch how one sometimes pads things to make poems go with the music, and these poems don't do as well on the page—unless you cut them down.) I've worked on these poems for a long time, and I've written hundreds and hundreds of them, but a lot of stuff is just not worth keeping.

There has to be the right kind of synergy for a jazz poem or performance. You have to feel the ambiance of the place. You have to get some sort of feeling of what's going on in the lives of the musicians when you hear the music—because what I write about is live performance. I'm not writing historical stuff. It might turn out to be history by the time it gets out, but what I'm really writing about is a performance that I have been to. It may be a street performance on Martin Luther King's birthday, "King"; it may be in a club, "Ellis Marsalis at Snug Harbor with Jason on Drums"; it may be where I live, "Babe Stovall"—but it's always a live performance, as it is what's going on in my life. The poems are not always just about the music; they should be on at least six different levels. They should have something to do with more than just the sound you hear.

FEINSTEIN: Otherwise you'd be writing liner notes, not poems.

GRUE: Exactly.

FEINSTEIN: At what point do you feel you can call a poem a jazz poem?

GRUE: The poem can either be influenced *by* the music, or it's something I feel works with music. But always I hope they're more, as you said, than just liner notes.

FEINSTEIN: Your initial performances took place a couple of years after the wildly popular poetry and jazz performances on the West Coast. What did you think of the recordings made by Ferlinghetti, Rexroth, and others?

GRUE: I knew very little about it. My experience was of people actually doing it. I had [Ferlinghetti's] *A Coney Island of the Mind.* I had some of [Kenneth] Patchen's things. I knew about [Charles] Bukowski. But I didn't really know the LPs. It was just ignorance on my part. The thing about New Orleans is, we think we start everything here. [Fein-

stein chuckles.] We don't realize there's a bigger world out there sometimes. You'll notice that most New Orleans musicians want to come
home to New Orleans; they don't want to go live in anyplace else. Not
too long ago, a friend of mine took some French people down to hear
Kermit [Ruffins] on the corner at Vaughn's Place. Right away, when
they heard Kermit would soon be playing in Paris, they said, "Oh,
Kermit! We'll take you here, we will take you there," and Kermit said,
"Oh, that's okay. I'd rather stay in my room and eat red beans and rice."

FEINSTEIN: [Laughs.] Which poets in New Orleans do you feel have a
real affinity for jazz?

GRUE: I think Jimmy Nolan writes well. He's now also doing song lyrics,
and he's translated Spanish poets. He did a translation of Jaime Gil
de Biedma, who was one of the Spanish poets of the '50s who wrote
a book called *Longing*, a beautiful book. There's something about the
sensibility of those poems. I bet you could read them with music.

John Sinclair reads with a band all the time. There are some of his
poems that I like a lot and other poems that I don't like as well but,
nevertheless, are very popular poems. He has one jazz poem where
the main metaphor is baseball. Now, maybe I'm just not as interested
in baseball, but a lot of people really are excited by that poem—and
that is one of my least favorites of John's poems. He has really beautiful poems that talk about different jazz and blues performers. I like
it when he talks about the blues.

FEINSTEIN: In Sinclair's baseball poem, many of the players are musicians who probably weren't on the field much. Do you object to him
changing history that way?

GRUE: No, it probably is more likely that I'm just not interested in baseball.

FEINSTEIN: I'm asking specifically because I don't like the jazz poems
that, for example, manipulate the lives of these great artists just to
make the poems more immediately (or obviously) explosive. I mean,
if you're going to create a fictitious character, fine. But if you're going
to incorporate someone's life into your work, it seems to me that the
writer has a responsibility to be true to that person's character. I know
a lot of people don't agree with me.

GRUE: There's a wonderful poem by Brenda [Marie] Osbey [called "The
Evening News: A Letter to Nina Simone"] about hearing Simone at the
Jazz Fest. (Simone, of course, is known for going off on tirades.) And
Brenda talks about hearing Nina when she [Osbey] was just a young
girl, being so impressed with Nina Simone, and the sensibility of Nina

Simone. And then Brenda tries to get into the mind of the singer to know what has made her life so astonishing. It's a wonderful poem—one of my favorites by Brenda Marie Osbey, who is a very different writer. That's a jazz poem that I think really works. I've never heard it read to music.

FEINSTEIN: Those are rare and wonderful moments when a writer can suggest the spirit of an astonishing musician.

GRUE: Absolutely. Do you know Eudora Welty's story "Powerhouse"?

FEINSTEIN: Of course!

GRUE: Isn't that a great story?

FEINSTEIN: I guess that's one of the two or three most famous jazz-related short stories.

GRUE: She was an amazing writer; her short stories are unbelievable. But you see now, people are always asking me, "Are you a poet or are you a fiction writer?" I resist that, and that resistance was something I felt I got from African American poets: I knew all these African American poets who wrote journalism, fiction—all sorts of things, and I saw no reason why I should call myself a fiction writer rather than a poet just because I started writing fiction. So when people ask me about my short stories, I say, "They're just long poems." They don't have the same kinds of line breaks (I wish they did!), but they certainly are musical.

FEINSTEIN: It's really more an issue in literature, I think. People aren't quite as compartmentalizing, say, when they look at the sizes of paintings, or the length of songs.

GRUE: Many of my poet friends, who publish a lot of books, feel that jazz poems are repetitive, that they're not as interesting, that I should get on a different kick, you know? And I say, "Well, I do get on a different kick, but this one happens to be one that I can continue and that I always go back to."

A good friend, the painter Jim Sohr, will sometimes get on my case: "Aren't you jealous of Anne Rice?" And I say, "Why in the world would I be jealous of Anne Rice?" And he'll say, "Well, Anne Rice makes a lot of money," and I tell him, "Jim, if I wrote from here until eternity I could not *write* like Anne Rice, so how can I be jealous?" You do what you have to do. That's it. And what I have to do is write whatever I'm writing at the moment. That happens to be the way I am. It would be nice if I could write on order, but I can't.

FEINSTEIN: I see a lot of poetry and jazz events advertised around town. What turned things around, made them so popular?

GRUE: There are many poets now who are working with jazz, but five years ago Burt and I were the only ones working on a regular basis. Some of the African American poets—Tom Dent, Quo Vadis Gex [Breaux], Kalamu ya Salaam for NOMMO, and, later, Kysha Brown— read over the years. Kalamu organized The Word Band. Lately, there are wonderful young African American poets reading their work in New Orleans at Ebony Square, Sweet Lorraine's, Flora's Gallery, The Dragon's Den, and other venues.

But I haven't yet shown you the double-parlor, which I call the Front Room. We have performances here. I think it was '95 when The Jazz and Heritage Foundation gave us a small grant to pay poets and musicians for a performance here, and we had poetry performances with jazz and began having them often. John Sinclair read with us a lot, and young poets, too. People come to our shows, and I think it is because young audiences have become interested in the Beats again. I think even *The Jazz Poetry Anthology* helped with the revival.

But when Eluard Burt and I played, we always had good audiences. We played in clubs, but we also played in people's houses and little festivals around town—like the festivals in Joe Brown Park and St. Augustine churchyard—and some colleges invited us, too: Dillard and Tulane. In the clubs, there were usually younger poets attending, particularly Dave Brinks, who was one of Andrei Codrescu's students. Every time we looked around, there was Dave Brinks, wearing his beret, hanging out and asking us questions. He's now the person who organizes many of the jazz-poetry events in town as well as The School for the Imagination; he's kind enough to include us in everything he does. Dennis Formento and Professor Arturo Pfister have a series at Zeitgeist Gallery and Sweet Lorraine's.

Dave used to ask Eluard Burt a lot of questions, because Burt knows a lot about early rhythm and blues; Burt played saxophone with Chuck Willis when he was only fourteen. Burt knows a lot about the New Orleans sound—how, for instance, young men whistling a certain way as they passed through their neighborhood identified themselves as from that neighborhood. He was also in San Francisco for a while in the late '50s, knew Bob Kaufman there, so he brought some of that scene back with him.

I just loved the music, so the possibility of putting the poetry with the music was perfect for me. Now I write all kinds of poetry, though some people say, "You write nothing but New Orleans poetry" (accusingly or admiringly). Not true, but that's what I'm most interested in.

FEINSTEIN: Let's talk a bit about Tom Dent.

GRUE: Tom Dent! Oh, yes. In fact, the last poetry reading that Tom did was with Quo Vadis Gex, Andrei Codrescu, and me at [the club] Snug Harbor. Tom organized the reading and it was supposed to be poetry and jazz, but I don't think Andrei ever reads with jazz. Tom loved Andrei's humor. We ended up just doing our own work. (Tom had accidentally given me a different order of topics than he had given the other poets, which kept me out of synch, and made us all laugh; I was reciting on food when the others were on music.) It was a fun reading. The tape is in the archives at Amistad Research Center [at Tulane University], if you're ever interested.

FEINSTEIN: One of my great disappointments is that I never got to meet Tom Dent.

GRUE: Wonderful man. When Tom died, there were about 2,000 people at his funeral. Andrew Young gave the eulogy, and there were African chieftains in full tribal dress who came to his funeral. Yet, if you had known his manner, you would not have known he was an internationally famous man.

I wrote a poem about Tom after his death ["In the Garden"] and sent it to his mother, and she sent me one of his hand bags; he used to carry beautiful leather bags.

FEINSTEIN: I'd love to see that poem. I admire him as a poet, and also as someone who truly promoted jazz.

GRUE: *Fantastic* . . . There's a video we made with another poet. He has a hard African name. Willie—

FEINSTEIN: Keorapetse ["Willie"] Kgositsile?

GRUE: Yes, that's right. He was the guest of honor. Tom read with jazz. I read Maxine Cassin, a few others. Tom was just an incredible person, and we knew each other for about thirty-five years. He was a lovely man. Funny—yes, very funny—dry. In fact, at that last reading, he did an audience participation poem about New Orleans that had the audience reply to him by name (I don't think it's ever been published).

I used to try to get black poets involved in the Poetry Forum. I called Tom several times. He'd say, "Oh, some of the poets are so militant, we're not going to be able to do that." But there was a poet who came called Ahmos Zu-Bolton. He had poetry Speak Easies at his Copastetic Bookstore.

FEINSTEIN: Yes, I know some of his work.

GRUE: Very, very fine poet. Ahmos said something about Tom, and I said, "I know Tom, but I've been turning my cheek to Tom for years." Ahmos told Tom that, and from then on, Tom and I were very close friends. He appreciated that expression.

FEINSTEIN: You mentioned militant black writers, some of whom dominated the sound of jazz poetry in the '60s. What was your take on their poetry at the time?

GRUE: I think people have the right to be angry when their lives are cramped by prejudice. The idea of political poetry doesn't bother me. When governments don't want the people to think too much, they lock the poets up first.

Whenever I'm teaching a workshop I say, "We don't know who the great poets are. Only time will tell. We should not be too judgmental because the very person that you're criticizing right now might be the poet whose work lives, and yours may be in the dust bin, and mine may be in the dust bin." We *don't* know who the great poets are. All you have to do is look at a list of Laureates of England and you can see that for sure. Time takes care of all that.

FEINSTEIN: Did you ever feel any friction from the African American community—you know, "What is this white woman doing with jazz?"

GRUE: No. The only friction I've felt has been from white academics, and white people in general: "Why are you doing what you're doing?" But never from the African American community. I think the African American community knows where I'm coming from. At least they do in New Orleans.

I'll have people get mad at me for some other small thing, like teasing somebody, because I'm inclined to tease at times if I think anybody's getting a little pompous. Whatever color we are, we all get a little pompous at times. [Feinstein laughs.] So I'll say something that punctures that. My words are not always appreciated.

All poetry is political. If you have written a poem that you feel strongly about, and you've done it as honestly as you possibly can, it can change things. I've written with that idea in mind—though that's an idea that's in the back of my head, not the front of my head when I'm writing poems, because I'm translating: I'm writing from the language I have in my head, which has nothing to do with what finally gets down on paper. We *want* to get that poem down, but it's always a translation. That's the best you can get—a translation.

FEINSTEIN: How long have you been editing *New Laurel Review*?

GRUE: Since 1982. The founding editor was Alice Moser Claudel. She died suddenly in '82. Her husband, Calvin Claudel, and her son asked me if I would get the issue out that she was working on at that time.

Because I edit a journal, I don't get to read as many books as I like; I'm always reading manuscripts. One of the other things I've done is read tarot cards at Marie Laveau's House of Voodoo in the Quarter. (For a while, I was the Visiting Writer at Tulane University and a tarot reader.) The voodoo shop is the old house where Marie Laveau lived. I sometimes read there a couple of days a week. I think of it as my office. I used to read cards a few hours a day; the rest of the time, I would read great books and write. It was perfect. Right now, I'm trying to avoid going back to work, but my house is usually so busy, it's easier to work outside of it. There's a new little coffeehouse in the neighborhood called Café Picasso that looks perfect. It's nice. I often go to write at PJ's on Frenchmen Street, which is owned by Ken Ferdinand, Kalamu's brother.

I used to write at Café Brasil at night. I have a long poem called "Street Life Meditation," which is about the life on Frenchmen Street. I read that poem with jazz.

FEINSTEIN: Did you have jazz in mind when you wrote that?

GRUE: There was a jazz background. I could hear it because I was sitting out on the street. They used to have tables outside before the police made them push everything inside. The owner, Ade, is open to anyone who's trying anything new. So you have jazz students from UNO [University of New Orleans] who come to play early before the regular band. The music may change two or three times during the evening. A lot of times, well-known musicians come and jam there, so I'd just sit on the street and write. In New Orleans, it's strange to write *without* music. There's so much music; you can't go anywhere without hearing music.

FEINSTEIN: Most writers insist on absolute silence when they're writing.

GRUE: I can write to jazz when it's instrumental and I don't recognize the lyrics. The minute I hear words in my head, it doesn't work. I have a poem on that CD called "Terminal," and we did it in performance a lot. I loved what Burt was doing with it; it was just the flute. The first time we performed it, he played "Lover Come Back to Me," and I said, "That sounds really good, but it bothers me when I hear words." If you listen to that [cut on the] CD, it is still [based on the chord changes to] "Lover Come Back to Me," but you don't *hear* the words to "Lover Come Back to Me." You hear the poem and a jazz improvisation.

I can listen to live music and it doesn't bother what's going on in my head at all, but let me sit down here and put on a CD . . . Do you know who Danny Barker was?

FEINSTEIN: Sure—the great banjo player.

GRUE: We had a grant from the National Endowment for the Arts to pay poets to read in The First Backyard Poetry Theater, so I hired Danny (everyone called Danny "Danny") and the clarinetist Dr. Michael White to play at intermission. So the poets came to listen. Yusef [Komunyakaa] was here in the audience. I don't remember who the poet was who was reading, but came intermission, all of the poets rushed outside to talk to the reader! Yusef and I and maybe a couple of other people sat, but everybody else rushed out. Well, Danny, who must have been in his eighties at that point, and Michael, being the kind of musicians that they were, must have thought, "Well, we're going where the audience is!" So they ran out, sat their chairs down, and played on the patio.

A lot of poets don't even listen to music. Poetry is one kind of music to them, and I've had many, many parties with poets, and sometimes they'll turn the music off.

FEINSTEIN: *Really?*

GRUE: I've had that happen many times.

FEINSTEIN: I don't think anyone would *dare* do that in my house . . .

GRUE: [Laughs.] As I told you: My house is open ground. People do all kinds of things here.

FEINSTEIN: Let's talk about the theater in the back. You've hosted such a variety of creative productions—poetry readings, concerts, plays. When and how did that start?

GRUE: It ended in 1990 and had gone on for ten years. I had been directing The New Orleans Poetry Forum, though I didn't know how to direct a group of poets. I just fell into it, as I fall into a lot of things.

FEINSTEIN: [Smiles.] You keep making statements like that—but you know *exactly* how to direct people.

GRUE: When I say I don't know how to direct things, I mean I was not schooled in it. So I did not have the workshop jargon (and when I say "jargon," you know that I'm not thinking it's a wonderful tool, sometimes), and I did not consider myself an authority. I would always put my own work in, because I considered myself a *poet*, and I wanted to be part of the mix, which relaxes people. The whole idea of a poet is a person who is an authority on themselves. I think that's what we are, because that's what we're writing about. I was trying to develop the individual voice. That's what I was and am interested in.

I had started doing poetry all over town. Once, they were going to take the ferries off the river and replace them with new ferries, and we weren't so happy about that. "Oh, that's a terrible idea!" So I decided that we'd have poetry readings on the ferries, going back and forth ("We were very tired, we were very merry . . ."), for the last running of the old ferries. We were going to spend the whole night reading.

Well, the dock board, or the levee board, or whoever, got wind that all these crazy poets were going to ride back and forth and probably drown themselves off the back end of the boat.

FEINSTEIN: [Laughs.] Homage to Hart Crane.

GRUE: Right! So they set about stopping us, and instead of the ferries running to such and such an hour, they quit early. "What are we going to do? What are we going to do?" So I said, "Well, we'll have it in Spanish Plaza. It will be for the demise of the ferries, and we'll all write about that and talk about that." So we went to Spanish Plaza, which is by the river.

By this time, we had hundreds of people because this was interesting and exciting. And then they turned the lights out. They really didn't want us to perform there. So I said, "Well, we'll get flashlights," and we read by flashlight. Then, of course, it was a *big* thing; what they did was take something that probably no one would have noticed and turned it into something that newspapers picked up and people read about it the next day—all these poets reading by flashlight. [Both laugh.]

FEINSTEIN: That's great!

GRUE: So that type of stuff happens.

We were reading all over town. One of the funniest readings was with a woman who had written the scene in the TV show "Dallas" where J.R. gets shot; she was one of our poets in the '70s. I had set up a series of poetry readings in a mall. There were people selling cars with the microphone we used (it was a terrible mike), and there was a walkway for fashion shows, and that's where we had the poetry reading. She had written a poem that used words that you didn't hear anywhere in public at that time—a poem about female genitals and the fact that we have a lot of moisture and mildew there. It was a very funny poem; she used some very basic words referring to female genitals—and this is in a shopping center.

Now, I've never censored anybody on anything. If you want to read what you want to read, you read it. Got nerve enough to read it, read it. So she reads this poem to all these women who are sitting around with shopping bags. I heard two words and I went, "Wow!" and then I hear *rustle, rustle, rustle.* [Feinstein laughs.] All these shopping bags rustling. And then they must have said to themselves, "I didn't really *hear* that." Everything quieted down, and there was never a word about it. Isn't that interesting? They just couldn't believe they heard what they heard, because at that time you didn't hear what you hear on television now.

We had a series of readings—once or twice a month—at a place called the People's Playhouse, founded by Lyla Hay Owen. My husband would help. He said he never worked so hard in his life as he did for poetry. So many people were using the space, you had to clean the place before you could have a reading. That's the reason we ended up with The First Backyard Poetry Theater. He said, "We need a place to have the poetry readings. It will be a theater for a while, but we'll put in the plumbing and, one of these days, when we need it to be an apartment, it will be an apartment." That was how we did it. It was his idea to build the theater. I named it. I thought The First Backyard Theater would be memorable.

FEINSTEIN: And did you have poetry and jazz events from the start, or just poetry readings?

GRUE: We had music, but not poetry and jazz together. There was a poet who was part of the Poetry Forum—I guess late '70s, early '80s—by the name of Ron Cuccia, who did a series of poetry and music performances, and a record with the Neville Brothers. Cyril Neville is a good poet (he plays drums with our readings sometimes), and so is Ron; the Nevilles wanted to work with a poet. The record [*Brother's Keeper*] is well worth hearing. (Sometimes Ron worked with other poets and got most of the credit, but he worked best with the Nevilles.) He used to say to me, "When are we going to do what you used to do—what you talk about all the time: poetry and jazz?" Well, I had little kids, and when you have little kids you can't hang out as much as you used to.

FEINSTEIN: I sure know that.

GRUE: Burt and I did do some readings with attorney/poet/musician Shael Herman at Lou and Charlie's on North Rampart Street. Lou and Charlie's was a famous jazz club run by Charlie Bering in the early '70s. Charlie was the first club owner in New Orleans to pay us.

But I couldn't hang out during those years. Ron went on and made a record.

Years later, there was a party at my house for Quorum Club people. Many of us had not seen each other for years. Eluard Burt and Kichea Burt, a great photographer in her own right, had come back to town from L.A. They came to the party where she and I became great friends. Kichea Burt is the reason why we have the CD; she recorded us with a single mike.

FEINSTEIN: I remember talking to Jayne Cortez about her recording *There It Is* where, because of a rudimentary sound system, she had to scream to balance her voice with the musicians. It's so difficult to achieve that kind of balance.

GRUE: That's what happens to so many performances. At times, I don't have much voice. Many of the poets we work with now have *beautiful* voices. (I've always said that in my next life I would like to be a dancer, but now I think I would like to be a singer.) Under the right circumstances, it's fine. Universities usually have good mikes and podiums. But if you're working on a stage that you've never seen before, and then you invite people to play with you, and they've never played with a poet before, they can drown you out.

We've got all kinds of versions of our performances on videotape. Kichea Burt documents everything. Some of them are good; some of them are ghastly; some we look really good but sound terrible, or the other way around. We kept trying to get the right sound for the CD. That's why we did it live, but we did it in Kichea and Burt's living room, with Burt on flute and keyboards and Rodger Poche on bass.

It's strange how people at different colleges have been excited about our doing these jazz poems, but they never come up with money for the musician to travel with me. So I often end up reading with musicians I've never worked with before in my life. I did this in Austin, Texas, a number of times. I did it on a tour in Michigan—that's when I worked with a guy named Kesuku Mafia, a former Motown studio musician. He plays several saxophones, the flute, keyboards, and he has this little trampoline-like thing he jumped up and down on while playing. We worked together in a college coffeehouse in Michigan— just the two of us—and they gave us something like four hours to fill.

FEINSTEIN: *What?*

GRUE: That's right. Four hours to fill. I talked to him on the phone; I had never performed with him before.

FEINSTEIN: Poet and saxophonist together for four hours?

GRUE: Right. But he was a one man band. When I talked with him on the phone, I relaxed, because he said, "Oh, don't worry about it. I played with Freddie Hubbard. I played with Aretha Franklin. I played with so and so. Don't worry about it." I said, "Baby, I'm not worried about it. After talking to you, I'm not in the least worried about it." (If I can find the video, I'll play a bit for you.) He's got one of those little Islamic hats on. Handsome old guy. And he's on this trampoline with a saxophone here and a flute there and a keyboard here.

So he would do thirty minutes, and then we'd get up together. I read short stories, too. (I wasn't about to fill *hours* with poetry, even with breaks and all that. So I said, "I'll read a story," and he said, "I'll accompany you on the story." [Grue laughs.] I start reading the story, and we'd do call and response. Then he'd go off stage; I'd read; he'd come back on his little trampoline to play. [Feinstein laughs.] We had the best time—and I've got a video to prove it.

FEINSTEIN: What was your audience like?

GRUE: These were people at tables. A great audience of students and people from the community. I had done coffeehouse type things before. The woman who put this together is a poet and friend, Margo LaGattuta. She invented something called "Inventing the Invisible" for radio. I had done a coffeehouse for my children's elementary school; we had The Meters on stage for one of those shows. Great shows. Free form. So I was used to a coffeehouse audience.

I don't memorize my stuff, which Burt gets furious about. But I say, "Burt, I love to change things, and once you memorize it, it's kind of set in stone." I like what my friend Yictove says. He says, "I always read my work. Because, you know, some people can't read."

FEINSTEIN: Do you play an instrument?

GRUE: Many years ago I played the piano.

FEINSTEIN: Do you have fantasies about playing any particular instrument?

GRUE: No, as I said, I always wanted to come back as a dancer, but now, because I get laryngitis, I'd like to have a stronger voice. Sometimes I end up without a voice if I'm forced to shout. Actually, I do better if I'm in a room without a microphone, where I know I have to project.

FEINSTEIN: It's never easy to have a fully successful evening of poetry and jazz. Apart from the technical challenges, of course, you need good writing (and good readers of that writing) and fine musicianship.

GRUE: That's right. So when I have a Sunday afternoon thing in The Front

Room, we invite certain people to read. We can't afford to pay the musicians, unless we have a grant; usually it becomes a party. (I've let bands use The Front Room to practice, and I always cook something good for them to eat; if you cook for the band, they'll play.) Most of the time, there's also art shown with the performance. I want as many enthusiastic workers as possible. My idea is, if you want to hang your work and you want to read, then you have to do some other part of it. Now for the musicians, since they're usually forfeiting money, we don't ask for much.

FEINSTEIN: But this kind of community—what you have here—is a rarity. You must know that.

GRUE: I know it only because there was a retired publicist who came here from New York—Marty O'Farrell, no longer with us, a wonderful guy—and he said, "New Orleans is the only place I've ever been where they didn't tell me they were as good as New York." People here don't think about that. They think about what's happening here, what we're doing. Everybody loves to *go* to New York, but most musicians want to come back here to the well. The Marsalis brothers, Wynton and Branford, may not live here, but they're back all the time. They have a strong commitment to family and community. Delfeayo Marsalis plays here. Irvin Mayfield plays with Jason Marsalis here. There is something here that revives you artistically. I do see some similarities between New Orleans and New York, and it has to do with neighborhoods. I love the idea of a community, and I love the idea of artists supporting each other, helping each other. Maybe I need to lean today; maybe you need to lean tomorrow.

Fred Hersch. *Photo by David Bartolomi.*

8

Respiration and Inspiration
Fred Hersch

Unlike a stereotypical jazz musician, I do my best to be punctual, so when I plan for an interview, I leave early, find the location, then mark time in a coffeeshop, bookstore, or whatever looks most interesting. In this case, I had twenty minutes to spare, so I walked up the block and into a New York landmark I'd never experienced, Dean & DeLuca. Inside were the ingredients for a meal at Versailles: lobster and Alaskan crab on ice; whole foie gras and smoked sturgeon; cases of international cheeses; chocolate-covered berries and nuts; cocoa from Holland, coffee from Sumatra, tea from Xi Ping. I gained ten pounds just looking.

Although appealing on many culinary levels, the bourgeois nature of Dean & DeLuca reflects the yuppie transformation of the Village, and in that respect, it contrasts absolutely with Fred Hersch as a person and musician; in this interview and his performances, one hears honesty and passion. He composed and recorded *Leaves of Grass,* for example, because he felt instructed by and genuinely grateful for Whitman's poetry. As he writes in his articulate liner notes: "I was on tour in Paris and, wandering the city, I was mysteriously seized with the urge to read Whitman. I found an English-language bookshop, bought *Leaves of*

Grass, sat at an outdoor café, and read 'Song of Myself' in one sitting. It was a revelation."

Fred Hersch's *Leaves of Grass* represents a musical departure for him. (In the interview, I point out that it's not really a jazz session, and he agrees, calling it "Fred Music.") But the fact that it doesn't sound like his previous recordings makes it all the more in keeping with his exploratory sensibilities. And if there are similarities between the breadth of Fred's music and the appeal of Dean & DeLuca, they have to do with being cosmopolitan: encountering in one location the disparate sounds and tastes of the world. That kind of universal embrace also embodies the spirit of Whitman. After all, what did Allen Ginsberg title his famous Whitman tribute? "A Supermarket in California."

Pianist and composer Fred Hersch has recorded more than twenty albums as a solo artist or leader and co-led another twenty sessions; he has appeared as a sideman or featured soloist on eighty others. His recent recordings include *The Fred Hersch Trio + 2, Live at the Village Vanguard, Fred Hersch in Amsterdam: Live at the Bimhuis,* as well as *Leaves of Grass,* the focus of this interview. His honors and awards include a fellowship from the Guggenheim Foundation, grants from the National Endowment for the Arts, and four composition residencies at the MacDowell Colony. He has taught at the New England Conservatory, The New School, and The Manhattan School of Music.

The interview took place at Fred's apartment in SoHo on September 26, 2005.

* * * * * * * * * * * * * * * * * *

SASCHA FEINSTEIN: Did you start to play the piano when you were three or four?

FRED HERSCH: Around four. I don't really remember. I was told I went to the piano and started picking up themes from TV shows.

FEINSTEIN: And then you were classically trained, correct?

HERSCH: Yes. They started me at age five with class lessons—this was '59/'60, thereabouts—and that was considered standard, but it just didn't work for me. For one thing, I always liked to improvise because it was more fun. But I was also clearly more advanced and got bored, so they sent me to a woman who was considered, locally, to be the best teacher, a woman named Jean Kirstein who had gone to Juilliard and won the Naumburg Competition in New York, and had settled in Cincinnati. Then in third grade, when I was about eight, I started taking theory and composition with a guy named Walter Mays.

I recently played a benefit concert for a local AIDS service organization in Kansas, and Walter Mays is on the composition faculty there [at Wichita State University]. This is somebody I hadn't spoken with since I was twelve, and I was able to thank him for, basically, giving me a musical tool kit: how harmony works, how to notate things, how to analyze a score. These are things kids do in their freshman and sophomore years in conservatories, and I did them in elementary school. He said, "When you came to me, I hadn't taught any private theory students, nor had I ever taught a child. When I asked my wife—who I'm still married to, forty years later—'What should I do with this kid?' she said, 'Well, give him what you give your grad students and see what happens.'" So he did, and I guess I did well enough.

Then I went through some changes in grades seven through twelve, kind of getting away from classical music and composing, but always playing music: improvising on pop tunes, playing the violin, singing in shows and in choirs. It really wasn't until I was a freshman in college when I heard real jazz, and that was the real eye opener. It changed my life.

FEINSTEIN: And at that time, how influential were the radio broadcasts by Oscar Treadwell?

HERSCH: Oh—that's great you know about that. Radio was so important in Cincinnati and Boston when I was there in the mid '70s, and it pains me so much that young musicians are not going to have that kind of exposure via the radio to the real stuff—not just whatever female singer the record labels are pushing, or some reissue. Even here in New York, jazz radio is not great. You would expect that there would be a really interesting, independent jazz station, and there is not. That's very distressing. Because radio provides an opportunity for audiences to hear a wide range of jazz music, obviously for free, and get some input from a DJ, and it may make them go to the record store or order recordings online.

In Cincinnati, we had an AM station called WNOP, which was all jazz, and a lot of it was pretty straight-ahead, but not when Oscar Treadwell was on. His program was called "The Eclectic Stop Sign," featuring jazz and poetry, and he had the most beautiful speaking voice. I mean, this guy could have made millions in voice-over. Unbelievable speaking voice . . . Anyway, this guy used to offer free Friday night classes at the conservatory in "jazz listening." There'd be a roomful of people with a record player and each week he'd talk about one artist: One week it would be Ornette Coleman, or Mingus, or Bix Beiderbecke. (He probably had 50,000 LPs.) One of the hippest things he did—and I've passed this on to my students: Whenever he'd play musical examples, he would turn off the lights. It was a great idea because it eliminated visual distraction and you had to concentrate on what was being played.

Now, some of the poetry that he read I remember as being particularly awful. [Feinstein laughs.] But maybe I wasn't ready to appreciate that. It was a great place to learn.

But I learned mostly from hanging out with older musicians and asking what they listened to. Those were the days of used record stores, so all my LPs were a buck-and-a-half, two bucks, three at the most; a retail LP was only seven or eight dollars, so it was very inexpensive to build a library. (That's another thing that kind of breaks my heart: With the cost of CDs, young musicians can't really afford to build the same kind of libraries.) But the older musicians were fantastic to me; I was a novelty then—a young guy with *any* talent wanting to play jazz. There was no jazz education . . . And these were guys playing fifty-dollar bar gigs, or eking it out playing private parties on weekends, or doing what little bit of studio work there was, or playing on local TV shows. But they were very welcoming to me, and they could tell that I had ambition. Even then I was drawn to things that were a little edgier, and that led to some battles. Most of the local pianists thought that Oscar Peterson was the be-all and end-all, and I certainly respect Oscar Peterson as a pianist, but as an artist, he's not a very interesting artist. You can listen to one Oscar Peterson album from any era and you've pretty much got it; he does what he does, and that's sort of it. Not much development, not much challenge, not much interest. It's like a good cheeseburger. I mean, Earl Hines is *way* further out, and completely takes chances, almost more than anybody. He's like the original "Let's let it all hang out and see what happens." And I gravitated towards those kinds of players.

This was also the early days of ECM records, and I would wait for each release: [Chick Corea's] *Crystal Silence* or *Light as a Feather,* or [Keith Jarrett's] *Facing You,* or [Dave Holland's] *A Conference of the Birds.* Those records really had an impact—the way they were packaged, the fact they didn't have liner notes—and it was also the heyday of [the record label] CTI, and there were some *great* CTI records:

Freddie Hubbard, Joe Farrell . . . Blue Note was a dead label then, and Verve was a dead label, and Columbia had Miles and Stan Getz and not much else. (A lot of little indie labels don't even exist anymore.) So that was where the interesting music was happening, and I would go to the used record store several times a week.

I often tell this story about the pivotal moment of my life as a musician: I had started at Grinnell College in Iowa, and chiefly it was a non-choice. I did not want to audition for Eastman or Juilliard; I hadn't really been practicing and I knew my heart wasn't in it. A friend of mine was going to Grinnell, it was easy to get in, and I figured, "Okay, a liberal arts school in the middle of the country— I'll figure it out." I got there, and there was a piano teacher named Cecil Lytle, and he asked me if I knew that Herbie Hancock had gone there. I didn't know who that was. Lytle was African American, and he gave me LeRoi Jones's (now Amiri Baraka) *Black Music*. So I read that, and I started listening to [avant-garde artists such as] Pharoah Sanders, Cecil Taylor, Coltrane, as well as [Chick Corea's group] Return to Forever and whatever people were playing in the dorms. Plus, in '73 Marvin Gaye was peaking, Stevie Wonder was peaking—it was an interesting time.

Anyway, I went back to Cincinnati on a Christmas break and went to a little jazz club I'd heard about. A quartet's playing, about a couple dozen people in the audience, maybe. I sat in front and was pretty knocked out by this really fantastic tenor player, Jimmy McGary. They were just calling tunes, it was a no-big-deal Tuesday night. On the break, I went up to him and asked if I could sit in. He looked me up and down and asked, "Do you know any tunes?" and I said, "I know 'Autumn Leaves.'" I got up and played, but I had never played with a professional rhythm section—I'd only played with a high school jazz ensemble rhythm section—and I made a lot of errors because I was trying things. So he took me to a back room where there was a portable record player, and he said, "Look, you clearly have a passion for this, and that's great, but you need to get your rhythm together, you need to get your time together." He had the '56 *Ellington at Newport* recording, where Paul Gonsalves plays twenty-seven choruses on a blues ["Diminuendo and Crescendo in Blue"], and he made me listen to that whole track. Of course, I wanted to ask questions, and he'd say, "Shut up and listen." [Feinstein laughs.] "This is all so good." And he just looked me dead in the eye afterwards and said, "Now *that's* time.

If you want to be a jazz musician, you *have* to be able to swing. So go get some records, and once you learn some more tunes, you can always come back to play."

I was very excited, but I didn't know any other jazz musicians. Where do you go? So I went to the record store and I bought every LP that had "Autumn Leaves" on it. There were twelve or thirteen: a few versions by Miles; Ahmad Jamal; Oscar Peterson; Chet Baker, I think; Sarah Vaughan with strings. I went home and I just dropped the needle on that track on all those records, and I realized, "Okay. They're all great. They're all different." I couldn't really pick one that I liked more than the others—or if I liked one more one day, I'd like another the next morning for a different reason. So I realized if you're going to play a tune, you'd better make it your own.

Then I dropped out of Grinnell and starting hanging in Cincinnati, listening to sides, hanging out with the cats, and working little gigs. As I said, there were not that many players—period, young or old—and I soon found myself being a professional and attending the [Cincinnati] Conservatory [of Music] by day (to keep my parents off my back). After about a year-and-a-half of that, I felt as though I just had to get out of there. I thought, "I need to be around a higher level." And Jaki Byard was teaching at the New England Conservatory, so I got in a car, drove to Boston, auditioned—which meant just being in a room with him and playing a couple of tunes; it was very easy—and I joined the famous class of '77: Marty Ehrlich, [clarinetist] Michael Moore—

FEINSTEIN: Jerome Harris—

HERSCH: Yeah. Just awesome. Guenther Schuller was still there. It was the peak of that place and I, just by dumb luck, ended up there. I got to play contemporary music and I learned about all sorts of things—as much or more from my peers as I did from my teachers—just listening and talking, having heated debates about Stockhausen, all those sorts of things that people get into in college. I got out, somehow, in two years and moved to New York in '77 and have been here ever since.

FEINSTEIN: And it was at the [New England] Conservatory where you had the American literature course that introduced you to Walt Whitman, right?

HERSCH: Exactly. And I also had a boyfriend then—sort of—who read me the poem "What I Heard at the Close of the Day," and that really knocked me out. Then I wanted to read more of Whitman, and I ended up in that class. And it wasn't just the "gay thing" that resonated with me; it was the purity of his intent. The language. The fact that you could tell this is a guy who really found a personal way of expressing himself. You find that in Picasso and Stravinsky and late Beethoven, and lots of other great artists who were onto something because, well, they had the guts to put it out there, even if it wasn't popular. And certainly Whitman was an odd bunch of contradictions. On the one hand, he was selfless in his service to soldiers and young people and the community; on the other, he was a relentless self-promoter and enjoyed being the Great Gray Poet and all that sort of stuff. And he wrote a lot of crap. Let's face it: Beethoven wrote a lot of crap, too. No artist hits home runs every time. But even the stuff that's kind of self-indulgent and rambling can be like a jazz solo.

Here's what I mean: I played with Joe Henderson for ten years, and he could play some *long* solos—twenty-, twenty-five-minute solos. The first ten minutes would be Joe doing what Joe does, and then all of a sudden, at the moment when you think, "Okay, he's phoning it in," all this new stuff would come up. For me, playing with Joe was graduate school. He was so resourceful in his improvising without it being overly brainy. It wasn't worked out. This guy was really thinking and trying stuff. Sometimes it got messy. (And, of course, Joe, at his "average," was better than 99 percent of saxophonists in history on their best night.) And Whitman is like that, too. You can read some of the poems that go on and on, and suddenly there will be a line or a stanza that blows you away, and it's almost as though you needed all the preceding stuff to get to that.

FEINSTEIN: Given the wealth of material by Whitman, how did you decide what texts to include on your CD?

HERSCH: *That* took much longer than writing the music. It was a six- to nine-month process. Unscientifically, I got the 1892 edition of *Leaves of Grass* (basically, the complete edition) and, from the first to the last page, marked with a pencil things that attracted me: a title, a part of a poem, a whole poem. And then I went back and looked at them again, whittled things down, and typed things into my computer that I thought I wanted to work with. Then I cut the pieces of paper out and put them on the floor. My studio was a sea of these little pieces of paper, and I would move them around, see if I could find a through line. Finally, I realized I needed help, that I was so close to it I couldn't see it, so I had this friend of mine, Herschel Garfein—a first-rate composer, director, librettist—and I went to him because I had a deadline looming. (This was October; the first performance was [scheduled for] March and I hadn't written anything yet.) So I went to him and said, "I think I have a torso here. Can you look at it and help me?" And he did, and he's the one who suggested repeating a couple of phrases—"a child said What is the grass?" that begins the second half—then I came up with the idea of ending "After the Dazzle [of Day]" with "I celebrate myself" as a recap. I had a working libretto around November and went to the MacDowell Colony in January with the basic text, and I wrote the music in about three-and-a-half weeks—

FEINSTEIN: Wow—

HERSCH: Chiefly by singing, or by finding rhythms and then trying to slide Whitman's words into rhythm, because, you know, there's no [set] meter, there's no rhyme. And in a way, that's cool; it allowed me to be very fluid with the melodies. But I also covered my ass by hiring musicians and singers that I knew could do *anything*. So if it ended up being really edgy—let-the-animals-out-of-the-barn kind of stuff—they could do that; if it was classical, they could do that; if it was jazz, they could do that. Because I just didn't know where it was going to take me. So it took about three-and-a-half weeks to compose, and about a month to orchestrate it. Then I had to hand-copy the parts because I don't use a computer [for musical compositions]. And that got done about ten days before the first performance. Right to the wire.

I didn't know if it would work at all: I didn't know if people would react, I didn't know if the musicians would like it, I didn't know if *I* would like it. I knew I had great singers [Kurt Elling and Norma Winstone, who was replaced by Kate McGarry on the CD] and a great band. But I was concerned, first because of the current state of composition, what you might call the split between uptown and downtown: "Uptown" you might refer to as Elliot Carter, Milton Babbit, post-serial-kind-of guys; "downtown" I associate, chiefly, with those more concerned with rhythm. (I think the greatest composers in the world, like [György] Ligeti and John Adams, are themselves at this point but they've been through aspects of all this stuff.) I was a little concerned this was perhaps too tonal, too tuneful, too whatever, but it was what I could write. Because of the text that I picked—and I avoided the Civil War poems, the New York poems, the overtly gay poems—I was left with what I call the spiritual Whitman: Most of the poems are about love or nature or the present moment or being excited by life. I just felt, with all the crap going on in the world, that's the message I wanted people to hear.

I got this really snotty review, and it's the first time ever that I've responded to a reviewer, on some English webzine. This guy wrote a long, pompous article about how I missed the point of Whitman, blah blah blah. His tone was really nasty. So I went to the website's home page and read his credentials, which were all literary (I think it said, "He played the saxophone in high school"), and I wrote an open letter that said, "Look, if he wants to write about literature, that's fine. Obviously his view about what Whitman *is* is not mine, but I think he's way off base, and, furthermore, I think he's really nasty and ill-informed." There have been other people who have fought [with the recording]; they see Whitman as "messier" or "edgier" and there are some messy places, but, for me, I found it more intimate, spiritual.

From the beginning, I was determined not to have just a male singer; I thought it needed a female singer. Even though her role is smaller, it's equally important. He's sort of the voice of Whitman; she's sort of the voice of all women, a kind of universal woman. The one poem I knew I couldn't avoid doing was "Song of Myself." I was also determined not to do "[When] Lilacs [Last in the Dooryard Bloom'd]" and "O Captain, My Captain"; they've been set *so* many times. And because Whitman is conveniently dead, I had no estate to argue with. "No, if you're going to set a poem, you have to use the whole poem." I could cut and paste—nobody cared. And that was helpful because it allowed me the freedom to use what I wanted. I could use two or three stanzas, say, of an eight-stanza poem. I mean, if you do an opera based on a Shakespeare play, you know that already half the characters are going to have to go, and at least two or three of the subplots, and even if you use his words, you're going to have to reduce it by two thirds or you're going to be there all night. So it's distilled and very personal. I don't make any claim that this is an academic project. It's an artistic project.

We recorded it in October [2004] and got it out in March [2005] and toured six cities in the U.S. in March. And we had this gig in Lincoln, Nebraska, at the end of March. Now, I'm an avid reader of the *New York Review of Books,* and suddenly I see this big ad that says, "*Leaves of Grass,* Sesquicentennial Symposium," and then it dawned on me: 2005 was the sesquicentennial year. I didn't even *know* that. It was just dumb luck. So that helped me get a lot of press: I was on [National Public Radio's] "Fresh Air" and "Morning Edition"—partly because they liked the piece, but also because it was timely. Sometimes you get lucky.

. . . .

FEINSTEIN: You mentioned how many times Whitman's verse has been set to music, and I was wondering how important it was for you to know, or not to know, the recordings of Whitman by, say, Paul Hindemith or Joan Baez, or John Carradine from the 1959 LP *Jazz Canto*.

HERSCH: I didn't listen to any of them. I tend to be that way.

The next thing that I'm doing is a song cycle with the poet Mary Jo Salter called "Snapshots." It's going to be staged. There will be three men, three women, an orchestra of twelve, lighting, and costumes. It's all going to be new songs to new lyrics about different aspects of photography, everything from cyberdating to food stylists to finding old photos of yourself or loved ones, photography right after the Civil War, photography in space and underwater. We have lots of ideas for songs. This [*Leaves of Grass* project] got me into working with texts in a personal way. If the next thing goes well, then I might tackle a small opera/music theater piece. Now, this has nothing to do with my jazz career.

FEINSTEIN: I wouldn't file your *Leaves of Grass* recording under "jazz."

HERSCH: No, it's just American music, or whatever you want to call it: I call it "Fred Music." It's got elements of jazz and contemporary music and Americana and whatever—it's just a soup. But the last thing I want to do as I'm working on this song cycle is listen to a bunch of Stephen Sondheim or Adam Guettel or Ricky Ian Gordon. I need to just work with the words, let them inspire me, try to get out of the way. That's my goal. I'm vaguely familiar with some of the settings of Whitman. I've heard some that I just loathe. [Feinstein chuckles.] Especially—and this is not particularly nasty—those that are done by classical singers. That was another deliberate decision on my part: not just to use miked singers but jazz singers, because they understand diction and can finesse things intuitively that even a good music theater singer would have to be told how to interpret.

FEINSTEIN: In the eleven sections of "Song of Myself," for example, how much of Kurt Elling's vocals—and I'm talking about the melody, the vocalization—was improvised?

HERSCH: Even though he is a very fine improviser, everything's written. He improvises a handful of notes. But "The Mystic Trumpeter" is all improvised—the front part, the duet between voice and trumpet. That was another decision. In performance, there is an intermission between part 1 and part 2, and part 2 is only a half hour. (Part 1 is just shy of an hour, so theoretically you could do it without an intermission, but I felt that at the end of "Song of Myself" [which concludes part 1], everyone needed a break, just to stop and consider.) If it was up to me, I would give people the text [only] on their way out of the hall. "Okay, you've heard it; now go and look at it." (You can't always control things that tightly.) So the type of voice was really important to me, and, you know, I've worked with many of the great classical singers, but text like this is often not their strong suit. For them it's more about sound and tone and projection and singing over large orchestras in large opera halls. I really wanted a different sort of sound, so it's very hybrid. Most of what I do is a hybrid of some sort or another. This is just the biggest one so far.

FEINSTEIN: Your recording brought me back to Whitman's love of opera.

HERSCH: Yes, yes.

FEINSTEIN: He once claimed that he simply could not have written *Leaves of Grass* without opera, and to another friend he wrote how his youthful vitality saturated his verse, adding, "A real musician running through *Leaves of Grass*—a philosopher-musician—could put his finger on this." I thought it might be an interesting way for you to see yourself in relation to this project—as that "philosopher-musician."

HERSCH: Well, the philosophical point is, as I said, how I selected the texts, what order. Something that became clear to me as I got into the libretto with Herschel's help: I think of this whole piece as a cycle of seasons. "A Riddle Song" is spring, when things are starting to pop; it introduces everybody. "Song of the Universal" is birth. "Song of Myself" is a kind of summer, when things are going riot and all sorts of changes of mood and style. But the second half becomes more reflective: "The Mystic Trumpeter," "The Sleepers," "Spirit That Form'd This Scene / On the Beach at Night Alone." Those are kinds of fall/wintry moods. Then the final anthem, "After the Dazzle of Day," is moving back into the spring, triumphant. So it's a cycle. I don't claim to be either a literary expert or a philosopher, but, as an intelligent human being who's lived a certain amount of years, I have a point of view.

As I get older, I really give less of a shit what people think. "You have your Whitman, I have mine. I have my way of playing the piano, my artistic choices, and you have yours." If I can keep creating projects and keep the wolf from the door, and continue to challenge myself—

you know, as long as my health holds up—that's all I really care about. I went through this period in my thirties of being obsessed with being a jazz star: having a record deal, being in the critics' poll, playing at the Vanguard. Now that that stuff is all happening for me, it's like, "Oh, that's nice . . ." Of course, part of that was fueled by my health anxiety, which has lessened, thank God, but is still there. I mean, I'm going to be fifty in less than a month, and a good friend of mine—my recording engineer—says, "The good thing about being fifty is you feel perfectly within your rights to say 'Piss off' to anybody or any project." You've proven yourself; you don't really have to do anything you don't want to do—unless you have to pay the bills, or something like that. But, in general, you should be at that point in your life where you make choices based on what you feel and what you want, and I had no idea that this piece would become such a big thing in my musical output. I wanted it to be large enough in sound to be significant but not so large that it needed a conductor. It's not a cheap thing to tour, but I wanted it to be tour-able. (I didn't want to go to other cities and deal with a strange bunch of musicians, although I've done that, and sometimes it works out.) Frankly, it's a lot of work dealing with nine other people and logistics and travel, but I'd like to keep doing it.

We tried it once in Antwerp. Didn't work. Ironically, they had the best intentions and had commissioned this wonderful essay on Whitman, beautiful photographs, a booklet. But they didn't put the words in. Also, they were expecting more of a jazz piece: long, screaming solos. Edgy kind of stuff—and it isn't. I mean, I could certainly extend some of the solos, but I really wanted to keep the focus on the words.

FEINSTEIN: I had intended to ask if you had plans to work with contemporary poets, and you began to answer that without a prompt. How did you encounter Mary Jo Salter's poetry?

HERSCH: We've been at MacDowell two or three times together. I've always liked her; she's a really great person. Last fall, I got a little commission to write a song for baritone voice, soprano, and piano at a celebration for a close friend of mine, so I wrote to Mary Jo, who edits *The Norton Anthology* [*of Poetry* with Margaret Ferguson and Jon Stallworthy] and is the closest I know to a poetry goddess, and I said, "Mary Jo, here's the situation. Do you know of anything that I could possibly set that's not Emily Dickinson?" She wrote back for more details, and about three days later, a lyric [that she had written] arrived called "I've Got Your Picture." I loved working with it; I wrote this song in an afternoon—it just popped right out because the lyrics were interestingly constructed and the premise was very cool. It was clever without being too clever. Very interesting and unexpected. So I set it, and then, together, we decided to tackle an opera, and I tried unsuccessfully to get the rights to *The Baron in the Trees* by [Italo] Calvino, which is one of my favorite books of all time—how great to write a book set in the 1700s in an Italian garden *in* an Italian garden (I got a Rockefeller Fellowship for August of 2005 at Bellagio on Lake Como!)—but the widow Calvino (or somebody at the estate) decided to deny us the rights to adapt the novella. I started to see there would be lots of legal fees and God knows if I'd ever get the rights. But after I wrote this song with Mary Jo, and after we got turned down, I just said to Mary Jo, "Let's create a song cycle about photographs and photography." Immediately we started brainstorming. E-mails went back and forth furiously. So now I've written three pieces of a projected eighteen, but there won't be a book; it'll just go song to song, hopefully with clever staging and lighting and costumes.

FEINSTEIN: And she's writing all the lyrics?

HERSCH: Yeah. But what we're doing is discussing the scenario of each song, what the focus is. We may write more songs than we need, and then, as I did with *Leaves of Grass,* we'll put them on the floor and think of what might be an interesting flow: an ensemble song, a duet. Practical issues: how to get people on and off the stage. And so on.

FEINSTEIN: You play on two cuts of Luciana Souza's *North and South.* What do you think of her work with poetry texts, such as the poetry of Elizabeth Bishop and Pablo Neruda [*The Poems of Elizabeth Bishop & Other Songs* and *Neruda*]?

HERSCH: I think her Neruda album is really strong. Of her compositional efforts, I think that's the one I'm drawn to. (I'm impressed that Lu got the rights to those poems. I've always wanted to set a handful of Neruda's love sonnets. There's just something about them that I think is extraordinary, and within the sonnet form there are so many possible variations.) Of her non-compositional efforts, the stuff I like best are the Brazilian duos. Lu is a great, great singer. She's pretty fearless. She's like me in a certain way: She straddles some worlds. She's sung Osvaldo Golijov's music. But when she sings in English, except for this Neruda project, it doesn't, sometimes, have the same life as when she sings in Portuguese.

Setting poetry is really hard. I've heard so many contemporary "art songs" that are just unlistenable, either because of the singing or because they're sort of putting square pegs in round holes. To me, in any kind of singing, I always prefer a more natural sound. My favorite classical singer before the public now is Lorraine Hunt Lieberson. I've worked with her and Renée Fleming, who's also brilliant, and I'm recording with Audra McDonald this week, who's also incredibly brilliant, and Dawn Upshaw. They all, in the right context, have a certain naturalness about their singing, a connectedness. It's not just about sound and showing off. Among jazz singers, this is also so important. To me, Kurt Elling and Andy Bey may be completely different singers, but they're both *honest* singers. I also love non-singer singers, like Jimmy Rowles and Chet Baker, or people with limited voices, like Blossom Dearie. Irene Kral is a heroine of mine; I think she's one of the great, unheralded jazz singers. And there's even debate about what *is* jazz singing: Is it defined by scat singing, for example? To me, it has to be spontaneous.

And then there's a great jazz singer named Nancy King, who lives in Portland and who's in her mid-sixties. She's completely fearless, and she's an incredible scat singer, which, ordinarily, I don't care about, but she's so good you want her to keep going. Pretty much as good as any horn player. So with singers, whatever style you're coming from—whether it's music theater, classical, jazz, pop, singer/songwriter—as long as it's the right approach for the song and it somehow gets me, that's all I care about. It's not about who has the more beautiful instrument. I don't care. (And the bar for singing isn't that high right now. There aren't a lot of *great* singers.) It's the ones who use what they have in the most intelligent way that tend to get me. That's what I look for.

FEINSTEIN: One of my favorite cuts on *Leaves of Grass* is your instrumental response to "At the Close of the Day." Recently, there have been other instrumental responses to poetry, such as Tom Christensen's *New York School,* inspired by Frank O'Hara's poetry but without any vocals. Would you ever consider a purely instrumental album that responds to poetry?

HERSCH: Yeah, I think so. I think that would be interesting. The next instrumental project that I have in mind—and I've already written one of a projected two volumes—is what I'm calling at this point *Well-Tempered Preludes and Tunes.* There would be twenty-four pieces, all major/minor keys; twelve of them would be solo pieces (the preludes) and twelve of them would be trio pieces, so there would be a prelude, a tune, a prelude, a tune. (There would be twelve on a disc, and then the next disc would be the opposite keys, so they'd all be covered.) I like to work from that kind of perspective when I compose.

"At the Close of the Day" was the first of my Whitman pieces.

FEINSTEIN: It's gorgeous.

HERSCH: Thank you. And "Riddle Song" I originally wrote for my drummer, Nasheet Waits, and it's built on perfect fifths. I thought, "This would make a really dandy overture."

FEINSTEIN: I thought it was a little chancy—maybe "gutsy" would be a better word—to open two new releases [*Leaves of Grass* from 2005 and *The Fred Hersch Trio + 2* from 2004] with the same tune ["A Riddle Song"].

HERSCH: I know. We debated about that. When we put the sequence together, I said [to Palmetto producer Matt Balitsaris], "I have a feeling it's going to be first on *Leaves of Grass* [as well]," and Matt said, "I don't care. I think it's a great opener." And of course, on *Leaves of Grass,* it's much more concise and more orchestrated.

FEINSTEIN: Quite a different treatment.

HERSCH: Right. And yes: I think there are nice instrumental moments throughout. The bass solo on "On the Beach at Night Alone"—I mean, it's not a very good poem, but it's such a great title. I could *see* Whitman, walking around on the New Jersey shore. In the Calamus poems, he talks a lot about bathing in the cool waters and waiting for his lover. Water was clearly a part of his life: the Brooklyn ferry, the shore, the beach, the rocks. "Spirit That Form'd This Scene" is a nature poem. I'm not sure how much of the American landscape Whitman actually saw, but just that wildness and comparing it to his poetry—I thought that was interesting. And then to have that sung by a woman, which I also thought was intriguing.

So, yes. I'm drawn to instrumental responses. I've also used poem titles as tune titles, and roughly half of the tunes that I've written are dedicated to specific musicians, mostly people I've played with or admire, and friends. It's not that I want to imitate them, but I want to think about them as I'm writing. It's a nice hook-in.

About five years ago when I was at MacDowell, I discovered a new process for composing. I was really struggling with myself. So I had a baseball cap there and an index card, which I cut into twelve little pieces. I put the names of the twelve pitches on the scraps, and I had a kitchen timer that I would set for forty-five minutes. I'd pull out a letter, which would represent a key (minor or major) or starting note, think for a minute of a title, hit the timer, and in forty-five minutes I'd have to finish a tune. "At the Close of the Day" came out that way, as did "Endless Stars," as did "Riddle Song."

FEINSTEIN: Remarkable—

HERSCH: I'd say most of the tunes that have come out of my repertoire in the last five years have come that way. First of all, it eliminates waiting for "the great idea," because you don't have time. Also, it focuses you on one or two elements. In a lot of contemporary jazz composition, I find, it's like, six pounds of shit in a five-pound bag. [Feinstein laughs.] It's just too much stuff, and so when it comes to the improvisation it either sounds anticlimactic or like the players are struggling to get through this roadmap of stuff. For me, great tunes—if you look at [compositions by] Kenny Wheeler or Wayne Shorter or Ornette Coleman or Monk—are built on one or two elements, and they have a vibe. I was once teaching a class on what makes a great tune, and this one kid, who was particularly smart, said, "I think the most important thing about any tune is that it should be memorable." I thought, "That's pretty good." What are the tunes that we remember, and what are the zillions of tunes that have just fallen by the wayside? And *why* do we remember good tunes? Is it the lyric, the construction, or who sang them? So that's very important to me as a composer. *Leaves of Grass,* obviously, is a hybrid, but I was really shocked at how tune-like most of it really is.

So having an inspiration—whether it's restricting yourself to certain intervals, or a vibe or personality, or something in nature, a rhythm—and starting somewhere, just grabbing at something, saying, "Forty-five minutes, go!"—it just gets you out of the way. And when I play live, I don't have the luxury of time to sit and think, "Well, I could have played *this* chord . . ." I just have to play something. And that's why I started *Leaves of Grass* by singing, because I wanted to see if I could find the internal, natural rhythms. And they *are* in there.

FEINSTEIN: Absolutely. It's why I mentioned Whitman's letter and his image of the "philosopher-musician" finding the musical vitality and rhythms in his verse.

HERSCH: Right. You can dig them out. But in some cases, it takes a long time for them to appear.

FEINSTEIN: Whitney Balliett in *The New Yorker* once referred to you as "a poet of a pianist." How do you feel about that phrase?

HERSCH: Well, you know . . . I think it's nice. It's alliterative. [Feinstein chuckles.] Some people have thought it means "romantic / gay." There's an element of that. But I'd say I'm a reasonably poetic pianist.

FEINSTEIN: Very much so.

HERSCH: So I suppose it's accurate. In my early career, I got dumped into the Bill Evans box constantly.

FEINSTEIN: You know, I never understood that completely. For one, there's a determined propulsion to a lot of Evans's phrasing that I don't particularly hear in the majority of your pieces. I heard more—if one *has* to make comparisons—Ahmad Jamal. But I don't recall Jamal being mentioned, at least early on.

HERSCH: Right. They see a white guy, playing with a trio, who plays ballads, and they just say, "Bill Evans." Now they just say, "Bill Evans or Keith Jarrett"—who is basically Bill Evans and Paul Bley combined, essentially. It's true. I mean, Kenny Barron is essentially early McCoy Tyner and Tommy Flanagan. Chick Corea is McCoy Tyner and Bud Powell, with a Latin accent. Again: essentially. And Bill Evans was a much more edgy player when he started. He was more delineated; his touch was different, the rhythm was different. (And then there was the junkie period, and the coke period, and various other bored periods.) But I just got lumped in there.

One writer for a prominent New York magazine used to mention Bill Evans every time I played. Finally, I just wrote him: "Maybe twenty-five years ago . . . but can we just get past that?" Even pianistically, and with all due respect, I'm a much more expansive pianist. I mean, it's better than comparing me to [New Age pianist] John Tesh or somebody really awful, but I think I have a *very* broad musical outlook and output, and Bill pretty much played with a trio for thirty years until he killed himself. That's all he did.

When people ask me who my influences are, my top five are Earl Hines, Ahmad [Jamal], Paul Bley, Tommy Flanagan, and Monk. And then the next rung is Bill Evans and Herbie Hancock—the usual suspects—and some idiosyncratic piano players, like Jaki Byard or Art Lande or John Taylor, who I think are really important. The state of jazz piano? Yeah, I'm a little mystified, but that's another whole story. All I can do is do what *I* do. As I said, I'm about to be fifty; I'm just starting to get some big-time juice here. I've paid a lot of dues. When I mentor or teach young musicians, whether they're pianists or not, I try to give them a perspective: "Look, this is not about getting out of college and getting a record deal, because that's not going to happen."

FEINSTEIN: Right. I teach poetry . . .

HERSCH: Exactly, and how many poets have been ruined in high-profile
MFA programs? The soul of the true poet is there. You want to nurture it but not interfere with it. Support it but not dictate to it. Painters:
the same thing. I was up at [the] Bellagio [Center] with this very interesting painter who said, "So many good painters have been ruined
at MFA programs," and most of the people I know who do *anything*
well are autodidacts through most of it. When we get stuck, hopefully
we have the wisdom to consult with someone who can help us.

At least I can make a living doing what I'm doing. As Mary Jo
[Salter] says, "Maybe four poets in the U.S. can make a living without
teaching." Maybe.

FEINSTEIN: I'm not sure if I could come up with four.

HERSCH: Less than one hand. And whether or not the people you teach
poetry to end up being poets or not, they're going to have a greater
appreciation of language. You're also building an audience: people
who might go to a reading, or buy poetry books. There are kids who
play second alto in the college big band who are going to be lawyers,
but they might make sure that their kids pick up an instrument, or
they might support their local jazz society, or frequent concerts. For
the people who are really going to have careers, it's a combination of
talent—although that's not necessarily the case—and luck and per-
severance. Right place at the right time. Breaks. I mean, if you heard
some of the more popular female singers these days in a hotel lobby,
you might say, "Nice," but you wouldn't think, "Six million records."
Our country does not reward fine artists very well.

When I came to New York in '77, there was, obviously, no Jazz
at Lincoln Center. The idea of doing jazz concerts only happened at
the Newport Festival. (Once in a while, Miles would play at Carnegie
Hall or the Beacon Theater.) I still play the [Village] Vanguard and
The [Jazz] Standard and isolated clubs around the country and Europe, but now the majority of my performing in the course of the year
is at concerts, performing arts centers, and universities. And on one
level, it's better money, better conditions, nicer pianos. But the music
doesn't thrive quite as much. After a week at the Vanguard, I feel like I
could pick up a piano with my fingers. Because you *really* play—night
after night—and you can't phone it in (you never know who the hell is
out there). It's the Carnegie Hall of jazz clubs. If you can't play well in
there, you should sell insurance.

I hear a lot of young jazz musicians who play with a lot of fear, and

young poets—some very gifted poets whom I've met at MacDowell—
who write with fear. The editor is always over the shoulder. But we
learn by fucking up: "Okay, I made a mistake. Nobody died. Now:
What can I learn from this?" And we learn by taking chances. Had I
not done this piece [*Leaves of Grass*], other things might not have followed. You have to take those risks.

David Jauss

9

Stolen Moments
David Jauss

In an essay titled "Contemporary American Poetry and All That Jazz," David Jauss writes, "If we want to understand the poetry of our time fully, then we must try to understand why it so often turns to jazz for inspiration." Making comparisons to poetry, he discusses "the crucial element of jazz: a sense of 'seeking' for something not immediately available in our culture, or ourselves." It is interesting, though hardly surprising, to note that his own jazz poems connect to the music in precisely this way: Jazz allows him to imagine lives spectacularly different than his own.

In 2004, David Jauss spent a week at Lycoming College as a writer-in-residence, visiting a range of literature and creative writing classes, including my advanced poetry workshop. I had tailored my syllabus to include his work, and since a number of his poems allude to jazz figures, I thought it would be helpful if I made an accompanying recording. (These days, most undergraduates haven't even heard of the most innovative jazz musicians; our nationwide ignorance of jazz remains an American tragedy.) Dave's poem "Brutes," for example, invokes Ben Webster playing "Prisoner of Love," and the CD includes that particular cut from 1957. But a number of his poems referred to performances not captured on record, and I strongly suspected the gigs had been researched rather than experienced. This struck me as being fairly unusual, and very much worth discussing.

Of course, it would *not* be worth discussing if research removed from the poetry the essence of music—if the poems became, say, mere exercises—but that's not the case. His work consistently approaches emotionally charged topics—from personal despair to the politics of race—and, by controlling his form, he challenges the stereotype of jazz poetry. (To quote his essay again: "The term 'jazz poetry' may conjure up in many readers' minds the image of a black-garbed, goateed beatnik solemnly reciting his pseudo-poem to the accompaniment of a similarly garbed and goateed 'cat' on a bongo drum.") A deep listener, he brings to these imagined sessions the wise perceptions and gratitude of a humble devotee.

David Jauss is the author of two books of poetry, *Improvising Rivers* and *You Are Not Here,* as well as two short story collections, *Crimes of Passion* and *Black Maps.* He is co-editor of *Strong Measures: Contemporary American Poetry in Traditional Forms* and editor of *The Best of Crazyhorse: 30 Years of Poetry and Fiction.* His numerous awards include an AWP Award for Short Fiction, the Fleur-de-Lis Poetry Prize, a National Endowment for the Arts Fellowship, three Arkansas Arts Council Creative Writing Fellowships, the O. Henry Award, and two Pushcart Prizes. He teaches at the University of Arkansas at Little Rock and in the MFA in Writing Program at Vermont College.

Some of the poems mentioned in our discussion have been reprinted. The interview took place in my home in Williamsport, Pennsylvania, on March 17, 2004.

* * * * * * * * * * * * * * * * * *

Traps

> The Buddy Rich Big Band, Avalon Ballroom, St. Paul,
> Minnesota, 1968

David Jauss

Right off, I wanted to escape. Jazz
was dark, smoky bars, chicks in sunglasses,

dope deals in the john. Not this ballroom's glitz,
grandmas in evening gowns, and Traps

the Boy Wonder grown old. This wasn't the hip scene
I craved, just my parents' wet dream

of pre-war innocence and fun. But then Buddy
(whose name fit him the way Tiny

fits a sumo wrestler) swung his Mussolini glare
on his longhaired bass player. The kid must have erred

in some way my rock 'n' roll ears couldn't hear
yet it mattered so much it made Buddy glower,

his hate white-hot, the rest of the set.
And I began to listen, ears pried open, caught.

Black Orchid

> Miles Davis, New York, August 1950
> *for Lynda Hull*

David Jauss

Tonight he's playing the Black Orchid,
the old Onyx where before his habit
he played with Bird, looking cleaner
than a motherfucker, Brooks Brothers suit,
marcelled hair, trumpet floating over
that hurricane of sixteenth notes no one
could have played sober—19, a dentist's son,
on stage with *Bird* and laying down shit
nobody ever heard before or since!—but now
his fourth cap of heroin's wearing off,
its petals closing up inside his chest so tight
he can barely breathe. Drunk again,
Bud hangs heavy over the keys, left hand
jabbing chords that break his right hand's
waterfall arpeggios: "April in Paris,"
and that strangely tropical odor of coconut
and lime in rum comes back to Miles,
the smell of Paris, Juliette Greco's sweet lips
as she sang, each syllable a kiss
for him alone. *Juliette,*
his trumpet moans, *her small hands*

on the small of my back, long hair black
on the white pillow . . . Even Sartre
tried to talk him into marrying her
but he'd gone back to America, to Irene,
and a habit. And though numerology proved
he was a perfect six, the Devil's number,
he drove the Blue Demon, top down, to East St. Louis,
Irene silent beside him, the kids crying
in the back seat, one thousand miles
to escape heroin and the memory
of Juliette's white shoulder. But now
he's back, alone, long sleeves
hiding fresh tracks on his forearms,
and it's not Bird but Sonny who's unraveling
the melody, looking in it for a way
to put it all back together again.
Then Wardell leaps in, *This is it, man,*
can't you hear *it?* They're dueling
like Ground Hog and Baby, the junky tapdancers
who buck-and-winged for dope on the sidewalk
outside Minton's, feet turning desperation
into music, and Miles joins them, his mute
disguising the notes he fluffs. He sounds
as bad as Fats, last May when they recorded
Birdland All-Stars. Glassy-eyed, nose running,
Fat Girl had to strain to hit notes
he used to own. 26 and just two
months to live. *I'm going to kick this shit,*
Miles vowed the night Fats died,
but here he is, blowing a borrowed horn
because he pawned his own to play
a syringe's one-valve song. If only
he'd stayed, if only he'd never come back . . .
Behind him, Art plays Paris dark
as a jungle, and Miles falls into her pale arms,
the dark hotel room, and he's lost, lost
and free, released from some burden he's borne
across the ocean, to this bed, this woman,
a burden that, lifting, lifts him
like music, one clear unwavering note piercing

the silence that defines it . . .
When he tries to explain, she tells him
that's *existentialisme.* "Existential,
shit," he says, "Let's fuck."
And she laughs, her mouth a red flower
opening under his. Then he kisses
two whole notes out of his horn, their beauty
painful as they vanish into the swirling
smoke of the Orchid, each note
unfurling, an orchid itself, its petals
falling and settling on the nodding heads
of grinning white Americans
who will never understand jazz, or Paris,
or him. He closes his eyes,
and for as long as his solo lasts,
it's not August, it's not New York,
and he is not dying.

Brutes

     Listening to Ben Webster play "Prisoner of Love"
David Jauss

The Brute, they called him, because he loved
to brawl. But one night some scrawny drunk spit
the word *nigger* at him, and Ben just shrugged,
unfurled his fists, and said, "No, I've got to save it
for my horn."
     Now Ben's in prison
on my stereo, all his rage transformed
by breath and metal into music so warm
it could save us all. But you, J. C. Wilson,
who slugged my wife's dear face for five
goddamned dollars, you're free . . .
         For months I've dreamed
of beating your face until my fists bleed,
but now, listening to Ben, I hope someday love
imprisons you as it does him. And I hope you find

your own horn, as I'm trying to find mine.

Hymn of Fire

John Coltrane, Huntington Hospital, Huntington, New York,
July 17, 1967

David Jauss

Once he told Elvin, *If we only knew*
the right notes, we could eliminate all friction
in the universe, and all matter would fall
away from itself, nothing would hold anything
together. Later he chanted the seven breaths

of man—*A um ma ni pad me hum*—as if breath
were spirit and body the mere instrument
it played. Meanwhile, each night the news
got worse: riots at Fisk, Jackson State, Texas Southern,
and now twenty-five brothers in Newark have fallen

and the ghetto's ablaze. Everything's falling
apart, the country, himself, and music is a fire
that can neither purify nor destroy . . . He breathes
slowly, carefully, open-mouthed, the cancer
in his liver making each breath a new

reminder of what his music foreknew:
the desire to live forever is the darkest fire,
a fire that cannot cancel the Fall
or its aftermath, though it consumes
everything but the spirit, the breath

he releases now, the seven breaths
become one at last in the final
blissful, burning rise and fall
of his chest, a last hymn
so ancient and eternal it's new,

as he falls, like Newark, in flames, breathless.

SASCHA FEINSTEIN: I'd like to discuss how you create poems from other
texts—as opposed, say, to live performances—because I think this

could be educational for writers who never had the opportunity to hear seminal figures in jazz. But I'd like to begin by breaking a classic creative writing workshop rule of separating speaker and author: Is the narrative in your poem "Traps" true to the origin of your actual infatuation with jazz?

DAVID JAUSS: No it's not, but it's very close. I had a friend in high school who was a jazz fanatic and a drummer, and he's the one who introduced me to jazz. He played Dave Brubeck constantly—his hero was Joe Morello—and he was the guy who talked me into going to the Buddy Rich concert. I didn't know Buddy Rich from anybody and I wasn't really all that excited about going, but I went, had a great time, and the incident that I describe in the poem is actual. Rich did turn and growl at this longhaired bass player. A couple of weeks later, Buddy Rich was on *The Tonight Show*, and Johnny Carson was talking about his reputation as a demanding, hard-to-please bandleader—apparently he was the George Steinbrenner of Big Band leaders—and he said, "Yeah, I just had to fire a bass player."

So all that part of it's true, but to torque up the drama of the moment, I acted in the poem as though I'd been dragged to the concert by my parents and didn't want to be there. But [in actuality] it was my choice and I was with my friend.

FEINSTEIN: Was this the first major jazz musician you heard?

JAUSS: The only one I'd heard at that point. I was seventeen. We did not hear jazz on any of our radio stations [in Minnesota]. We didn't hear much beyond the predictable pop. In fact, for my tenth birthday in 1961, I was given one of those radios they had then, the kind with vacuum tubes in them, and at night I could get KAAY in Little Rock, which at that time was a rock and roll station, and they were playing things that I was not hearing on the radio stations in Minnesota, songs by people like Chuck Berry and Little Richard. And I just thought they were local boys. [Laughs.]

FEINSTEIN: And how, after the Buddy Rich concert, did you nurture your new attraction to jazz?

JAUSS: Largely by listening to my friend's jazz records. I bought a few records of my own, too—the first album I bought was a Coleman Hawkins record. I didn't know anything about Hawkins, but the album was called *The Genius of Coleman Hawkins* and I figured he had to be good if he was a genius. [Both laugh.] Mostly I was like everybody else my age, listening to Dylan, the Stones, the Beatles, that sort of thing, but I was liking jazz more and more. And in my senior year in high school, I wrote my English research paper on the history of jazz. I somehow managed to get it down to about nine pages. [Both laugh.] That was the first time I felt the desire to read about it, to find out the sources behind the music. I didn't feel that desire from the Buddy Rich concert, but when I started to hear the jazz that really spoke to me, I felt that this was the language I had wanted to hear all my life. It was like the unconscious talking, expressing everything that you can think and feel in a language you cannot rationally explain. It just communicated so intensely compared to anything else I'd ever heard before. I wanted to read about the people who made it and learn how this music came to be, so I wrote this research paper.

When I went to [Southwest Minnesota State] College [in 1970], I had a really bad Introduction to Music class; it was not a good experience for me and I never took another music class. I didn't have much money to buy records, and in graduate school I spent most of my time reading and writing. But while I was at Syracuse University [1972–74], I spent a lot of time at Stephen Dunn's house—Stephen was my first creative writing teacher, back in Minnesota, and we'd become friends—and I listened to just about everything in his jazz collection. But jazz didn't really take me over heart and soul until I moved to Little Rock [in 1980]. In part it was because there was a good jazz and blues scene there, but mostly it was because my son Steve began to be interested in jazz. We went to clubs together almost every week for years—he was always the youngest person in the room—and watching his love for the music grow brought me back to the way I felt when I first discovered it. And now that he was interested in jazz, and playing it himself—he played guitar in jazz bands in high school and college—I had a good excuse to buy all the records I wanted—I was furthering his education, after all! [Laughs.] But of course, I was also furthering mine at the same time.

FEINSTEIN: Was there a parallel moment to the Buddy Rich experience when you realized that writing would be at the center of your life?

JAUSS: Not really, because I always wrote—I started writing stories when I was in first grade and I've never stopped. I always assumed I would have to stop someday when I grew up: I'd have to find something practical to do. Even after a couple of creative writing classes in college, which I really enjoyed, I thought, "You can't be serious about this." And then I just got selfish and said, "I'm going to learn as much about literature and writing as I can. Regardless of what I'm going to do for a living, I'm going to spend the rest of my life reading books and writing poems and stories." So it was more of a gradual giving in to an impulse that had been there forever.

FEINSTEIN: Given the fact that you are nationally recognized in poetry, fiction, and nonfiction, why has jazz so much more strongly influenced your poetry?

JAUSS: I would like it to more strongly influence my fiction as well. I have tried to write jazz stories and have always failed. For some reason, jazz seems more congenial to poem form. Part of it is that I am conscious of feeling inadequate, of not knowing enough about that world, since I'm not a musician myself. I think in a story I would have to know more, whereas in a poem all I have to do is try to capture a moment. Usually in capturing a moment, I bring in some of the past life—like in that Ornette Coleman poem ["The Master Musicians of Joujouka"], which summarizes his past leading up to the poem's present moment—but that moment takes center stage and it's the only one I feel I really need to inhabit imaginatively. I figure I can enter a moment better than I can a life, so that's probably why I write poems about jazz but not stories.

Also, I think I'm drawn to certain moments more than to the overall stories of their lives. It's the same with the music. There are certain passages in, say, Coltrane's *Crescent:* Every single time I hear them, the hair stands up on the back of my head, I can feel my heart rate go up. There's just something about it, and I couldn't possibly tell you why. The combination of the notes, the tones, the feeling that's put into it—it just nails something inside me that nothing else does. And that happens when I read about jazz musicians' lives, too—certain moments just leap out and beg to become a poem.

FEINSTEIN: In terms of genre, though, if you had a student who said, "I'm not a musician but I love jazz and I'd like to write about it in a short story," wouldn't you encourage that student?

JAUSS: Oh, absolutely. And I would encourage myself, too. [Feinstein laughs.] I have tried. But I don't want to write something bad about jazz—it means too much to me—and I work hard at the jazz poems that I write because I feel part of the impulse behind them is to honor the people who made this great art and who have not gotten the recognition that they deserve. I mean, they're famous among those of us who know something about jazz, but I always have to explain to my students who Coltrane is, who Billie Holiday is, who Thelonious Monk is. But I can't blame them. I can remember the first time I heard Coltrane's name, and I didn't have a clue who he was, so when I encounter students and other people who haven't heard of him, I can empathize with that, but I feel the need to spread the word because these people are missing so much. I feel that very strongly. As I told you the other day, I was once teaching Frank O'Hara's poem "The Day Lady Died" and talking about Billie Holiday and one of my students said, "Well, in order to really get this poem, we need to know who *he* was." (Even though it's "The Day *Lady* Died"!) I asked everyone to raise their hands if they knew who Billie was. Only one hand went up. And that upset me. The fact that some of these students were African American upset me even more: If they're losing this astonishing contribution to American culture, what's happening to the WASPs out in the suburbs?

*   *   *

FEINSTEIN: Your Miles poem "Black Orchid" seems to have been inspired by Miles's autobiography [*Miles*].

JAUSS: That's right.

FEINSTEIN: In the book, Miles mentions—in passing—that he *may* have played in the club [Black Orchid] at that time [1950]. You've taken a possible gig and turned it into a lengthy poem. How did that happen, and why?

JAUSS: Partly because, since we don't have a record of it, no one can accuse me of describing it incorrectly. [Both laugh.] Throughout my life of writing jazz poems, I have strategically picked as often as possible moments that were not recorded. [Both laugh again.] For example, in the Sun Ra poem ["After the End of the World"]: I could have set it in 1970, when he actually recorded there [in Berlin], but then people might say, "Well, no—this didn't happen, and that didn't happen," so I picked another year in which he did tour Germany but didn't record there.

FEINSTEIN: But the Miles Davis autobiography includes many interesting stories. It's a fairly hefty book—unless, of course, you edit the swear words, in which case it boils down to a third of the size. [Both laugh.] There must have been something about the moment, or title of the club, that offered such an energizing trigger.

JAUSS: I think it was the club's name, to an extent, but I also wanted to set the poem in 1950 because that was such a crucial year for Miles. It was a time in his life when he was in danger of losing his genius, because of the drugs and the emotional turmoil of leaving Irene and all that. Since it was such a dramatic, important time, and since the Black Orchid gig wasn't recorded, I did what I do as a fiction writer, which is to try to get into the mind of the character. I thought imagining Miles playing "April in Paris" would be a good way to bring in the Juliette Greco story. The story of his marriage. Heroin addiction. The death of Fats Navarro. All of that. Basically, I just tried to imagine what someone in that spot would be thinking while playing a song that would bring back all these memories.

FEINSTEIN: Two issues ago [Summer 2003], *Brilliant Corners* published a tribute to Lynda Hull, which included your excellent essay on her poem "Ornithology." We've often discussed our admiration for Lynda, how we both think she's one of the greatest voices in twentieth-century poetry. Why did you dedicate this particular poem to her?

JAUSS: My first instinct is to say that I dedicated it to her because she helped me so much with it. But now that you ask the question, I think that's only part of the answer—and probably just a small part. After all, I could have asked any of my other poet friends for their advice. So why did I choose Lynda? Partly because she wrote so well about jazz herself, I suppose, but also, I suspect, because I feared she was like Miles in the poem, at a point in her life where her genius was threatened by her addictions. But I don't think I was conscious of this when I dedicated the poem to her. At that time, I think I was just thanking her for all of her help. And I needed her help badly—it was the first jazz poem I ever wrote.

FEINSTEIN: Since then, of course, you've written quite a number, and you've crafted many of them in sonnet form. Why's that?

JAUSS: I don't know. It's a congenial form to me, and I've used it for other subjects as well. My long poem for Lynda ["Requiem"] is written in hobbled sonnets—

FEINSTEIN: Thirteen lines—

JAUSS: Yes, they're all one line short. (That wasn't my original intention. It's just that the first section was thirteen lines and I thought, "Well, keep it going." It seemed to me to make sense, eventually.) But the sonnet form seems to work for me and, again, I think it goes back to this idea of capturing a moment, especially a moment in which there is a change of some sort. The sonnet form seems so wonderfully designed for that, the way everything turns in another direction at the end of the octave in the Italian sonnet or right before the final couplet in the Shakespearean sonnet. And sonnets end with a punch line of sorts—

not necessarily a funny one, of course—and that's something that appeals to me about the form, and that's a main reason I used it for the poems about racism.

FEINSTEIN: You mean the four sonnets that comprise "Diminuendo and Crescendo in Blue"?

JAUSS: Yes, those anecdotes about racism. I thought it was a very appropriate form and length for them.

FEINSTEIN: [The sonnet] "Brutes," I know, began as a considerably longer piece.

JAUSS: Yes, it was much longer, and it was awful (and I'm not all that pleased with the way the final version turned out, either). It was a hard poem to write because it was based on an actual event: My wife was indeed mugged by the person named in the poem, and we had several months of worry and trouble—intimidating phone calls from jail, several court appearances in which he either bolted or didn't show up at all, et cetera. Finally, when it was all over, he was given probation. It was a very traumatic experience for both of us. And I don't say this to brag in any way, but I rarely get mad. (I get depressed easily, but I rarely get mad.) And I was so furious at this guy. I felt so much rage, and I wanted to hurt him. I had never felt like that about anybody before, and I didn't know what to do with that kind of emotion. So the first versions of the poem were, I believe, letters to him. Loose and sloppy—they just weren't poems.

Eventually, after some time had passed, I was listening to *Coleman Hawkins Encounters Ben Webster,* and listening especially to Webster on "Prisoner of Love"—I put that song on repeat and listened to it over and over again. And for some reason, I kept thinking about that old anecdote about him refusing to get into a fight and saying, "I've got to save it for my horn." That fit in with what I was trying to get to in my response to this fellow who mugged my wife for a whopping five dollars.

So in the early versions, there was no Ben Webster, but through Ben Webster, I found a lens through which to view the experience. Finding that lens—that's often the key to making a poem better, if not make it work, at least for me.

⋆　⋆　⋆

FEINSTEIN: For someone eager to read interesting accounts of the jazz world, what books have been important to you? What would you recommend?

JAUSS: That's a little hard to answer because the books that have been important to me—or at least to my poems—aren't always books I'd recommend. The books I'd recommend—the books I most admire—are probably David Hajdu's biography of Billy Strayhorn [*Lush Life*], which is the best jazz biography I know, Art Pepper's *Straight Life,* and Miles's autobiography. I also like Geoff Dyer's book *But Beautiful,* which does in prose some of the things that I try to do in poems: He imagines his way into various musicians' lives, expanding brief anecdotes into full-fledged scenes, complete with dialogue and thoughts for which there's no record. Essentially what he does with their lives is what jazz musicians do with melody: improvise. And I like [Charles Mingus's autobiography] *Beneath the Underdog* too, bizarre as it is at times. But only a couple of these books have helped me write my poems. I got one poem from Miles's autobiography, and I got another one from *Beneath the Underdog*—"The Hatchet" is based on Mingus's description of a painting Monk did while he was in Bellevue. Actually, I got two from *Beneath the Underdog,* but one of them wasn't publishable—or rather, I did publish it, but I shouldn't have. It dealt with his Mexican experiences . . . [Both laugh.] But mostly my poems have come from biographies I don't really admire all that much—[C. O.] Simpkins's biography of Coltrane [*Coltrane*], John Litweiler's *Ornette Coleman: A Harmolodic Life,* Ross Russell's *Bird Lives!* I guess it goes back to what I said about why I write jazz poems instead of jazz stories—it's the moment that grabs me more than the whole life, and even in these less accomplished books, there are moments that made me want to write a poem.

FEINSTEIN: You mentioned that Bill Crow's book *Jazz Anecdotes* inspired the sections of "Diminuendo and Crescendo in Blue," and that makes sense since Bill's book reads like a series of snapshots.

JAUSS: Right. And the sonnet seemed the right form to capture the snapshot quality of those anecdotes. To a large extent, all I did was put the information in the anecdotes into sonnet form. For the Dizzy Gillespie section, the details about the Greek skull-cap, the Turkish slippers, the Italian sunglasses, and the Sheraton towel draped over his shoulder—all of those things are in the anecdote. I didn't have to make anything up in that poem. The same is pretty much true of the other three sections, though I confess I couldn't resist making up the part about Red Rodney singing "Hava Nagilah."

FEINSTEIN: Do you think writers can get trapped by anecdotes?

JAUSS: Yes. What actually appeals to me most are the poems where I'm allowing myself to go into the character and imagine what that person was like. I have a great sense of curiosity about great artists of any kind. The first book [*Improvising Rivers*] has a lot of jazz poems, but it also has poems about Flaubert, Chekhov, and Kafka; I've done the same thing with them. More often, it's the moments where I *don't* know what happened, where I don't have all the information, that I'm most interested in writing about.

FEINSTEIN: And what do you think distinguishes a strong poem based on an anecdote as opposed to the anecdote itself?

JAUSS: To be honest, I don't think too much of "Diminuendo and Crescendo in Blue," partly because the sonnets were almost prefab. I knew virtually everything that was going in them; I didn't have to imagine much of anything. They don't mean as much to me as some of the other poems, though I like the content.

FEINSTEIN: Which jazz poems mean more to you?

JAUSS: The ones I care the most about are the ones where I worked my imagination the most. I don't know if "Black Orchid" is one of my best jazz poems, but it's one that matters a lot to me, simply because of that effort to enter into Miles's mind. I like to try to collapse a whole life into one moment, so I try to bring many facts about his life into that one moment of playing that song. Same thing with the Ornette Coleman poem ["The Master Musicians of Joujouka"]; I tried to suggest that in this moment he found, in a sense, a home—that through his immersion in the ancient, timeless music of the Master Musicians, he found a self within all his previous selves, a self that had always been there but had remained hidden. Whether or not that's how he felt, I have absolutely no idea, but when I listened to the music, it seemed like some incredible release. So that's how I interpreted it.

FEINSTEIN: Aside from the strength of the poem itself, I'm interested because, frankly, the album that inspired the poem [*Dancing in Your Head*] is not one of my favorite Ornette Coleman recordings.

JAUSS: It's not mine at all. I like the early Ornette [recordings for Atlantic] much more than anything else, although I do like *Sound Museum: Three Women* and *Sound Museum: Hidden Man* a lot. But his early stuff, with Charlie Haden and Don Cherry, that just knocks me out.

FEINSTEIN: I guess I'm surprised that you chose an album that means much less to you, at least in terms of the musical impact.

JAUSS: If I was to write about an Ornette Coleman composition that means a lot to me, it would probably be "Lonely Woman," which is one of the most moving songs I've ever heard. But I was more interested in the psychology of his character than my emotional response to the music. For some reason, I felt this had been a big moment for him, that it changed him in some significant way.

FEINSTEIN: Would that explain why you've also written about [smooth jazz saxophonist] Art Porter? I can't imagine his music being played in your house.

JAUSS: Art Porter was from Little Rock, and I saw him play a lot around town. He'd been performing with his father [Art Porter, Sr.] since he was a young boy, and he had an enormous amount of talent. I have been very moved by things that I heard him play in Little Rock clubs. (One time I heard him play "In a Sentimental Mood" with such gentleness, such reverence, such a beautiful tone—it was just extraordinary.) So, years later, when he came back to town shortly before his first CD was released, I was really anxious to go hear him play. And, honestly, I walked out. There were dance steps. Everything was choreographed. The music was slick. Whether his musical taste had changed since he left Little Rock or whether he was playing beneath his abilities just to get a record contract and make money, I don't know. But I was very, very disappointed by the change in his music.

FEINSTEIN: I like your elegy for him very much, though as a fate versus free will poem, it's a little heavy on fate for my taste. [Jauss laughs.] But it's very moving.

JAUSS: I'm always interested in the chain of coincidences that lead to any major event in life. I had a student years ago whose father was killed in an accident—his car was stalled on a railroad track and was hit by a train—and I've never forgotten something he said: "If my father had stopped to comb his hair, he would still be alive."

FEINSTEIN: Oh—

JAUSS: Just that little pause, that one small thing, would have changed everything. And with Art Porter, Jr., I thought about all the coincidences that led to him drowning in Thailand. It goes all the way back to the Benny Goodman records young King Bhumibol heard in 1946. When he heard them, he became a lifelong lover of jazz, so in 1996 he invited jazz musicians from around the world to perform for him at a celebration of his fiftieth year as king. Art Porter was one of them. It's not the king's fault, obviously—or Benny Goodman's—but in a way, Art died because the king listened to Goodman's records fifty years before.

FEINSTEIN: Your Coltrane poem "Hymn of Fire" has the feel of a sestina, though you've obviously pulled it out of form. Could you talk about that?

JAUSS: It began as a sestina. I was trying to write a legitimate sestina, but it wasn't working, and I realized part of the reason was the content: The poem was about things falling apart, and at some point it occurred to me that maybe the sestina should fall apart too. So I shrunk it. I shrunk the stanzas from six lines to five and shortened the number of end words from six to three, leaving two lines in each stanza without repeating end words. And instead of the three-line *envoi*, I put all three of the repeated end words into one final line. So there's a sense of things funneling down, that all of these things that are apart are gradually getting closer and closer, and in the final moment they come together. It seemed appropriate for this poem because of what was happening in the world at that moment when Coltrane died: the riots in Newark, and so forth.

FEINSTEIN: It also pays homage to the late Coltrane performances when he explored circular, sometimes diffuse themes and then suddenly pulled them together at the composition's close.

JAUSS: Yeah, I meant that. [Laughs hard.] I'd love to say I intended to imitate that structure, but if it's there—and I guess it is—it's just a lucky accident. What drew me to the sestina form was its principle of repetition with variation, which is of course the principle behind all improvisation but especially, I'd say, behind Coltrane's improvisations. If he can play "My Favorite Things" for twenty-nine minutes with Eric Dolphy, you know? That's a sign that someone can really explore repetition and variation. So maybe that's why I turned to such a repetitive form, and maybe one of the reasons I shortened it is because I've always loved that Miles quote. Coltrane asks him for advice on how to end a solo, and Miles says, "Take the damn horn out of your mouth!" [Both laugh.]

FEINSTEIN: Why focus on the end of Coltrane's life as opposed to his performances with Dolphy?

JAUSS: What I'm able to connect to—if anything—is the life. Since I don't have access to the musical sides of their lives—the technical aspects of music—my way of connecting to the music, apart from the sheer pleasure of listening, is through their lives, through them. Since I'm also a fiction writer, my natural impulse is to try to enter another character's mind, and, in my jazz poems, to pay homage to these people whom I wish I had heard and known. One of the reasons I write about these musicians, I guess, is my sense of loss, the fact that they were gone before I could hear them. Because I *know* the difference between hearing something live and hearing it on record. I know how much more moving and powerful it is. I know what it feels like to sit in a room and feel the vibrations in your chest that you don't get from your CD player.

FEINSTEIN: Michael Harper once said to me that he thought people should only write about musicians they've actually heard.

JAUSS: Well, I'd be in bad shape!

FEINSTEIN: I was blessed to hear quite a number of astonishing musicians before they died, but most people of my generation—certainly the next—will never have that opportunity. So, sad though it might be, it seems important to address art as artifact.

JAUSS: There have been some musicians I have heard that I have tried to write about. My daughter Alison and I went to hear Joe Lovano play in Little Rock a few years ago and it was one of the most powerful sets of music that I've ever heard. But I wasn't able to get it in writing, partly because I was there. I couldn't convey the music; I don't think there *is* language that can convey it. But I couldn't even convey what it felt like to be there. In some ways, it's easier for me to enter into something that I haven't actually experienced, a performance I haven't heard but only imagined.

Another example: Recently, I was visiting my son and his wife in Philadelphia where we heard Dave Holland with Chris Potter— I've heard Chris Potter play several times; I love his playing—and the others in the band: the wonderful trombonist, Robin Eubanks. Steve Nelson: I'd like to be able to describe just his body movements. They're almost a part of the music he makes, I think. And Holland was as solid and wonderful as could be. It was a great night of music, and I have since tried to write about it. But all my efforts just turn into vapor. I would like to be able to capture something that I've heard, but I have yet to be able to do that. Even in the Buddy Rich poem, where I *was* there, I'm not really writing about the music; I'm writing about his fury at the bass player's mistake.

FEINSTEIN: But I also love the aspect of the poem where the speaker realizes there's a lot happening on stage that he doesn't know—why Rich is so upset—and thinking, "I want to know more. I don't want to miss that next time."

JAUSS: And of course, I continue to miss it . . . [Both laugh.] But the concert also showed me how important this was for Rich. This wasn't just about money; this meant so much to him that he was furious when someone made a small mistake.

FEINSTEIN: I think, too, you very cleverly use the word "traps," not only to describe the drum kit but also the traps on stage (playing for Buddy Rich, say) and the positive trap: being utterly captivated by this music.

JAUSS: Yes. I think the last word of the poem is "caught." That's how I felt. For the rest of that concert, I was paying as close attention as I was able to. I was trying to hear what was so important to Buddy Rich. And I think now I can hear it, at least a little, and I wish more people could. Jazz is such an important contribution to our culture. [Federico García] Lorca once said, "The only things that the United States has given to the world are skyscrapers, jazz, and cocktails," and, obviously, the most important has been jazz. It's behind the music that everyone listens to, and the people who created it never got the respect that they deserved. Classical musicians are sort of like the golfers of music: They're in their orchestra halls, everyone's quiet, so much respect, everyone's dressed up. Meanwhile, the jazz musicians are having to play over conversations and the *ching* of registers. To create great music in that environment is astonishing. And it is great, great music.

I firmly believe that jazz is the greatest contribution to American culture, and I believe that the jazz created in the '50s through the mid '60s is the equivalent in music to what happened in the middle of the nineteenth century in literature with Melville, Hawthorne, Whitman, Dickinson, Emerson, and Thoreau. And to have those people disappear . . . People just don't know about them, and if their albums don't get transferred to CDs, the names disappear, and they're gone.

FEINSTEIN: I can't say "they're gone." Maybe gone from general consciousness.

JAUSS: Right. You know all those nasty books about cultural literacy that have been published recently? Well, they didn't really talk about *African American* cultural literacy, especially given the great cultural contributions African Americans have made to our culture. It seems to me a form of racism that we're ignoring it. It seems to me a form of racism that we make fun of the Rolling Stones for still performing in their old age and yet we consider it normal for an old blues musician to still be playing. And that's partly why some of my poems have focused on moments of racism in jazz history.

I once tried to write a poem about Dizzy Gillespie's one experience in Arkansas, where he was beaten up in a restroom for being black.

FEINSTEIN: Oh God . . .

JAUSS: I would like more people to know about it and about all the obstacles jazz musicians had to overcome to create their music. But mostly I'd like more people to *listen* to the music, to give it a chance. I've found that people who think they don't like jazz don't know the breadth of it. They don't know that there's some part of it that absolutely will speak to them. They think, somehow, that it's homogenous: just one thing, one sound. It's a word that . . . As Duke Ellington always said, it would be better just to call it "music" and not try to categorize it. But a lot of people will hear one tune, not like it, and then reject everything. I know people who've heard early Ornette Coleman and said, "That's too avant-garde." Well, that's fifty years old! [Both laugh.] Can't they catch up?

I remember the first time I heard "Lonely Woman"—the fact that it began with a bass solo was something of a shock: I'd never heard a tune that began with a bass solo before. But with Coleman, it was, "We're all in this together. I'm not the star; you're not the star." That was such a wonderful thing, and as avant-garde as that may be, it was also a return to the very earliest jazz instinct: the idea of group communication.

And that's maybe what I love most about jazz: the depth of the communication, both between the musicians themselves and between the musicians and the audience. I have enormous envy for people who can play jazz. It seems to me that they're able to communicate in so many ways that writers can't. To me, art exists because of a desire, a need to express, and I get a certain amount of satisfaction from writing poems and stories, but the alphabet isn't large enough, and the musical vocabulary is so *large,* so expressive, so emotive—far beyond what can be done on the page. It's amazing. I just remain in love.

Yusef Komunyakaa. *Photo by Tom Wallace.*

10

Survival Masks
Yusef Komunyakaa

In 1995, Yusef Komunyakaa telephoned to ask for valuable biographical sources about Charlie Parker. He explained that he was writing a libretto, a long poem about Bird that would eventually be set to music by an Australian composer and producer. Over the next couple of years, he mentioned the poem in passing. (Yusef never easily parts with information about himself; when he won the Pulitzer, for example, he taught his class and told them *nothing*.) When he eventually said he'd completed his libretto, I fantasized about publishing the piece in *Brilliant Corners,* but I didn't want our friendship strained in any way so I simply asked if he would let me read it.

I received "Testimony" a few days later, and found it to be linguistically spectacular—a monumental tribute worthy of Charlie Parker's music. I called him right away and asked if he had sent it out for publication. He had. Worse: He'd sent it to a handsome, prestigious journal. I said, "I'm sure they snapped it up." Remarkably, though, this journal felt the poem was too long to run and wanted to print selections. The rest of our conversation went something like this:

I shouted, "*Excerpts?* Are you kidding me? That poem's not meant to be excerpted."

Yusef said, "Hmmmm."

I said, "That poem is symphonic."

He said, "Hmmm."

"Yusef, that poem's a very serious poem."

"Yes."

"That poem's meant to be read in its entirety."

"Yes, yes. I think you're right"—and shortly thereafter, he agreed to publish "Testimony" in *Brilliant Corners.*

At the last, however, this literary coup took place because of Yusef's generosity and kindness. The least I could do was feature the libretto as prominently as possible, which is why this taped conversation accompanied the poem.

Yusef Komunyakaa has published many books of poetry, including *Pleasure Dome: New and Collected Poems, Talking Dirty to the Gods,* and *Taboo.* He is also author of *Blues Notes: Essays, Interviews & Commentaries,* and co-editor of *The Jazz Poetry Anthology* and its companion volume *The Second Set.* His many honors include the William Faulkner Award from the Université of Rennes, the Hanes Poetry Prize, the Thomas Forcade Award, fellowships from the National Endowment for the Arts, and the Pulitzer Prize. He also received the Bronze Star for his service in Vietnam. In 1999, he was elected a Chancellor of The Academy of American Poets. He teaches at New York University.

This conversation focused on "Testimony," which has been reprinted. The interview took place at The Runcible Spoon (a coffeehouse in Bloomington, Indiana) on June 25, 1997.

Testimony
Yusef Komunyakaa

I
He hopped boxcars to Chitown
late fall, just a few steps
ahead of the hawk. After
sleepwalking to the 65 Club,

he begged Goon for a chance
to sit in with a borrowed sax.
He'd paid his dues for years
blowing ravenous after-hours
till secrets filled with blues
rooted in Mississippi mud;
he confessed to Budd Johnson
that as a boy playing stickball,
sometimes he'd spy in a window
as they rehearsed back in K.C.

It was Goon who took him home,
gave him clothes & a clarinet.
Maybe that's when he first
played laughter & crying
at the same time. Nights
sucked the day's marrow
till the hibernating moon grew
fat with lies & chords. Weeks
later, with the horn hocked,
he was on a slow Greyhound
headed for the Big Apple,
& "Honeysuckle Rose"
blossomed into body language,
driven by a sunset on the Hudson.

II

Washing dishes at Jimmy's
Chicken Shack from midnight
to eight for nine bucks a week
just to hear Art Tatum's keys,
he simmered in jubilation
for over three months. After
a tango palace in Times Square
& jam sessions at Clark Monroe's,
in the back room of a chili house
on "Cherokee," he could finally play
everything inside his head,
the melodic line modulating

through his bones to align itself
with Venus & the Dog Star.

Some lodestone pulled him
to Banjo's show band on the highway
till Baltimore hexed him: a train
ticket & a telegram said a jealous
lover stabbed his father to death.
He followed a spectral cologne
till he was back with Hootie,
till that joke about chickens
hit by a car swelled into legend.
Now, he was ready to squeeze
elevenths, thirteenths,
every silent grace note
of blood into each dream
he dared to play.

III
Purple dress. Midnight-blue.
Dime-store floral print
blouse draped over a Botticellian
pose. Tangerine. He could blow
insinuation. A train whistle
in the distance, gun shot
through the ceiling, a wood warbler
back in the Ozarks at Lake
Taneycomo, he'd harmonize
them all. Celt dealing in coal
on the edge of swing. Blue
dress. Carmine. Yellow sapsucker,
bodacious "zoot suit with the reet
pleats" & shim sham shimmy.

Lime-green skirt. Black silk
petticoat. Velveteen masterpiece &
mindreader twirling like a spotlight
on the dance floor. Yardbird
could blow a woman's strut
across the room. "Alice in

Blue" & "The Lady in Red"
pushed moans through brass.
Mink-collared cashmere & pillbox.
Georgia peach. Pearlized facade
& foxtrot. Vermillion dress. High
heels clicking like a high hat.
Black-beaded flapper. Blue satin.
Yardbird, he'd blow pain & glitter.

IV

Moving eastward to the Deep
South with Jay McShann,
on trains whistling into dogwood
& pine, past shadows dragging balls
& chains, Bird landed in jail
in Jackson for lallygagging
on the front porch of a boardinghouse
with the lights on. For two days
he fingered a phantom alto
till "What Price Love" spoke
through metal & fluted bone.
The band roared through the
scent of mayhaw & muscadine,
back into Chicago & Detroit.

When the truckload of horns
& drums rolled into Manhattan,
Bird slid behind the wheel.
The three-car caravan
followed, looping Central Park
till a mounted policeman
brandished his handcuffs.
Days later, after moving into the Woodside,
after a battery of cutting contests,
Ben Webster heard them & ran downtown
to Fifty-second Street & said
they were kicking in the devil's door
& putting the night back
together up at the Savoy.

V

Maybe it was a day like today.
We sat in Washington Square Park
sipping wine from a Dixie cup
when Bird glimpsed Anatole
Broyard walking past & said,
"He's one of us, but he doesn't
want to admit he's one of us."
Maybe it was only guesswork
contorted into breath. We sat
staring after Anatole until he
disappeared down Waverly Place.
Bird took a sip, shook his head,
& said, "Now, that guy chases
heartbreak more than I do."

Maybe it was a day like today.
We were over at Max's house
as Bird talked Lenny
before Bruce was heard of,
telling a story about a club owner's
parrot squawking the magic word.
Maybe it was sunny or cloudy
with our tears, like other days
when Max's mama slid her key
into the front-door lock. Bird
would jump up, grab the Bible
& start thumbing through pages,
& Mrs. Roach would say, "Why
aren't you all more like Charlie?"

VI

If you favor your left
hand over the right, one
turns into Abel & the other
into Cain. Now, you
take Ikey, Charlie's half-brother
by an Italian woman, their father
would take him from friend

to friend, saying, "He's got good
hair." Is this why Charlie
would hide under his bed & play
dead till his mother kissed him
awake? No wonder he lived
like a floating rib
in a howl whispered through brass.

Always on the move, Charlie
traversed the heart's nine rings
from the Ozarks to le Boeuf
sur le Toit in Montmartre.
Though he never persuaded himself
to stay overseas, his first day
in Stockholm glowed among fallen
shadows. Always on some no-man's
land, he'd close his eyes
& fly to that cluster of Swedes
as he spoke of his favorite artist:
"Heifetz cried through his violin."
Charlie could be two places at once,
always arm-wrestling himself in the dark.

VII

Like a black cockatoo
clinging to a stormy branch
with its shiny head rocking
between paradise & hell,
that's how Yardbird
listened. He'd go inside
a song with enough irony
to break the devil's heart.
Listening with his whole body,
he'd enter the liquid machine
of cow bells & vibes,
of congas & timbales,
& when he'd raise his alto
a tropic sun beamed into the club.

Machito & his Afro-Cuban
Orchestra peppered the night

till Yardbird left ash in the bell
of his horn. He swore Africa
swelled up through the soles
of his feet, that a Latin beat
would start like the distant
knocking of tiny rods & pistons
till he found himself mamboing.
He must've known this is
the same feeling that drives
sap through mango leaves,
up into the fruit's sweet
flesh & stony pit.

VIII

He was naked,
wearing nothing but sky-
blue socks in the lobby
of the Civic Hotel in Little Tokyo,
begging for a quarter
to make a phone call. The Chinese
manager led him back to his room,
but minutes later a whiff of smoke
trailed him down the staircase.
This was how six yellow pills
sobered him up for a recording
session. He was naked, & now
as firemen extinguished the bed
cops wrestled him into a straitjacket.

Camarillo's oceanic sky opened
over his head for sixteen months
when the judge's makeshift bench
rolled away from his cell door.
Eucalyptus trees guarded this
dreamtime. Yardbird loved
working his hands into the soil
till heads of lettuce grew round
& fat as the promises he made
to himself, lovers, & friends.
Saturday nights he'd blow

a C-melody sax so hard
he'd gaze into eyes of the other patients
to face a naked mirror again.

IX
I can see him, a small boy
clutching a hairbrush.
This is 852 Freeman
Street, just after his father
took off on the Pullman line
with a porter's jacket
flapping like a white flag.
A few years later, he's astride
a palomino on Oliver Street
where a potbellied stove
glowed red-hot as a nightclub
down the block. Rudee Vallee
& late nights on Twelfth
haven't marked him yet.

When I think of Bird, bad
luck hasn't seethed into his body,
& Kansas City isn't Tom's
Town. This is before the silver
Conn bought on time, before Rebecca's
mother rented the second-floor,
before prophecies written on his back
at the Subway Club by Buster & Prez
on "Body & Soul," long before
Jo Jones threw those cymbals
at his feet, before Benzedrine
capsules in rotgut & the needle's
first bite, before he was bittersweet
as April, when he was still Addie's boy.

X
My darling. My daughter's death
surprised me more than it did you.
Don't fulfill funeral proceeding until
I get there. I shall be the first

one to walk into our chapel.
Forgive me for not being there
with you while you are at
the hospital. Yours most sincerely,
your husband, Charlie Parker.
Now, don't say you can't hear
Bird crying inside these words
from L.A. to New York,
trying to ease Chan's pain,
trying to save himself.

My daughter is dead.
I will be there as quick
as I can. My name is Bird.
It is very nice to be out here.
I am coming in right away.
Take it easy. Let me be the first
one to approach you. I am
your husband. Sincerely,
Charlie Parker. Now, don't
say we can't already hear
those telegraph keys playing Bartok
till the mockingbird loses its tongue,
already playing Pree's funeral song
from the City of Angels.

XI

I believe a bohemian girl
took me to Barrow Street
to one of those dress-up parties
where nobody's feet touched
the floor. I know it was months
after they barred Bird
from Birdland. Months
after he drank iodine,
trying to devour one hundred
black roses. Ted Joans
& Basheer also lived there,
sleeping three in a bed
to keep warm. A woman dusted
a powdered mask on Bird's face.

I remember he couldn't stop
talking about Dali & Beethoven,
couldn't stop counting up gigs
as if tallying losses: the Argyle . . .
Bar de Duc . . . the Bee Hive . . .
Chanticleer . . . Club de Lisa . . .
El Grotto Room . . . Greenleaf Gardens . . .
Hi De Ho . . . Jubilee Junction . . .
Le Club Downbeat . . . Lucille's Band Box . . .
The Open Door . . . St. Nick's . . . Storyville.
I remember some hepcat talking about
vaccinated bread, & then Bird began
cussing out someone inside his head
called Moose the Mooch. I remember.

XII

Bird was a pushover, a soft
touch for strings, for the low
& the high, for sonorous catgut
& the low-down plucked ecstasy
of garter belts. He loved
strings. A medley of nerve endings
ran through every earth color: sky
to loam, rainbow to backbone
strung like a harp & cello.
But he never wrung true blues
out of those strings, couldn't
weave the vibrato of syncopated
brass & ghosts
till some naked thing cried out.

Double-hearted instruments breathed
beneath light wood, but no real flesh
& blood moaned into that unbruised
surrender. Did he think Edgard
Varese & Stefan Wolpe could help
heal the track marks crisscrossing
veins that worked their way back
up the Nile & down the Tigris?
Stravinsky & Prokofiev. Bird
loved strings. Each loveknot

& chord stitched a dream to scar
tissue. But he knew if he plucked
the wrong one too hard, someday a nightmare
would break & fall into his hands.

XIII
They asked questions so hard
they tried to hook the heart
& yank it through the mouth.
I smiled. They shifted
their feet & stood there
with hats in hands, hurting
for headlines: *Baroness Pannonica* . . .
I told them how I met my husband
at Le Touquet airport, about decoding
for De Gaulle, about my coming-out ball.
I said I heard a thunderclap,
but they didn't want to hear
how Charlie died laughing
at jugglers on the Dorsey show.

The Stanhope buzzed with innuendo.
Yes, they had him with a needle
in his arm dead in my bathroom.
They loved to hear me say that
he was so sick he refused a shot
of gin. I told them his body
arrived at Bellevue five hours
later, tagged John Parker.
I told them how I wandered
around the Village in circles,
running into his old friends,
that a cry held down my tongue
till I found Chan, but they only
wanted us nude in bed together.

XIV
They wanted to hold his Selmer,
to put lips to the mouthpiece,
to have their pictures snapped

beneath *Bird Lives! Bird Lives!*
scrawled across Village walls
& subway trains. Three women
sang over his body, but no one read
The Rubaiyat of Omar Khayyam
aloud. Two swore he never said
"Please don't let them bury me
in Kansas City." Everyone
has a Bird story. Someone
said he wished for the words
Bird recited for midnight fixes.

Someone spoke about a letter
in *Down Beat* from a G.I.
in Korea who stole back
a recording of "Bird in Paradise"
from a dead Chinese soldier's hand.
Someone counted the letters in his name
& broke the bagman's bank. Maybe
there's something to all this
talk about seeing a graven image
of Bird in Buddha & the Sphinx.
Although half of the root's gone,
heavy with phantom limbs, French
flowers engraved into his horn
bloom into the after-hours.

SASCHA FEINSTEIN: What initially inspired you to write a libretto?

YUSEF KOMUNYAKAA: Well, Chris Williams at the Australian Broadcasting Corporation first approached me in early 1995 with the idea of a libretto, something that celebrated jazz's relationship with blues and gospel. I chimed to this wonderful idea because I feel that my work, my poetry, has evolved out of this musical tradition. In this first discussion, Chris described his admiration for Charlie Parker's musical ideas and then he mentioned that most likely Sandy Evans would compose the music.

Immediately I felt this was a healthy challenge. I had heard one of her three groups, Ten Part Invention, at a local pub a week earlier in

Sydney and I remembered going away highly impressed. She has exciting musical ideas, and she blows that sax as if she was made for the instrument. However, the more I thought about the impending piece, the more I wanted to write something new and different. I began to play Charlie Parker, everything he did, and I clothed my psyche in his sounds again. Though I'd listened to him through the years, he was still new and traditional in the same breath, old and cosmopolitan.

I think Chris was thinking of a more traditional libretto but I wanted a flexible definition. With Parker, I felt that a traditional libretto would pull against his experimentation and his whole trajectory of working things out as he went along. I wanted the piece to emulate the musical ideas, how they would flow for him.

FEINSTEIN: In essence, what did you keep and what did you pull away from?

KOMUNYAKAA: I pulled away from the structure of the libretto. I wanted something to excite me and surprise me, so what I went for was a kind of composite. I started thinking about the actions of Parker, and also about the fact that many of the stories were erroneous, misleading. A good example is the story that Parker died in Baroness Pannonica's bathroom at the Stanhope Hotel with a needle in his arm. This is the story I had been told. So everything was rather melodramatic and less complex, and what I wanted to do was capture the complexity of this man.

FEINSTEIN: Of course, the truth of his death—that he died watching a juggler on the TV—has often become melodramatic in the way that it's been presented and reported—

KOMUNYAKAA: Yes, right. But at least there's something pleasing about the truth. Let's face it, he's *laughing,* and not sitting on the commode grimacing with a needle in his arm.

FEINSTEIN: I know that often in your career a particular poem has triggered many others, even an entire book. Did a particular section or image generate the rest of this poem?

KOMUNYAKAA: I tell you, the first idea that came to me was based on a photograph I'd seen of Parker where he's about one year, holding a brush in his hand. There's something about the severe innocence.

FEINSTEIN: He looks like a girl.

KOMUNYAKAA: Yes, very much so. I kept glancing from that photo to the photo of him at the Bird's Nest in Los Angeles in 1947. He's with Harold Doc West, Red Callender, and Erroll Garner, and he has a smile that suggests he has been initiated by hard times and joy. It is a visual moment of knowledge and acknowledgment. Cocky.

And, also, there's another photograph of Parker as a young boy, maybe a year and a half, astride a Palomino pony. I began to weigh this image against the image of him carefully listening to two Apache visitors, Swift Eagle and Bad Wolf, at the Royal Roost. He seems so attentive, it parallels something glimpsed of him in those early images. I wanted to at least attempt to unearth a moment of this something-ness, this mystery, through "Testimony." But I was also drawn to the later photographs of Parker. So I am interested in that contrast—the innocence and, later on, something close to a visual ferocity.

We tend to think of jazz and gospel as opposites. Blues is called "the Devil's music." One is secular, the other sacred. I tend to think of Parker as blowing both at the same time. I feel that the technology of sound through brass is his religion.

FEINSTEIN: Obviously the music itself was the primary influence on your poem, but you also address biographical issues. Were there any literary sources that you found helpful?

KOMUNYAKAA: I've read a number of works on Parker, such as Ross Russell's *Bird Lives!*

FEINSTEIN: Which in fact takes many liberties with the truth—

KOMUNYAKAA: That's the first one I read. Then I went to [Gary] Giddins's *Celebrating Bird* and Robert Reisner's *The Legend of Charlie Parker*—even to liner notes [especially Phil Schaap's writing for *Bird: The Complete Charlie Parker on Verve*], which are quite informative as well. So it was all of those things plus the imagination. I tried to create an emotional composite of the man.

FEINSTEIN: I love how you make the effort to talk both about his life and the aesthetics of jazz, and my favorite section may very well be the third, with all the lush colors.

KOMUNYAKAA: It's interesting, that idea of Parker being associated with visual arts. Colors and textures. Textured motion and emotion. I believe many visual artists have been influenced by jazz and the atmosphere it creates. I am thinking about Romare Bearden, Matisse's "Jazz" series, Otto Dix, Picasso, and so forth. Recently I saw an exhibit and I was quite taken with the fact there were so many visual images of Armstrong—literally hundreds—and there must be hundreds of Parker as well. I know at least one sculpture that captures him in stone, a piece by Julie MacDonald.

The idea of blowing colors is interesting to me, and I do think that there are certain tones that parallel certain colors. In a sense, that's the way I approach poetry. I think I've said somewhere that I wish I were a visual artist at times.

FEINSTEIN: Many poets have said that.

KOMUNYAKAA: Right. [Laughs.] The very first time someone asked me, "How do you define your poetry?" I remember saying, "I think they're word paintings." In a certain sense, I think of Parker's tunes as pictorial.

FEINSTEIN: "Testimony" seems to have changes in speaker. Do you hear vocal shifts?

KOMUNYAKAA: I see this as many speakers, people telling different stories, or, at times, telling riffs on the same stories. Dealing with the space, I couldn't do *too* much of that. But this again emphasizes the complexity of Parker. I wanted a few of the pieces as multiple voices, with two or three people talking. I also wanted to give room to the director, where he could deal with these different voices. I think what Chris has planned so far is to use a thirteen-piece band and two actors, and a male chorus of four voices. So I kept thinking, "How would I do it?" and in certain cases I could see bringing in another voice in the middle of an idea or sentence.

This sort of parallels the way I construct poems often, in the sense that I love the idea of shifts happening where things are not completely resolved, where narratives do not necessarily have a lineal chart or continuity. In that way it parallels the idea of the psyche where there are many shifts.

Let's face it, Parker would have observed all kinds of things. He was a very troubled man, growing up in the Midwest, traveling around America and Europe, never really making much money, always living on the edge. But at the same time, I've seen so many photographs of him smiling—one where he's smelling a flower—which is interesting to me.

FEINSTEIN: William Claxton selected the photograph that will be on the cover of this issue [Winter 1997] because he said he never caught Parker looking happier.

KOMUNYAKAA: Parker seemed capable of being happy in the most troublesome moments, and I think that is the energy that people often relate to when they say "Bird" and give him this sacred dimension. I'm thinking of that Jack Kerouac poem ["239th Chorus" from *Mexico City Blues*] where he attempts to elevate Parker to Buddhahood. Parker had this capacity of embracing others, and at the same time he appears as a Trickster—trying to survive his habit, on the edge. But I don't think he ever tricked himself.

He wore many masks, multiple masks. I would classify them mainly as survival masks more than anything else. I don't know if he grew up lonely, but maybe he began creating survival masks early on, within the context of his family.

FEINSTEIN: In the 1950s, poets dispersed Bird poems like napkins. [Komunyakaa laughs.] Some poets were much more successful than others, and I remember a few years ago when you said that Bob Kaufman had been an influential figure on your [early] poetry. Kaufman, of course, was almost obsessively attracted to Parker—

KOMUNYAKAA: To the extent that he even named his son "Parker."

FEINSTEIN: Do you still feel his presence guiding your sensibilities as a poet?

KOMUNYAKAA: I'm not as quirky as Bob Kaufman. At times I wish I were! [Laughs.] He's full of surprises, and the other thing is his obsession: There's a body to that obsession which propels the music of the poems. You see that in Parker as well. I'm still quite taken with Kaufman, with his obsessive imagination.

FEINSTEIN: You can tell that he really listened, and that he genuinely loved Charlie Parker as a human being and as an artist.

KOMUNYAKAA: He respected Parker.

FEINSTEIN: I think Kaufman's poems for Bird [compared to many others from the '50s] were most in tune with Parker's spirit.

KOMUNYAKAA: Yes. He was able to penetrate the internal terrain, to get to the essence of Bird, the man. Maybe he saw part of himself in Parker. I don't know if I see part of myself in Kaufman, but it's interesting that Kaufman grew up in Louisiana [as I did], born into a complex family, with a black mother and Jewish father.

FEINSTEIN: Many of Kaufman's contemporaries who tried to write Bird poems were, I think, emotionally removed from Parker. How did you solve that problem?

KOMUNYAKAA: I really had to find myself meditating on the essence of Bird, and I'm glad I didn't attempt these poems early on—say, fifteen years ago. I don't know if I understood Bird early on, and I think it takes a certain amount of maturity to understand where Bird is com-

ing from. I had to understand important things about myself in order
to understand Bird. I was able to place myself, at times, in his situation. And at first it was terrifying, because people often talk about
Bird and his habit—

FEINSTEIN: Which, needless to say, did not literally parallel your life—

KOMUNYAKAA: Of course. But I do empathize with him and understand
how history helped to create him. I think he was more tender than he
often wanted to appear—as hard edged as possible (maybe because he
grew up in Kansas City). I was taken by the fact that Bird would wash
dishes at Jimmy's Chicken Shack just to hear Art Tatum.

I think with Bird's alto there's a great lyricism, almost a tonal narrative. I'm also interested in the fact that he had such an intricate relationship with the blues—and a blues is not always a dirge. [Grins.]
There's wonderment. There's laughter. There's a wholeness to his vision that I admire, and a bravery as well. There's also an ego he constantly wrestles with in his work.

FEINSTEIN: The title of your poem changed several times.

KOMUNYAKAA: Originally, Chris [Williams] suggested the title "Call and
Response," and this idea of call and response as a dramatic device still
interests me of course. Then it changed to "Seance," but there's something about "seance" that didn't work because there's this idea of con-
juring the dead. But "Testimony" is a kind of coming forth, telling a
story—a number of stories, contradictions—braided into the fabric
and design of the piece. At the same time, it's a celebration.

FEINSTEIN: Bringing emotional extremes together has been a central
concern of yours throughout your career as a poet, and this poem
certainly does that, sometimes quite directly: "Maybe that's when he
first / played laughter & crying / at the same time." And that's also at
the center of the blues.

KOMUNYAKAA: Yes. I think so.

FEINSTEIN: Did you ever have an experience in your life that was similar
to Parker's artistic breakthrough when playing "Cherokee"?

KOMUNYAKAA: That's an interesting question. When I went to Irvine
in 1978 after living in Colorado for seven-and-a-half years, I wrote
a poem called "Safe Subjects," and after writing that poem I realized there was something that taught me what I should try to accomplish in my work. It really became a directive: "Let truth have its way

with us / like a fishhook holds / to life, holds dearly to nothing / worth saying—"

FEINSTEIN: You've said before that you'll start a poem with a refrain and then later extract it. I'm so glad you left the repetition in "Section V."

KOMUNYAKAA: It's a riff on how stories come about, on possibilities.

FEINSTEIN: What made you bring in [Anatole] Broyard [in section V]?

KOMUNYAKAA: I wanted something to complicate the situation, and I visualized Broyard walking through Washington Square Park, actually going past Bird. I think Parker was very aware of race, even in relation to his half-brother, Ikey.

FEINSTEIN: Those issues certainly arise in section VI. And I love that image of Bird being awakened by his mother's kisses.

KOMUNYAKAA: When you think about it, the two brothers become a metaphor for the tensions of race in America, with Parker as a child hiding under the bed.

Perhaps it was that tension of growing up in the 1920s that helped to create the lyrical tension beneath Parker's alto. In Amiri Baraka's *Dutchman,* the character Clay says that Yardbird wouldn't have played with such urgency if he had gone out into the streets and killed a white person. (Of course, this existential act in *Dutchman* echoes Richard Wright's *Native Son.*) Indeed, I feel muted screams underneath Parker's lyricism. There's a rage just below the surface of a blues tonality that has been created out of need. He is sensitive to what is happening around him and to him.

FEINSTEIN: Where did you first encounter the telegrams [in section X] that he sends to [Parker's wife] Chan after their daughter's death?

KOMUNYAKAA: I don't even recall when I first encountered them. Maybe they are in Robert Reisner's *The Legend of Charlie Parker.* I do remember feeling that a cry sounded through the room as I read them. There's a quiet desperation in those telegrams—quiet because of the words chosen, but at the same time there's something frantic about them as well.

FEINSTEIN: Phrase against phrase—

KOMUNYAKAA: One after the other, almost as though he's forgotten the previous line, like words strung together by pain and regret.

FEINSTEIN: And those strange signatures, "Sincerely, your husband."

KOMUNYAKAA: Yes—almost as if he had to remind himself, out in L.A. I don't think he ever got along too well in L.A., that he was more at home in New York. He suffered in L.A. and found himself doing bizarre things.

FEINSTEIN: At what point in making "Testimony" did you visualize the wondrous final images of the Chinese soldier and the engravings on Parker's horn?

KOMUNYAKAA: That came to me as a breakthrough. One of the agonies of writing poetry is the question, "Where am I going to end this poem?" But midway through I started writing about the soldier, and the horn. For some reason I put that aside and then got back to it close to the end, and said, "Yes. This is the ending." It surprised me, and I do think it is the right stroke on the canvas.

* * * *

FEINSTEIN: "Testimony" is an individual section of your next book, *Thieves of Paradise,* which has seven sections. How does the poem function in this context?

KOMUNYAKAA: It functions as a bridge. I think it's different from anything else in the book, and I'm glad that it's different because it sort of switches gears, but the emotional trajectory isn't broken.

FEINSTEIN: Switching gears from what?

KOMUNYAKAA: I think the subject matter's different, more urban. There are many shifts in "Testimony" that have to do with the possibility of many voices. Tonally it's different, though it's hard to say how exactly.

FEINSTEIN: That's all right. Let other people chew the fat over those questions. [Komunyakaa laughs.] "Testimony" may very well be the longest poem you've ever written. Did you find the length liberating?

KOMUNYAKAA: I had to surrender to its structure. I knew I wanted symmetry—not as a mold but as an organizing principle—and it liberated me in that sense. Two fourteen-lined stanzas. Fourteen sections. I seem to always get involved with numerology and destiny.

FEINSTEIN: And you chose fourteen because—?

KOMUNYAKAA: You can divide seven into fourteen twice. [Laughs.] Often this becomes an obsession of sorts, what I call an emotional symmetry.

FEINSTEIN: There's a knockout line break in section VIII: "Wearing nothing but sky- / blue socks." That break on the hyphen is quite unusual for you. [Komunyakaa grins.] You often avoid breaks that might be seen as almost too clever—that bring attention to themselves. But I think it works marvelously well here.

KOMUNYAKAA: For a long time, that was the very first image [in the poem] for me. And for some reason, when I initially wrote it, the break was there, and I kept it.

FEINSTEIN: There's a truth to that image.

KOMUNYAKAA: I hope so.

FEINSTEIN: And I admire the way you address his stay at Camarillo [State Hospital] not merely as an emotional breakdown but also as a more positive revelation.

KOMUNYAKAA: I was quite taken with the fact he experienced so much pleasure getting his hands into the dirt. It says something about Parker, and in a way it takes him back to his beginnings. For years I thought of the Midwest as restrictive and reactionary, but recently I've been having this idea about all the experimentation that came out of that part of the country.

So I could see Parker embracing a certain kind of space early on. It might even have something to do with his creative dexterity, you know? He was able to move from one musical idea to the next, and to embrace different people and musical situations. I think it has everything to do with the fact that physical space parallels emotional and psychological space. He was at home under that blue sky.

Philip Levine. *Photo by Frances Levine.*

Detroit Jazz in the Late Forties and Early Fifties

Philip Levine

First, the obvious: I did not interview Philip Levine. But the creation of this essay, from notes to final form, evolved over many written exchanges and phone calls, so the essay, for me, feels like an interview. Here's what I mean:

In 1996, while preparing to launch the inaugural issue of *Brilliant Corners,* I solicited work from Phil, and he generously agreed to send a poem, "Now and Then," which appeared in the first issue. At that time, he said he might also have some notes about jazz in Detroit during the 1950s. I leapt at this possibility—did I beg?—and he sent them along. But the notes were just that: shards of memory, jotted down in no particular order. They required more direction and, ultimately, substance.

When I read the submission more carefully, however, I realized these notes helped elucidate several of his jazz poems written over the last thirty years. Like a poet's casual conversation that often precedes the reading of a particular work, and not merely as superficial garnish, they presented the cultural landscape that ignited his passion for jazz. After reorganizing the prose to frame his poems, the piece became both a statement about Detroit jazz in the '50s and a document about poetic inspiration and process.

With more than a little chutzpah, I retyped the notes, inserted his poems from various collections, suggested areas for expansion, and sent him the revised manuscript, hoping he would shine on the revision. He did, and as we continued to exchange ideas (between March 1996 and May 1997, he wrote fourteen times) his appreciation for the project escalated, culminating in his final approval: "I decided to make no changes. I know you came a long way to placate me."

After the publication of this essay, we met a number of times, from my home in Pennsylvania to his in Fresno, and I could have interviewed him on one of those afternoons but the material from this reflection, I suspect, would have been the heart of such a discussion.

Philip Levine is the author of many collections of poetry, including *Breath, The Mercy, The Simple Truth,* and *What Work Is.* He is also the author of a collection of essays, *The Bread of Time: Toward an Autobiography,* as well as a book of interviews and two books of translations. His awards include the Lenore Marshall Award, the National Book Critics Circle Award (twice), the Ruth Lilly Prize, two fellowships from the Guggenheim Foundation, the National Book Award, and the Pulitzer Prize. In 2000, he was elected a Chancellor of The Academy of American Poets. He lives in Fresno, California, and Brooklyn, New York.

I Remember Clifford

Wakening in a small room,
the walls high and blue, one high window
through which the morning enters,
I turn to the table beside me
painted a thick white. There instead
of a clock is a tumbler of water,
clear and cold, that wasn't there
last night. Someone quietly entered,
and now I see the white door
slightly ajar and around three sides
the light on fire. I remember once
twenty-seven years ago walking

the darkened streets
of my home town when up ahead
on Joy Road at the Bluebird of Happiness
I heard over the rumbling of my own head
for the first time the high clear trumpet
of Clifford Brown calling us all
to the dance he shared with us
such a short time. My heart quickened
and in my long coat, breathless
and stumbling, I ran
through the swirling snow
to the familiar sequined door
knowing it would open on something new.

The title "I Remember Clifford" comes from a fabulous melody written by the saxophonist Benny Golson as a tribute to his departed friend, the astonishingly gifted jazz trumpeter Clifford Brown who died at age twenty-five in an auto accident. Where do talents such as Brown's come from—& how do we come to deserve such gifts? The poem is concerned with the sudden generosity of the world, the unexplainable giving that occurs in the midst of deprivation, for I discovered the moment of Clifford deep in the misery of one of the hardest years of my life. A door opened, and this music—unexpected & unearned by me—was suddenly mine, pure, free, clear, as water was in my early years. Yes, I'm trying to say that music like water is essential to life, for in fact I can't imagine a life without music.

Do I truly remember Clifford? I honestly don't know, for this was almost fifty years ago. I am simply not sure I ever saw him at the Bluebird, but every time I hear that tune I think of the Bluebird & the excitement of going to that place. (It may be that the trumpet I actually heard that night was that of Thad Jones.) The place was a big rectangular café with a bar on your left as you entered & the bandstand on your immediate right with maybe a dozen tables facing the bandstand. The place was unusually well behaved—the owner, who was reputed to have served time for murder, kept the patrons subdued. My favorite among the "regulars" was the young alto man, Eddie Jamison (who inspired a section of my poem, "The Angels of Detroit," though my guess is the events recorded in the poem have nothing to do with fact); Jamison's style was based on Bird's, & Charlie Parker was then my favorite musician. The other regulars included Art Mardigan on drums, Phil Hill on piano, & Abe Woodly on vibes.

The Bluebird was home for me on Friday nights. I remember Thad Jones playing there often, his power & delicacy were not to be forgotten. Billy Mitchell was there often—a big, full tenor sound; he played with great energy & fire. Frank Foster, another great tenor. And when Wardell Gray was present he brought a special excitement to the place. (I later learned that Miles Davis played there for some months during the fall & winter of '51, but all that year I was working afternoons—4 PM to midnight—& was too worn out even for music.)

I had the good luck to discover Pres early, at age eighteen. In my first semester at Wayne, then the city university of Detroit, I was seated in an English class next to a big Irish brawler whose passion was Lester Young, whom I had never heard of. My new friend so loved the music of Pres he arranged a dance at his old high school & talked them into inviting Pres to play. A couple hundred kids, mainly white, showed up for the event—held on a Saturday night—& staged in the gym. My friend & I watched from the track, which served as the balcony that night; this was the autumn of '46 & Pres was breathtaking. Of course almost no one danced. We were too mesmerized to even move.

Eight years later I saw him again in Detroit playing at a toilet on Grand River not far from where my grandfather had his used car-parts grease shop. That night it seemed as though everything had abandoned Pres except his horn. When he wanted to he could revive the real Lester Young from memory, playing some of the great old pieces brilliantly, though at any moment he might stop playing & do a little graceless dance on the bandstand. During the second set he lost control, demanded to be paid on the spot, & would not listen to the young Detroit trumpet man who begged him to behave. Except for one drunk in the place the audience was listening—we knew he was Pres—; this jerk had come up to the bandstand & insisted on "directing" the musicians. Lester didn't seem in the least bothered by the man & let the guy carry on, though the other members of the band were clearly distracted or worse. And quite suddenly Lester exploded, not at this fool but at the owner of the place who was tending bar. A shouting match ensued; Lester was demanding to be paid for something else he'd done that day—as I recall it was a radio appearance for some DJ—& the owner claimed he'd had nothing to do with that. Finally the exasperated owner paid him off & Lester stomped off into the night while the young band members packed up. I was reminded of seeing Zero Mostel, down on his luck, in a cheap nightclub in Miami Beach during the summer of '49. A woman in the audience began to heckle him—he was doing a stand-up routine & getting no laughs—& he suddenly pulled down his pants revealing long flowered boxer shorts. He grabbed his crotch & shouted to the woman, "You don't even deserve this."

One Word

Western High School gym, Friday night dance,
spring of '47. Lester Young
playing for the edification
of two hundred mainly white teenagers
four of whom are off dancing in a corner.
Up on the indoor track my buddy Conway,
the Irish brawler and hockey player,
who organized the entire evening,
turns to me and says a single word
that justifies his rapture, his hard eyes
watering: "Pres." By which he means Lester
is the president not only of
the greatest tenor sax of the world and
of our hearts, he means Lester has made
it back from eight months in an army stockade
for merely being who he is, from
what we two, being kids, have no words for.

The years were there to teach us. Conway
would battle his father for the old house
in Del Ray and win only to lose out
to the bank. He'd get his first real kill
in the air over Korea. I would find
him in '59, drunk in a white bar
on Second Avenue, an Air Force Major,
ready to fight even me. Lester
would return from Paris that year, alone,
to die in New York of malnutrition
and the need not to live. If I close

my eyes I can still hear him come in late
on "Easy Living" and sail out just
behind the beat, lightly, to sing and sing
until Conway turns to me his eyes filled
with all he must learn and says the one word.

Early '50s, in one of the less grand downtown picture palaces, I heard
Billie Holiday for the first and only time. I was seated high in the second
balcony and looking almost straight down on Billie and her pianist. The
stage dark except for the spots on the two of them. The theater completely sold out, everyone let out a breath when she came on stage. Billie
in a white dress, her hair adorned with a white gardenia. I was stunned
by her physical beauty and grace; I'd heard so much about her difficulties
and addictions I was not prepared for such a powerful woman. For years
I'd listened to those early records with Teddy Wilson, Lester, Chu Berry,
Benny Goodman, so I was not expecting this huskier, deeper voice. She'd
lost that floating quality that had delighted me with its lyric understate-
ment and ease. The new power was different: frank, pained, and unrelenting. She was a different singer, probably a different woman, and
still the greatest jazz singer ever. I was surprised by the perfect clarity
of her articulation: above all else it was the songs she presented. She
ended with "Strange Fruit" and brought the house down, but I liked best
"Foolin' Myself," "Easy Living," "Mean to Me," and "I Must Have That
Man," the songs I knew so well, sung with an unexpected authority. Almost thirty years later, home after a difficult & lonely journey of some
months, I played "Easy Living," & that night years earlier in Detroit came
back to me with undeniable force.

Songs

Dawn coming in over the fields
of darkness takes me by surprise
and I look up from my solitary road
pleased not to be alone, the birds
now choiring from the orange groves
huddling to the low hills. But sorry
that this night has ended, a night

in which you spoke of how little love
we seemed to have known and all of it
going from one of us to the other.
You could tell the words took me
by surprise, as they often will, and you
grew shy and held me away for a while,
your eyes enormous in the darkness,
almost as large as your hunger
to see and be seen over and over.

30 years ago I heard a woman sing
of the motherless child sometimes
she felt like. In a white dress
this black woman with a gardenia
in her hair leaned on the piano
and stared out into the breathing darkness
of unknown men and women needing
her songs. There were those among
us who cried, those who rejoiced
that she was back before us for a time,
a time not to be much longer, for
the voice was going and the habits
slowly becoming all there was of her.

And I believe that night she cared
for the purity of the songs and not
much else. Oh, she still saw
the slow gathering of that red dusk
that hovered over her cities, and no
doubt dawns like this one caught
her on the roads from job to job,
but the words she'd lived by were
drained of mystery as this sky
is now, and there was no more "Easy
Living" and she was "Miss Brown" to
no one and no one was her "Lover Man."
The only songs that mattered were wordless
like those rising in confusion from
the trees or wind-songs that waken
the grass that slept a century, that
waken me to how far we've come.

Went one spring to the Paradise Theater on Woodward Avenue—the main drag of Detroit—to see Art Tatum & instead got Erroll Garner. A guy came out on the stage to announce that Tatum's flight was delayed, but he was going to make it, and until he did we would have Garner playing without bass or drums. With short breaks Garner went on bravely for what seemed like several hours. I confess it felt like a lot of Garner. Finally after 11 PM the great man arrived with a bassist and a drummer. They got right into it after Tatum thanked the audience for staying—I would guess more than half of us had declined the offer of a refund & stayed to hear him play non-stop for hours. The next evening, near the Flame Show Bar, on John R, I saw Tatum & the bass player. I crossed the street intending to thank him; I was also curious to know what a genius would talk about: I suspected it would be a discussion of the works of Darius Milhaud or Stravinksy. What I actually heard I recorded in the poem "On the Corner."

On the Corner

Standing on the corner
until Tatum passed
blind as the sea,
heavy, tottering
on the arm of the young
bass player, and they
both talking
Jackie Robinson.
It was cold, late,
and the Flame Show Bar
was crashing
for the night, even
Johnny Ray
calling it quits.
Tatum said, Can't
believe how fast
he is to first. Wait'll
you see Mays
the bass player said.

Women in white furs
spilled out of the bars
and trickled toward
the parking lot. Now
it could rain, coming
straight down. The man
in the brown hat
never turned his head up.
The gutters swirled
their heavy waters,
the streets reflected
the sky, which was
nothing. Tatum
stamped on toward
the Bland Hotel, a wet
newspaper stuck
to his shoe, his mouth
open, his vest
drawn and darkening.
I can't hardly wait, he said.

It took me years to realize how beautiful was the modesty of Erroll Garner that night at the Paradise. He knew the audience had come to hear Tatum, he certainly knew—as a gifted musician—how great a difference there was between his command & Tatum's, yet he did his best. I didn't then appreciate how heroic Garner was; I hadn't yet learned that the world is over-populated with people who never tire of hearing themselves. I was only just starting to meet other poets.

Saw Bird in an intimate setting in Detroit only once. (First saw the legend with JATP at Masonic Temple, but those evenings were dominated by Illinois Jacquet playing "How High the Moon" with such fervor & showmanship he got us all to screaming.) At the Flame Show Bar, Parker seated in a wooden kitchen chair did not even stand to solo. He looked both stunned & stoned. His playing was absolutely Bird, a succession of the very miracles I'd heard on records. The tone seemed even more pure, the slow numbers even more plaintive. Before I left I went up to shake his hand; haggard and pale, he never stood to take my hand nor even looked up.

One Friday afternoon I heard that Sonny Stitt was going to sit in with Gene Ammons that night at a dance hall on the east side. I was going to Wayne part-time & working full-time afternoons; I decided to skip work. All of my jazz buddies were busy with one thing or another, so I read in the library until it closed that Friday night and then walked the long blocks alone to find an enormous mob of kids my own age & younger waiting to get in, and it was worth the long wait. Stitt & Ammons battled good-spiritedly for hours with Sonny mainly playing tenor with a huge tone & wonderful resourcefulness. A dance hall where no one danced. Forty years later, living in a tiny apartment in Nashville, I heard Sonny on the radio (a fortuitous event in Tennessee) & was inspired to try to catch the magic of that long-ago night:

> Sonny was dazzling. The story went
> he'd just gotten out of Lexington
> the day before, was still clean, and could
> do it all on tenor and alto.
> When the last set ended I waited
> to thank him but so many people
> crowded around I gave up and left,
> walked the seven blocks to the streetcar,
> stood stamping in the cold, humming "My
> Funny Valentine" feeling happier
> than I ever expected to feel . . .
>   "It just gets you
> some kind of way," somebody once said.
> The man was talking about Ma Rainey,
> but it's all the same, music with words,
> music without words, words alone,
> the city streets silently turning
> toward the light, the still darkened houses
> holding their tongues while a man dances
> before them, content to be alone.

Dizzy's great band, the orchestra, playing on a Saturday night at the Paradise Theater, 1948 or '49. I walked in while they were playing "One

Bass Hit": the brass went off like the 4th of July, & then Dizzy himself came on, faster & higher than even Little Jazz. I'd never heard anything so powerful and disciplined.

In '51 in a huge place in Flint, size of a basketball stadium, I heard him again with John Lewis, Cecil Payne, & the wonderful tenor player James Moody, who insisted I was an FBI agent: he could tell by my shoes, the big heavy, black clodhoppers I wore to work. I couldn't tell if Moody was serious or not; he & Cecil Payne accepted a ride back to Detroit in my little Ford two-door. By the time I got home the birds were singing. I was struck that night by the number & loveliness of the young groupies hanging around the band & the degree to which the musicians seemed to ignore them. Reminded me of Dylan Thomas at the 92nd Street Y in NYC, except Thomas did not ignore them.

An afternoon jazz concert on the second floor of the student union building at Wayne, a converted hotel used mainly to house students. Began with duets with Kenny Burrell & Tommy Flanagan. Kenny, tall & shy, looked all of seventeen, & had already grown into that blues voice that would mark his playing. Tommy, short, compact, perhaps a few years older, barely looked at the audience. His mastery for so young a player was remarkable: one heard echoes of Tatum, Bud, but he was less ornate than the former & more lyrical than the latter. He was then just twenty but already an accomplished artist.

In the second session they were joined by Pepper Adams, whom I'd known as a great wit & aspiring fiction writer (he'd said he hoped to be the F. Scott Fitzgerald of the Be-Bop age, our age). When he opened up on the baritone it was hard to believe that skinny, baby-faced boy wonder could get so much sound out of the great machine. Tall, bespectacled, with the complexion of a squid, Pepper looked like a candidate for a degree in mortuary science, but in fact he was already bringing to his playing the wit & drive that later marked his style.

Bess Bonier & then Barry Harris replaced Tommy; Elvin Jones joined them on drums. What my classmates were in truth teaching me was that it was possible to be a kid from Detroit & an artist. And that if you worked hard enough at your art you could create original, beautiful works and just possibly live off your art. This was the first proof I saw it could be done, and those young musicians—several younger than I— were my early inspiration, living proof it could be done if you had the discipline & the desire; nothing was more obvious than that these young players knew their instruments & the history of the music they played & that they burned with the need to make music.

About that time Bess & I were classmates in a humanities course, & she & I wrote both music & poetry together. In fact it was the first time I showed my poems to more than one person. Her poems were better than my musical compositions; she taught me a lot about chord structures & musical accent & I helped her with the use of imagery. One time we were together on the Woodward streetcar when a woman, seeing Bess was blind, gasped & said, "Oh, my dear, you've lost your sight!" Bess: "How careless of me." Later Bess said, "She tried to make me feel like a penny waiting for change." I have never regretted not going to the University of Michigan or east to one of the Ivy League schools with their much published English departments, for what I got from Wayne was unique & changed my vision of what was possible.

A summer evening in the early '50s, Bess & Elvin playing behind Stan Getz in an outdoor venue. Getz I'd already seen with the Woody Herman band at one of the big downtown picture palaces, & I'd fallen in love with his sound. Up close he looked like a movie star; up even closer you could tell he knew it. Bess was pissed off at him for playing the great man. The Getz sound was gorgeous, clearly cooler & slicker than any of the local tenormen, but the playing was minimal at best. He seemed determined to give just as much as he was being paid to give. Bess said he regarded her & Elvin with mild respect & the audience with contempt. The truth was the audience was used to better stuff. It must have been hard on these brilliant young musicians, people like Bess, Elvin, Tommy, Kenny, Pepper, & Barry Harris, who knew they had the gift as well as the musicianship to play with people their own age & with big names but no more artistry. My classmates were in there for the long haul, & the best & the luckiest later made their names, but what they seemed far more determined to do was to make their music.

Kenny Burrell got a Sunday gig at some sort of hotel in the downriver area of Detroit, a very unlikely place to hear jazz; it was not as far downriver as Dearborn, where the only blacks welcomed were those on their way to work at the giant Ford Rouge plant. These were wonderful sessions, for not only were all of the best of the local musicians present, but the best of the visitors from the big bands would drop in & were usually invited to play. And it was so inexpensive that even I could attend regularly. Curiously, the Sunday I recall most clearly was one on which I arrived too late to hear the music. Years later, living in Somerville, Massachusetts, & hearing of the death of Pepper Adams, I was moved to record it in a poem.

The Wrong Turn

There are those who will tell you
that the shortest way to get
to NYC is by way of Buffalo,
but back in 1949 if you left
Detroit at 2 AM when the clubs
were closing down, and the car—a '48
Studebaker that looked as though
it were going in two directions
at the same time—was owned by
Frenchman Jack, who along with
Pepper Adams was about to be
drafted, then why not misread
all the road signs and go by way
of Columbus, Ohio? Pepper was not
yet the greatest baritone saxophonist
—he was 21—, but he was good,
so on a Saturday night he was working.
And he was tired. The Frenchman
had been out all day scrounging
money and supplies, so he was tired.

I, the driver, had been recovering
from a week of polishing plumbing parts,
which meant sleeping in until noon,
then clearing the debris out of my room,
which meant sweeping the rug with
precision and intensity so the reds
glowed like fire in the afternoon
and the Persian blues settled in.
Oh, how a man can love a rug

when it warms his only floor!
35 years ago, so I've forgotten
why I went to NYC and even
how I got back, I've forgotten
who I stayed with and whether
or not I walked the streets at night
wondering that so many lives
behind glass were not mine or if
I filtered through the bookstores
on 3rd searching for words that could
become mine so that I might say
what I did not yet have to say. I
recall that night I stood in the rain
for almost an hour, too shy even
to speak to the girl who waited
beside me for the bus. I recall
that I arrived too late to hear
even a single number. The bar
was closed, so I watched Pepper
remove the mouthpiece and wipe
it carefully with a handkerchief
and stow the huge sax meticulously
in its garnet plush lined case
which I carried out to the car
while he said goodbye to Kenny,
Elvin, and Tommy. In the dark
the Frenchman gave me a swig
of something hot and vile and I
almost gagged. They settled down
in the back, we decided to go
by way of Toledo, and they
talked and smoked and snoozed by turns
until there was silence. After
Toledo it was all two lane,
no cars and no lights. The wet
fields of Ohio rushed by, rich
and autumnal, looming with presences
I couldn't imagine. I remember
the first sign that read "Columbus 45,"
and the next that said "Columbus 14,"

and I pulled over on the shoulder
of the road and turned on the map light.
Out of the back Pepper asked, "Where
are we," and I answered, "Columbus"
because I thought that was where
we were. When Jack awakened
Pepper told him "Columbus."
We all three began laughing,
until we cried we laughed so hard.

In 1953 I escaped a terrible marriage & a host of financial problems
& so decided to pursue seriously a life in poetry; I wandered in the East
for a time, & except for a night of Bud Powell on 52nd Street saw almost
no jazz & lacking a record player heard only what my car radio gave me.
Out of money in the summer of '54 I returned to Detroit; & at Klein's
Show Bar on 12th Street my first night home heard Milt Jackson. An extraordinary performance: Good as he was on record, it was only a shadow
of the playing I heard that night in a bar jammed to overflowing. During the months to come I heard many of the emerging jazz giants of
our town: Paul Chambers, Frank Rosolino (who filled whatever room he
played in without ever sounding too loud), and Elvin playing better than
ever. I was working long days refinishing used bearings that were probably sold for new, so I had the time & money to discover Yusef Lateef & to
hear Tatum out on Livernois. One night Kenny Burrell sat in & the place
rocked with that Detroit blues sound destined to become more & more
the signature of my city.

I've always envied the jazz musician, the ability to break into new
song day after day, night after night, to be able to listen and answer to
his or her fellow musicians. I love the fact that jazz has so much room
for so many; you don't have to be Bird or Pres or Tatum to play with a
genius; the art leaves room for the good journeymen who do their best.
By comparison poetry is so utterly solitary & interior. I think of young
Wardell playing at the Bluebird with abandon & control, his artistry become body, muscles, breath, the stuff of life, maybe even digestion. I see
in memory the whole person alive in the song, body & soul. Fantastic to
experience something so total. The thrill of speaking through those ancient, inert metals mined from the earth & perhaps themselves stunned

to be making music. What must it be like to make these *things*—this horn, this big bellied wooden bass, this skin stretched over steel—make all that is lifeless come to life.

❄ ❄ ❄ ❄

Above Jazz

> A friend told me
> He'd risen above jazz.
> I leave him there.
> —Michael Harper

There is that music that the hammer
makes when it hits the nail squarely
and the wood opens with a sigh. There is
the music of the bones growing, of
teeth biting into bread, of the baker
making bread, slapping the dusted loaf
as though it were a breathing stone.
There has always been the music
of the stars, soundless and glittering
in the winter air, and the moon's
full song, loon-like and heard only
by someone far from home who glances
up to the southern sky for help and finds
the unfamiliar cross and for a moment
wonders if he or the heavens
have lost their way. Most perfect
is the music heard in sleep—the breath
suspends itself above the body, the soul
returns to the room having gone in dreams
to some far shore and entered water
only to rise and fall again and rise
a final time dressed in the rags of time
and made the long trip home to the body,
cast-off and senseless, because it is
the only instrument it has. Listen, stop
talking, stop breathing. That is music,
whatever you hear, even if it's
only the simple pulse, the tides

of blood tugging toward the heart
and back on the long voyage that must
always take them home. Even if you
hear nothing, the breathless earth
asleep, the oceans at last at rest,
the sun frozen before dawn and the peaks
of the eastern mountains upright, cold,
and silent. All that you do not hear
and never can is music, and in the dark
creation dances around the single center
that would be listening if it could.

Haki R. Madhubuti

12

Where the Call Needs to Be Heard
Haki R. Madhubuti

At the time of this interview, the downstairs offices for Third World Press did not have air conditioning, and when I arrived, the whir of fans sounded like the inside of an airplane. In the hallway, a framed print by Romare Bearden warped dramatically from years of humidity. The receptionist said that Mr. Madhubuti would be down in a few minutes. I opened my shirt a bit and prepared for an uncomfortable afternoon. But shortly after his appearance, those concerns disappeared: Madhubuti's expansive office upstairs wasn't at all humid, and his demeanor—direct, friendly, open—let me know conversation would not be strained.

In addition to displaying Third World Press publications and other books, his office featured a variety of art and artifacts, including a large, colorful painting of Madhubuti from the 1960s when he was known as Don L. Lee. Its prominent location almost demanded a response, although my commentary could have been more astute: "That's nice," I said. Haki pointed to the portrait and, in a half-disconnected tone, replied, "Yeah—look at old Don up there."

For most of his career, Haki Madhubuti has promoted the work of other writers, and in listening to him speak, it became clear that his generous spirit has been energized by his own inspiring mentors. Throughout the conversation, for example, he repeatedly mentioned the importance of Gwendolyn Brooks, at one point saying, "Ms. Brooks—well, Gwen—she's like a mother. That's how close we've become over the years."

Just prior to going to press—on December 3, 2000, almost exactly three months after the interview—he telephoned to say that Ms. Brooks had died. I stopped production of the journal so as to reprint several of his tribute poems to Brooks (he's written many), and to dedicate the issue to her memory. It gave the publication an inescapably elegiac tone, but I'm glad that during our conversation he could speak of her as he did.

Haki R. Madhubuti is the author of more than twenty books, including *GroundWork: New and Selected Poems; Black Men: Obsolete, Single, Dangerous?;* and *Yellow Black: The First Twenty-one Years of a Poet's Life.* His many honors include fellowships from the National Endowment for the Arts and the National Endowment for the Humanities, as well as the Illinois Arts Council Award and the American Book Award. In 1967, he founded Third World Press, for which he remains publisher and chairman of the board. In 1969, he co-founded the Institute of Positive Education/New Concept School, and in 1998, he co-founded the Betty Shabazz International Charter School.

The following reprinted material corresponds to works and themes raised during our conversation. The interview took place in Chicago at Third World Press on September 1, 2000.

Don't Cry, Scream

> *for John Coltrane*/ from a black poet/
> in a basement apt. crying dry tears of "you ain't gone"
> Don L. Lee / Haki R. Madhubuti

into the sixties
a trane
came/out of the
fifties with a
golden boxcar
riding the rails
of novation.
        blowing

a-melodics
screeching,
screaming,
blasting—
> driving some away,
> (those paper readers who thought
> manhood was something innate)

> bring others in,
> (the few who didn't believe that the
> world existed around established whi
> teness & leonard bernstein)

music that ached.
murdered our minds (we reborn)
born into a neoteric aberration.
& suddenly
you envy the
BLIND man—
you know that he will
hear what you'll never
see.

> your music is like
> my head—nappy black/
> a good nasty feel with
> tangled songs of:
>> we-eeeeeeeeee   sing
>> WE-EEEeeeeeeeee   loud &
>> WE-EEEEEEE EEEEEEEEEE   high
>>   with
>>   feeling

a people playing
the sound of me when
i combed it. combed at
it.

i cried for billie holiday.
the blues. we ain't blue
the blues exhibited illusions of manhood.
destroyed by you. Ascension into:

```
scream-eeeeeeeeeeeeee-ing        sing
SCREAM-EEEeeeeeeeeeee-ing        loud &
SCREAM-EEEEEEEEEEE EEE-ing  long with
                                 feeling
```

we ain't blue, we are black.
we ain't blue, we are black.
      (all the blues did was
      make me cry)
soultrane gone on a trip
he left man images
he was a life-style of
man-makers & annihilator
of attache case carriers.

Trane done went.
(got his hat & left me one)

naw brother,
i didn't cry,
i just—

```
Scream-eeeeeeeeeeeeee e-ed             sing loud
SCREAM-EEEEEEEEEEEEEEEEEEE-ED          & high with
  we-eeeeeeeeeeeeeeeeeeeeeee ee        feeling
  WE-E-EEEEEeeeeeeeee EEEEEEEE         letting
  WE-EEEEEEEEEEEEEEEEEEEEEEEE          yr/voice
  WHERE YOU DONE GONE, BROTHER?        break
```

it hurts, grown babies
dying. born. done caught me
a trane. steel wheels broken
by popsicle sticks. i went out
& tried to buy a nickel bag
with my standard oil card.

blonds had more fun—
with snagga-tooth niggers
who saved pennies & pop bottles for week-ends
to play negro & other filthy inventions.
be-bop-en to james brown's
cold sweat—these niggers didn't sweat,
they perspired. & the blond's dye came out,
i ran. she did too, with his pennies, pop bottles

& his mind. tune in next week same time same station
for anti-self in one lesson.

to the negro cow-sissies
who did tchaikovsky &
the beatles & live in
split-level homes & had
split-level minds & babies.
who committed the act of
love with their clothes on.

> (who hid in the bathroom to read
> jet mag., who didn't read the chicago
> defender because of the misspelled
> words & had shelves of books by
> europeans on display. untouched. who
> hid their little richard & lightnin'
> slim records & asked: "John who?"
> instant hate.)

they didn't know any better,
brother, they were too busy getting
into debt, expressing humanity &
taking off color.

SCREAMMMM/we-eeeee/screech/teee   improvise
aheeeeeeeee/screeeeeee/theeee/ee   with
ahHHHHHHHHH/WEEEEEEEE/scrEEE   feeling
    EEEE
we-eeeeeWE-EEEEEEEEWE-EE-EEEEE
the ofays heard you &
were wiped out. spaced.
one clown asked me during,
my favorite things, if
you were practicing.
i fired on the muthafucka & said,
"i'm practicing."

naw brother,
i didn't cry.
i got high off my thoughts—
they kept coming back,
back to destroy me.

& that BLIND man
i don't envy him anymore
i can see his hear
& hear his heard through my pores.
i can see my me. it was truth you gave,
like a daily shit
it had to come.

can you scream—brother?   very
can you scream—brother?   soft

i hear you.
i hear you.

and the Gods will too.

Are Black Musicians Serious?
(excerpt)
Haki R. Madhubuti

The black musician's inability to deal with the economic and business side of their profession has ruled them ineffective in the real world. This deficiency is not necessarily due to ignorance or stupidity of the economic and business world, but to the immediate priority—their music. In the end, their priority ends up being anti-music and anti-black. There is a saying among black musicians that is articulated in many ways—"we make it and they take it." Who own the record companies? White people. Who own the major publications that write about music? White people. Who own all the clubs? White people. Who have authored the so-called "major" texts on black music? White people. Who are the major record distributors? White people.

However, at some point in a man's life, it becomes not enough to keep blowing hot air at the *man;* when do we as responsible people begin to critically assess the collective problem we face? After all, the white boy didn't force musicians to sign padded contracts—all he did was provide a pen. We, ultimately, at some level have to admit failure in doing the necessary homework. From the concert hall to the basement "jazz" clubs; from AM and FM radio to the airwaves of UHF and VHF; from record companies to record clubs; from the college concert to neighborhood jukeboxes—we have let Anglo-Saxons, Italians, and Jewish pimps dictate to our people what they must hear and what they must buy. We have let them, in effect, define what "soul" music is. . . .

The positive side of the whole black music disaster is that we have learned much from what little black music we've received. Most black writers/poets, known and unknown, have at some time or another given credit to black music for inspiration and direction. Black artists have, time and time again, used black music as a source for their growth and vision. Black music is the major impetus other than black life itself for the whole wealth of creativity that we possess. Black music is used at every level of human involvement in the black community.

Amiri
Haki R. Madhubuti

baraka
"always
come in a
        place
later."
rushin to catch words that came before him
tho that don't much matter,
him got his own words, music, dance, dramatics
& bright ideas even if some of them used cars
& don't work.   but baraka works
works harder than 15 men his age,
da, da da, do   who been around
long enough to tell his time
in places where people have tried to
beat the beat & tempo out of his talk & walk.
monk, trane & duke played secrets
that saved him and us even if we didn't
accurately hear their da da, doos
baraka did, they spoke musically to him.
he gave us his many languages and genius.
his comin in time is gettin better & best & less late,
even for this sage still makin up stories
actin on his own stage & firing truthpoems
that compel liars & politicians to exit early and often.

SASCHA FEINSTEIN: I want to start in the past and move to the present. How central do you think jazz was to the Black Arts Movement of the 1960s?

HAKI MADHUBUTI: It was more than central. Jazz—or our classical black music—was probably like blood and oxygen. I'm really serious about that. What people have to understand is that the serious musicians have always been ahead, consciously and culturally. Many of them cannot handle their *personal* lives. Many of them do not understand anything about finance. But in terms of philosophical thought, in terms of black thought—between African American people and their connections to Africa—they've just been ahead.

I found the music early. I came out of the Lower East Side of Detroit, Michigan, and the West Side of Chicago, coming from a very disadvantaged and materially impoverished background, and the music was almost like a schoolmate for me, primarily because I had to grow up very quickly. I didn't have a childhood. (I always say I grew up around pimps and hoes slammin' Cadillac doors.) I was always around the music. My mother was a barmaid at one of the best nightclubs in Detroit, Sonny Wilson's, and Billie Holiday seemed to be her alter-ego. Certainly Motown was there—popular music, rhythm and blues— and my father, who was never with us, *did* attempt to play trombone. And I fell in love with the trumpet.

I listened often to Louis Armstrong, but I was really too young to realize the artistry of Louis Armstrong. Then I found Miles Davis, and I said, "God, I want to be like *that* guy." I was in the seventh or eighth grade—junior high school—and I went to the band master in this basically all-white school and asked if I could join the band, learn how to play trumpet. And he said, "No." I asked, "Why not?" and he said, "Well, you don't have enough air in you." [Laughs.] I'm six-one, about a hundred and thirty-one pounds, all right? I said, "What?!" and he said, "Well, you're not big enough." That was his way of saying, "You're not getting into this band," because the band was all white.

At that time, I was working two paper routes. I was cleaning up bars and taverns at night. And on the way home from work one day— I was about thirteen or fourteen years old—I passed a pawn shop (the poor man's bank). This trumpet's in the window, so I go into the pawn shop and ask the man who owned the shop, "How much is that trumpet?" He said, "Thirty-three dollars." This is the '50s. I said, "I don't have thirty-three dollars, but can I work out a deal with you?" This is a Jewish pawn shop owner. He said, "I'll let you have the trumpet for a dollar a week, and I'll give you lessons." For a dollar a week! I said, "Yeah." He said, "But before I give you the trumpet, you have to bring in a down payment—let's say, three dollars." I thought, "This is amazing." This was my first introduction to credit.

So I worked hard, 'cause most of my money went to help the household, but I told my mother I wanted to do this, and she said, "Okay. Go ahead and try it." And I got the trumpet, and I began to take lessons.

FEINSTEIN: Was he any good as a teacher?

MADHUBUTI: He was good enough to teach *me*. He played several instruments, and evidently he was teaching other young people, too. But the next semester, I went back to the band and not only got in but took first chair.

By then I was listening closely to Miles and Louis Armstrong and, of course, Dizzy Gillespie—[Madhubuti points to a poster of Gillespie hanging above and to his left]—who became a model. And I was very good—through high school—and I got a scholarship, but things happened in the family and I ended up not taking it, I had to move.

FEINSTEIN: A scholarship for—?

MADHUBUTI: For the trumpet, to college. See what happened was, I came out of junior high school and went to one of the finest high schools in the country—Cass Tech, in Detroit. I studied music, and was pretty good, although I realized then that I was not as good as I needed to be or could be, primarily because the white trumpet players there had been playing practically since infancy, with private lessons and everything. What held me down in terms of high school was that I didn't have the time to develop my musical skills. In Detroit, I was also in the All-City band. My mother OD'd when I was sixteen years old. And as a result of that, I left Detroit and came to Chicago—on my own.

But music has been a cultural companion for me, and I would dare say that this is true for most of the serious writers that I was associated with in the Black Arts Movement. All the poets that we work with in Chicago [at Third World Press] have their own musical tastes. Sterling Plumpp is basically into blues. (I was primarily into jazz and doo-wop.) The women poets . . . Carolyn Rodgers and Johari Amiri, they both like progressive black music. Hoyt Fuller, who was in many ways one of my mentors: He liked progressive black music, also. Kalamu ya Salaam is an authority on black music. [Sonia] Sanchez, Baraka, and [Keorapetse] Kgositsile are inspired by black music.

I don't think I could have done the work that I have—and been involved with many of the poets nationally—if music had not been a part of my life. In fact, we have published three musicians who are also poets: Gil Scott-Heron, Mari Evans, and Kahil El'Zabar.

FEINSTEIN: As a poet, you're probably best known for the poetry collection *Don't Cry, Scream.*

MADHUBUTI: Probably so—as Don L. Lee, yes. Over its life, and it is still in print, *Don't Cry, Scream* has sold close to half a million copies. We never hear of these kind of sales in the United States. I understand that it was not unusual in the former U.S.S.R. for poets like Yevgeny Yevtushenko to sell in the millions.

FEINSTEIN: The title poem to your collection is driven by the music of John Coltrane.

MADHUBUTI: Absolutely. And all of that plays into where I'm at today. John Coltrane was a man of integrity more than anything else. Obviously, his music drove me. But for me, he set a standard, set a bar, that a lot of other musicians had not done. Because, indeed, I was influenced by Lee Morgan, Freddie Hubbard, and many of the other trumpet players of the time, but John Coltrane had a spiritual side of him, and I think he was on a different mission than the other musicians of his time. And that's how that poem came out.

When I was writing *Don't Cry, Scream* [in the late 1960s], I lived in an apartment about the size of my desk over there and I shared it with other animals. The only luxury I had was music. I didn't have money to go to clubs and things like that, but I would buy many of my records secondhand. My books, too—everything. I grew up in secondhand stores; I grew up in used books stores; I grew up in Salvation Army stores. So it was not a problem for me to go into dusty bins. My personal collection of albums from the '60s and '70s—and I really started buying a lot in the '80s—[totals] about six thousand albums. (I'm still trying to decide what I'm going to do with them.) So, yes: The music was critical, crucial.

FEINSTEIN: What about the politics of Coltrane's music? That poem ["Don't Cry, Scream"] was published in '69, within a year of dozens and dozens of John Coltrane poems—which has a lot to do with his death in '67, but more with his music.

MADHUBUTI: Right.

FEINSTEIN: So many of those poems interpret his music as political statements related to Black Nationalism.

MADHUBUTI: Right. It was highly unlikely to be a black musician coming out of the '40s and '50s and not be political. The black musicians lived in legal apartheid in the United States. John Coltrane had experienced pain and rejection like most black people. However, it is indeed the artist who must try to transcend one's own suffering in order to paint a picture of a better world. Yes, we hear black suffering in his music, but when he left Miles Davis to organize the Coltrane Quartet—with McCoy Tyner, Jimmy Garrison, and Elvin Jones—his music sounded like what Albert Ayler called "a visit from another planet," noting that his music was deep peace and spiritual.

FEINSTEIN: Why do you think Coltrane himself shied away from talking about politics?

MADHUBUTI: I think he reached a level in his life [in the late '60s] that he truly became himself. He was born in 1926, and by '66 he was just forty years old, which is still young for an accomplished artist.

I no longer go on marches or take part in much street demonstrations. For me, the mission is to write as well as I can, and to build this company [Third World Press], and to build our schools [Institute of Positive Education/New Concept School and Betty Shabazz International Charter School]. Three missions. (My children are pretty much grown now.) For Trane . . . I mean, you grow up in the music community, you see a lot of death, you definitely see a lot of poverty— poverty of spirit, poverty of the material—and you get to a point in your life when you say, "I may not have that much time." Whether he knew that he was ill or not doesn't really matter. You just know that what you see around you is not going well. I think he had moved into another realm of spirit, another realm of knowledge. His knowledge base had increased tremendously. Alice Coltrane obviously was a big part of his life. And I think he thought, "Now I've got to concentrate totally on this music." And he did.

When I heard his music, I heard that very spiritual side. At the same time, I heard anger—but the anger seemed to be a mature anger, saying, "We've got to deal with the problems, but they've got to be dealt with in a way in which more people are not hurt." This is very important, because after I really got into Trane, my whole philosophy changed: "How do we move this community?" Prior to Trane, I was more "anti": anti this, anti that. And when I started seriously listening to Coltrane's music, and reading a lot more outside of my culture, I realized that was not the way to go. I began to concentrate on: "What are we *for*?" Define what you're for, and then do the thing that's not expected of poets: Try to build it.

And that's when I hooked up with Margaret Burroughs and Charlie Burroughs at the DuSable Museum [of African American History] in Chicago; hooking up with Dudley Randall, who was my first publisher, and who passed about two weeks ago [August 5, 2000]; started Third World Press [in 1967]; and in '69, started the Institute of Positive Education. And I began to write about what we could do. I moved away from what I consider to be very boisterous rhetoric to ideas that work.

I think that's what Coltrane was doing in his music: He was moving out toward ideas that inspired. That's how I felt, and that's how the poem came to be. And that's why I think he remains one of the most important musicians to come out of the twentieth century, or any century. His music will live and endure. He was so far ahead of everybody else that when Impulse! finally released *Transition* and *Sun Ship* in 1972—they'd been put on tape in 1965—some people thought that he was still alive because his music was so fresh and innovative.

The Coltrane Quartet was the group all serious musicians listened to and copied. Coltrane reinvented the sound of the saxophone. Most saxophone players incorporated the licks of John Coltrane. The great Pharoah Sanders and Archie Shepp quickly come to mind.

FEINSTEIN: Who would you say are some of the strongest writers to incorporate jazz into their work?

MADHUBUTI: Baraka would be close to the top of the list. Quincy Troupe. Eugene Redmond. Sister out of New York—Jayne Cortez. Sonia Sanchez. I think music has influenced them a great deal, especially Jayne Cortez. She's just marvelous, what she does with the music. Ntozake Shange, also; she's very influenced. Michael Harper has that very important poem, "Dear John, Dear Coltrane." Ishmael Reed is also very good. He's close to Baraka in his use of musical motif. A lot of people don't know that because he's primarily known for his fiction. Askia Touré and Kalamu ya Salaam are master poets who incorporate music in their work.

FEINSTEIN: Reed's fiction is infused with jazz, too.

MADHUBUTI: Oh yeah. He's on it, as is Al Young, Clarence Major, Lucille Clifton, and A. B. Spellman. Larry Neal and Sherley Anne Williams are poets who helped to set new standards in musical poetry.

FEINSTEIN: Why do you think they've incorporated the music successfully?

MADHUBUTI: Well, most of them are still alive and still functioning. Coming out of the '60s, you know, there were a whole lot of poets, like Askia Touré, that hit the scene, but very few of us are still around. They may still be alive, but they stopped producing. But those I mentioned, with the exceptions of Larry Neal and Sherley Anne Williams, are still going very strong, and all of them realized the developmental aspects of good music. The two oldest arts are music and dance, and most black poets and writers understand rhythm and the source of rhythm: The beat, or meter, is music.

I think that listening to Trane, Miles, Louis Armstrong, Duke, Billie Holiday, Bird, Quincy Jones, Shepp, Wynton Marsalis, J. J. Johnson, Ella, Nancy Wilson, and hundreds of others may not be enough to satisfy one's intellectual demands. Over the last twenty-nine years or so, there has been a sizeable body of literature on black music published. Baraka's *Blues People* and *Black Music* [published under the name LeRoi Jones] are excellent. *Miles: The Autobiography* by Miles Davis and Quincy Troupe, *Jazz People: As Serious as Your Life* by Valerie Wilmer, *I Put a Spell on You* by Nina Simone, *Coltrane: A Biography* by Dr. C. O. Simpkins, and *Mingus/Mingus: Two Memoirs* by Janet Coleman and Al Young are all serious books on the lives of black musicians and their music. Two excellent books on the cultural history of black music are *The Death of Rhythm and Blues* by Nelson George and *What the Music Said* by Mark Anthony Neal.

FEINSTEIN: You've publicly attacked the quality of recent African American literature anthologies because of important voices that you feel have been omitted. Is Touré among those writers?

MADHUBUTI: Yes, he'd be among them, and Redmond. And Jayne [Cortez]; she's left out of most of them. Sterling Plumpp, Angela Jackson, Julia Fields, Kalamu ya Salaam, Samuel Allen, Naomi Long Madgett, to name a few.

FEINSTEIN: [Henry Louis] Gates [Jr.]'s anthology [*The Norton Anthology of African American Literature*] included just one of Jayne's poems. One poem.

MADHUBUTI: That was the main anthology I was talking about. Houston Baker was the person who did the part about the Black Arts Movement, and a lot of the material that he wrote about me was just totally inaccurate and unscholarly.

FEINSTEIN: What would you have changed?

MADHUBUTI: He made a statement about my feelings towards Jewish people in general, as if I'm anti-Semitic, and I'm not. I'm critical—not only of Jewish people but black people, Irish people, Polish people, and so forth. So I thought it was a very small statement.

That's one. Two: He doesn't have any idea what I am doing. He has never been here [to Third World Press or the schools]. He's never *been* here. I think the last time Houston Baker came through, we were over on Cottage Grove in a store front. This is now a multi-million dollar investment, and I have not changed my values, okay? I'm trying to say, we can be black and conscious and cultural, and we don't have to sell out. The black public intellectuals are at Harvard, University of Pennsylvania, Yale, and so forth; I'm at Chicago State, which is a black university on the South Side of Chicago, and that is a choice. I left Iowa and came down to Chicago. My choice is: If one is true to the calling, then you go where the call needs to be heard the greatest. I felt that the call was not being heard in Iowa, but here on the South Side of Chicago is a university that services about 7,500 black students, about 500 Hispanic students, and maybe 500 white students. Some people *talk* blackness, but when it comes to putting your money and your actions where you said your values are, it becomes another question.

I will say that Cornell West *does* work with some structures that he's trying to build, but as far as a lot of these other people, I don't know what they're doing in the black community other than writing and speaking about it and making an excellent living—a living that most black musicians will never experience.

FEINSTEIN: What works of your own would you say have been most influenced by jazz?

MADHUBUTI: "Don't Cry, Scream." Probably *We Walk the Way of the New World,* because I was back and forth between an African sensibility and African American sensibility, and music was a large part of that. There's an essay in *From Plan to Planet* ["Are Black Musicians Serious?"] on black musicians—how, for the most part, they've lost control of their music from the business side. I never wrote too much about the music because I never felt qualified. I could do it, I think, more in the poetry than the prose. In *Book of Life,* a lot of those poems, especially in the first part of the book, were heavily influenced by music. And a lot of the poems I'm working on now go back to it.

One of the problems with me has been trying to work a job to make a living, keep our school going, build the publishing company, travel to make money and to spread the word, and maintain a family—my wife [Dr. Safisha Madhubuti] and I have been married twenty-seven years; we have three children, and I had two children before, and all our children are doing very well. (I've always felt that if I don't do well by my children, I don't have no right to write about family-building.) So I've been trying to maintain all of this, and I feel that, if you talk about revolutionary work, this is what my life has been about. I've learned this from Dudley Randall and Margaret Burroughs, primarily, because I feel that one of the most revolutionary acts that we can be about in terms of autonomy is building independent black institutions and making a payroll. It'll age you rather quickly. But in the over twenty-seven years of our school, and over thirty-three years of our press, I haven't missed a payroll, or filed for bankruptcy, though I've been close to both of them, many times. And I have lost many, many hours of sleep because what I do or don't do impacts on the economic livelihood of many people.

FEINSTEIN: One of the reasons why I admire your accomplishments is because of your selflessness, the amount of time and energy that you've spent on behalf of others—especially the schools and the press. I find that truly important. The books are beautiful, and so many of the voices would not be heard without your efforts. So I want to thank you.

MADHUBUTI: That means an awful lot. You know in your own work that there are very few thank you's. I've worked a lot with black people who most certainly have experienced horrors in this country and the world, but sometimes black people, even the people that we publish, forget to say, "Thank you." That means an awful lot.

That's one of the reasons why I love Gwendolyn Brooks so much. She taught me a lot about friendship and kindness. Gwendolyn Brooks's creed is kindness. How do you express kindness? Well, you express it whenever you can, and one of the easiest ways of doing that is to say, "Yes." Just say, "Yes" to life, and try to do it. My mentors—Malcolm X (El-Hajj Malik El-Shabazz), Margaret Burroughs and Charlie Burroughs, Dudley Randall, Hoyt W. Fuller, and Gwendolyn Brooks—they were saying, "You have promise, young man," and backing it up with resources, helping me out when I needed it the most. So when I got my first 400 dollars, I bought a mimeograph machine and started publishing. Been going ever since.

It's been a struggle. Even this morning, when I met with some Chicago bankers [to help fund future projects for Third World Press] who were so far away from any kind of cultural enlightenment, they could at least see the passion, and the sincerity. (Of course, one of them's been out here and seen our operation.) And Sascha, if I get those resources, you're going to see a lot more. I mean, you're going to see some things that are almost unbelievable. Because we never *had* any money; if I get this money, what I borrow will be, like, double, since my overhead, unlike other companies, is remarkably reasonable. We're going to go into spoken word. We're definitely going to do music, because there are a lot of black musicians in this city, so I'm going to start a spoken word/music label.

When I leave here [at the end of the day], I go home and put the music on. It's an integral part of my life. And I recently decided to bring my records back out, because my children have been into rap, and rap is a music that's sampling a lot of traditional black music, and I just don't like much of what's happening. I think that they don't know what to listen to. But for me, music is like a lifeline, and for those of us who have had this privilege to work in black struggle and to still be alive—it's always going to be a struggle, but so many people got their souls broken—but for those of us who have been able to survive and develop as a result of our movements, the music has been a kind of bridge that we cross over.

People have a lot of negative things to say about Wynton Marsalis, especially in the *New York Times* about Lincoln Center. I don't know Wynton—I've only met him once—but I know his work, and what I appreciate about this man is that he *does* know the music. I appreciate his great respect for Louis Armstrong. I put my horn down primarily because of Louis Armstrong. I realized, "I cannot do that. I cannot even get *close* to doing that." I was technically skilled. I could read—but I could not think music. Once I turned from the page, I could not play. Maybe if I had just stayed with it . . . I ended up in the military at eighteen, so I quit. I put my horn down. I had a new Martin.

FEINSTEIN: Nice horn.

MADHUBUTI: One of the best. But at the time, due to my economic circumstances, I had to pawn it, which is an interesting circle: I bought my first trumpet from a pawn shop and ended up pawning my new horn to eat.

FEINSTEIN: That's terrible.

MADHUBUTI: But listening to Louis Armstrong taught me I needed to find another profession. [Laughs.] So I said, "Okay, I'll let Langston Hughes take over." Go to the poetry.

FEINSTEIN: One of my favorite tributes to Hughes is Dudley Randall's "Langston Blues."

MADHUBUTI: Langston was, of course, a blues poet, a black music poet, a poet who always reached out to help others. Gwendolyn Brooks gives Langston Hughes a great deal of credit for her success. Ms. Brooks loves music. She was really moved by the music in one of Melvin Von Peebles's Broadway shows. [Madhubuti points to her portrait above his chair.] Ms. Brooks—well, Gwen—she's like a mother. That's how close we've become over the years. What I saw in her, and what I see in her, is this unselfishness—this giving—*every* place she goes. I also saw, on one level, others from one segment of this community patronizing her . . . Let me put it this way: Why is it that she has not won a MacArthur? Why? This is my question. Many of these other people [who have received the award] are worthy; I don't want to disparage them. But why is it that this eighty-three-year-old master poet, one of the finest poets in the world, hasn't won a MacArthur? She could use it—but she wouldn't use it on herself. She would very deliberately and very carefully distribute the money around the community. That's what she would do; I know exactly what she would do.

Now *I*, as her cultural son—as Dudley Randall's cultural son, Hoyt Fuller's cultural son—have the responsibility to keep that line going. I would be not only a failure but a traitor if I did not stay in the line that she set, that Hoyt Fuller set, that Dudley Randall set, that Margaret Burroughs and Charlie Burroughs and El-Hajj Malik El-Shabazz set. That's the mission. These are very large footsteps, but I'm up to it.

In the final analysis, you can say, "Why do you do this?" Well, I essentially love black people. By extension, I love all people. But I can say this without hesitation: I love, and deeply, deeply care for, all children. Why? Because children are not racists. Racism is *learned.* Prejudice is *learned.* I can get along with any children. That's why we started the school. Our responsibility to these children is to make sure that we are developing exceptional young boys and girls. When they come out of our school, they love themselves. They're not going to be involved in drive-by shootings. They're not going to be involved in rapes. They're not going to be involved in stick-ups and all that stuff. Last year, we had five engineers graduate from the nation's top schools.

That is the reward, ultimately. So for you to come in here and just say, "Thank you," that's part of the reward.

FEINSTEIN: Maybe that kind of selflessness—that giving to the public—is also one reason why the music is such an important part of your life, how it has helped to educate you as a writer but also acts, as you said, as blood and oxygen, as a lifeline.

MADHUBUTI: I practice yoga, and when I'm doing my exercises, music is on. I'm a vegan; if it runs from me, I'm not going to eat it. If I gotta chase it, it's not gonna be cooked. [Feinstein laughs.] I guess I'm a Strange Vegetable. But a part of growing, at least for me, was knowing how to stay healthy. How do you *live* health, and how do you *give* health? See what I'm saying?

Now, with John Coltrane, most certainly in his last eight or nine years, this is where he was at. He was passionately pushed to put the best out. What can you say about "My Favorite Things"? If you talk about the major compositions of the last four or five hundred years, it's going to be there.

FEINSTEIN: His *versions* of the tune.

MADHUBUTI: Yeah, the versions. Or most certainly *A Love Supreme,* which is probably more applicable, because I think *A Love Supreme* said everything he wanted to say.

FEINSTEIN: That whole album was a gesture of thanks, though I'm not sure if it "said everything he wanted to say"; I think he was trying to find new forms of musical expression every day of his life.

MADHUBUTI: Absolutely, and I guess that's where I want to end up as a writer: to put words together at the same level as he put together his notes. (We saw that Trane was not finished with the release of *Transition* and *Sun Ship* in 1972.) I'm trying to get there; it's just taking a little more time.

FEINSTEIN: In reprinted versions of "Don't Cry, Scream," you've extracted the stanza that's disparaging towards homosexuals.

MADHUBUTI: Right.

FEINSTEIN: As a writer, where do you think your greatest revisions have been, politically or aesthetically?

MADHUBUTI: I grew up in a culture that was really homophobic, and although I've never personally involved myself in trying to disparage anybody, the use of the term was used throughout the black community. So that revision was very important, and it came about because I had hired gay people [at the press], and they asked me about it. I tried to explain it within a cultural context, and then I realized about the best way to explain it was just to take it out. And so I did.

I wrote one other poem that actually dealt with a part of the gay situation—that's in *Don't Cry, Scream,* also—but I didn't change that because that's a different kind of poem. As you know, the major part of writing is revision, and sometimes the revisions come kind of late, after pieces have been published. But I'm not above criticism—ever. I think that one of the things that I've learned from the best musicians and from black struggle is that you listen to your critics. You look at the criticism, obviously—

Feinstein: That's very important—respecting the source—

Madhubuti: Who's doing the criticizing, yes. But if it's legitimate, you learn from it and make some changes. I think that's what life's all about. I was talking about health earlier. How can one be healthy if one is not writing healthy, or living healthy? I will always want to look my children in the eye—not only my biological children but my *cultural* children—and never say, "I don't want you to read this." If they can't read it, why write it?

Feinstein: I wonder if Coltrane's relentless struggle to play new music kept him from being healthy.

Madhubuti: I think that's why we have to pace ourselves. By his early death, we learn something: Stress can take you out in a minute, and you have to be able to manage your body, spirit, psyche, psychology—everything. You have to manage that and do it in a way that allows you to function at an optimum pace so you can be productive. It's a struggle. I travel all over the place and see all kinds of confusion—people fighting among themselves—and I'll come back home, and I'll just be thankful for what we have. Because within all that confusion, I didn't see any production; at least in our struggles back home, we were producing something. When I got frustrated, I'd walk over to the school and be with the children. That'll just cool you down in a minute. There is something therapeutic about being around children full of innocence, hope, and laughter.

And having the right kind of friends. I'll never forget Gwendolyn Brooks, Hoyt Fuller, and two of our beautiful critics, who are no longer with us, George Kent and Darwin T. Turner. I'd been working very closely with Baraka at the Congress of African People and they thought I'd lost my mind. So they asked me to come over to Hoyt's place and have dinner, and they had a long talk with me. It was basically, "We think that you're going too far this way," or "Step back." It showed me that my elders loved me.

Feinstein: Too far which way?

Madhubuti: Well, really, politically traveling with Baraka in the late '60s and early '70s. At that time he was making this big split away from his Black Nationalist, Pan African roots; he was going totally Mao Tse-tung-ist. Communism. And I told them, "I'm not going there. I'm not leaving this community." This was 1974, and we went our separate ways; Baraka and I didn't speak for a long time. We finally came back together as brothers in struggle, but it was a long split—about eight or nine years.

But I'm saying this because I think all people should be connected to the best of their culture, and the best of our culture, or most certainly a part of it, is classical black music, which other people call jazz. That music is foundational. If it wasn't for the music, I wouldn't be here. I know that. Because that's what inspired me. It gave me direction and forced me to question the world in other ways—much more than doo-wops and rhythm and blues.

I guess that's why I tried to play trumpet. You try to copy that which is so important to you. You try to do it, and I really tried. I just did not have the talent for the trumpet, but I tried. I tried. [Shakes his head.] I tried awfully hard.

William Matthews. *Photo by Star Black.*

13

Mingus at the Showplace
William Matthews

One evening after a poetry reading, truly pleased that he had caused a roomful of listeners to guffaw at his clever retort, Bill Matthews turned to me and said with a flushed grin, "Why come up with a new anecdote when an old one will do so well?" In that spirit, here's a story I've told often, one that's been quoted by others, including his son, because it holds up pretty well:

In 1996, Bill was Poet-in-Residence at Bucknell University, just half an hour south of where I live. During his residency, he visited my house frequently—partly, I like to think, for the company, but also for my expansive jazz collection and my wife's extraordinary cooking—and he gave a reading at our college that March. His was the first reading I hosted as the new director of the school's reading series, and though I had no concerns about Bill's performance, I felt unusually self-conscious about the event.

For that particular night, Bill had to read in the only available large room on campus: an antiseptic chemistry lab with many rising rows of seats. I introduced him, the crowd applauded, and, as he walked to the podium, an elderly couple from the very back of the room stood up, walked slowly down the aisle, and exited through the door just a few feet away from where he stood. I can only assume the couple had expected a lecture, or maybe a movie, and Bill knew as well as anyone that every reading has at least one idiot in attendance. Still, it was an awful moment—but it was *only* a moment, because as soon as the door clicked shut behind them, Bill turned to the audience and said, "How am I doing so far?"

Bill's poems for Charles Mingus and other jazz geniuses celebrate the art of improvisation; linguistically, Bill could improvise as fast as anyone I've ever known. When he was in his element—and when was he not?—he delivered lines "the way we like / joy to arrive," to quote from his Art Tatum poem: "in such / unrelenting flood the only / way we can describe it / is by music."

During his lifetime, William Matthews published many books of poetry and prose, including *Selected Poems & Translations 1969–1991, Curiosities,* and *Time & Money,* which was awarded the National Book Critics Circle Award. His posthumous collections include *After All,* a book of poems; *Search Party: Collected Poems,* a finalist for the Pulitzer Prize; and *The Poetry Blues: Essays and Interviews,* which reprinted this interview. He received many national honors, such as three awards from *Poetry* magazine as well as fellowships from the Guggenheim Foundation, the National Endowment for the Arts (two), the Rockefeller Foundation, and the Woodrow Wilson Foundation.

This interview focuses on his four poems (reprinted on the following pages) about or inspired by the bassist Charles Mingus. The interview took place in my office at Lycoming College on February 23, 1996.

Mingus at The Showplace
William Matthews

I was miserable, of course, for I was seventeen,
and so I swung into action and wrote a poem,

and it was miserable, for that was how I thought
poetry worked: you digested experience and shat

literature. It was 1960 at The Showplace, long since
defunct, on West 4th St., and I sat at the bar,

casting beer money from a thin reel of ones,
the kid in the city, big ears like a puppy.

And I knew Mingus was a genius. I knew two
other things, but as it happened they were wrong.

So I made him look at the poem.
"There's a lot of that going around," he said,

and Sweet Baby Jesus he was right. He glowered
at me but he didn't look as if he thought

bad poems were dangerous, the way some poets do.
If they were baseball executives they'd plot

to destroy sandlots everywhere so that the game
could be saved from children. Of course later

that night he fired his pianist in mid-number
and flurried him from the stand.

"We've suffered a diminuendo in personnel,"
he explained, and the band played on.

Mingus at The Half Note
William Matthews

Two dozen bars or so into "Better Get It
in Your Soul," the band mossy with sweat,
May 1960 at The Half Note, the rain
on the black streets outside
dusted here and there by the pale pollen
of the streetlights. Blue wreaths
of smoke, the excited calm
of the hip in congregation, the long
night before us like a view and Danny
Richmond so strung out the drums
fizz and seethe. "Ho, hole, hode it,"
Mingus shouts, and the band clatters
to fraught silence. There's a twinge
in the pianist's shoulder, but this time
Mingus focuses like a nozzle
his surge of imprecations on a sleek

black man bent chattering across
a table to his lavish date:
"This is your heritage and if you
don' wanna listen, then you got
someplace else you'd better be."
The poor jerk takes a few beats
to realize he'll have to leave
while we all watch before another
note gets played. He glowers dimly
at Mingus, like throwing a rock
at a cliff, then offers his date
a disdained arm, and they leave in single
file (she's first) and don't
look back, nor at each other.
"Don' let me constrain you revelers,"
Mingus says, and then, tamed by his own rage
for now, he kick-starts the band:
"One, two, one two three four."

Mingus in Diaspora
William Matthews

You could say, I suppose, that he ate his way out,
like the prisoner who starts a tunnel with a spoon,
or you could say he was one in whom nothing was lost,
who took it all in, or that he was big as a bus.

He would say, and he did, in one of those blurred
melismatic slaloms his sentences ran—for all
the music was in his speech: swift switches of tempo,
stop-time, double time (he could *talk* in 6/8),

"I just ruined my body." And there, Exhibit A,
it stood, that Parthenon of fat, the tenant voice
lifted, as we say, since words are a weight, and music.
Silence is lighter than air, for the air we know

rises but to the edge of the atmosphere.
You have to pick up The Bass, as Mingus called
his, with audible capitals, and think of the slow years
the wood spent as a tree, which might well have been

enough for wood, and think of the skill the bassmaker
carried without great thought of it from home
to the shop and back for decades, and know
what bassists before you have played, and know

how much of this is stored in The Bass like energy
in a spring and know how much you must coax out.
How easy it would be, instead, to pull a sword
from a stone. But what's inside the bass wants out,

the way one day you will. Religious stories are rich
in symmetry. You must release as much of this hoard
as you can, little by little, in perfect time,
as the work of the body becomes a body of work.

Mingus in Shadow
William Matthews

What you see in his face in the last
photograph, when ALS had whittled
his body to fit a wheelchair, is how much
stark work it took to fend death off, and fail.
The famous rage got eaten cell by cell.

His eyes are drawn to slits against the glare
of the blanched landscape. The day he died,
the story goes, a swash of dead whales
washed up on the Baja beach. Great nature grieved
for him, the story means, but it was great

nature that skewed his cells and siphoned
his force and melted his fat like tallow
and beached him in a wheelchair under
a sombrero. It was human nature,
tiny nature, to take the photograph,

to fuss with the aperture and speed, to let
in the right blare of light just long enough
to etch pale Mingus to the negative.
In the small, memorial world of that
negative, he's all the light there is.

SASCHA FEINSTEIN: Throughout your career, you've written about a number of astonishing jazz musicians, including John Coltrane, Coleman Hawkins, Lester Young, Bud Powell, Ben Webster, and Sidney Bechet. I'd like to talk this afternoon about your recent poems for the bassist Charles Mingus and your visits in 1960 to the Showplace, which featured Mingus's Jazz Workshop for half of that year. Nat Hentoff said that he inevitably brought friends visiting New York to the Showplace because at that time "[t]here was no other experience in jazz at all like it."

WILLIAM MATTHEWS: Various accounts of what the business arrangements were have by now attached themselves to this legendary gig, but Mingus was in effect guaranteed a six-month stint at the Showplace. He was not just the entertainment, but also the artist-in-residence. The group expanded its repertoire not in someone's loft or in a rented rehearsal space, but in front of an audience every night. It allowed the audience a look at Mingus's terrific willfulness. He could gather and focus enormous vitality and purpose when he could arrange not to be distracted by his own personality.

I agree with Hentoff. The Jazz Workshop was unique in jazz at that time. And not just unique in format, but in the daring and quality of the music. It was also unique in that it was truly a group enterprise and at the same time driven by dictatorial Mingus. How they managed this is hard to say, but here's one way to think about it.

Mingus's greatest influence as a composer, I've always thought— and it doesn't require a genius grasp of jazz history to know this—is of course Ellington. Mingus learned something crucial to the enterprise of the Jazz Workshop from Ellington. He didn't learn it firsthand, for he didn't spend that much time around Ellington. But he understood deeply the way Ellington wrote not just some music for the trombone, but for a particular trombonist in the band—Juan Tizol, let's say. He wrote for the individual style and tone and strengths of the Workshop members, and, like Ellington and Strayhorn, he sometimes incorporated phrases from his sidemen's improvisations into his written compositions. Mingus did his composing half at the piano at home and half on the stand.

No doubt Mingus was so hard on his pianists and fired so many of them, and often melodramatically and humiliatingly in public, because it was his teaching instrument—his classroom, in effect. He knew what he could hear from it, and when others wouldn't or couldn't hear likewise he forgot that they were not he, and thus the frustration he might otherwise have eaten he spat at them. The other musicians he wrote toward, but the pianists had to play toward him. And that was why the most unstable thing about the group was the identity of the pianist.

FEINSTEIN: He went through so many piano players—

MATTHEWS: He used Horace Parlan. And he used people who sounded so unlike Horace Parlan you'd think they were from different planets.

FEINSTEIN: Jaki Byard, Sir Roland Hanna, Kenny Drew, Paul Bley, Sy Johnson . . .

MATTHEWS: Nico Bunick, Tommy Flanagan . . . The remarkable combination of tightness and exaltation that marks *The Complete Candid Recordings of Charles Mingus* was built during that stay at the Showplace. Of course, Hentoff supervised (or is the right word "abetted"?) the Candid recordings, and thus speaks of those days with special authority.

Mingus would often stop the band during a number to work on some detail or other. The sessions were not nightclub "entertainment," but more like a master class at Juilliard.

A lot of stuff got reworked on the stand and not written down. It was only going to get written down after the fact, or not at all. The famous debacles concerning the copyists for the Town Hall concert suggest that "not at all" was the correct answer. Mingus fulminated at copyists for not getting down what was only in his head. This dynamic duplicates with depressing neatness his relationship to his pianists.

You never knew if Dannie Richmond, who was having smack problems in those years, was going to show up shivering like a cymbal or in fine form. Every so often he was so close to being on the nod it was like going back fifteen years in jazz and drug history, or so I imagined, for I was too young to know firsthand. But Mingus never let Richmond go. I've always thought some temperamental fit between Mingus and Richmond was the emotional glue of that group, which was built from the rhythm section up in a way that's not true of any other jazz organization except Basie's early band, and maybe the MJQ. No matter what a pain in the ass Richmond might be—and Mingus showed his discontent now and then—he knew not to get rid of him. Richmond's might well have been a broken career with any other leader.

I wasn't living in New York in those years and went into the city on weekends when I could, so I never sat in the Showplace three or four nights in a row listening to the group work its way slowly through the same piece. But from weekend to weekend you could hear the pieces evolve and the repertory grow. It was like watching time-lapse photography.

FEINSTEIN: But you were there a lot.

MATTHEWS: I was there a lot.

FEINSTEIN: And this was when you were seventeen years old, right?

MATTHEWS: Yes. I turned eighteen in November of 1960.

FEINSTEIN: Why did it take you thirty-five years to digest this experience and write about it?

MATTHEWS: I don't know why it took me so long to understand it. I knew in some visceral way I was witnessing a genius at work. I think most geniuses are monsters of a sort, but there's a difference between a pure monster—a loathsome thing—and a genius tinged by his gift with monstrosity. Perhaps I was scared as well as excited by the intensity and difficulty of what happened at the Showplace.

No doubt in some way that was adolescently romantic, but not therefore necessarily false, I realized that artists, black people, and others marginalized by mainstream American culture were dramatizing my possible lives far more accurately than mainstream American culture could. That would explain both the fear and the excitement.

I wasn't one of those white kids who thought he was secretly black. The gap between whites and blacks seemed to me immense and tragic. Norman Mailer's essay "The White Negro" was in the air in those days, but it seemed to me a kind of hipster's wet dream. I thought, "Hang out with some non-literary blacks for a few days, Norman, and learn how full you are of shit." [Laughs.]

Also, Mingus's music was dense and layered, at the same time it was immediately exciting. It took a while to understand how complex and sophisticated it was, for all its emotional force. The combination of the two is unusual in art, though there's no self-evident reason why one must be achieved at the cost of the other, and work in which the two cohabit usually takes a while for partial understandings of it to grow full.

The more interesting our experience is, the more slowly it submits to understanding. That tenacity may be our first sign how interesting a particular body of experience is.

Recently someone asked me when it first occurred to me to translate Horace (I've been working on his satires the last couple of years), and I remember thinking in my late twenties, not knowing if it meant anything more than bravado, "I'll translate Horace one day, when I'm older and more skillful." I started in my early fifties. I guess I'm a slow study! [Laughs.]

FEINSTEIN: A few years ago, you told me that your poem "Mingus at The Showplace" was 98 percent autobiographical, and I love that moment when this seventeen-year-old speaker, "casting beer money from a thin reel of ones," shows Mingus his poem based on what he considers "miserable" experience. Did you show Mingus the poem because Mingus himself was interested in poetry?

MATTHEWS: Mingus was *said* to be interested in poetry, and Al Young, who was around Mingus in those years . . . Al and I must have spent some nights in the same room.

FEINSTEIN: He was there at the same time.

MATTHEWS: But neither of us remembers that, of course. We met years later. Well, given the narcissism one has at that age, it would be a wonder if I remembered *anyone* else being there.

FEINSTEIN: Al has a wonderful reflection on the Showplace in his *Mingus/ Mingus* book, written with Janet Coleman.

MATTHEWS: Yes, I like the book a lot. I've talked to Al about Mingus and his interest in poetry. I think Al's memory may be more trustworthy than mine, in this sense: Once I've transformed some memories by writing about them, the resulting poems tend to shadow the originating memories. I think that for Al the source and the poems co-exist more equably. And Mingus certainly respected poets and poetry, as remarks in his liner notes, *The Village Voice,* and elsewhere in that period suggested. I don't know how avid a reader of poetry he was. I think he cared about it some, quite genuinely, and if he got a reputation for caring about it more than he really did he wasn't about to offer a public correction of that misconception.

FEINSTEIN: He wasn't a great reader of poetry, perhaps, but poetry crept into several of his records—*The Clown,* for example—and he played on the Langston Hughes date [*Weary Blues*].

MATTHEWS: Yes, and not perfunctorily, either. He really showed up for that one. That's the kind of gig some musicians would phone in.

FEINSTEIN: Sure. Hughes noticed it, too, and said he preferred the session with Mingus.

MATTHEWS: Of course, the poets are so thrilled to have the musicians there they often don't care if the musicians play anything interesting or not.

FEINSTEIN: That's often true.

What do you think of Mingus's autobiography, *Beneath the Underdog*? That's a very complex question, I realize.

MATTHEWS: Well, let's dispose of the accuracy question right off and assume that the truth of the autobiography is not historical but emotional truth. If you can read it that way, it's very moving. I love Mingus's descriptions of his early years as an acolyte bassist in L.A. and of how grateful he was to his teachers and anyone with skill who gave him any time at all. We're both teachers and know how rare gratitude can be. [Laughs.]

I love about the jazz tradition the way musicians tip their hats and pay their dues. By contrast, poets tend to act as if they'd discovered their abilities under a cabbage. Thanks are important.

FEINSTEIN: They're a necessity.

MATTHEWS: Oh yeah. Absolutely. There was no schoolhouse for this class, so names have to be named.

The early part of Mingus's book raises the fewest questions of truthfulness, chronological accuracy, et cetera. I find his account of his personal and musical boyhood very moving. It has some of the same wacko confidence that [James Joyce's] *A Portrait of the Artist as a Young Man* has, as if to say, "I'm going to make this character so interesting that you won't mind spending all this time on his earliest years." There's less grandiosity and myth-making here than anywhere else in the book, but still there's a sense that his teachers were not only fine teachers and musicians but important the way the guy who tutored Alexander the Great was important. Alexander doubtless thought that was the most distinguished thing his tutor ever did.

Perhaps the hardest things for Mingus to come to terms with, and the aspect of his book to which my proposition that an emotional truth is captured by laying waste to other kinds of truth, is the impact of race on jazz in Mingus's world. He had a Martin Luther King side to him and a Malcolm X side, and they never got along. They're at war, contesting for the microphone, whenever the subject comes up in the book, as it crucially must come up early and often. He lived with white women. He hired Jimmy Knepper to play trombone for him because he thought Knepper the best available trombonist even if Knepper was a honky. He kept exciting the conflict.

To compare and contrast, let's think of Art Blakey, who just hired hip and talented young black musicians and saved himself all the drama.

Mingus kept making decisions—erotic decisions, sideman decisions, recording contract decisions—that kept the problem on his plate, and then his contesting instincts on the matter made grandiloquent and "false" reactions, like Siamese twins turned on one another. One thought himself a Jeffersonian and the other a bilious, brokenhearted black nationalist. The other thought his counterpart a Tom and himself a clear-eyed racial realist.

· · · ·

FEINSTEIN: Both "Mingus at The Showplace" and "Mingus at The Half Note" conclude with the image of the music pushing forward: the first ending, "and the band played on"; the second, "he kick-starts the band: / 'One, two, one two three four.'" There are other striking similarities. Do you see these as variations on a theme? Do you see why I would think that?

MATTHEWS: Yeah, I do. They're both apparently anecdotal pieces, but both end with Mingus's will and urgency in command. I wanted to register my own naïveté and voyeurism. I wanted to admit, without making a big deal of it, that the person who goes to hear these things does so for love of the music but also for complicated reasons of his own—thus the passage about "the excited calm / of the hip in congregation," and my description of myself with "big ears like a puppy." I wanted to register what a rube I was and the pleasure I took in being someplace cool without switching the ardor of the poem from Mingus—a shot of the ears in silhouette, with the focus not on the foregrounded ears but on Mingus. [Chuckles.] After writing them was perhaps when I first noticed that the poems knew something I hadn't, except by writing the poems, of course: The rhythmic drive of the music and Mingus's willfulness are nearly identical in the poems. I had to know that in order to write the poems, one might say, but I think it's truer to say I had to write the poems to know that.

While I was working on *Time & Money,* I kept thinking there should be two more Mingus poems—one about him after his death (what happens to the dynasty) and one about his death and the way it became instantly mythologized. I couldn't get the second one right, and then the deadline for adding anything to the manuscript passed. Within a week I was able to get that poem, too.

FEINSTEIN: Naturally—

MATTHEWS: It will follow in my next book. The poem's called "Mingus in Shadow" and it's about the last photograph of Mingus, which appears in the biography of Mingus by—what's his name?

FEINSTEIN: Priestley.

MATTHEWS: Right, Brian Priestley, who wrote that "critical" biography, using the word critical fairly loosely. You know the photo, and I think you've heard that poem, haven't you?

FEINSTEIN: Yes. It's a terrific piece, as is the third Mingus poem that appeared in *Time & Money,* "Mingus in Diaspora." That's not nearly as anecdotal as the other two in the book. What's the history behind that poem?

MATTHEWS: Two things I can think of.

One is the phrase from Auden's elegy for Yeats, "He became his admirers." That's the literal diaspora, the scattering: the homeland, in this case the body, is gone and irretrievable.

The other is the long process of accumulating expertise. Let's imagine it as an emotional and intellectual version of aerobic gain— the way repeated exercise forms new tributaries to the circulatory system. An artist spends years ramifying these new passages, and then at death they're gone, winked out, absolutely ceased. How do artists make complex and accurate decisions fast and intuitively? How do musicians teach themselves to improvise? How do chess players look at the board and sense that they're in dire trouble in the upper left corner of the board six moves from now? They provide a kind of alert flexibility for themselves the way a pond "makes" algae. If you die comparatively young, as Mingus did, this beautiful construction, not the work itself but the attention that made the work possible, dies early, too.

FEINSTEIN: He lived to be fifty-six, older than many of his contemporaries, but still he died *far* too young.

MATTHEWS: There are players from his era still building—[Tommy] Flanagan, Kenny Barron . . .

FEINSTEIN: Barron actually played at the Showplace with Mingus. He must have been remarkably young. [Born in 1943, Barron would have been sixteen or seventeen.]

MATTHEWS: I was surprised by the apocryphal stories that attached themselves to Mingus's death, such as the one that fifty-six whales beached themselves in Baja on that day.

But the "Diaspora" poem has nothing anecdotal in it, and it mourns the winking out of Mingus's hard-won expertise. I even give Mingus's music a possibly longer period of incubation than his own life span by bringing his bass and its maker into the poem.

Mingus had an old bass and a new bass. Maybe sequentially, but I suspect he had them together. He referred to the one in his hands as The Bass, but there were two of them—two halves of a whole personality, perhaps. It always seemed right to me he would have a Jekyll and Hyde bass. [Laughs.]

FEINSTEIN: Mingus remains such a mythic figure, as are several jazz musicians from the '50s and '60s, and, like many poets, you have focused your jazz poems on those musicians. I know that you're not locked in time, that you often go downtown to hear contemporary players—but why do you keep returning to the past?

MATTHEWS: I think the period in jazz history that has the most emotional voltage for a person is that period when he fell in love with the music. To return to the music recapitulates the beginnings of a grand affair.

FEINSTEIN: Certainly, but—

MATTHEWS: Of course, I think it's one of the crucial periods in jazz history.

FEINSTEIN: It *is*.

MATTHEWS: And it's coincidental that I happened to have been listening attentively to the music then. It was a period so rich and complex, so difficult socially and racially, that after those years spent themselves jazz entered some doldrums. Much dull stuff. Jazz in New York, if New York is still an accurate jazz microcosm, and I think it is, has *some* of the health now that it had in those years, but not the same sense of reckless and unstoppable growth. In the halcyon years, if you were trying to keep up, you might need to go to two or even three clubs a night. Not now: There's usually one clearly stellar attraction a week.

One reason that those great years lost their momentum was an increasing polarization of musicians along racial lines, stylistic lines, et cetera. The network grew smaller, there was less cross-pollination, and jazz broke up for a while into small islands of the saved, always a dreadful situation.

I remember going to hear Coltrane and Dolphy, and the act they alternated sets with was Stan Getz.

FEINSTEIN: No kidding?

MATTHEWS: They were coming from different places, but listened to one another. But soon you heard people say things like, "I can't learn anything from anyone who's not into free jazz."

Getz and Dolphy were on nearly opposite ends of some bar graph or other, but they were both great musicians and so listened to one another. Coltrane tended always to listen for some cloud nobody else knew the location of, but Dolphy and Getz each listened carefully to something he had no inclination to play.

And Coltrane once said, "We'd all play like Getz if we could." It's not a compliment without a faintly serrated edge, but I think he meant it in some generous way, too.

FEINSTEIN: One of the reasons I was eager to talk to you about these Mingus poems is that this seems to be the first time in your career when you have, at least publicly, presented a series of poems about the same figure in jazz. It's not as though you couldn't have. I mean, you've written about some stunningly inspirational figures, and I imagine there are a number of Lester [Young] poems in you. But what was it about Mingus that inspired this series?

MATTHEWS: I had the most complicated relationship to Mingus. I set that up for myself rather deliberately. Call it hero worship, call it role model . . . I picked him as a tutelary figure.

What would it be like to take a complicated and obsessive project and say to yourself, "It doesn't matter that this seems foolish to everyone else and often to me. It's important. I'm going to do it. I'm willing to waste my breath, my energy, my love on it."

Of course, I was dimly preparing myself for something and didn't want to say very clearly to myself what it might be. For one reason, I didn't know. For another, it would have been a little scary to say to myself, "Well, you're probably longing for some impossible project yourself, you fool, and don't want to look like an idiot."

Self knowledge might be fine, but it could come later, as Saint Augustine said about chastity. [Laughs.]

I have certain dopey identifications with Lester Young, it's true. There's a combination in Young of strong emotion, not so much concealed as released by diffidence, irony, and sweetness of tone, that doesn't sound far off from certain textures in my poems, unless my ear is off.

FEINSTEIN: No, you're absolutely right.

MATTHEWS: I'm a little more angular and boppy, being a child of a later age. But a sense of fellow-feeling is strong. Young went into hiding more than Mingus's temperament would have permitted him. Possibly Mingus is a better tutelary figure for a younger writer, who needs the courage of his brashness and anger. Maybe, then, Young would serve a writer in his later years, when all the important confrontations are internal.

These are also, of course, two black styles, like Richard Wright's on the one hand and Ralph Ellison's on the other, and as a white man I'm somewhat to the side of that. But only somewhat. One point of the music and of poetry is that we can imagine what it means to be each other, and that we'll be made by that empathy, well, if not free, then more human and more nearly whole.

I didn't, of course, set out to write about Mingus in some political way, or as an instance of how a white boy starts to think seriously about race in American life, or about the relationship between the intuitive and emotional to voracious will—sometimes Mingus seemed to be 300 pounds of frontal lobe. But I wound up having to think about all those things, and whatever else I could get into the poems. He's just so large that I think one poem wouldn't do it.

Dan Morgenstern. *Photo by Ed Berger.*

14

Consideration

Dan Morgenstern

Like anyone remotely involved with jazz, I had known for years about the extraordinary archives at the Institute of Jazz Studies at Rutgers University, one of the world's largest collections of jazz materials, but until this interview, I had not made my pilgrimage. Shortly after I arrived and began to comprehend the depth of the holdings, I realized the stupidity of this delay. From my cell phone, I called my wife and spoke in a tone that was both enthusiastic and utterly insincere: "Honey, I'll be home in a couple of years."

For more than three decades, the Institute of Jazz Studies has amassed many thousands of jazz LPs and CDs, as well as music videos and DVDs. In addition, the institute houses a startling number of books and periodicals, reels of taped interviews, rooms of instruments formerly owned by legendary musicians, Grammy Awards, and so on. One can easily imagine a jazz enthusiast equating it with Mount Olympus, and if there's any accuracy to that analogy, then Dan Morgenstern would be Zeus.

Before and after our discussion, Dan said that he used to be quite reserved but has gotten better at speaking about his life. Since this was our first meeting, I can only confirm the latter: He talked until I ran out of tape. In fact, I asked relatively few questions—fewer than this text suggests, since we trimmed the digressions rather considerably. But, one-sided or not, I'm very pleased to know of his newly found comfort. It made my job easy, and it provided a wealth of information from someone who has for decades worked behind the scenes in order to place jazz in the forefront.

His more reserved side emerged after the interview, when he walked me through the inner sanctum to unearth some genuinely arcane resources, including a Joe Albany video that I'd wanted for years to view. As he glanced at the spines of DVDs and video tapes, he became, for the first time that afternoon, strangely distant, as though he had teleported into one of the recording studios from this ever-expanding collection.

Dan Morgenstern was raised in Vienna and Copenhagen and came to the United States in 1947. He has served as editor of *Metronome, Jazz,* and *Down Beat,* and has been a jazz critic for many publications, including *The New York Post,* the *Chicago Sun Times,* England's *Jazz Journal,* and Japan's *Swing Journal.* His liner notes have appeared on many recordings, and he has won seven Grammy Awards for Best Album Notes. He is author of *Jazz People,* and co-editor of both the *Annual Review of Jazz Studies* and the series *Studies in Jazz.* Since 1976, he has been the director of the Institute of Jazz Studies at Rutgers University. He lives in New Jersey.

The following selections from *Living with Jazz: A Reader* correspond to various moments in our discussion. The interview took place at the Institute of Jazz Studies on October 2, 2004.

· · · · · · · · · · · · · · · · · · ·

Bill Evans

(excerpt)

Dan Morgenstern

Evans's music—lucid, lyrical, melodic, and infused with a sense of, and search for, beauty and balance—is firmly grounded in an astonishing command and organization of the musical materials in the mainstream of the jazz tradition. And his approach to his instrument reflects a firm commitment to the heritage of Western keyboard music that began with Bach and perhaps reached its final splendor in Debussy.

Such an orientation is not exactly typical of the trend in contemporary jazz, sometimes called the "new thing," sometimes "avant-garde," and which seems more concerned with discarding tradition than with building on its foundations. The watchword of this school is "freedom"— a word open to many definitions.

Evans, too, is concerned with freedom in music. But he said recently, "The only way I can work is to have some kind of restraint involved— the challenge of a certain craft or form—and then to find the freedom in that, which is one hell of a job. I think a lot of guys either want to circumvent that kind of labor, or else they don't realize the rewards that exist in one single area if you use enough restraint and do enough searching. . . .

"When I'm playing with a group, I can't do a lot of things that I can do when playing by myself, because I can't expect the other person to know just when I'm going to all of a sudden maybe change the key or the tempo or do this or that. So there has to be some kind of common reference so that we can make a coherent thing."

Evans becomes emphatic.

"This doesn't lessen the freedom," he continued. "It *increases* it. That's the thing that everybody seems to miss. By giving ourselves a solid base on which to work, and by saying that this is accepted but our craft is such that we can manipulate this framework—which is only like, say, the steel girders in a building—then we can make any shapes we want, any lines we want. We can make any rhythms we want, that we can feel against this natural thing. And if we have the skill, we can just about do anything. Then we are really free."

Paul Desmond
(excerpt)
Dan Morgenstern

Paul Desmond is perhaps the most famous sideman on today's jazz scene. For fourteen years, he has been the alto saxophonist with the Dave Brubeck Quartet, from the group's early days of struggle to the notably successful present. Over the years, the quartet has often been the target of hostile criticism, but Desmond usually has been singled out for praise, even by the group's strongest detractors.

Considering these circumstances, and the common urge of jazz sidemen to become leaders, Desmond's reluctance to step out on his own is indeed an exception to the rule. But then, the tall, slender, soft-spoken altoist is an exceptional person in many ways.

He is indifferent to publicity. "I still think you should save this whole story for some significant event," he said during the course of this interview, "like when I die—you could have a picture of an alto and an empty chair and a bottle of J & B . . . I always wanted to be a romantic jazz player."

His sense of humor—or, rather, his wit—notwithstanding, Desmond *is* a romantic player. This is evident both in the graceful, warm lyricism of his playing and in his stage personality: somewhat diffident, introspective, and slightly withdrawn. This image has given rise to frequent speculation that Desmond is detached from the rest of the quartet—though both his playing and his words belie that interpretation.

"It's weird," he said; "so few people really know or care what we are trying to do—which isn't really that complicated. The questions people come up and ask after we play run like this: 'How do you know when to come in and when to stop?' or 'Who writes the choruses?' or 'How many of you are there in the quartet?' . . . It gives you a feeling of futility. . . .

"I'm working on a play (it's too formless yet to say anything about it much) and a couple of magazine pieces, things like that. I have this great reputation as a writer, primarily because I haven't written anything, and it almost seems a shame to spoil it, but sooner or later I'll have to make a move."

Lester Young: The Pres/Pres
(excerpt)
Dan Morgenstern

The message of Lester Young was intensely personal. Pres *spoke* into his horn, and what came out was always a story. As one listens to these creations torn from the womb of indifferent time, one marvels at the measure of this man, who in his own gentle way had the strength of a giant and the patience of an angel. What marks these moments from the life of Lester Young as the heritage of genius? The warm, breathy, life-filled sound; the marvelously relaxed, flowing conception utilizing so subtly all the possibilities of time; the innate sense of form that shapes each interpretation or the message that is the sum of all the describable elements of what was truly a *style*? Whatever they may make of it on paper, the sounds spell Lester Young—and there never was and never will be another Pres. . . .

There are many dimensions to Lester's music: fantastic humor and high comedy (dig the stop-time business in "Lester Leaps In," here taken at lightning speed); passion and yearning ("Body and Soul"); near resignation ("I Cover the Waterfront"); surrealistic happiness ("Lester's Blues No. 2," better known as "Neenah"); preaching in the great tradition ("Lester's Blues No. 1"); and relaxed, gentle strength ("Sunday"), to name a few. No note Lester played was wasted or meaningless. Technique is a term that has little function here. Lester knew what he wanted and how to get it out of the horn. Technique. Who swings more than Lester? He was a master of the dramatic entrance. The now conventional idea of beginning a solo on a break was reintroduced to jazz by Lester, within the context of swing. Tonguing is an act he raised to perfection. His tone *was* large and vibrant, in its own unique way. Sub-tone playing, a lost art these days, is admirably demonstrated on the opening choruses of "Waterfront." Melodic imagination, without which there can be no great jazz playing, is present here on every track. Lester's ballad improvisations were always involved with the creation of new and fresh melodies, which, miraculously, never tore asunder the underlying original. And although these were free sessions, Lester never solos at grotesque length—he leaves you knowing there is more, and wanting it.

Breakfast with Champions
(excerpt)
Dan Morgenstern

The promoters had wisely refrained from playing favorites and advertised their function at New York's Americana Hotel immediately following the most widely publicized fight in history simply as "Breakfast Dance in Honor of the Champion." (For those too young to remember, a breakfast dance is an affair that starts anytime around midnight and goes on from there. In the old days, it could last well into daylight; this one happened from 11 till 5—a rare enough treat.)

Nevertheless, Joe Frazier had his victory party around the block at the Hilton with Duke Ellington's band featured, so that's where his close people were—at first. But the Americana event was the more public one (and at $25 a head, a ten-spot cheaper) and could boast three bands (Count Basie, Buddy Rich, and King Curtis), so the good-sized crowd on hand was not a partisan one. . . .

The Imperial is a huge rectangular room in contemporary hotel style. It lacks the warmth of the cheerfully ugly, gilt-edged, stuccoed, and muraled ballrooms of another day, but a good-time crowd creates its own atmosphere, and the feeling inside was already happy. Basie's set had begun, and as I got my bearings and made my way toward the bandstand, the blues (was it "Splanky"?) wafted through the air, lubricated by that special Basie oil. . . .

It's early in the morning. A champ has been dethroned (Ali was the champ, no doubt about that, until tonight), a new champ has been born, and on that occasion, two all-time champions [Count Basie and Buddy Rich] and their great seconds and corner men and fans have had a chance to get together and trade not blows but embraces. It's been a good night, and there should be more nights like it, for jazz is a music that thrives in a social setting.

Once, the many big bands that roamed through the nights of this land often met, in serious battle or friendly jousts. Today, the few surviving giants seldom cross paths. When they do, it brings them and all of us a little closer together, and in these times, that counts a lot.

* * * * * * * * * * * * * * * * * * *

SASCHA FEINSTEIN: You've conducted so many interviews over the decades. Among the musicians, who would you say were the most literate, the most interesting in terms of language?

DAN MORGENSTERN: One of my favorites was Bill Evans. Bill was totally amazing. He was anything but glib. Everything he said had substance. He was so responsive to questions, his answers so intelligent—and he spoke in complete sentences. It was a pleasure to interview him. I could have talked to Bill for hours. Another very pleasant interview—though different because it was more like having a wonderful conversation with a very witty person—was Paul Desmond.

FEINSTEIN: They were both good writers, too.

MORGENSTERN: Yes. But Bill was amazing, and it's such a pity that he did such damage to himself. But there was something there that caused him to do that, because he was much too intelligent not to realize what he was doing.

FEINSTEIN: Did you ever talk about books with them, or did you focus exclusively on jazz?

MORGENSTERN: Usually the situation was that you're working on deadline, you know pretty much what the magazine wants, and the people you are interviewing don't necessarily have all the time in the world. So generally it was confined to jazz, but we would sometimes talk about other things. Very often you would have a lot more than you could accommodate in the confines of the magazine. As far as reading goes, I can't really think of anyone who was really into literature. But with people that I would be friendly with and talk to in a non-interview situation, other things would come up. We'd talk about good movies, and so on. Then there were people I was really good friends with, like Roy Eldridge, so we would talk about all kinds of things, including sex, and where the world was going. But Roy wasn't much of a reader.

FEINSTEIN: What about your most difficult interviews?

MORGENSTERN: I think probably the most difficult interview—not because of interviewing, because I didn't have to do hardly anything—but the most difficult interview to transcribe and edit appropriately was Ornette [Coleman]. This was in the '60s. Ornette hasn't changed in the way he thinks about his relationship as an artist to the world, and his way of looking at what he calls "the business." It's interesting that in all these years his outlook remains the same: that he, in this culture, is looked at as a marketable item, and he's had a lot of problems with that. I already knew Ornette quite well by the time he came to my apartment for the interview. He sat down in a chair and I turned the recorder on. I asked him one question, and, except for [my] turning over the reel, he talked for an hour and a half, and only very rarely would I ask him anything. So I had all that [conversation] in his unique way of speaking, his unique way of connecting and sometimes *not* connecting thoughts. I really worked hard on it, and it came out to his approval, so I was very proud of that! It would be quite something if everybody talked like that. He has his own way of looking at things and his own way of using the language, too.

FEINSTEIN: Let's talk about your own use of language and jazz. When was the first time that you knew jazz would be at the center of your life?

MORGENSTERN: It was a gradual process. I became very much involved in jazz as soon as I came to this country at the age of seventeen in 1947. I was already what you might call a jazz fan, but I had no idea of putting it to any kind of use other than the pleasure of listening to the music. I came to America with my mother. My father was already here. It's a long story, a bit complicated. I started out in Austria, and in 1938, when Hitler came in, I was eight years old. My father was a writer. He became a novelist after being a prominent contributor to a major German newspaper, and he had written some things that were anti-

Nazi before they took over. Someone he knew told him he was on the Gestapo blacklist, and he got out in a hurry. He got on one of the last trains to Switzerland and then to France, where he'd been before.

My mother was by birth a Danish citizen, and in those days it wasn't so easy to get from one place to another, but she managed to get into Denmark and take me along. In the intervening time, the Danes wouldn't let my father in, but we visited him briefly in France in 1939—for about three weeks in Paris—and then I didn't see him again until here [in America]. The French put him in an internment camp. (He managed to get out with some intervention of some French writers, but then they put him in another one.) Eventually, he made his way to Marseille where everybody who was trying to get out congregated at that time. He had applied for an American visa even before 1933, because he could smell what was going to happen. Then he made his way to Casablanca, and then to Lisbon, and finally he came here in 1941, right before Pearl Harbor. By '46 he had his citizenship and was able to bring us over.

Meanwhile, my mother and I were in Denmark, and then we managed to escape to Sweden. In Denmark during World War II, like so many other countries in Europe, jazz was extremely popular: It was symbolic of America and something that the Nazis hated. This was the Swing Era and you heard that music all around you. I already had some records. And in 1938, when I was eight, I saw Fats Waller in Copenhagen. My mother took me to see him because she was a little interested, and it so happened that we were living half a block from the concert hall where he was appearing. I really liked him. He was unlike anything I had seen before. Fats was huge, and I hadn't seen very many black people at all. (I could count them on one hand. In the movies, yes. And there was an old black woman in Vienna who I would occasionally see on the street.) So there was Fats, and he was just tremendous. He gave off what we would now call a vibe. [Laughs.] You definitely couldn't help tapping your foot. So anyway, Fats got me started. Then I heard the Hot Club of France with Django [Reinhardt], and the Mills Brothers. And then the war broke out, and that was the end of Americans coming to Europe. But there was good Danish jazz. Svend Asmussen, who is still alive, God bless him—in his eighties and still playing violin. There was a lot of good jazz there.

What I really wanted, though, was to go to California to become a film director. But my father, after he came to America, traveled with a friend to California and spent about a year and a half, and he didn't like L.A. at all. He had friends there, including John Brahm, who was a friend from Vienna who had become a fairly well-established director. But my father was adamant: "No, if you go to California, you will get the wrong impression of what this country is like." As a compromise, he got me an interview at Time, Inc., where they had something called the March of Time. So there I was, eighteen, a recent import from Europe. My English was good because they teach you very well in Denmark, and I was intent upon learning, anyhow. (I would go to the movies but not read the subtitles. I read everything—things like mysteries that were written in slang—and I read Dashiell Hammett, but I also read lesser things because they gave you a good flavor. There was a guy named Horace McCoy—he's famous for *They Shoot Horses, Don't They?* and another one called *No Pockets in a Shroud.* Very cheerful stuff. [Laughs.] But he was very good with dialogue.) So my English was good. But this nice man at Time said, "You know, there is something called television, which has just come in"—this is late 1947. "What we have at the March of Time is going to be gone within a year or two. We're cutting back rather than hiring anybody, and there's no trainee program or anything. But you're interested in film and you're interested in writing, and one way to do it is to write screenplays, or become a journalist." So he sent me over to TimeLife, where I got a job as a kind of glorified messenger/mail room trainee. That was interesting and fun, but it did away with my film stuff; I no longer had that great ambition. And jazz became more and more a part of my life because I was making enough money—certainly not a lot of money—but I was making enough money to hang out on 52nd Street, and started meeting musicians.

I hated jazz critics because I became friendly with jazz musicians and they hated jazz critics—[both laugh]—though even in Denmark I got [Charles Edward Smith's] *The Jazz Record Book* [1942]. There was a very nice clerk in a music store in Copenhagen who suggested I should buy this book. It was very expensive, but he said I could buy it on time. And that was a very good primer; it taught me a lot. But basically I had no use for the Leonard Feathers and other critics. I would read stuff that I didn't care for. Musicians would tell me about records and things, and there would be things that you didn't read about in books.

And then I got drafted, sent to Germany, which was very peculiar. In the fall of 1951, I was back in Europe. It was nothing personal—my whole outfit was sent over—and it was certainly better than being sent to Korea, but it was strange to be in Germany. Of all places, we were stationed in Dachau.

FEINSTEIN: Oh my God—

MORGENSTERN: It was very cheerful. [Laughs.] That was known as the Munich Military Post Service Center. It was outside of the village— Dachau is basically nothing more than a large village. The camp was some distance from there. We were actually quartered in what had been the S.S. barracks.

FEINSTEIN: You're kidding me—

MORGENSTERN: Anyway, that's a whole other story.

FEINSTEIN: Did you manage to sustain your interest in jazz at that time through the radio?

MORGENSTERN: We would go on the army bus to Munich, which was only sixteen miles away and where we spent all our free time (nobody ever went into Dachau—there was nothing to do there). The best jazz I heard was in Frankfurt, where I came across a band playing in an American service club: Jutta Hipp and Hans Koller. It was a terrific quartet; Koller was then very much into Stan Getz, and wherever you went in Germany at the time there was always an alto player trying to sound like Lee Konitz. That was what they liked there. But there was some nice music in Munich. One place where I used to hang out had a good little house band. The leader was a Yugoslavian drummer. But the best band in town was tenor saxophonist Max Greger's, with American trumpeter Sonny Grey. They played at a hangout for black soldiers, and I'd go there with a black buddy who was a jazz fan.

When I was first stationed at Fort Benning, Georgia, we couldn't find any good jazz at the record store in Columbus, Georgia. You could find run of the mill [Benny] Goodman or whoever was on a big label, but you couldn't find any bebop or Jazz at the Philharmonic. But we met some black soldiers who told us that there was a hip record store called Doctor Jive in the black section, so we went there and it was a great place. This was in the era of ten-inch LPs and we bought some Jazz at the Philharmonic. They had [jazz labels such as] Prestige and Blue Note. We went there a couple of Sundays and got to be friendly with some of the people there. Then one day this one white guy comes in who obviously wasn't a jazz fan. He was not in uniform and turned out to be a plainclothes cop. "Come with us." There was an unmarked car outside with this other guy at the wheel. They put us in the back and drove us out of the black section, and while they were driving they gave us a lecture in very nice, southern dialect: "What you do up where you're from is none of our business, but when you're down here, we don't want to see you there. If we ever see you there again," he said, not raising his voice, "when we turn you back over to the MPs, they won't recognize you." Very nice little message.

Once we got to Europe, though, they integrated our unit. I was still reading *Down Beat* and had a few records. A girlfriend sent me a copy of [Ralph Ellison's] *Invisible Man,* which had come out then in 1952, and that was a great experience to read. It's still one of my favorite books. Then when I came back, I had already decided I would go back to school because when I came here from Denmark I hadn't quite finished matriculating. (I would have matriculated in June, but I had no eyes to stay any longer in Denmark.) They put me in a high school when I first came here, but I couldn't stand it because it was stuff that I'd covered. You do a little better in European schooling. That's when I said, I want to go to work; I don't want this. So by the time I got out of the army, there was the G.I. Bill, and my father had friends at Brandeis, which was a very new school then, so he presented me with more or less a *fait accompli:* I would attend Brandeis, which was all right with me because I was going to do it anyway. And that's where I really started writing. It was '53. I was older than most of the students, and I became editor of the school newspaper.

We also started to bring musicians to campus. There was an excellent jazz club in Boston called Storyville run by George Wein. (Downstairs he ran Mahogany Hall, which featured traditional jazz.) I had become friendly with other student jazz fans, and George helped introduce us to these musicians. So we began to bring them to campus, musicians like Stan Getz. That concert was nice—the music was great—but it didn't have much personal resonance. Stan and his guys were all on a different kick than hanging out with students. It wasn't that they were unpleasant, but they were in and out.

But then: Art Tatum. And that was important to me.

FEINSTEIN: You brought Tatum to campus?

MORGENSTERN: We brought him to campus. Tatum was appearing with a trio—that's what he was doing then, of course, at Storyville—but we wanted him solo. So we went in and talked to George, who said, "Fine," and then talked to Tatum and asked if he'd do a solo thing, and he said, "Yes," right away. We were able to offer him some decent money, and he was just delighted to do it. I had to get the best piano on campus, get it tuned. It was a wonderful, marvelous recital. Actually, we didn't have much time to promote it, but there were people who came. Machito, of all people, happened to be in Boston, and he came! We had a very good turnout, because even the classical people came, wanted to check it out. Anyway, he played marvelously, and then we drove him back to Boston, and we thanked him, and he said, "I want to thank *you*. Believe it or not, this is the first time"—and this is late '54—"this is the first time I've done a solo concert all by myself." I was flabbergasted. So that was one of the things that subliminally told me something should be done about this kind of injustice.

FEINSTEIN: How did you begin writing for journals?

MORGENSTERN: As editor of the school paper [at Brandeis], I could write what I pleased. I wrote some things about jazz. Nat Hentoff was in Boston at the time—he was *Down Beat*'s Boston correspondent, and he also had a very good radio program, and I liked what he had written— so we brought him out to give a lecture on jazz. Then I showed him some of the things I had written and he said I should write more.

[After college] I got a job at the *New York Post,* starting out as a copy boy and then I became an editorial assistant in the drama department. I had a byline on the Neighborhood Movie column. [Laughs.] The *Post* still was a [reputable] newspaper then. I was working night side from two in the morning to nine, so I would be around in the daytime and knew a lot of musicians who would say, "Hey, I'm recording to-morrow. Why don't you come by the session?" So I'd go to afternoon sessions.

I liked all kinds of music, and certainly I was a fan of Charlie Parker's and liked bebop, but I was really very much into what was then called mainstream. I really loved people like Coleman Hawkins, Lester Young, and Roy Eldridge. The Metropole was a great nexus for that. Besides, the Copper Rail, just across the street from the Metropole, was a great bar where they gave you a nice big drink for not very much money, and they had a wonderful soul food counter.

One night, [British jazz critic] Stanley Dance, who was then not yet [permanently] in the U.S. but had been on a long visit, said to me at the Copper Rail, "You're a journalist and you seem to know all the musicians. *Jazz Journal* has lost their American correspondent. They can't pay you anything, but you'll get books and records, some of which you can't get here, and it might be fun to do. Send them a monthly column." So I started doing that, and it grew, because at first it was kind of short and then the editor, the late Sinclair Traill, said, "Why don't you write a little more?" Then my old nemesis Nat Hentoff rec-ommended me to the editor at *Down Beat,* and I got a couple of as-signments.

Things had deteriorated at the *Post* when the editor who some-times assigned me a jazz piece (all but one got spiked) was demoted to columnist, and then I got an offer from *Metronome,* which was a terminally ill magazine. I realized it was on really shaky ground, but I got an offer to be assistant editor, and I thought to myself, "What the hell?" Although there were some hip people at the *Post*—Pete Ha-mill was a rewrite man, and Bill Dufty was a reporter (I watched him do his Billie Holiday series there)—when I got this offer, I said to my-self, "Here's a chance to do something about jazz," which I was getting more and more into. I was now writing for *Jazz Journal* and getting a feel for it, and people seemed to like what I was doing. The greatest thing—the first big thing I wrote—was a piece on Lester Young. They made it into the cover, which I didn't know they were going to do.

FEINSTEIN: That was for *Metronome* or *Jazz Journal*?

MORGENSTERN: *Jazz Journal.* (That's one of the reasons why they offered me the job at *Metronome.*) Lester Young's then drummer, a real sweet guy who's gone now, like everybody—Willie Jones—saw it. Willie was from Brooklyn, and, you know, not many people would read an En-glish jazz magazine, but you could find *Jazz Journal* at Times Square. Anyway, Willie said, "I showed the thing to Lester and he liked it. Would you like to meet him?" So that's how I met Lester Young, and we spent some time talking in the kitchen of the Five Spot, which was the artists' dressing room. He was so sweet, and he apparently really liked what I had written. He asked if I played anything and I said I had struggled with the violin when I was a kid but it didn't go very far, and he told me about some great fiddle player in the Midwest that he had heard in the '20s who didn't get to be known or anything. And we had a really nice talk. Then he said, "You know, I'm going soon to Phila-delphia, and then I'm going to France. When I come back—I'm at the Alvin, you know where the Alvin is—give me a call." So I said, "Yes," and got up to say goodbye, and he said, "That's a date, now. Don't forget." And I said, "Of course." There was a little step going up from the kitchen, and I was sort of looking around and stumbled a little on it. And he said, "Don't stumble, now. You might fall." That's the last thing he said to me.

I was still at the *Post* then. I had switched from night side because I was in the drama department. At four o'clock in the morning I got a call from a guy who knew me from the night side rewrite: "Dan, I'm sorry to wake you up but Lester Young just died. What can you tell me about him?" [Shakes his head.] He came back from France, went to the Alvin from the airport, and died.

So I took this job at *Metronome.* A crazy guy named Dave Solomon had become the editor, and Dave was a brilliant guy but he was a dreamer. He knew something about jazz; he even had a cornet on his desk and he could play the first half of Bix Beiderbecke's solo on "I'm Coming, Virginia." Anyway, Dave had come over from *Esquire,* where he actually wasn't an editor but he had been on the promotion side. He was very much involved with people like Kerouac and Ginsberg and Burroughs, who were new then, and he knew a lot of cartoonists, and he wanted to make *Metronome* into a kind of avant-garde magazine that would have poetry and art and, of course, jazz as well. There was a photography editor, Herb Snitzer, who's a very good photographer, and they really got me because Dave didn't feel that secure about his jazz chops. It was a very interesting magazine. We printed Burroughs before *Naked Lunch;* we knew who he was. We reprinted something by Henry Miller. We did Lenny Bruce. We went to see Lenny at his hotel on 44th Street and talked to him about jazz and wrote it down. Lenny was extremely hip; we didn't have to do very much with it at all. It was fine the way he talked it. (I remember I had to go to the bathroom and there was a stack of what would now be called very soft porn— he called them "stroke books." [Laughs.]) During Dave's regime, we published LeRoi Jones [later Amiri Baraka] in a big article called "The Blues: Black and White America," which is how he got the contract for *Blues People.* I worked on that baby with him really hard, editing that long article. We published A. B. Spellman for the first time, a piece about Archie Shepp. We had some good stuff going.

Metronome at that point in time had a very low circulation, mostly subscriptions to high school and college libraries. Even before [the journal emphasized] jazz, it was a music teacher's magazine, so there were still subscriptions that had carried on for fifty years or something. Anyway, Dave featured a photographer who had taken some very mildly sexy photographs of a stripper at Coney Island. She wasn't even showing anything—she had, like, a bikini thing. And he put that on the cover. It was nothing. And none of these high school libraries had looked at the stuff inside the book, which was Burroughs and Henry Miller and some pretty racy cartoons! But when they saw that cover, we literally got tons of cancellations from these libraries, and that hurt. Dave could have handled that in a different way and would have been able to sustain himself, but he got fired, and he felt that I should have quit with him, but I had no intention of letting personal loyalty prevent me from at least trying to salvage the damn magazine, and the only way to do that, I figured, was to make it a jazz magazine again. So then I became the last editor.

Pretty soon, our nice publisher was no longer able to use *Metronome* as a tax write-off, and I was out of a job. Then my old friend Stanley Dance came to me and said, "Do you know [record producer] Bob Thiele?" and I said, "Yes." And Stanley said, "Bob wants to start a magazine." (Bob had a magazine when he was eighteen years old. He had a rich father. It discontinued in 1942, but he had eyes to start up again.) So I said to Stanley, "Why don't you take it on?" and he said, "Well, I can't. You know, I'm English, and I'm too old." This was a great non-paying job—[Feinstein laughs]—to start this magazine, but Bob paid me off in liner notes, and he paid seventy-five bucks for liner notes, which was a pretty good price. [The label] Prestige would pay me thirty-five dollars.

FEINSTEIN: The liner notes commissioned by Bob Thiele, they were for his Impulse! label?

MORGENSTERN: Impulse!, yeah. It was a good label and Bob was a very good record producer, and of course he had this budding relationship with Coltrane. He hadn't signed Coltrane to the label; that was Creed Taylor who made the first LP, *Africa /Brass,* but then Creed had a falling out with ABC, who owned the label. Then Bob came in.

FEINSTEIN: So Thiele approaches you about this new jazz magazine [*Jazz*] and in between you're writing liner notes for cash.

MORGENSTERN: Yeah. This is '62. I did some finagling here and there and managed to stay alive. And then I was the editor of this magazine, so I got a lot of freebies. I'd go to nightclubs and eat. In those days, record labels were doing a lot of press stuff, and they even had junkets. You'd go to some party for an artist who had a new record coming out, and there would be music and lots of food and drink. (This continued into the rock and roll era, but when the rock journalists got into it, I mean, they were like locusts. If you didn't show up right on time for one of these things, everything disappeared. Within ten minutes it was gone! It was like these people hadn't eaten in weeks.) Anyhow, the magazine was interesting to do, but I realized very quickly that I had been hired to teach Bob's girlfriend, Pauline Ravelli, how to edit a magazine, because he was obviously grooming her for that. Pauline was a nice enough gal—she was not unintelligent. She had no experience as a journalist but she learned quickly, and I didn't mind. My leaving had more to do with an editorial that I wrote where I said that it was too bad records were now mostly being made in a studio situation where musicians had the pots on—the headphones—and, in addition, often didn't have eye contact. In jazz, it's extremely important that you have that. It just is not the right kind of atmosphere for recording an intimate jazz session. Well, Bob hit the ceiling. He wrote a letter to the editor, which, of course, we printed, though he never had identified himself as publisher. But I had had enough, and Pauline was getting ready to take over, which she did. The magazine then became *Jazz and Pop,* eventually, and lasted an amazing five or six years after that, which is pretty good for that kind of magazine. A sequel, *Pop,* was stillborn, which is sort of just.

Because she wasn't a writer, however, they got someone to replace me—the notorious Frank Kofsky! Frank didn't have a title or anything, but Frank started writing about half the magazine, and he indulged in great tirades against the jazz establishment. [After leaving *Jazz,*] I very quickly was offered the job as New York editor at *Down Beat,* and by the time Frank hit his stride, I was part of the establishment. So after all the work that I had done for this magazine, I was now subjected to all kinds of infamous slander in its pages. [Feinstein laughs.]

I've got to tell you a funny story about Kofsky. I was at [the] Newport [Jazz Festival], like everybody, and in those days, when Newport really was *Newport,* if you had a press badge, you could go to the photographers' pit right by the stage, a nice place if you wanted to hear. You had a little camera just for show. (The professional photographers eventually put a stop to this.) So I find myself in the photographers' pit standing next to Kofsky. He had flaming red hair. Most of the jazz people dressed fairly conservatively, but he was wearing very tight orange pants and a bright yellow shirt, a little fancier than a tee-shirt. He was so colorful; you couldn't miss him. We'd never met, but I saw his name tag, so I said, "Frank Kofsky, I'm Dan Morgenstern." He was a little taken aback, figured I would maybe do something to him or whatever. We shook hands. I had been going to Newport for many years and I knew he'd never been there before, so, just to make conversation, I said, "This is your first time at Newport, isn't it?" and he said, "Yes," so I asked, "What do you think?" And he said, "*Is that for publication?!*" [Both laugh.] I assured him that it wasn't. Kofsky was a trip.

Then I became New York editor at *Down Beat.*

FEINSTEIN: And you were at *Down Beat* for about ten years?

MORGENSTERN: Almost ten years. I was at *Down Beat* from the spring of '64 until '73—nine years.

FEINSTEIN: For *Down Beat*—and all sorts of other venues, some of which we've touched on—you have published *so much.* Why has it taken decades for your selected writings to be published?

MORGENSTERN: I think in part it's because I got this job here [at the Institute of Jazz Studies at Rutgers University]. The day after tomorrow [October 4, 2004] it will be twenty-eight years. I mean, I didn't stop writing. I would do liner notes and the occasional article, but it slowed me down (except for the liner notes). I never approved of some of the people (who shall remain nameless) who, every time they have enough stuff, put out a book, because it seemed to me too formless, even if you could find a good catchy title for the collection. Of course I don't mean such things as Gary Giddins's terrific *Visions of Jazz* and his other anthologies. Also, I had so much stuff and not enough time. I did a book—this comes in after I left *Down Beat*—called *Jazz People,* which is still in print because it was reprinted by Da Capo Press some years ago, but that was a collaboration with a photographer [Ole Brask], and I've contributed to anthologies and so on.

FEINSTEIN: So how did you begin to select work for *Living with Jazz?*

MORGENSTERN: Well, when my younger son, Josh, was home summers from school, I'd bring him here [to the Institute] to go through books and journals, and he'd Xerox everything with my byline. He did a tremendous job. But the project really began with Robert Gottlieb, who invited Sheldon Meyer, who'd recently retired from Oxford [University Press], and me to lunch at Sheldon's favorite restaurant, which is near Oxford—Keane's Chop House, a very old New York restaurant—and after we had our first course, he said, "I would like to do a book of Morgenstern's writings edited by Sheldon Meyer." He just sprang it on us, and, fortunately, Sheldon said, "Yes." When I later sat down with Sheldon, he asked me to pick some things that I thought really should be there. There are always certain things that you think are particularly good. But then it started taking shape, thanks to Sheldon. He suggested we do the first section on the two people I'd written the most about and that I was most strongly committed to, Armstrong and Ellington, and I thought that was a great idea. Then he offered ideas on how to organize the other pieces. We have a section called "Profiles," which includes both interviews and things from liner notes where I would have written a lengthy biographical thing. Then there's a section called "Festivals and Events." You know, I covered a load of Newport Festivals, and at one point we thought of putting together a whole Newport section, but, obviously, we came up with too much stuff and had to cut back; there's only one Newport piece in there. But there's the Lester Young thing ("Lester Leaps In"). There's "One Night in Birdland," which I did for the Charlie Parker/Columbia [double LP]. There is something called "Breakfast with Champions," which is about the post–Muhammad Ali/Joe Frazier fight; there was a big thing at the Americana with the Count Basie band and the Buddy Rich band after the fight until early in the morning. Things like that. The big blues festival at Ann Arbor. Then there's a section "Caught in the Act," reviews of live performances and record reviews. There is a section of articles about topics—it's called "The Outreach of Jazz"—such as a piece I did many years ago for a *Down Beat* annual on jazz and film (before Krin Gabbard, and without too much phallic symbolism). [Both laugh.] And a piece on Jazz on Television, for the Museum of Broadcasting; they did a show, and I wrote the catalog text. I updated both of them a little bit because they needed it. And the piece from [Bill Kirchner's] *The Oxford Companion* [*to Jazz*] about recorded jazz, which Sheldon wanted in, and a piece I did for Martin [Williams] for the Smithsonian LP of Hot Chocolates, which I like a lot; it's a well-researched piece. That's somebody I miss a lot: Martin was sort of my conscience. When I wrote something he liked, he'd send me a postcard with a few well-chosen lines, and when I stumbled, he'd do the same, always right on the mark.

The last section is called "Controversies." It's pretty short, but it has some things in it like a piece where I defend [disk jockey] Willis Conover when he was being attacked by this very nice but mistaken black journalist in Washington, and there's a piece about commercialism in jazz—"In Defense of 'Commercialism'"—and another thing which, if anybody really bothers to review the book in any kind of depth, is the essay they might pick on: a review of a very strange concert, "Titans of the Tenor." A really weird concert. It started out with Zoot Sims, and then Coleman Hawkins, and then Sonny Rollins, and then John Coltrane. It was surrealistic. Zoot played two numbers. Dave Lambert was the emcee, and you could tell Dave knew things weren't right. Then Coleman came on. He was in pretty good shape considering he was near the end of his life. But he played one number—he told me he was contracted just to do one number—and, even though there was a lot of applause, he disappeared. Then Sonny Rollins came out with Yusef Lateef, who's unannounced. Sonny played a little bit of "Sonnymoon for Two" and then let Yusef play. After only fifteen or sixteen minutes, Sonny says, "I'll be back," and they left, but they never came back.

Then Coltrane comes out, and what happened was similar to something that had happened at the jazz festival in Chicago, the only jazz festival that *Down Beat* had produced, where Coltrane came on with Archie Shepp in tow. [In Chicago,] Coltrane played for about five minutes and then Archie took over, and soon everybody split. Really, like 90 percent split. [*Down Beat* editor] Don [DeMicheal] was driving me, and Archie hitched a ride, and Archie was roaring. But I mean, he wasn't even hired and he really spoiled the thing for Coltrane fans. But that was Trane. I'm convinced that Coltrane toward the end of his life felt responsible for all these people who latched onto his coat tails. He got Archie the Impulse! contract, and Pharoah Sanders as well. He was a really sweet man, and he let them take advantage of him.

So here he comes [at the Titans of the Tenor concert] with a bag of stuff—maracas and God knows what—and with him are, aside from his rhythm section, Pharoah and the Ayler brothers. What happens? Coltrane plays "My Favorite Things" for a few minutes, and then the others take over. There's pandemonium. That's why Sonny Rollins never came back, I think. There was a chance that Sonny would have come out to do a thing just with Coltrane, which would have been great, but that never happened.

And I did develop a kind of appreciation of Albert Ayler, although I've said some nasty things about him. (When they were playing at Newport, I said that they sounded like a Salvation Army band on LSD! [Laughs.]) I did write some favorable things, quite a few times, as a matter of fact. But I could never stomach Donald [Ayler]. I have a thing for the trumpet—I'm really a trumpet fan—and, you know, my favorite trumpet player is Louis Armstrong! So I couldn't handle Donald, and Donald played quite a lot at this thing. It was just a shambles. It was the most peculiar concert I think I've ever attended.

FEINSTEIN: What are some of your favorite pieces that didn't make it?

MORGENSTERN: A long piece on Kenny Davern, a dear friend. A George Wallington [essay]. There are some other pieces . . . It was hard to edit the book. Some of the stuff I looked at I thought, "Is that really worth considering?" Some things that people suggested to me I would have liked but Sheldon didn't care for them that much. (Sheldon's favorite expression is, "That's not a very strong piece.") Still, we had very few disagreements. Sheldon is fun to work with; I'm very fond of him. And if there was something that we were not in agreement about, Gottlieb would be the one who would decide. He's a very experienced guy. Of course, there were things that should have been in there that fell by the wayside because there was too much. There's a nice Art Farmer piece, but it wasn't that significant. There's a very nice interview with Cozy Cole, but it wasn't deemed that significant. So there are other things to balance that.

FEINSTEIN: Apart from that interview with Ornette Coleman, what were some of the toughest pieces to write? I'm not talking just about transcription. I mean, in terms of trying to capture the music or the musician.

MORGENSTERN: It was difficult covering a whole long event, like a Newport festival. Of course, by the time I got to *Down Beat,* we would split the coverage up, though I think there was one Newport Festival that I wrote for *Down Beat* myself. I did all the ones for *Jazz Journal* by myself, and, frankly, I think they came out pretty well. It's a challenge, and of course you really have to do it chronologically, but you can tie things together a little bit.

FEINSTEIN: That's in terms of volume. I'm talking about aesthetics: the difficulty of the music, or the complexity of the musician.

MORGENSTERN: Let me say this about that, as Nixon used to say: It was very good discipline for me, both as a writer and more importantly as a listener, to be in a situation where you are a working reviewer, where you have to cover things that as a fan or, in the best sense of the word, as an amateur of the art, you wouldn't feel compelled to attend or write about. But I had to do this, and that's where Don DeMicheal was really great, because without any kind of pressure he would quite frequently send me records to review and assign me things to cover that he knew were not my cup of tea, necessarily; because he himself had to go through that process, he put me through it, and it was very valuable. It also helps teach you one of the more difficult things about reviewing: how to retain your sense of fairness, because, ultimately, it's of the utmost importance that you should be fair.

The one success that I had in achieving a personal wish had to do with getting Dexter Gordon into full focus. Dexter hadn't come back here [to the United States] yet, and I wanted to make absolutely sure that his records were featured and that they got really strong reviews. (This wasn't any kind of compromise because the records were great.) So we could do a little bit there. On the other hand, putting Jaki Byard, whom I loved, on the cover of *Down Beat* didn't do anything for Jaki, you know? Maybe it brought a few people to his attention, but it didn't do anything for his career. When I first started working for *Down Beat,* some musicians would ask, "How much does it cost to get a piece in *Down Beat*?" I'd say, "There's no such thing." They wouldn't believe me. Of course, the only attempt to do something like that would come from record companies, though they wouldn't say it as crassly. "How about a cover story on Maynard Ferguson?" If it's legitimate, it's legitimate. Again, it's the issue of being fair. This happens, too, when you review a whole festival: you have to review acts that you're not necessarily attuned to, but you want to be fair. And it's also really good to be exposed to all this. It's just like any art form: You should expose yourself to anything that you may not feel attracted to on first sight. You may not particularly like a certain genre, but you want to give it a shot, you try to be fair.

Of course, you don't want to extend that to the degree where you say things that you feel are not true. You wouldn't want to smooth over stuff. You want to raise the consciousness of your readers. You want to bring attention to deserving people, deserving records, deserving books. At the same time, you are obligated with a magazine like *Down Beat*—which, in spite of the fact that its influence is less than a lot of people in the business think it is—to give exposure to other people. Not, of course, if you feel that somebody is a charlatan or a no talent, but if somebody you're not particularly crazy about is nevertheless popular, you still need to give him or her time and space.

What's really important, I think, is that you take into consideration things that critics often don't: If you know an artist's work, you must take the whole body of work into consideration if you happen to catch him on a bad night. Say Sonny Stitt makes a not-very-good record, or you hear Sonny Stitt on a night when he's not at his best. You don't deal with it as a totally abstract thing, which is what some critics do. They just say, "Well, Sonny Stitt this that and the other." They don't say, "On this particular night, he wasn't in tune with his rhythm section," or, "He was drunk." Whatever the reason is. I didn't particularly like John S. Wilson as a critic because John would do precisely that. He always dealt with things out of context. In other words, he would go review, say, Mingus. God knows he knew how volatile

Mingus was, but he would simply deliver a judgment in this kind of neutered *New York Times* style, which sounded like it was some kind of definitive opinion of this person's work. A critic should adjust to that. Not every public performance is the end all. I mean, I appreciate opera, an art form that is in some ways very similar to jazz insofar as it demands a lot of stamina: You're exposed, and you have a demanding audience. But whatever you do, the human voice is subject to all kinds of things that are not within the artist's control. So I appreciate opera reviewers who, if they know their business, will usually take that into consideration. They will say that the singer did not have a very good night, or had a lot of trouble with her upper range. They do that. But a lot of jazz reviewers don't. They seem to deal with everything as a unique or self-contained event. Even with records, the leader may not be in complete control over what is done and what is put out. And you take that into consideration. You don't have to bend over backwards, but you try to be fair.

FEINSTEIN: You've been pretty tough on jazz critics—John S. Wilson, for example. Earlier you said you had no time for the Leonard Feathers of the world. You called Nat Hentoff your nemesis—

MORGENSTERN: Jokingly, because he got me into the big time. I liked Nat's stuff a lot when he first started writing for *Down Beat,* and also because he did a great interview with Lester Young, who was not an easy interview. He did Coleman Hawkins at a time when everybody was into bebop and these people were being neglected. He was also, I thought, a fair record reviewer, and he was someone who had quite a lot of scope. Actually, Nat and I are on very good terms, but I fired Nat from *Down Beat.* [Both laugh.]

FEINSTEIN: I didn't know that!

MORGENSTERN: Nat was a columnist for *Down Beat,* and he was certainly a notable name. But at the time, jazz was no longer Nat's main thing. That's the reason why, in a friendly way, I told him, "I think you're not really spending that much time listening to jazz, or being around jazz, and I think that you just don't have that much to say about it at this time." And he agreed with me. So that's why I let him go, because I thought he was straining to write a column on a regular basis about something he really wasn't all that in touch with. He was then very much into his education crusade, and he was writing biographies, and he was very much into politics. I think he was trying to keep his name alive in jazz, and for that reason he may have been a little miffed that I did this, but I wanted to put somebody else in that space. I had a great deal of respect for Nat, and I still do. And in the last few years, he's really had a sentimental return to jazz. A few years ago, I was at a little jazz festival—more like a jazz party—in Florida, and Nat was there. I said to him, "It's great to see you here." But it was the first jazz party that he had ever been to; he missed that whole era of Dick Gibson [a wealthy fan known for hosting extravagant jazz gatherings, beginning in 1963] and all that. He and Joe Wilder had a reunion, and they hadn't seen each other in forty years! But Nat's back in the fold now.

As far as Leonard [Feather] goes, Leonard was a very complex individual. I admired Leonard as a professional. There was one thing I could rely on Leonard for without any doubt: If I was in a hole for something—if some piece had dropped out because somebody didn't come through with it, or whatever—and I needed something on short notice that I knew would be of professional caliber and would come in when I needed it, all I would have to do is call and say, "Leonard, can you do this and that?" And it would come in. If I asked Leonard for 1,500 words, I would get 1,500 words; with many others, I would get 1,200 or 2,000. He was a total pro, and he also would listen. You could edit him. If there were things that I really didn't agree with, I wouldn't have any problem with him. There were other people with whom you couldn't do that. I even got to like Leonard, but Leonard was a strange duck. In the history of this peculiar trade of writing about jazz, Leonard was the most influential critic of them all because, at one time, he was an editor of really important magazines (co-editor of *Down Beat*, then *Metronome*); he was a record and concert producer, and quite an active one; he was a successful songwriter; he had a syndicated radio show called "Platterbrains." For quite a while, he was everywhere, so he had tremendous influence, and that's why some musicians came to resent him.

Again, my attitude towards critics was shaped by being friendly with and knowing a lot of musicians. I got to look at it from their perspective. They would tell me specifically if something came up [in a review or interview]—what it was they didn't like about the way they were being treated in the press. That was important. And also I learned from being around musicians how unexpected events can affect them: how you could come to work at a club and find that the piano is out of tune, and you're stuck with that and have to adjust. Or your regular bass player is sick and you've got a not-first-choice substitute and you haven't had any time to rehearse. Or you've had a very bad flight, a terrible trip, or you simply drank too much or ate too much, or you got high on some bad shit, or whatever. [Laughs.] That does matter. My dear friend Ira Gitler is one critic who understands such things.

Of course, you can say that a critic can't consider these things because his only responsibility is (a) to the art form, and (b) to his readers. That's all good and well. You have to take these things into consideration, or you can withhold judgment. You don't issue an edict, a verdict. You can find ways of avoiding that. It's not that you shouldn't point out when something is wanting or undistinguished, or meretricious, or simply of no value. You have to say that—but you have to be sure you're on solid ground and that you can defend it. By the same token, if you praise something, you should be able to justify that as well. Empty praise or pandering is no good, either.

Hank O'Neal. *Photo by Milt Hinton. Courtesy of the Milton J. Hinton Photographic Collection.*

15

The Greatest Equalizer in the World
Hank O'Neal

In the late '70s, when jazz became a central part of my teenage life, Chiaroscuro Records represented one of the few active companies to focus on jazz. By the end of that decade, financial restrictions ended its production, but in 1987, Chiaroscuro reacquired the rights to produce the music in its catalogue and began issuing new recordings as well. By then, I was a graduate student in Bloomington, Indiana, and I wrote to the company to request a brochure. It arrived about a week later, accompanied by a note from the founder of Chiaroscuro Records, Hank O'Neal.

O'Neal explained that he rarely wrote to people who requested catalogues but my address had triggered good memories: As a boy, he spent about four years in Bloomington. I wrote back, of course, and we shared several exchanges: I sent him a copy of *The Jazz Poetry Anthology,* which I edited with Yusef Komunyakaa; he sent me a copy of Allen Ginsberg's LP *First Blues,* which he produced with John Hammond. And in 2002, I queried him because I wanted to get in touch with someone he knew well—the great album-cover and book-jacket designer, Paul Bacon.

When I met Bacon in New York at the Society of Illustrators, we spoke about the covers he designed for Thelonious Monk LPs. I later transcribed the conversation and pieced together an essay about those covers; it ran in the Summer 2003 issue of *Brilliant Corners*. Part of that essay also incorporated liner notes that he had just completed for a Monk tribute forthcoming on the Chiaroscuro label. Naturally, Hank O'Neal became part of our discussion. "You should interview him," Bacon said. "He's remarkable, and he's lived a truly interesting life. He was in the CIA—all sorts of things."

Three years later, as I walked to the door of O'Neal's home, I wondered, since we'd never met before, how long it would take for him to feel comfortable discussing the more personal aspects of his history. Turns out, it took only minutes.

Hank O'Neal is an author, photographer, and record producer. His books include *Eddie Condon's Scrapbook of Jazz; A Vision Shared: A Portrait of America and Its People 1935–1943; Berenice Abbott: American Photographer; The Ghosts of Harlem;* and *Charlie Parker: The Funky Blues Date.* He founded Chiaroscuro Records in 1970 (selling the company in 1979 and then, with Andrew Sordoni, reacquiring the catalogue in 1987); in its history, Chiaroscuro has released nearly 200 jazz recordings. Chair of the board of governors for Jazz and Contemporary Music at The New School, he lives in New York City and Thornhurst, Pennsylvania.

The following essay from Chiaroscuro's *The Dave McKenna Quartet Featuring Zoot Sims* has been reprinted, with one change: In the original notes, "How Deep Is the Ocean" erroneously appeared as "I Cover the Waterfront," and that mistake has been corrected. The interview took place on April 3, 2005, at O'Neal's home in Thornhurst.

Liner Notes for *The Dave McKenna Quartet Featuring Zoot Sims*
Hank O'Neal

An idea to make a record and a finished disc in your hand often takes longer than most people imagine; it always surprises me. An old mentor, Sherman Fairchild, used to tell me that I had too many ideas; this is probably the case, but I keep plugging along and no matter how long it takes some of my more persistent ideas work out as records. This recording is one that worked out.

The Dave McKenna and Zoot Sims project began in April 1974 sitting at Shea Stadium watching the Yankees do badly against Cleveland (this was when they were refurbishing Yankee Stadium). Dave and I were discussing a possible recording; I was eager and he was stalling. Dave is the all-time champion reluctant recording artist and no matter how much I schemed and plotted it just never worked out to get a quartet record done. Everyone, including Dave, thought it would be terrific to record a quartet with Zoot, but there were just always too many hurdles in the way and in the end nothing ever seemed to happen.

Dave arrived back in New York in October to play for a month at Michael's Pub and who should turn up in the group he was to lead but Zoot, along with Major Holley and Ray Mosca. This, I thought, was too good to be true, but unfortunately I had about $1.37 in my record account; the perils of a small independent record producer might make a swell soap opera. I let things drift, knowing I was out of cash, but at the beginning of the last week of the quartet's run I decided that perhaps it might be possible to borrow the money necessary to pay everyone. I managed to float a loan on Thursday of that last week the quartet was at the club and by Saturday afternoon everything was arranged to start recording the following day.

On Sunday afternoon I walked over to Washington Square to get Dave; he was staying at Phyllis Condon's and busily engaged in watching Buffalo beat New England. Dave likes New England; he lives there. They lost by one point that day; nice start, I thought. By 6:00 everyone had arrived at my studio; Fred Miller had a good level on all the instruments and we were ready to go. Zoot wanted to do "Linger Awhile," a tune you either love or hate. I have approved of it ever since I heard Cliff Jackson do it and it worked out very well with the quartet. The next item on the agenda was Bill Perkins's "Grooveyard." There were many takes involved; Zoot wanted to make certain there were many to choose from because he is very fond of the song. A ballad was the next choice; Dave wanted to do Eddie Condon's "Wherever There's Love" as a thank you to Phyllis for the hospitality. I called Phyllis and left the telephone off the hook while the quartet first rehearsed it and then made two very good takes. John DeVries, who wrote the words for the song, was also there, and he made certain no one sang any of them.

Three tunes in two hours is pretty good so we adjourned to play a little ping pong. Zoot won the only complete game and then we went back to record some more. We wanted to do an up tune and "There'll Be Some Changes Made" turned out to be the choice. Zoot picked up his soprano for this one and then put it down for the next song, Erroll Garner's "One

Good Turn." At the time nobody knew the name of the song; it was just called "Erroll" on the take sheets and there were many takes. Another up tempo number was selected, "Limehouse Blues," and it was fun to watch the window in the recording room jump as the group stomped their way through it. The last choice for the group was a ballad; both Zoot and Dave agreed on "How Deep Is the Ocean." Two takes were completed but the day wasn't over; two solos for Dave were next in line.

Dave had an original he wanted to do and he did it. He wanted to record a second version but Zoot wouldn't let him and perhaps that was just as well. There was a good deal of worrying about his last solo and it took some while to come to any sort of agreement, mainly because Dave, Zoot, and Louise Sims wanted to know where to go for a good Mexican dinner that late on Sunday. Finally Dave decided on "'Deed I Do," made two versions of it, and that was that, or so we thought.

The system was shut down, everything was packed up, and the house was empty except for Dave, Zoot, Louise, and myself. Just as Zoot started to leave, he asked to hear a playback of "How Deep Is the Ocean." I wound up the system and played it back; he wanted to do it again, as a duet. That is why there is a duet on this album, something I had asked Dave about ten hours earlier that we had never found time to discuss any further. The duet version is really a special one; I'm glad Zoot asked for that playback. Someday maybe I'll issue the quartet version but not for a year or two.

Well, that's how Chiaroscuro records are made; a relaxed atmosphere, no big-time studio clocks ticking, a few friends around and the best guys in town to play. Maybe it's a little too informal, but the results are generally good and when it's over everyone still likes everybody else, because no one is ever told what to do; they are just allowed to do what they do best. I will be the first to admit this is not the way to make records that sell a million copies in today's market, but in fifty years somebody might still listen to Dave and Zoot and most of those million sellers will probably not even count as mediocre nostalgia.

. . . .

SASCHA FEINSTEIN: I'd like to know how your passion for jazz developed.

HANK O'NEAL: You can trace everything back to certain kinds of things that happened to you, and I guess you can trace it back to RPI [Rensselaer Polytechnic Institute] when I decided I didn't want to be a chemical engineer. I had to be an engineer, I was told. Sputnik had just gone up; you had to be a scientist, and I had good SATs in science. I was taking a test in the physics department, and there was a question about some hockey player (RPI's a big hockey school) who'd hit the puck and it had crossed the blue line at such and such, and the coefficient of friction between the puck and the ice was such and such—when does it get to the net? And I said, "I don't give a shit." [Feinstein laughs.] "I don't care." That was the light bulb moment: "I'm going to be a mediocre scientist. I don't want to do this." So I went back home and told my dad, who was a school superintendent.

FEINSTEIN: This was in Syracuse?

O'NEAL: Yes. I'd gone to high school there [in the late '50s]. Anyway, I said, "I don't want to do this. Why don't you make a couple of phone calls and see if I can get into Syracuse University. I'll start in the summertime and make up my liberal arts," and he did, and I did. Then I took a class about Russian politics, and it turned out that the guy who was teaching that class was the CIA spotter on campus. I remember him calling me into his office and saying, "Hank, what are you going to do when you graduate from school?" and I said, "Dr. Bishop, I don't know what I'm going to do *tomorrow* let alone when I graduate." So he said, "I have somebody I'd like you to talk to." I agreed. (I'd talk to *anybody*. I was nineteen.) So I talked to this CIA guy, and he liked what he heard, I guess, and he talked to me each year. Finally, in my senior year, they brought me to Washington and gave me all sorts of tests—psychologicals, the foreign service test, and all that kind of thing—and they made me an offer.

So I went for training, and then, about nine months later, was pulled out of training, which took me out of Clandestine Services, because they needed someone with the funny background that I had: I had a minor in African Studies. (My professor, Eduardo Mondlane, was leading the revolution in Mozambique.) Somebody had suddenly resigned, and they decided they wanted me back in Washington in the Office of National Estimates, where I remained for about eight months.

FEINSTEIN: National Estimates?

O'NEAL: Yeah. Remember the great big brouhaha about the weapons of mass destruction? I was in the office that wrote those [kinds of estimates], but I was only twenty-three. I was way over my head; it was just a holding position, and they told me so. (They wanted a forty-five-year-old Ph.D. from Princeton to be in that position, and I was just holding it until someone like that could be found.) And I had a marvelous time. I actually guessed right on a few things. [Feinstein laughs.] But when it was over, I was out of a job because I'd been in true name for eight months and the Clandestine Services were no longer an option. So they said, "Well, Hank, we're going to put you in domestic activity," and I was sent to the Office of Operations, had no idea about anything (again, I was just twenty-three), and I was told to meet the Director of Domestic Operations. They said, "Hank, you will go in, and you will shake his hand, and you will sit down if he asks you to, and you will talk to him for five minutes, and you will leave." So I'm sitting there while people are coming and going, saying, "Mr. Ashcraft this, Mr. Ashcraft that." Then an older gentleman said, "Well, Squirrel says we've got to do this or that." I asked Annie Redman, the secretary, "Ma'am, is the director a piano player?" and she said, "I don't know. He plays at Christmas parties. We sing along . . ." So I went in, but I didn't spend five minutes; I spent five *hours,* because the Director of Domestic Operations was [Edwin M.] "Squirrel" Ashcraft [III], who, in the '20s and '30s and '40s, had been a legendary jazz figure.

That meeting started everything. He introduced me to everybody. I got him *back* into music, because he was effectively retired (except for calling people and saying, "Howdy do"). We started having parties at his house with the McPartlands [Marian and Jimmy] and Tom Gwaltney and Steve Jordan and Bobby Hackett—just like the old days. When I was transferred to New York in 1967, he had made all the calls. I would call up [record producer] John Hammond, and John would say, "Come on over!" and I would call [record producer] Nesuhi Ertegun, and he would say, "Come on over!" Whoever it was. One thing just led to another—and it's still going full cycle. I mean, the day before yesterday, we started a documentary film about Nesuhi Ertegun. I spent two and a half hours in back of the camera with [record producer] George Avakian talking about Nesuhi, then that night had dinner with Nesuhi's brother [Ahmet Ertegun, founder of Atlantic Records]. The parade goes on, and you can trace it all the way back to that test and the hockey puck. I could have decided to grind out the answers and become a mediocre chemical engineer at some ethylene glycol factory in New Jersey. That's what I would have been: really mediocre. I would have probably been worse than I was as a piano player. (I was just the worst; I recognized early on that I wasn't going to be any good so I stopped doing it.)

FEINSTEIN: You must have had some introduction to jazz in order to pick up on the name "Squirrel."

O'NEAL: No.

FEINSTEIN: No? How did you recognize his name?

O'NEAL: It was part of a natural progression. My parents loved music. My mom was an adequate piano player; she played operetta, light opera, and stuff like that. My father didn't play anything. I remember him buying a piano for thirty-five dollars for me to take lessons. Big old upright. My father tried to learn how to play the aria from *Samson and Delilah*—"*Mon Coeur s'ouve à ta voix*"—and he never could do it. I never could, either. But he had all the records, so I started listening to classics a lot and continued. I didn't listen to anything else, and we certainly didn't go to concerts or to clubs. We were in Fort Worth, Texas. Today, Forth Worth has Bass Hall and all that fancy stuff, but in 1948 Ornette Coleman was probably playing in some jump band, and Dewey Redman was doing what he was doing, but not much was going on that an eight-year-old kid would know about.

From there we went to [Bloomington] Indiana [from 1949 to 1953], and then to Syracuse when I was thirteen. And I remember very distinctly: They let me play their records. I had to be very careful with them because they were 78s, and I played them all, just to hear what they were. As I said, my mom liked operetta, and sometime back in the '30s, she had gone to the record store and wanted an operetta record, but they sold her the wrong one. She wanted a copy of Victor Herbert's "Indian Love Call" from *Rose-Marie*, and I put it on and it was Artie Shaw. I said, "Oh my. This is very different." From that point on, I started liking that kind of music.

When I was a freshman in high school, around fourteen, I was given a little record player that came in a kind of suitcase, and it played 78s, 45s, and LPs. They gave me two 45s with it: Rosie Clooney singing "This Old House" and the McGuire Sisters singing "Muscrat Ramble." I had a job at the grocery store on the block, and I would save my money, and the first record I bought was one that George Avakian did: It was called *I Like Jazz*, a Columbia record. And there was an EmArcy one called *Jazz of Two Decades*. They cost ninety-nine cents— or maybe they cost $1.98.

Then I got a part-time job at Bruce Wilson's record store for about fifty cents an hour, and every bit of it went into buying records, and not necessarily from him. I had started going to the library, and one book said that you could find 78 records in junk stores. So I started going to the Salvation Army and Goodwill. (The other day I played a Django Reinhardt record for a young cousin of mine, and I told her, "When I was a kid, you couldn't buy records like this. You had to *find* them.") I remember the first Salvation Army store that I ever went into in Syracuse. I found a whole pile of records, and the one on the top was an original Victor [recording] of Jelly Roll Morton and the Red Hot Peppers doing "Black Bottom Stomp," and I thought, "Wow! This is easy!" [Laughs.] I think it was another two or three years before I found another Jelly Roll Morton . . . But I kept looking for those records, and finding people who liked them.

I discovered early on something that works all the way to this very day: A certain kind of jazz music for people of a certain age and era becomes a common bond. It's a link. I remember, for example, when I got a summer job as a plumber's assistant. I mean, I had to carry the slop from the basements. And I thought this was the most ignorant, buffoonish guy I'd ever seen in my life—until I found out that he had actually *seen* Bix Beiderbecke at the Alhambra in Syracuse, and that he had *seen* Django Reinhardt in wartime France. So he was okay. And later, with people who were 110 times fancier than I was, I was just a kid, but I was okay because I knew who, say, [bass saxophonist] Joe Rushton was. (Squirrel Ashcraft was astounded; Joe Rushton was his best friend.) And it has continued that way to this day. I mean, the little dinner party that Ahmet Ertegun had the other night consisted of Shelly and myself; a young Turkish investment banker (probably a cousin); George Wein and Joyce Wein; Ahmet's niece, Leyla; and a doctor from France. And, as often as not, you could not get in a word edgewise because Ahmet wanted to talk about [alto saxophonist and clarinetist] Boyce Brown and others. It's quite a common bond that has always existed. Jazz is the greatest equalizer in the world. And it should be.

Another interesting thing that came up on Friday in the talk with George [Avakian] about Nesuhi Ertegun concerned people who worked it out so that the music could get done in the first place, who put their money where their mouth was, their reputations on the line. I mean, George had to find a whole lot of Johnny Mathises and people like that to underwrite signing Miles Davis. But none of the credit flows back to the fact that a Nesuhi Ertegun or a George Avakian or a John Hammond or a Bob Thiele not only put it on the line but, occasionally, had the ideas of what they should do.

Here's a classic example of that. Everybody talks about Louis Armstrong having this great enormous hit on "Mack the Knife." Well, this is how it worked: George heard the song at the Theater de Lys when they did *The Three Penny Opera* down on Christopher Street in the early 1950s, and said, "This is a great song." And he talked to every single person on the CBS roster to do it; everybody said no. He finally asked Turk Murphy if Turk would do it, and Turk said, "No, I won't do it, but I'll tell you who *should* do it: You should ask Louis Armstrong to do it." So George said, "That's a great idea," and he got him to do it. Turk wrote the arrangements and gave them to Louis on the [West] Coast. Louis *lost* the arrangements, and when he got back to New York, they had no arrangement. They did five or six takes of it, and every single one was wrong, messed up, but they had to quit after one session because Louis was going on tour the next day. George took all the takes home and started cutting them up. What you hear as the finished version is bits of this and bits of that. Louis went out on tour to Europe, and when he came back, the record was a hit. He played his first job and people yelled, "Play 'Mack the Knife'! Play 'Mack the Knife'!" He didn't even know how it went! He had to go down the next day, put a nickel in the slot, and learn it off the jukebox.

Now, George gets no credit for that. It's Louis Armstrong's performance of "Mack the Knife." And when George recorded Ellington at Newport doing "Diminuendo [and Crescendo in Blue," which sent the crowd into a frenzy], it reinvigorated Ellington's career. And it's not just George. I mean, it's Nesuhi who put his neck on the line to get Ornette Coleman into the studio, or to develop the Modern Jazz Quartet. Not that the musicians' music was any less—of course it wasn't; it was great all the time. But nobody cared, and it was this handful of people like Norman Granz that enabled them to get their stuff out there because, left to their own devices, it wouldn't get out there. Not enough credit is given to these legendary, hard-working guys. Of course it was their job, but their job could easily have been recording some pop person. They recognized what few people recognize now: You must have a balance. The people at major record companies today are so non-musical, for the most part. What are they going to reissue in forty years of what they're doing today? Nothing—they're going to reissue what was done in the '30s and '40s and '50s because they aren't going to have any product from today.

Now, when we did the project on Friday, the young sound engineer, Fiona McBain, turned out to be a fine vocalist, and she had her

CD with her put out by Sony. She's part of a group called Ollabelle that sings very eclectic things—two Blind Willie Johnson songs—but T-Bone Burnett was in back of them, so, because it was T-Bone Burnett, Sony took a chance and did about 40,000 units and they aren't going to do any more, but that's not enough [for most large companies]. My God—if I could do 40,000 on one of my records, I'd stand on my head. (I haven't been standing on my head recently, or ever.) But that's the kind of thing that, a long time ago, you'd be happy to put out and balance with something that's going to sell 200,000 or a million copies, and it's also the kind of thing that in thirty or forty years still has some validity.

The enablers who fixed it so Bobby Hackett and others could make records—they were important people who are not as recognized as they should be. The ones who get recognized are the ones that also had pop hits. I mean, [record producer] Milt Gabler is not in the Rock and Roll Hall of Fame because he did Louis Armstrong and Billie Holiday; he's in there because he did Bill Haley. One of the first conversations I had with Ahmet Ertegun was about an old blues singer, Blind Willie McTell. That's all he wanted to talk about: finding an old blues singer in Atlanta. But that's not what he's in the Hall of Fame for, either. It's the Rolling Stones and Ray Charles and all of that. I mean, you realize one of the very first records that Atlantic Records ever made was a 78 of Eddie Condon.

People of a certain age and era—someone from, say, fifty to eighty— who grew up in the '50s and '60s, would come to New York and go to [clubs such as] Condon's or Jimmy Ryan's or Birdland, and they would form lasting friendships. They would remember all this with great affection, as do I. It's been a wonderful ride. Jazz is just a portion of what I'm up to, but it's always the fun portion. Everything that I've done has grown from the music. I mean, the stuff that I'm doing in photography is a direct result of that book. [O'Neal points to the table where I placed my copy of *Eddie Condon's Scrapbook of Jazz,* which he co-authored with Condon.] When we were doing that book, Eddie was talking to friends, and one friend had taken this picture—[O'Neal displays the photo on the back]—and her name was Genevieve Naylor. Through Gen, I met [her friend and mentor] Berenice Abbott. I remember asking Gen, "Does she sell photographs?" (I was so naïve . . .) She said, "Of course she does. How do you think she makes a living?" I said, "I don't know . . . but I'd like to buy two." She asked which ones I wanted and I told her Jean Cocteau and James Joyce. A week or so later, she called back and said, "Well, they're 100 dollars for an eight by ten, 150 for eleven by fourteen, and 200 for a sixteen by twenty." I said, "I'll take an eight by ten." [Both laugh.] About two or three months later, I get this phone call. [O'Neal lowers his voice considerably:] "Hello. This is Berenice Abbott. I'm in town. I've got your photographs. It's 300 dollars. I know you wanted eight by tens but they ought to be eleven by fourteens. Take it or leave it." [O'Neal mimics himself mumbling.] "And bring cash." So I got the money and met her, and that started nineteen years of working with Berenice Abbott.

I actually got Mary Lou Williams to go to Maine and hang out with Berenice. I had given Berenice a record of Mary Lou's that I had made, and she loved it.

FEINSTEIN: Which record—*Live at the Cookery* or *Night Life*?

O'NEAL: No, the one that excited her first was the Buddy Tate one [*Buddy Tate and His Buddies,* with Mary Lou Williams on piano] because there was a song on there called "Paris Nights" and Berenice loved things that were from Paris, even if it was only a title. Even though Berenice hated church more than just about anything, she drove Mary Lou, who was a very devout Catholic, along with Father Peter O'Brien, Mary Lou's spiritual adviser, to a church in Greenville. Berenice sat in the car during the whole service. [O'Neal growls.] Mad, probably— but she'd do it because it was Mary Lou Williams. Music has always been the most marvelous common denominator.

FEINSTEIN: *Eddie Condon's Scrapbook* [*of Jazz*] opens with a wonderful letter from John Steinbeck, part of which you later quoted in liner notes for the Bob Wilber/Scott Hamilton record [*Bob Wilber and the Scott Hamilton Quartet*]. It's very much in keeping with what you've been saying: "Let a filthy kid, unknown, unheard of and unbacked sit in—and if he can do it—he is recognized and accepted instantly. Do you know of any other field where this is true?"

O'NEAL: Oh yeah. He really believed that. It makes you friends with board chairmen and plumbers, if they like the same thing and have the ability to talk about it.

FEINSTEIN: Who would you say writes well about jazz?

O'NEAL: Of the people I've ever read, the best was probably Otis Ferguson. Unhappily, Otis Ferguson was blown up off Sicily during World War II on a merchant marine ship. He primarily wrote for *The New Republic*. He had a two-parter in *The New Republic* in the '30s about Bix that was absolutely wonderful. His writings were collected in a small little book (he didn't write very long) in the early '80s [*Otis Ferguson Reader*]. He wrote a very insightful piece about John Hammond that I had not seen [before the reprint]. At that time I was working very closely with John, and I said to him, "Hey, I've got this new book by Otis Ferguson. There's a piece in there about you." John said, "Oh, yeah. I remember that." I said, "He's not very complimentary," and John said, "Well, you know, he had it pretty much right."

FEINSTEIN: Wow. That's generous.

O'NEAL: John recognized where his faults were, and he also recognized that the guy knew how to spell and was very perceptive. Otis Ferguson was absolutely terrific.

Of the people who write today, clearly Whitney [Balliett] is the best writer. You sometimes may not agree with what he says about this or that. There are other people I might agree with more, but as a wordsmith, Whitney is first rate, and always has been. Some writers have an agenda beyond the music, beyond the people. They have a sociological point of view that they want to put forward: "The music evolved this and that way *because* of oppression, or because of this or that." And I think that's a disservice.

I also enjoy almost everything that Gary Giddins does, and I still read everything Nat Hentoff writes and speak with him about once a week, but mainly about political matters.

FEINSTEIN: Of your books, I have yet to see *The Best of Jazz: Noted Writers on Great Jazz Records*.

O'NEAL: Boy, I haven't, either! [Laughs.] I had a good friend whose name was Ben Raeburn who ran Horizon Press, best known, perhaps, for the wonderful things that he did with Frank Lloyd Wright. Ben always did really good books, but they were not necessarily really successful financially. He was the original publisher of *The Encyclopedia of Jazz* [by Leonard Feather]. He was originally going to do my Berenice Abbott book but had gotten sick, and that's when it went to Jackie Onassis and, eventually, McGraw Hill. Anyway, sometime in the early '80s, he said, "Let's think of a project," and the next week I said, "Ben, here's what I would like to do: a book based on liner notes." It would be liner notes written for LPs and 78s by people that you didn't associate with being liner note writers. The people out there in liner note land basically say the same things over and over. That's their job: They write reviews for *Down Beat* and they write record liners, and there's not a hell of a lot of sizzle in what they're doing. So I said, "What I'd like to do is find fifty or sixty really important artists and combine them with fifty or sixty really good liners by people who are not professional liner note writers." He said, "That's a great idea. Go do it."

So he went out and got a Library of Congress number for the title and so on. I put it together. I called all the record companies; if I wanted something from Atlantic, for example, I'd call Nesuhi Ertegun. In some instances I had to talk to the writers. Everybody said yes. And then, before anything happened, Ben went out of business, and I never took it anyplace else.

About eight or nine years ago, Tom Piazza did a book on the same subject [*Setting the Tempo: Fifty Years of Great Liner Notes*], but he didn't do it the same way. I chose things that were just a tad more obscure: Mort Sahl writing about somebody, or Paul Desmond writing about somebody. It had to be a combination of two things: an artist who was moderately well known, like George Fraser writing about Glenn Miller (there was an early one from the '50s that was just as good as it got). I've still got the manuscript; it's probably in a file downstairs.

FEINSTEIN: But it never appeared? I've seen it listed—

O'NEAL: It's listed on Amazon as the 347,823 most popular book in the United States. [Feinstein laughs.] That shows you how bogus that system is. Never came out. Never even was handed in! But I finished it. I wound up taking photographs of all the record covers. (Some of them were 78 albums.) You're interested in cover art for *Brilliant Corners*. Well, if you go back far enough, Jimmy Ernst was doing covers for Circle Records. Ben Shahn did Columbia's. Stuart Davis [was] on lots of things. But that book never happened, and there were a number of things like that. In 1981 or '82, for example, John Hammond introduced me to Allen Ginsberg, who I didn't know personally. John had wanted to do a record with Allen but Columbia wouldn't let him. So we now had our own company—

FEINSTEIN: But he did, didn't he? *Blues*—

O'NEAL: *First Blues*. Anyway, I started working with Allen on this project. At that time, Allen was getting interested in photography, so he would come over to my house and go through all the pictures. For about ten years, starting in the early '70s, I had taken pictures of the Gay Parade on Christopher Street. Allen saw these and he thought they were great.

We cooked up a scheme whereby he was going to pick out his favorite 120 pictures and was going to write poetic captions on them, which he did. A few months later, William Burroughs got involved and wrote an introduction. Well, we must have shown that to a dozen different people who were just *horrified.* The gay editors only wanted muscle books and books about looking good and gay romances and that kind of stuff. The straight editors: *blaaaah!* [Feinstein laughs.] So it went back on the shelf. Now, twenty-something years later, somebody's interested—because now it's history. I mean, the book was to support AIDS research, but in 1983, the *New York Times* wouldn't even use the acronym AIDS in print.

I've always found it to be very, very hard to get books done. Once, when I was talking to Jackie Onassis about the Berenice Abbott book, I said, "Jackie, the only books that get sold these days are cookbooks, books about cats, or books about you." [Feinstein laughs.] I said, "Why don't we do a book and call it *Jackie Onassis's "How to Cook a Cat" Book.* [Both laugh.] She laughed and laughed. Never did that one, either.

FEINSTEIN: You recently took some excellent portraits of a favorite poet and friend, Hayden Carruth. I know that Hayden dedicated his book *Sitting In* [*Selected Writings on Jazz, Blues, and Related Topics,* 1986] to you and Brad Morrow. I think *Sitting In* is a marvelous collection of poetry and prose.

O'NEAL: It's a terrific book.

FEINSTEIN: When did your relationship begin?

O'NEAL: I have all the correspondence in the basement; I'd have to go back and check, but I think it was 1983. I had gotten a journal that had one of his jazz poems in it. What struck me, and what caused me to write the letter to him, was that he was talking about Buck Clayton, and he said that Buck was dead. [Laughs.] I wrote him a letter and said, "No, he's not. I had dinner with him last week! Unless something happened between now and then that I don't know about . . ." And that just started a lively correspondence that has continued to this day about music and politics and taking pictures.

Hayden's somebody who writes letters; most people don't. Letter writing is a vanishing art. Nobody wants to write a letter. They'll send you an e-mail and so forth. There are a handful of people that I write letters to on a regular basis, and they are clearly ten or twenty years older than I am. For example, Ahmet Ertegun writes letters. Hayden Carruth does. William F. Buckley does. Most people don't. I work with [university president] Bob Kerry at The New School; Bob writes letters, and they're often in longhand, which is *very* unusual. Of course, there is telephone conversation as well. Maybe I should have taped them because they're fun and interesting, but I don't tape people's phone conversations—

FEINSTEIN: Despite all your years in the CIA—

O'NEAL: Despite all my years of training. [Both laugh.] (I wasn't trained on doing that anyway.) But that was my connection with Hayden. He's quite a remarkable, wonderful poet and a very generous person. Like all poets, he has difficulty knowing where his next typewriter ribbon is going to come from. People say that modern dancers are the most scuffling of all artists, but I say, "Naw, probably modern poets are the most scuffling of all the artists."

FEINSTEIN: You've also photographed Amiri Baraka. What do you think of his writings on jazz?

O'NEAL: I thought he was very interesting. I have a wall full of books on jazz and music, and, frankly, most of it I use as a reference resource—except for the ones that I read early on. I mean, I do not need another book about Duke Ellington or Louis Armstrong. My problem is, there is only X number of hours in a day to read something (or to do anything, for that matter), and I've never been a biography person. For example, I've recently finished up a book about Berenice Abbott, just about working with her: what she thought about doing this or that, how we accomplished one project or another. Now, a good friend of mine is doing the formal biography [of Abbott] and is now 800 pages into it. It's going to have every fact anyone would ever want to know. But I think that if you have worked with somebody or you know the basic outlines of what, say, Louis Armstrong did, and then you look at his work, that's basically what you need to know. With Berenice, you know the basic outlines, you look at the work, you know the way she did it, what she thought about; if you learn of a relationship that she had in 1933, that might be very nice, but it's not anything that's going to change the overall appreciation of her great pictures. And if you find out that Louis Armstrong had an affair with a billy goat in 1942, it's not going to change "West End Blues" one bit.

FEINSTEIN: So what do you think are the most positive qualities of jazz-related literature?

O'NEAL: That's a good question. By jazz literature you mean people who write stories about jazz?

FEINSTEIN: No—the books on your wall, for example, which I assume range from Hayden Carruth's poetry to encyclopedias of jazz to biographies—

O'NEAL: Everybody, yeah. Okay: If they can accomplish the same thing that four or five books that I looked at when I was fifteen or sixteen— that is, gave me a basic guide—like Marshall Stearns's book [*The Story of Jazz*] or Hugues Panassié's book [*Guide to Jazz*] that was mainly a listing of names, like who Johnny Dodds was. If it was something that could stimulate a young person or a teenager to get them interested in a non-prejudicial fashion. (I recognized early on that Hugues Panassié only put black people in his book, with a handful of exceptions.) If you can just simply listen . . . I think the great thing about those first jazz records that I had, *I Like Jazz* and *Jazz of Two Decades,* was that here on one LP [*I Like Jazz*] was Wally Rose playing ragtime all the way up to [arranger] Pete Rugolo, and in the middle was Brubeck and Louis Armstrong and Billie Holiday and Lester Young and Bix Beiderbecke and whoever. And on the EmArcy *Jazz of Two Decades,* the decades being the '40s and '50s, there was a track from *Midnight at Eddie Condon's,* and a track of Clifford Brown, and Clark Terry and Lennie Tristano and Sarah Vaughan. So, at the same time that I'm listening to Sarah Vaughan, I'm listening to Bessie Smith, and I don't think one is modern and one is old; they're just both good. People should just listen to whether something is good, not whether it's new or old. It's just whether somebody is playing well and sensibly, not because they're male or female, black or white, French or whatever.

And the same with literature: A biography of Charles Mingus three inches thick is not going to help a seventeen year old appreciate Charles Mingus. My eyes glaze over at anything about *anybody* that's three inches thick. You might get just as much from a poem about Thelonious Monk as you could in a three-inch biography, if that short poem can somehow stimulate someone to hear what was this man about. In today's world that wants to go like *that*—[O'Neal snaps his fingers]—a seventeen year old is not going to pay much attention to the three-inch book, any more than I would have.

The other books that I remember from early on were Leonard's book, the first version of it (I guess that was in the early '60s).

FEINSTEIN: You mean [Leonard Feather's] *The Encyclopedia of Jazz*?

O'NEAL: Yeah, just because it listed names.

FEINSTEIN: And addresses!

O'NEAL: Yes, exactly—it had addresses. I remember a paperback I had on Jelly Roll Morton, [Alan Lomax's] *Mister Jelly Roll,* and I had found a copy of Rudy Blesh's *Shining Trumpets*. I remember finding a copy of the great big *Esquire Jazz Book* [from the 1940s] with all the pretty pictures. And the book that Orrin [Keepnews] and Bill Grauer did, called *The Pictorial History of Jazz,* a remaindered edition so the pictures were not very good but you could still tell who was who. Since then, of course, there have been books and books and books on the subject. I don't know what part the writing does, but I know what it did for me early on. I'd go to the Syracuse Public Library to get these books, and when I had a quarter or thirty-five cents (or whatever it was), I'd get a copy of *Down Beat.*

In 1981 or '82, I was in the Argosy Bookshop on 59th and I found five bound volumes of *Down Beat* from my formative years: '56, '57, '58, '59, and '60. They were in big binders, all fifty-two issues, and they were Bill Grauer's copies (they had his name inside). Then, a couple or three years ago, when Ruby Braff was sick and dying, he called to talk, and I said, "Ruby, wait just a second." I pulled off 1957 and went through it with Ruby, the great reviews of his records and stories about him. He laughed a lot and enjoyed it. That I found to be very useful. Those are nice little time capsules.

FEINSTEIN: One of the many unusual aspects of Chiaroscuro Records is JazzSpeak [cuts of musicians talking, frequently included at the end of the CDs]. I'd like to know more about the inspiration for presenting these narratives, and maybe about oral traditions in general.

O'NEAL: When I was a kid first buying records, I remember a record that Coleman Hawkins had made that he talked on. And I also had a record—I was a little older, maybe twenty or twenty-one—that [writer and ethnomusicologist] Sam Charters had done about Blind Willie Johnson. I was a big Blind Willie Johnson fan. The first time I found a Blind Willie Johnson record, I was beyond thrilled. I said, "My God! What is *this*!" It was "Church I'm Fully Saved Today." Blind Willie and his wife with that real high voice in the back. (I said, "I've got to get more of these," and of course there weren't any more to get. You had to find them.) But the Sam Charters' Folkways record was the first LP, and half of it was Columbia 78s; the other side was Sam and Blind Willie's wife telling stories about him. I thought this was terrific because there wasn't anything written down. Here was his wife telling the stories, and then telling how he got cold and sick and caught pneumonia and died. I always thought this was important, and was also impressed with [Nat Shapiro and Nat Hentoff's] *Hear Me Talkin' to Ya* [*The Story of Jazz by the Men Who Made It*].

Somebody once wrote that the best thing in jazz literature, just by the very nature of the music and the people who play it, are the short little spontaneous things that happen in newspaper columns or places like that. They're not necessarily the things that are put down by scholarly academics who do a lot of research and make big fat books. So much of jazz is an oral history. A great deal of what has passed as history was really shoddy jazz journalism at best.

In the mid '80s, when I started *The Ghosts of Harlem* project, which is before I had Chiaroscuro back with Andy Sordoni, I had started interviewing all these Harlem guys, and they were telling all of this stuff, and I thought, "My goodness, some of this is *marvelous*." I was talking to some obscure people that nobody had ever cared about, and sometimes you get a better insight from the third trumpet player in Jimmy Lunceford's band than from some big star. When Andy and I started Chiaroscuro again in 1988, the CD gave you so much more room that I decided it made sense to start letting the musician talk about what he had done on this record, or anything else he or she wanted to. I know this annoyed some people who just wanted to put the record on and hear the music; they didn't want to hear some guy talking for the last fifteen minutes of it. "I want more music!" Well, that's very nice. But if we give you an hour and I still have twenty minutes to play with on a CD, why not put something else?

I guess it went all the way from having someone say five or six minutes' worth, all the way to having totally separate CDs of somebody talking. I'm doing one right now with Clark Terry: The first CD is his big band recorded in Switzerland; the second is *nothing* but Clark talking about how he was educated and how he educates others. I think that, at a certain stage with certain people, what they have to say with their voice is almost as important as what they have to say with their horns. This *is* an oral tradition.

I'm associated with The New School where we have 280 students, and I'm chairman of the board of governors for jazz and contemporary music. At the same time, I'm very suspicious of certain kinds of academic activity. When the New School program got started in 1985, they sent me the curriculum on what they wanted to do, and they listed a whole bunch of people who were going to teach, including Zoot Sims. As it turned out, that very night Zoot and Louise were coming over for dinner. He was very sick at the time, and I jokingly said, "Hey Zoot, I see you're going to be teaching at The New School next fall," and he said, "No . . . I don't think so." So I said, "Well Zoot, if you were going to teach a course at a university, what course would you like to teach?" and he said, "I'd teach a course on how to scuffle."

FEINSTEIN: That's perfect.

O'NEAL: "Teach 'em how to scuffle."

At a recent board meeting, a wonderful young guitarist named Peter Bernstein was telling how it really worked [at The New School] in the earliest years. They were given vouchers that were worth $100, or something like that. They would go to some great jazz person and take a lesson, giving the voucher to the musician who in turn could then cash it in for money. Peter said, "I've got to admit that for a couple of these things, my lesson was nothing more than talking to Roy Haynes." And I said, "That's enough. You got your money's worth. You got a whole lot more money's worth with that than sitting in with somebody who had graduated from a school and become a teacher automatically."

I did a record with Nat Adderley that probably annoys the hell out of everybody. It's down toward the end of Nat's career.

FEINSTEIN: *Live at the Floating Jazz Festival*?

O'NEAL: Yeah. In some instances, he has six- or seven-minute introductions to the songs. He's talking to get his energy back. So I left in all the introductions, turned it into a two-CD set, and had no more than probably sixty or seventy minutes of music—but I also have sixty minutes of him talking. No matter what I do on these records, they're not going to sell a zillion copies but, like that Eddie Condon book, these records will be around a whole lot longer than whatever's number one right now. They'll have validity because somebody's going to care about what Clark Terry or Earl Hines or Mary Lou Williams played *or* said in fifty or a hundred years, where they aren't going to give two hoots about your biggest rap guy or pop guy or whatever—any more than you can remember today what the number one record was in 1929, '39, '49, or probably even '59. Didn't matter, and it doesn't have any currency in that it is not going to influence anybody. It is not going to make anybody a better pianist; it's not going to make them a better *anything*. It won't even be a footnote. It'll be a blip.

And so consequently, if the people's music is that good, why not have them talk? I mean, wouldn't you have loved an hour of Charlie

Parker telling you about what he was doing? Maybe Phil Woods isn't Charlie Parker, but he's damn good, and today almost as important, because he's carrying on the tradition.

FEINSTEIN: And he's articulate.

O'NEAL: And if he has something to say, put it down. All these oral histories that people have done are really important. But most of these oral histories, as good as they are, are stuck away in libraries where you have to make a really concerted effort to go find them. These [Chiaroscuro] CDs are out there. Now, they're not out there in great quantities, but if they're out there in the quantity of 3- or 4,000, it's a hell of a lot bigger quantity than one library. So that's what it was all about. I thought it was important.

Eugene B. Redmond. *Photo by Lenora Anita Redmond-Spencer.*

16

Levels of the Blues
Eugene B. Redmond

Henry Dumas (1934–1968) was the author of several books of stories and poems, including *Knees of a Natural Man, Play Ebony Play Ivory, Ark of Bones,* and *Goodbye, Sweetwater.* All appeared posthumously; Dumas was killed by a New York City Transit policeman in a case of "mistaken identity." He was thirty-three. The people centrally responsible for keeping his works in print have been his widow, Loretta Dumas, and his friend and literary executor, Eugene Redmond.

I had been in contact with Eugene in the mid '90s while co-editing *The Second Set,* an anthology that included work by both Dumas and Redmond, as well as another blues-influenced poet, Raymond R. Patterson. When Patterson died in 2001, I thought *Brilliant Corners* should run a selection of his work in tribute to his largely unrecognized career; in addition, I thought of running a selection of blues poems by Henry Dumas. I telephoned Eugene at his home in East St. Louis, and he liked the idea. And when I asked if he was coming east—that I would love to interview him for the journal—he said, "Funny you should mention it now. I'm leaving in a few days for New Jersey." He had plans to stay with Loretta Dumas and said he would be pleased to set aside some time to talk. Like so many projects connected to *Brilliant Corners*, this interview seemed destined.

In terms of unfurling narratives, Eugene remains the most circuitous speaker I've interviewed. Some passages and ideas were completed two hours later, and this final version reflects a substantial amount of editing. When I sent him the proofs, he realized the magnitude of my changes and telephoned me. "I remember the course of our conversation," he said, "so I know how you've worked with the text." I steeled myself for an explosive objection. (As Fats Waller famously asked, "One never knows, do one?") Then he took his time expressing his gratitude.

I hope he knows it was my pleasure.

Eugene B. Redmond is poet laureate of East St. Louis, Illinois, and the author of six poetry collections, including *Eye in the Ceiling: Selected Poems,* which received the American Book Award. Other awards include a creative writing fellowship from the National Endowment for the Arts and a Pushcart Prize. He is also author of *Drumvoices: The Mission of Afro-American Poetry—A Critical History* and founding editor of *Drumvoices Revue;* since 1968, when he became literary executor for the Henry Dumas estate, he has edited several volumes of Dumas's prose and poetry. In 1986, a group of East St. Louis authors formed the Eugene B. Redmond Writers Club.

The following prose excerpts correspond to issues that we discussed. The interview took place in Somerset, New Jersey, at the home of Loretta Dumas on August 9, 2002.

. . . .

From *Drumvoices*
Eugene B. Redmond

The student of black poetry should arm himself to the best of his ability with the tools of criticism and a knowledge of black culture. He must understand the part "duality" plays in the lives of blacks and how such "twoness" is manifested in the poetry; he should recognize the key issues being raised and debated among black artists, scholars, and activists, and have some feel for the historical circumstances out of which these issues and debates grew; he ought to understand what Baraka means in his references to some black poets as "integrationists" and "arty poets"; he will have to know what many of the new poets mean when they say they reject Western "forms" and refuse to be judged by *white* standards (Baraka, for example, talks about post-American forms). He will also want to recognize black in-house humor and intracommunal disparagement in such words and phrases as "nigger," "Negro," "Uncle Tom," "oreo," "colored," "the man," "dicty," "bad mouth," "bust a nut," "brother," "crumbcrushers," "main squeeze," and "Mr. Charlie."

From *Drumvoices*
Eugene B. Redmond

[Fenton] Johnson writes about roustabouts, prostitutes, vagrants, laborers, and strong will, and is, as Jay Wright said (during the late 1960s) of Henry Dumas, "the poet of the dispossessed." He is also the poet of the blues. In breaking away from traditional black poetic diction and form, Johnson not only received influence from the white experimenters of free verse but he borrowed heavily from the blues and, at this level, must share some of the accolades usually reserved almost solely for [Langston] Hughes.

It is now widely accepted that the blues do not simply preach resignation. To the contrary, the blues, telling about heartache and personal failures, carry hope in the singing and the going on. Margaret Walker is only one of the many poets whose work seems to reflect the influence of Johnson. And do we really believe that Johnson meant for the children to be thrown in the river, any more than we take the blues singer literally when he promises to "lay my head down on some railroad track"? Johnson's "note of despair" is one more brilliant distillation of the strange psychological web that produced the sorrow songs, the spirituals, the ditties, jokes, rhymes, and blues.

From the Introduction to Henry Dumas's *Knees of a Natural Man*
Eugene B. Redmond

He came out of the vase *somewhere*—like the music—with the music, mounting Robert Hayden's "rocking loom of history."

He was tuned in. Turned on. Cultural stabilizer. Cultural modulator. Funkadelic verb-gymnast. Irreversibly switched to Everyblood.

And, like his Everyblood counterpart in that oft-sung scroll *Ark of*

Bones, Henry Lee Dumas (1934–1968) was *called* to bear witness to the terrible swish and sass and swoon of life; to bear and *bare* the word. To shuttle the word between its far/near distances and its points of distillation along the Blackhuman Continuum. Wordwise he was sent to honor and *re*-illuminate those ancient things that remain in the ears. To sculpt slavery into song and churn commotion into poetry. . . .

Like Hughes, Dumas sought spiritually and culturally to unite his Black World ("all you golden-black children of the sun"); he recalled the past, which can only be reconstructed and re-entered by dispossessed people if they "make heavy-boned ships that break a wave and pass it." Then, and only then, can they "Bring back sagas from Songhay, Kongo, Kaaba, / deeds and works of Malik Toussaint, Marcus, / statues of Mahdi and a lance of lightning."

From *Drumvoices*
Eugene B. Redmond

We have said the poet takes a stand not inherent in, say, the musician's, when he commits his thoughts to paper. And over the past few years of social change and unrest, the black poet whose aesthetic or religious position was not aligned with that of vested interest groups came up before many a *strange* court, at which times his own feelings and sensibilities were often neutralized in favor of the "popular latex brand." Serious critics and "cultural stabilizers" need to examine such "one-way" approaches to poetry/criticism, especially as they have occurred over the past ten years. We mention this "side" show of the contemporary poetry scene because its presence has often dirtied the waters of "open" thought and either crippled or destroyed many a budding talent. In a few cases, it has even muffled a rich or significant voice. However, it is time the critical flood gates were "opened" completely and honestly. Only in this way can Afro-American poetry continue to breathe the breath of the ancestors. . . .

Most poetic principles, and the language associated with them, rely on the vocabulary of sound and music. Music is the most shared experience— the most vital commodity—among Afro-Americans. And poetry is music's twin. Both the metaphysical and the metaphorical word stem from and return to the drum.

SASCHA FEINSTEIN: There were many different experiences in my life that brought together literature and music, but, early on, two of the major text sources were Stephen Henderson's *Understanding the New Black Poetry* and [your critical study] *Drumvoices*. What were your formative influences when you started making connections between music and literature?

EUGENE REDMOND: When I was a kid, *everybody* wanted to box, and everybody wanted to *play* something. Every male wanted to be a boxer—you were trained to defend yourself in boxing—and early on we recognized that it was not *just* boxing as a sport or as a form of defense, but it was art. Often when you talked, you were engaged in the drama, in the ritual of boxing. And I don't remember anybody who didn't want to play an instrument and who didn't try to sing. I remember people trying to sing like Sinatra, like Nat Cole, like Billy Eckstine, like Cab Calloway, like Joe Williams—and, later, like Johnny Hartman.

I played several instruments, and a lot of them were homemade, very rough: old mailboxes, lunch pails, old tin cans and buckets and abandoned tubs and boxes. Various kinds of bottles that you'd fill to various levels with water and hit on the sides with forks and spoons. So we had these "orchestras" all over the community. As soon as school let out, and sometimes even on the playground between classes, the doo-wopping started. We're talking about the '40s and '50s, so this activity was widespread. Entertainment that was original, spontaneous, extemporaneous, improvisational; it wasn't dependent on high-tech. *Everybody wanted to play an instrument or sing!* It was the culture. It was the south end of East St. Louis, Illinois, the black side of town.

FEINSTEIN: About how old were you?

REDMOND: Between the ages of about eight and fifteen. When I was about nine, I started tagging along with my older brother, John Henry Redmond, Jr., who blocked hats and pressed clothes at Division Cleaners and Hat Shop owned by Chris Poulous, a Greek man who had all black employees, with the exception of Ray, his cousin. People would hand their clothes to me from a makeshift booth and I would give them to the presser, who would press them right there. (This was very common—not getting clothes cleaned but just pressed—and many people would get suits pressed several times before they actually got them cleaned.) Division Hat Shop was an intersection of the races and the classes. East St. Louis was a gangster town: the home of white gangsters, black and Italian gangsters, Armenian gangsters, German gangsters, Jewish gangsters. And then you had the Irish detectives. So you had all these languages moving through. That cultural panorama played a very important role in my pre-teen and teen years.

The verbal sparring—the signifying, the dozens—was also very central to the way we came up. When I was in junior high school and through high school, I emceed talent shows. I would make up all sorts of rhymes and rhythms and puns and cuts and turns and twists of language in order to keep the audience jumping, keep the show going. So I got good at joning and signifying and playing the dozens and cutting and the verbal gymnastics. I was growing linguistically. I was growing in terms of style. I was singing and playing my instruments; many people thought I'd end up being a drummer. I was growing in my weaving and bobbing—the boxer thing.

FEINSTEIN: You must appreciate Gerald Early's essays that compare boxing and jazz.

REDMOND: Sure. And essays by other people—everybody from [James] Baldwin to [Norman] Mailer to Joyce Carol Oates—who look at cultural, artistic, social, political, racial connections between a sport and a "fine art" or "cultural art." I think somebody who does a good job of this in poetry is Cornelius Eady. He does a wonderful job of presenting physical movement, choreography in poetry. And Quincy Troupe "feints" nicely in "Magic Johnson" and other sports poems.

FEINSTEIN: So your appreciation for music and literature grew simultaneously?

REDMOND: The twin movement of music and literature has always been a part of my life. I heard some of everybody. I started buying records as a small kid. We played them on the Victrola and, later, the hi-fi. I was exposed to Miles Davis, who went to my high school; he would come home on occasion. Grant Green played at a club called The Peppermint Lounge. There was a popular piano player named Albino Red. Ben Thigpen. George Hudson, the great band leader and music teacher who trained Miles Davis and Hamiet Bluiett. Jerome Harris, whom we called "Scrooge." We're talking late '50s, early to mid '60s now. At the Blue Note, East St. Louis's premiere jazz club, we had Eddie Lockjaw Davis and Jimmy Forrest ("Night Train"). There was Eddie "The Third Cup" Fisher. These were area musicians [who were] in and out of Peoria, Chicago, Decatur, Springfield, Gary, Indianapolis, Detroit, Memphis, Jackson, Omaha, Des Moines. Kansas City, Kansas; Kansas City, Missouri. When they would come through, I would hear them.

Before I was old enough to [enter a club and] hear them, I would sell my papers or have my shoe shine kit. In those days, local boxers, such as Kenneth Silver and Wesbury Bascom (who were contenders for titles), served as bouncers in the clubs, and they all knew me. After I'd make my rounds to see if anybody wanted a paper or a shoe shine, the bouncers would let me stand near the door, sometimes for twenty minutes, a half hour—sometimes even longer. I heard a lot of the greats that way.

You know who was one of my high school classmates? Leon Thomas, who graduated a year ahead of me. "Amos." (We didn't call him Leon; that was his birth name—Amos Leon Thomas—but you can see why he gave up Amos. [Both laugh.] "Amos 'n Andy." That's what we heard on the radio.) In fact, the poem that I wrote for my high school class's forty-fifth reunion ["We're Tight, Soul-Tight—Like Lincolnites"] starts out:

> It wasn't Elmore James, Muddy Waters or Howlin' Wolf growling
> "Dust My Broom"
> Or Big Mama Thornton driving a "Hound Dog" from Big Sister's door
> Or the Coasters crooning "Charlie Brown" from hi-fis & juke boxes at
> the Green House or Masonic Hall . . .
> It was Lincolnite Amos Leon Thomas, expanding/contracting against
> wall lockers in the boys' room—

> "Who did they kill? . . .
> Emmett Bobo Till"—

We were coming in from ball practice at school in August of 1955, and some friend of ours drove up in his parents' black Cadillac and said, "Hey, they just killed this stud." (We used the word "stud" to mean "dude" or "cat.") [Whispers:] "They killed this stud down in Mississippi and cut his stuff out. His name was Emmett 'Bobo' Till." And we went into the locker room to shower, and Amos started banging, "Who did they kill?" [Redmond raps the chair, echoing the rhythm of the lines:] "Emmett 'Bobo' Till."

FEINSTEIN: When did you become more serious as a writer?
REDMOND: When I went into the Marine Corps, a year after high school. In my unit, many officers had degrees in English, and they helped me a lot with fiction (Hemingway, John Dos Passos, Faulkner). I wrote

my first and only novel at that time, a 187-page suspense novel called *A Superb Obituary*. I was reading pulp stuff and solid stuff, the hot books of the time. But I wasn't reading black literature (except for some popular magazines like *Jet, Sepia, Bronze Thrills*, and *Ebony*) because no one had prescribed it for me.

Then I got out of the service and went to college at Southern Illinois University in East St. Louis, where I started a more systematic study of literature. One of my teachers, Vernon Hornback, got me reading Langston Hughes and e. e. cummings. This was 1961. He saw that I was playing with the language but recognized that I needed more depth and more training, so he told me, "Hughes for your roots, cummings for the language."

After SIU, I went to Wash[ington] U[niversity] (where Gerald Early now teaches) for grad school. And after that [in 1967], I came back to SIU to teach in their Experiment in Higher Education (E.H.E.) where I met Henry Dumas [who was shot and killed in 1968]. Some of the people who taught there were the sociologist Joyce Ladner, who wrote several important books and was later interim president at Howard [University], and the painter Oliver Jackson. Another person there was Shelby Steele, who almost everybody hates! [Laughs.] Katherine Dunham and the brilliant linguist and Africanist Edward Crosby also taught at E.H.E.

We were putting on shows almost every day: drum ensembles, avant-garde groups, dancers. We were holding rallies. I might read poetry before [activist] Angela Davis spoke and right after [Black Panther co-founder] Huey Newton spoke. You get the point: We were publishing, teaching, reading, protesting, marching, and training a generation of writers and leaders. We were also flying out of town almost every week to set up black studies and ethnic studies and women studies and urban studies programs in Canada and the Carribean and Africa and across the U.S., because we were one of the first black studies programs in the country. We had more scholars—cross-cultural, cross-gender, inter-generational—than any other higher educational center in the country. Everybody there was a radical. My colleagues had come out of the Peace Corps and VISTA; they had traveled around the world and hitchhiked across North America; they had had some kind of experience with Black Powerites, or White Panthers, or were sympathizers, they'd read *The Other America*—and all these people were teaching in this college.

In '69 I went to Oberlin as writer-in-residence (I left after a year because I didn't want to babysit rich kids), and then I went to Cal[ifornia] State, Sacramento, from '70 to '83. I came across country every year on tour, though, and I would visit Loretta [Dumas] and her sons, who were alive then. I was editing Dumas's work—something was coming out every year in the '70s—working with Toni Morrison at Random House and Marie Brown at Doubleday. I was publishing my own stuff through Black River Writers [Publishing Company, founded by Redmond, Dumas, Jerry Herman, and Sherman Fowler], which was part of a bigger movement in the Illinois/Missouri area that included BAG (the Black Artists Group, from which we got the World Saxophone Quartet) and the Experiment in Higher Education. Across the street from E.H.E. was the Performing Arts Training Center, which was run by Katherine Dunham, who brought in the great drummer from the Senegalese ballet, Mor Thiam, who introduced the djembe into the Midwest. That's just a whiff of the ferment and foment that was taking place.

FEINSTEIN: At what point did you say to yourself, "I'm going to write a huge book that brings together these large, interwoven, cultural issues"?

REDMOND: First, I had to get away, and that was a very traumatic episode in my life. Henry [Dumas] was one in a long line of friends who had been killed violently. He'd preceded or followed Taylor Jones, Lyon Herbert, Sister Zubena . . . It seemed that every other week I was going to a funeral to read a poem about someone who'd been shot, either by a cop or during some intraracial conflict. (That was really deep, too—that Panther/Us thing. That was played out across the country.) People were calling SIU asking for us to be fired because they would come over to tour the school and see in our cubicles cartoons from Panther newspapers and pictures of Malcolm X and Che Guevara. For about six months, I'd check under the hood of my car for bombs every time I left it for more than half an hour.

FEINSTEIN: To witness all of that is one thing; to create the kind of document that you made in *Drumvoices* is quite another.

REDMOND: Yeah.

FEINSTEIN: *Drumvoices* does such a wonderful job of setting up the subtleties of black music in its varied forms, as well as the variety of poetic voices influenced by blues and spirituals and jazz and so on. I'm interested in knowing when you decided you were going to set this down, as a formal document.

REDMOND: *Drumvoices* did not begin as ambitiously as it turned out. I had [originally] been approached to do a monograph. My first move was to go to Oberlin. Too much of my non-academic time had been spent working the streets, working the movement. I knew I couldn't stay right at the center of the movement and become the scholar that I needed to become, even if I was only going to teach the literature. I just needed time to systematically study the black canon like I had studied the Euro canon. Oberlin afforded that opportunity.

I really boned up on the spirituals and the blues at Oberlin. They had a number of original texts and editions by people like John Work. I got into James Weldon Johnson and followed the line back into Africa, and then [back to] Zora Neale Hurston, and Katherine Dunham's work and Melville Herskovitz. I looked at the lives of the musicians and studied the history of the music: the New Orleans line and the San Francisco line, the African line, the mixes. I knew that something came before the written word. I knew it in my gut first, then I knew it intellectually, and then I had to go back and know it in my gut again so I could mix the two. That's when I started working on *Drumvoices.*

In the meantime, I started this journeymanship. Since I hadn't gone to a historically black college, nor had I been taught by any black teachers in college, I decided I needed to go to the major libraries in D.C., New Orleans, and around the country, and I went to teach for two consecutive summers at Southern University in Baton Rouge, which at the time was the most populous of the black colleges. There I encountered some people who were into what was known as "Negro Education." They were jazz buffs, blues buffs, folk buffs, and they had classical European education at the same time. It was a great learning time. Louis Armstrong died during my first summer at Southern, and his passing helped set a pace for courses I taught there: He was from Louisiana, and I used his life and music as a catalyst to get into the culture of Louisiana.

Initially, I didn't know what the book was going to be called, and I wasn't sure that it would take the shape of a study of poetry, as opposed to the study of culture with music at the center. I'm glad that I came up with the term "drumvoices"; it has both shadowed and directed me ever since then. But I would not have come up with the term "drumvoices" had it not been for the '60s, and had I not encountered Katherine Dunham. She was a major contributor to the genesis of the *Drumvoices* idea: her work on the drum, her study of dances of Haiti, the Maroons, the global approach to Pan-African humanism that she embraces. I knew about the Anglophone component of Africa, but she introduced me to the Francophone component, not just from Senegal but from Haiti, France, Antilles. That all comes into play when I'm trying to define the black experience. In one footnote in *Drumvoices* I say, "Most attempts to define the black experience have failed" because people are thinking about something narrow—maybe something as narrow as some food—[chuckles]—or some color, or some juke joint down the street.

FEINSTEIN: During the research for *Drumvoices,* were there blues-influenced poets who really surprised you? I mean, did you already know the work of Melvin Tolson, for example?

REDMOND: You know, I had hoped to work with Melvin Tolson, and then he died.

There were people that I talked to, anonymous blues musicians—people who played rot gut, people who chewed tobacco, people who smoked their pipes, people who played washboards and jew's-harps and bottles and guitars made out of cardboard boxes and wooden boxes—and I asked about what they did. This does not include [well known] people I talked to, like Albert King, Sonny Terry, B. B. King, or any number of musicians I ran into in Chicago, where I spent quite a bit of time to catch the blues. I would ask Buddy Guy a question—

FEINSTEIN: What kinds of questions did you ask these musicians?

REDMOND: I would ask for the definition of the blues. "What are the blues?" "What's the difference between the blues and being blue?" "Are blues always sad?" Some of the questions I thought I had answers to; some of the answers that I had changed. I found out that the blues existed on a number of different levels. There was a kind of cleaned-up blues that people would talk about, and they weren't talking about the same blues that Buddy Guy played, or Howlin' Wolf, or Sonny Terry, or Lowell Fulsom, or Muddy Waters, or Bo Diddley, or Elmore James.

I saw all of these musicians in East St. Louis as a kid. I always had odd jobs, and many of my jobs had to do with cleaning up establishments, emptying trash. I still have the posters. You could catch Elmore James for seventy-five cents. You could catch Muddy Waters for a dollar-and-a-quarter. Bo Diddley for this amount or that amount. So I would ask them, "What is the blues?" and some would say, "It's a botheration on your mind." Or, as my father would say, "The blues ain't nothin' but a good man feelin' bad, or a good man feelin' sad." That was sort of my journeymanship. Some of those innocently asked—non-direct—questions would be stored away for decades and then invoked when I began thinking about *Drumvoices*.

I knew there was a deep and abiding connection [between music and literature]. I read Ellison's essays and could see the connection. I read of Baldwin holing up in a room in Europe and playing Bessie Smith records to gain rhythm in his prose. I remember Sam Greenlee, who wrote *The Spook Who Sat By the Door,* saying that the typewriter and the musical instrument are interchangeable. From Michael Harper I gleaned a lot, watching how his poems seemed to be saxophone solos. Sterling Brown—I spoke to him, and he complimented me on *Drumvoices*. He said, "You did okay there. You did all right." But I had suggested [in the book] that Sterling Brown might not have thickened the line of the folk material that he kept collecting from the WPA in what he wrote himself, that sometimes the line was a bit too thin between the actual transcribed folk song or shout or expression and Sterling's own writing of it. I said that in *Drumvoices,* but he was apparently not too upset about that—or maybe he was too drunk to remember it, because he could put down some Rock 'n Rye! And he was doing just that when he entertained a group of us writers in his home in the '70s—that's when he made that comment.

FEINSTEIN: If a young scholar approached you and said, "I really want to study the poets who have embraced a true blues sensibility," which poets would you recommend? Would you begin with Brown or Hughes, and how would you tell them to progress?

REDMOND: I would first send them to the blues. You'd have to go to the blues first. So I'd send them to East St. Louis, Chicago, the Delta, Kansas City. I'd send them to any current or former packing house town, any current or former railroad center, any current or former place that relies on the river. I'd send them to the African cosmology—you know, I'd send them to Muntu. I'd send them to New Orleans. And of course, they wouldn't have to do it the way I did it—they wouldn't have to take that line—but I would say, "You have to understand that." Because there's a vast difference between, say, the blues of Henry Dumas and the blues of Sterling Plumpp; between the blues of Langston Hughes and the blues of Sterling Brown; between the blues of Frank Marshall Davis and the blues of Quincy Troupe; between the blues of Margaret Walker Alexander and the blues of Al Young; between the blues of Bob Kaufman and the blues of Robert Hayden.

FEINSTEIN: Those are interesting parallels between poets . . .

REDMOND: When I mentioned Kaufman, I thought of Robert Hayden, who was one of the greatest blues poets. As I stated at a Robert Hayden conference in 1990 at the University of Michigan, Hayden followed in the line of the scholar Alain Locke, who thought that jazz was a false form of black culture. Hayden didn't deal with jazz because he went to the root. (Whatever he was after, he went to the root of it.) When he went to the blues, he sidestepped jazz and came forward, combining African-inspired conversational English with the modernity of Ezra Pound, Yeats, and so on. He circumvented jazz. It's kind of ironic, because Hayden was a proper man—gay, but closeted—and you would have thought that jazz would have been closer [to his sensibility]. But it was blues and European classical, because they're both "classical" forms.

Hayden and Kaufman were both highly stylized poets who helped define areas of language cum music, and who haven't yet gotten their due. But they were very different in personality—who they were, where they came from. Hayden was a blues poet and not consciously a jazz poet, while Kaufman was very consciously a jazz poet. When I think of Kaufman, I think of Bird, I think of the avant-garde, I think of Dolphy. When I think of Hayden, I think of a high intellectual skill, a Euro-classical consciousness coupled with the blues-classical consciousness. I could take three or four other poets to set up the same kind of paradigm, but these two bookend all of what I've been saying.

And my comments about Hayden are not intended to say anything disparaging about jazz. Locke's comments about jazz I understand, but, I mean, I love jazz. I also heard from Sterling Brown and others that Locke was saying jazz is a hybrid, a mutant, and that blues is the real thing—but that Locke allegedly complained about people playing blues too much. It's like the difference between lip service and living it. That's what a lot of people in my area of the country and a lot of people of my generation think of [Henry Louis] Gates [Jr.] and [Nellie] McKay [the general editors of *The Norton Anthology of African American Literature*] and those people: They don't have any idea what this is all about, really. Not fundamentally. I mean, Sterling Plumpp [by contrast] has listened to eight to twelve hours of live blues a week. Ever since I've *known* him. I'd call his home and his daughter would say, "Daddy is at the club listening to the blues." If you go to see Sterling, he's going to drag you to a blues club. Even *I* don't want to hear blues *that* much. [Both laugh.]

I still like Sam Greenlee's idea of thinking of the typewriter as a musical instrument.

FEINSTEIN: Didn't he make that statement on the back of one of his books?

REDMOND: Yeah, it was on the back of one of his books of blues poems [*Blues for an African Princess*]. But those were some of the ideas that I had when I was trying to put together a frame for *Drumvoices:* the idea that Greenlee proposed; the story of Baldwin playing those Bessie Smith records over and over; Ralph Ellison's definition of the blues ("an autobiographical chronicle of personal catastrophe," and when you go back over it, you suffer/enjoy); some of the things by [Michael] Harper, though, for me, they're less edifying. I like some of the things that Yusef [Komunyakaa] has said about the blues. He seems to have picked up the line that was laid down by 1) the non-literary blues expressionists, and 2) the literary blues expressionists, going all the way back to Paul Laurence Dunbar, who was a *great* blues poet.

I'd send a student [interested in blues and literature] there. And I would say to the student, "If you want to write about folk culture having to do with the African American experience, you'd better know the church. Don't bring yourself here trying to say something about black culture or folk culture and you haven't studied the church." [Chuckles.] I think of the crossovers: "Stop in the Name of Love" / "Stop in the Name of God." "Jesus Is Close to Me" / "My Baby Is Close to Me." There's a thin line between the secular and the religious.

FEINSTEIN: I bet you had many wonderful discussions with Henry Dumas about the blues and blues-inspired poetry.

REDMOND: Oh yeah. We had great discussions, and one of his great heroes (or sheroes) was Margaret Walker Alexander. On several student papers, he wrote, "Read Margaret Walker! Re-read Margaret Walker!" (When Henry died, Margaret Walker would write, "The first time I read *Ark of Bones* [Dumas's posthumous story collection from 1970], the hair stood up on the back of my head.") We talked about the blues. And listening to him read: pure joy. While living in East St. Louis, Henry read everywhere. He read most frequently at a place called the Celebrity Club, but he also read at The Peppermint Lounge, Pudgey's, in Lincoln Park, on the grounds of IMPACT House. IMPACT was an acronym that stood for Innovative Messages of Positive Action to Improve Community Tranquility, something like that. [Chuckles.] It was one of those governmental cultural centers of the '60s, during the war on poverty, and it was supposed to help achieve tranquility by giving young people outlets so they wouldn't be violent.

FEINSTEIN: What a horrible irony . . .

REDMOND [nods]: Henry worked improvisationally. I think the person who comes closest to working the way Henry worked is Quincy Troupe. Quincy writes fast, and Henry wrote fast, and the writing is closer to the work of a musician. If you read Quincy, or read Henry, you hear riffs, and the riffs are spontaneous. In [Michael] Harper['s work,] the riffs seem a little more contrived. Dumas, of course, was "studied" in the tradition, but you find a more extempore nature— what is known today as spoken art. Open mike. Slam. And the best of the slam poets come close to what Henry was after. Someone like Quincy, Amiri Baraka, Sonia Sanchez, or Sekou Sundiata. Saul Williams. Tracie Morris. M. L. Liebler. Jayne Cortez. Michael Castro. Sarah Jones. The late Arthur Brown. Ahmos Zu-Bolton. Tony Medina. Bob Kaufman. Ntozake [Shange]. Simon Ortiz.

Henry was wary of the critics, of the kind of scholarship that's okay in the academy if you write a paper, and he was one of the greatest examples of how you can engage in "unorthodox" scholarship. He conducted the field research and put it into creative writing, and that made his research less "valid" than papers for the academy . . . Who knows where Henry would have gone had he lived, but we do know that he spent a great deal of his life collecting cultural memorabilia in an attempt to put together what John Henrik Clarke referred to as "a national black personality." Some call it "the bones of the black personality," or "the bones of black life." Toni Morrison once mused out loud: "I wish he [Dumas] were around to help straighten out all this mess." You can select which one of the "messes" she was talking about. [Laughs.]

There again I think you have an interesting paradigm if you look at Dumas and Sterling Brown, or Dumas and Zora Neale Hurston, or Dumas and Stephen Henderson. Zora Neale Hurston did both scholarly work and creative work. Sterling Brown was able to do both. He studied it; he did the field work; he wrote about it; and he wrote out of it. And he was an academician. Stephen Henderson did scholarly work, and he would spin his blues records sometimes all night, listening, trying to find connections, to understand.

FEINSTEIN: How would you describe the blues poetry of Raymond Patterson?

REDMOND: Patterson, for me, is a combination of Hayden and [Langston] Hughes. He's looser than Hayden and more structured than Hughes. Patterson was northern, and you don't really hear a lot of blues in New York. I mean, there's some, but it's not like you just walk out of your door and hear the blues, like I did as a kid. (Every time I walked outside my house, I could hear somebody under the bridge beating something, growling. Just the conversation among the men sitting around was bluesy.) He was a Lincoln University poet, and that includes Hughes, Melvin Tolson, Larry Neal—great poets.

I think Raymond is, if you will, *wrier* than some of the other poets. There's a sarcasm and an irony. There's no doubt that his language and themes come right out of Hughes. Raymond went to public school, went to the army, went to Lincoln University, got married, had a child, moved to Long Island—and that's his life, or is it? I mean, there was not a lot of experimentation in his personal life. He went south for a while to teach at a black college, and he came back and taught in New York City public schools. It wasn't nearly as varied as Henry's life or Sterling Brown's (I mean, he didn't go around doing a lot of collecting). But he didn't apologize. That's something I liked about Raymond. A lot of poets are liars, literally and figuratively, and Raymond was not. If Raymond lied in his poetry, he took a persona—not like Quincy, who's a tall-tale teller; one friend of mine said, "If *half* the things that Quincy said were true, he had to have lived four lifetimes." [Both laugh.] Raymond was sort of like Hayden, without the air or affectation. He was a straight person, and his poetry is straight-ahead, like straight-ahead jazz.

He also crosses the line between poetry and jazz, which is why I say he's like a blend of Hayden and Hughes. He's very modern. Some poets stay within cultures, and other poets cross the cultures. You can see, when you read Raymond's stuff, that he was a walking encyclopedia of black folklore: the proverbs, juke, jive, animal stories, jazz—and he *knew* modern poetry. We used to talk a lot about T. S. Eliot and his relationship with Pound, how they would excise each other's work.

I think Raymond was a wonderful blues poet.

FEINSTEIN: One of the best, I think.

REDMOND: Yes, I think one of the best. And there's a great difference between his blues poetry and, say, Sterling Brown's or Sterling Plumpp's.

FEINSTEIN: Patterson's work is very even.

REDMOND: Very even, yes. Patterson is a classical blues poet. It's almost always close to iambic pentameter—something that Alvin Aubert was critical of in a review of *Elemental Blues*. When Patterson and Aubert first met at the Furious Flower Conference in 1994—I presented Raymond with an award there—they were very cordial, but . . . [Laughs.] I think Aubert felt he had a corner on the blues, because he comes out of Louisiana and had been writing blues for a lot longer. Plumpp can be like that, too; he'll question your knowledge of the blues—and of Marxism, too, if you're around him long enough!

But I think Raymond's contribution to poetry is enormous, and will last.

FEINSTEIN: *Drumvoices* includes some strong criticism of some major figures from the Black Arts Movement, and part of the function of this book seems to have been an effort on your part to distance yourself from the movement, or at least to rethink some of the politics of the time. Am I off base here? Was that important for you?

REDMOND: You hit the nail on the head. In fact, the criticism was more severe than the book reports. There was some excising. I went into Baraka with a lot more depth, and Marie Brown, my editor at Doubleday, snatched it out; she didn't want the heat. (Part of it was the size. We were going beyond the length that Doubleday wanted to allot.) I know when I got to [Haki] Madhubuti I said some [critical] things, and I still have the feelings but I don't need to say them now. I think that Madhubuti took some wrong turns as a poet, but when I see him overall, I admire what he's done. He stuck to his guns. He's been there in Chicago for thirty-five years. You can't take that away.

As a poet, he did some stuff [that I admired] early on. After 1975, there's very little about his poetry that interests me. But there's a lot [to say] about his cultural work. His publishing. His fathering—biologically, culturally, politically. His building of institutions. Those things are all very important. (They're part of the approach I took to *Drumvoices*.) Looking at his last two or three books, you can see he's trying to proselytize. And he has a mission. I mean, the cities are in trouble. Our youth are in trouble. Our adults are in trouble. He's trying to work on that, and Chicago is the best and the worst place in the world to do it.

This has all become a lot clearer to me as I've seen the spoken word movement evolve—or, as some people would say, "devolve." [Chuckles.] I see the role of Baraka. I see the role of Kalamu ya Salaam. You know, in the '70s, Baraka and Kalamu ya Salaam had a big blowout. They were shooting at each other in various publications. And Baraka said, "I didn't tell anybody to follow me." Well, that's half true and half false, because he always has some kind of movement going and he's always recruiting, always proselytizing. At the same time, he demands that people be free thinkers, that you can take of him what you want; you don't have to follow so closely that when he takes a left turn your nose breaks off. That's part of his position, too.

But I can see their roles. I see the role of Haki. I see the split role of Quincy Troupe. Al Young, even, because of his musicality.

FEINSTEIN: Jayne Cortez?

REDMOND: Jayne Cortez in particular. I remember saying near the end of *Drumvoices* that the language holds promise in [Ishmael] Reed and Cortez. They're the people to watch, because they were doing it two different ways: One was coming out of the Vodounic catechism, and one out of a cultural Pan-African activism—music.

So there are some things I wouldn't say today. In fact, I haven't become the critic that *Drumvoices* promised. I went in another direction. You know what I mean—I would have been stiffer. The work that people do at Harvard and Princeton and the University of Wisconsin and places like that doesn't interest me that much (though I like what Craig Werner's up to). When the Cultural Studies and Deconstructionists and Marxist people came along, I didn't want to get into that fray. Now when you "construct" something, you have to fit into one of those slots. (When Stephen Henderson wrote his introduction to *Black Women Writers,* which was edited by Mari Evans, he lamented the fact that there wasn't any of that [theoretical material among the essays], as if he was saying, perhaps apologetically, "Maybe we need to know more about what they're doing, what Deconstructionism is doing.") I've been reading it but I haven't tried to integrate it into my teaching or writing. I suggest looking at the texts and using common sense. I'm not interested in a lot of neo-syllogisms or "isms" of any kind. I didn't go that way.

FEINSTEIN: "That way" is a pretty terrible way.

REDMOND: [Laughs.] Yes!

FEINSTEIN: Many writers whose work was shaped by music have been dismissed in academic publications, writers such as Tolson or Kaufman. The situation's improving—a bit—but a lot of people you've mentioned today are still painfully under-recognized. Sam Greenlee, for example.

REDMOND: That's right. Many of the people I've mentioned are not in the *Norton* [*Anthology of African American Literature*]. Greenlee. Patterson. You can go on and on—they're not in there. Other [popular African American literature] anthologies have similar problems. I see it like this: The Norton is the Eurocentric Anthology of African American Lit., and the Riverside [*Call and Response*] is the Afrocentric Anthology of African American Lit. Now we need an African American Anthology of African American Lit. [Laughs.]

FEINSTEIN: What do you make of the fact that Yusef [Komunyakaa] remains the only African American man to have received the Pulitzer Prize for poetry?

REDMOND: The battles are being waged, and we just have to stay in the trenches. That's what I tell the people around me: "If you're locked out, just stay in the trenches. Keep up the creativity *and* the activism." Baraka? Eady? Ethelbert Miller? Harper? Troupe? [Al] Young? Aubert? [Jay] Wright? [Calvin] Forbes? [Primus] St. John? The list of eligibles [for the Pulitzer Prize] is endless but the battles—and the racism—go on.

FEINSTEIN: Of the poets influenced by music, who would you like to see more well known?

REDMOND: I'd like to see Patterson more well known. Cortez. I'd like to see Kaufman much more exposed. Dumas. Melba Boyd. Certain early works by Haki. Mari Evans. In a blues and literature context: Robert Hayden. He's exposed, but not so much for music and literature. Alvin Aubert. Sam Allen / [also known as] Paul Vesey. Xam Cartiér's [novel] *Be-Bop, Re-Bop.* "Yardbird's Skull" [the poem by Owen Dodson]. Askia Touré. [Michael] Castro. Victor Hernandez Cruz. We mentioned Greenlee. Curtis Lyle. Kamau Daáood, Peter Harris, and Michael Datcher of the Los Angeles World Stage. Certainly the brilliant jazz poet and playwright Robert Earl Price in Atlanta. Lorenzo Thomas. Darlene Roy.

FEINSTEIN: Why do you think their work isn't more publicized? What makes the academic world so tight and closed?

REDMOND: Well, that's it. It's compartmentalized. And the academic world is unable or unwilling to apply the measuring rod that's needed to qualify this poetry.

I'm thinking about reissuing *Drumvoices*, and what I might have to do is write a new preface that looks at people who weren't mentioned, or who weren't even writing then—people like Elizabeth Alexander, whose work I think is really good, or Yusef and Rita Dove. I'm trying to decide whether I should write something cursory that reintroduces it or whether I should write an essay in which I summarize what has happened since the mid '70s. But I'm not sure if I want to do all that.

And then, what to make of spoken art? I've talked about that before. I've called for a definition of poetry that's performed. Some poets can only do spoken word.

FEINSTEIN: One way to continue your discussion, if you end up revising *Drumvoices,* might be to discuss how connections to music continue to be unfailing for poets.

REDMOND: As I say at the very end, "Music is the most shared experience . . . and poetry is music's twin."

FEINSTEIN: And in your work—both creative and scholarly—I think the "twin" would be the blues rather than jazz.

REDMOND: That's right. In fact, when my older brothers were trying to get me hooked on jazz, I would hear it all, but I was kind of veering off course. They wanted me to be a more straight-ahead jazz addict. And it took me a while. I had to go through people like [Earl] Bostic and the popular tunes by Duke Ellington. Now, Charlie Parker was very lyrical; I thought, "Hey, that's nice. I can follow that." With jazz, I was interested more in the melody. But the blues—the blues I could feel.

Sonia Sanchez. *Photo by Leandre Jackson.*

17

Cante Jondo
Sonia Sanchez

Given Sonia Sanchez's centrality to the Black Arts Movement and her on-going contributions to jazz-influenced poetry, I knew I would interview her at some point; in 2002, when she accepted a semester-long residency at Bucknell University, just thirty minutes away, I knew the time had arrived. I set up the interview with the help of Cynthia Hogue, then the director of Bucknell's Stadler Center for Poetry: I would pick up Sonia in the afternoon, and Cynthia would join us for dinner that evening. That November, when I arrived at Sonia's guest cottage, she opened the door and said, "Wow, you're right on time. That's great; I appreciate that. I'll be out in a minute." Then she added: "My son, Mungu, has arrived. It's okay if he joins us, isn't it?" I tried to veil my surprise and said, "Sure." When they emerged, Sonia rode shotgun, and Mungu, who had been on the road for several days before meeting up with his mother, stretched out across the backseat to catch up on his sleep.

Car rides that precede interviews can be a little strange, since it's wise to save questions that might be appropriate for the forthcoming discussion and kind not to strain the voice of the person being interviewed. But conversation flowed easily—without pause, in fact. When we arrived at my home, I apologized to Mungu ("I'm about to be a terrible host") but he assured me that he was completely content, then relaxed on the living room sofa as Sonia and I retired to the adjacent room.

Given the fluid conversation during the car ride, I feared Sonia might speak for about twenty minutes and then say, "That's enough." I shouldn't have worried; she spoke for almost two and a half hours, releasing story after story with unwavering energy and passion. The vitality of the afternoon carried into the evening with Cynthia's arrival and my wife's lavish meal. And that's when Mungu came to life: laughing and waving his hand in the air, rocking in his chair and occasionally reaching for my shoulder like a man in the aisle of an airplane who grabs someone's seat for balance.

Sonia Sanchez's many poetry collections include *Shake Loose My Skin: New and Selected Poems, Does Your House Have Lions?,* and *Homegirls & Handgrenades,* which won the American Book Award. She has also published books of criticism, drama, and children's literature. Her extensive list of honors and awards includes the Pennsylvania Governor's Award for Excellence in the Humanities, a National Endowment for the Arts fellowship, the Langston Hughes Poetry Award, and a Pew Fellowship in the Arts; most recently, she was named Ford Freedom Scholar and Frost Medalist. Sanchez was also the first Presidential Fellow at Temple University, where she held the Laura Carnell Chair in English until her retirement in 1999.

The following poems correspond to works mentioned in our conversation. The interview took place in my home in Williamsport, Pennsylvania, on November 18, 2002.

* * * * * * * * * * * * * * * *

a/coltrane/poem
Sonia Sanchez

my favorite things
                    is u/blowen
                                        yo/favorite/things.
                    stretchen the mind
                                        till it bursts past the con/fines of
                    solo/en melodies.
                                        to the many solos

of the
      mind/spirit.
           are u sleepen   (to be
           are u sleepen   sung
           brotha john   softly)
           brotha john
                 where u have gone to.
           no mornin bells
           are ringen here. only the quiet
aftermath of assassinations.
                   but i saw yo/murder/
the massacre
           of all blk/musicians. planned
in advance.
           yrs befo u blew away our passsst
       and showed us our futureeeeee
screech   screeech   screeeeech   screeech
a/love/supreme, alovesupreme a lovesupreme.
      A LOVE SUPREME
scrEEEccCHHHHH screeeeEEECHHHHHHHH
      sCReeeEEECHHHHHH SCREEEECCCCHHHH
      SCREEEEEEEECCCHHHHHHHHHHHH
a lovesupremealovesupremealovesupreme for our blk
people.
      BRING IN THE WITE/MOTHA/fuckas
      ALL THE MILLIONAIRES/BANKERS/ol
MAIN/LINE/ASS/RISTOOCRATS (ALL
THEM SO-CALLED BEAUTIFUL
PEOPLE)
       WHO HAVE KILLED
WILL CONTINUE TO
               KILL US WITH
THEY CAPITALISM/18% OWNERSHIP
OF THE WORLD.
          YEH. U RIGHT
THERE. U ROCKEFELLERS. MELLONS
    VANDERBILTS
         FORDS.
             yeh.
GITem.

PUSHem/PUNCHem/STOMPem. THEN
LIGHT A FIRE TO
THEY pilgrim asses.
TEAROUT THEY eyes.
STRETCH they necks
till no mo
raunchy sounds of MURDER/
POVERTY/STARVATION
come from they
throats.
screeeeeeeeeeeeeeeeeeCHHHHHHHHHHH
SCREEEEEEEEEEEEEEECHHHHHHHHHH
screeEEEEEEEEEEEEEEEEEEEEEEEE
EECCCCHHHHHHH
SCREEEEEEEEEEEEEEEEEEEEEEEEEEEEEEE
EEEEEECHHHHHHHHHH
BRING IN THE WITE/LIBERALS ON THE SOLO
SOUND OF YO/FIGHT IS MY FIGHT
SAXOPHONE.
TORTURE
THEM FIRST AS THEY HAVE
TORTURED US WITH
PROMISES/
PROMISES. IN WITE/AMERICA. WHEN
ALL THEY WUZ DOEN
WAS HAVEN FUN WITH THEY
ORGIASTIC DREAMS OF BLKNESS.
(JUST SOME MO
CRACKERS FUCKEN OVER OUR MINDS.)
MAKE THEM
SCREEEEEEAM
FORGIVE ME. IN SWAHILI.
DON'T ACCEPT NO MEA CULPAS.
DON'T WANT TO
HEAR
BOUT NO EUROPEAN FOR/GIVE/NESS.
DEADDYINDEADDYINDEADDYINWITEWESTERN
SHITTTTTT
(softly   da-dum-da da da da da da da da/da-dum-da

til it da da da da da da da da da
builds   da-dum-da da da
up) da-dum. da. da. da. this is a part of my
    favorite things.
    da dum da da da da da da
    da da da da
    da dum da da da da da da
    da da da da
     da dum da da da da
     da dum da da da da————

(to be rise up blk/ people
sung de dum da da da da
slowly move straight in yo/blkness
to tune da dum da da da da
of my step over the wite/ness
favorite that is yesssss terrrrrr day
things.) weeeeeeee are tooooooooday.
(f   da dum
a   da da da (stomp, stomp) da da da
s   da dum
t   da da da (stomp, stomp) da da da
e   da dum
r)   da da da (stomp) da da da dum (stomp)
    weeeeeeeee (stomp)
     areeeeeeeee (stomp)
       areeeeeeeee (stomp, stomp)
    tooooooday (stomp.
      day   stomp.
      day   stomp.
      day   stomp.
      day   stomp!)
(soft rise up blk/people. rise up blk/people
chant) RISE. & BE. What u can.
    MUST BE.BE.BE.BE.BE.BE.BE-E-E-E-BE-E-E-E-E-
     yeh. john coltrane.
my favorite things is u.
      showen us life/
        liven.

a love supreme.

              for each
         other
      if we just
lisssssssSSSTEN.

Blues
Sonia Sanchez

in the night
in my half hour
negro dreams
i hear voices knocking at the door
i see walls dripping screams up
and down the halls
                        won't someone open
the door for me? won't some
one schedule my sleep
and don't ask no questions?
noise.
          like when he took me to his
home away from home place
and i died the long sought after
death he'd planned for me.
Yeah, bessie he put in the bacon
and it overflowed the pot.
and two days later
when i was talking
i started to grin.
as everyone knows
i am still grinning.

Sister's Voice (read to "'Round Midnight")
Sonia Sanchez

this was a migration unlike
the 1900s of black men and women
coming north for jobs. freedom. life.

this was a migration to begin
to bend a father's heart again
to birth seduction from the past
to repay desertion at last.

imagine him short and black
thin mustache draping thin lips
imagine him country and exact
thin body, underfed hips
watching at this corral of battleships
and bastards. watching for forget
and remember. dancing his pirouette.

and he came my brother at seventeen
recruited by birthright and smell
grabbing the city by the root with clean
metallic teeth. commandant and infidel
pirating his family in their cell
and we waited for the anger to retreat
and we watched him embrace the city and the street.

first he auctioned off his legs. eyes.
heart. in rooms of specific pain.
he specialized in generalize
learned newyorkese and all profane.
enslaved his body to cocaine
denied his father's signature
damned his sister's overture.

and a new geography greeted him.
the atlantic drifted from offshore
to lick his wounds to give him slim
transfusion as he turned changed wore
a new waistcoat of solicitor
antidote to his southern skin
ammunition for a young paladin.

and the bars. the glitter. the light
discharging pain from his bygone anguish
of young black boy scared of the night.
sequestered on this new bank, he surveyed the fish
sweet cargoes crowded with scales feverish

with quick sales full sails of flesh
searing the coastline of his acquiesce.

and the days rummaging his eyes
and the nights flickering through a slit
of narrow bars. hips. thighs.
and his thoughts labeling him misfit
as he prowled, pranced in the starlit
city, coloring his days and nights
with gluttony and praise and unreconciled rites.

A Poem for Ella Fitzgerald
Sonia Sanchez

when she came on the stage, this Ella
there were rumors of hurricanes and
over the rooftops of concert stages
the moon turned red in the sky,
it was Ella, Ella.
queen Ella had come
and words spilled out
leaving a trail of witnesses smiling
amen—amen—a woman—a woman.

she began
this three agèd woman
nightingales in her throat
and squads of horns came out
to greet her.

streams of violins and pianos
splashed their welcome
and our stained glass silences
our braided spaces
unraveled
opened up
said who's that coming?

who's that knocking at the door?
whose voice lingers on

that stage gone mad with
>   *perdido. perdido. perdido.*
>   *i lost my heart in toledoooooo.*

whose voice is climbing
up this morning chimney
smoking with life
carrying her basket of words
>   *a tisket a tasket*
>   *my little yellow*
>   *basket—i wrote a*
>   *letter to my mom and*
>   *on the way i dropped it—*
>   *was it red . . . no no no no*
>   *was it green . . . no no no no*
>   *was it blue . . . no no no no*
>   *just a little yellow*
voice rescuing razor thin lyrics
from hopscotching dreams.

we first watched her navigating
an apollo stage amid high-stepping
yellow legs
we watched her watching us
shiny and pure woman
sugar and spice woman
her voice a nun's whisper
her voice pouring out
guitar thickened blues,
her voice a faraway horn
questioning the wind,
and she became Ella,
first lady of tongues
Ella cruising our veins
voice walking on water
crossed in prayer,
she became holy
a thousand sermons
concealed in her bones
as she raised them in a

symphonic shudder
carrying our sighs into
her bloodstream.

this voice, chasing the
morning waves,
this Ella-tonian voice soft
like four layers of lace.
        when i die Ella
        tell the whole joint
        please, please, don't talk
        about me when i'm gone. . . .

i remember waiting one nite for her appearance
audience impatient at the lateness
of musicians,
i remember it was april
and the flowers ran yellow
the sun downpoured yellow butterflies
and the day was yellow and silent
all of spring held us
in a single drop of blood.

when she appeared on stage
she became Nut arching over us
feet and hands placed on the stage
music flowing from her breasts
she swallowed the sun
sang confessions from the evening stars
made earth divulge her secrets
gave birth to skies in her song
remade the insistent air
and we became anointed found
inside her bop
        bop bop dowa
        bop bop doowaaa
        bop bop dooooowaaaa
Lady. Lady. Lady.
be good. be good
to me.
        to you.   to us all

cuz we just some lonesome babes
in the woods
hey lady. sweetellalady
Lady. Lady. Lady. be gooooood
ELLA ELLA ELLALADY
> *be good*
>> *gooooood*
>>> *goooooood . . .*

SASCHA FEINSTEIN: When did the crossovers between music and literature fully form in your life?

SONIA SANCHEZ: I grew up with music. My father was a drummer and
a school teacher in Birmingham, Alabama. He was inducted into the
Black Music Hall of Fame. And my father taught "Papa" Jo Jones how
to play the drums. They had an amazing friendship, and they argued
amazingly, sometimes, too. ("Papa" Jo Jones was a cousin of mine and
had asked me to do his biography, but when I would come up on weekends to interview him, the door would be open, he'd be gone with a
note [saying that] he's at the corner bar—it was an impossible situation. Being an academic, and trying to keep my children in line—
whatever—I just thought it had to stop because I couldn't pin him
down.) So I grew up in a house of music. I was probably one of the few
children who could recognize [the music of] Art Tatum. I'd walk into
people's homes, they'd have Art Tatum on, and I'd say very casually,
"Oh, I love Art Tatum." And they'd say, "What do you know about Art
Tatum?" They didn't expect children to *know*. But I grew up on musicians. I met Sid Catlett. He would put me on his lap while he talked to
my father. I met all of the musicians who played down on 52nd Street.
My father gave up music when he came to New York City because musicians had to travel, and he had a new wife, and she was saying, "If
you go overseas, that's it." My father had to make the decision between
a father who would stay home with an ordinary job, as opposed to [a
professional jazz musician]. But he still would do gigs in the Village—
for years, until he got too old—and he gave lessons. He gave one of
his drums—one of the old-fashioned drums with the pedal—to Max
Roach, and I still have his other drums at home.

I'm saying all that as background. Music has been a part of my life
for a very long time, and I think music has helped me to survive for a

very long time, too. I watched the motion and movement of music as it changed. I remember when bebop came in; my father didn't think it was music—[Feinstein chuckles]—because music was Duke Ellington, and we, who then began to listen to the new music, looked up at him and thought, "Huh. That's something 'wrong.' That's something *else* that we can be alienated with and about."

I learned about black literature from Miss Hutson—Jean Hutson—at the Schomburg [Library, now the Schomburg Center for Research in Black Culture]. After I got out of Hunter [College in 1955], I needed to get a job, so I answered an ad in the *New York Times*. The ad said the company needed a writer for their firm: "Would you please send a sample of your writing and your CV." I did. And I got a *telegram:* "Report to work on Monday at nine AM." I went down the hallway, knocked on my father's bedroom door, showed him the telegram, and said, "See? See? I *can* get a job as a writer." My father—I will never forget—gave this droll answer: "Well, go try it, but if I were you, I would really prepare to be a teacher." Right? I had *not* prepared to be a teacher at Hunter. I had prepared to go to law school with no money. (They weren't giving out money at that time.) But being a liberal arts grad, you could always get a job teaching.

Anyway, I go downtown that Monday. I have a blue suit on. Blue shoes on. Blue hat on. Blue purse and white gloves—I *know* I look good. I didn't go on C.P. time—

FEINSTEIN: Oh, you're terrible—

SANCHEZ: I was there at eight thirty. *Eight thirty.* Nobody was there, so I'm standing outside. Then in comes the secretary/receptionist, and she said, "Yes?" and I showed her this [telegram], and she opened the door. I sat down, and I'm thinking, "This is like really what I—." I mean, can you imagine? "I can make all this money before I go back to school. I have a chance to really write—they like my writing," because I was a closet writer. All of a sudden—they had another entrance there—I saw this face, and I smiled. And another face, and I smiled. And about ten minutes to nine, this guy walks up and says, "I'm so sorry, but the job is taken." I looked at my watch and said, "But I wasn't due to report until nine o'clock. How can I not have a job at ten to nine when I wasn't due here until nine o'clock?" He said, "The job is taken." I said, "But I have the telegram." He looked at it, and he looked at me, and his eyes said, "Whoa, did I make a mistake." He raised his voice—"I *said*, the job is taken"—and he walked away. I turned to the secretary and she looked down; she never looked up. I could see the offices back there, and I said, "You're discriminating against me! I'm going to call the Urban League." The guy turned around to me, like, "The Urban League? So what? What are they going to do?"

I go out, take off my hat, and I get on the train. But I was so angry that I didn't get off at 96th and it went all the way to the East Side. I had to get to the West Side, so I said, "Okay, I'll walk across. I won't pay any more money to go back downtown." I get off at 135th Street and start crossing the street. I look up. I'm hot, I'm sweaty now, and I'm angry. And there's this guy standing out on the steps. I said, "*Schomburg*? What is the Schomburg?" He said, "It's a library." I said, "What library?" He said, "Go inside and ask the lady inside." So I walked in and saw that long, long table with all of these men—black, white scholars—sitting down like this—[Sanchez bows her head]—working at this long table that took up this whole room.

Miss Hutson was enclosed in a glass office where she could look out. She had her back to me, and I knocked. (She used to tell this story to all my students, and I would be so embarrassed. She used to tell it with this very subtle, sly smile.) I said, "Hello?" She said, "Yes? I'm Miss Jean Hutson." I said, "What kind of library is this? I've never heard of this library. I just got out of Hunter College. I've never heard of the Schomburg." "Oh, dear," she said. "This library *only* has books by and about black folk." And I said, at age nineteen-and-a-half: "There must not be many books in here."

FEINSTEIN: Wow . . .

SANCHEZ: She sat me down, my brother, and she said, "I'm going to bring you some books." And she brought three books: [W. E. B. Du Bois's] *Souls of Black Folk,* [Booker T. Washington's] *Up from Slavery,* and the top one was [Zora Neale Hurston's] *Their Eyes Were Watching God.* She said [Sanchez taps the table]: "Okay. For you, dear." I looked around. These men have not looked up yet. Didn't matter who was sitting where. They were working with all these books spread out. I had this little tiny space. I started reading, and then I got into the black English part, and I was thrown for one minute, but I kept reading. And then, I started to cry.

I inched out, knocked on her door, and said, "How can I be an educated woman and not have read these books?" and she said [Sanchez grins widely]: "Yes, dear. Now go back and read." I inched back in and read some more, and came back out again. I mean, I was *stricken* by this, my brother. Then I sat back down, and one of the scholars said [Sanchez speaks in a gruff voice]: "Miss Hutson! Will you please tell this young woman either she sits still or she has to go!" [Feinstein laughs.] And I sat still, and I read those books. I came back every day. I stopped looking for a job. I would tell my father, "I'm going to look for a job," but I came to the Schomburg.

I had heard the music of poetry in the black schools of the South—because someone always recited Langston Hughes, Countee Cullen, or Paul Laurence Dunbar. So I knew that existed; I could hear the rhythm. Someone would do Paul Laurence Dunbar's [poem "A Negro Love Song":] "Jump back, honey, jump back." We had heard that. We had heard the music; this poetry had been planted in our subconscious already and in a sense was ready to come out.

I always heard music as I wrote. I ignored it for a long time, or I would write, "To be sung," on the side. Or, "Clap your hands." I would give all kinds of directions. I heard the music at the base of my skull, but I never, *ever* read any of my poems with music until I was making a trek from New York to Brown University, and we got caught in a snow storm.

FEINSTEIN: When was this?

SANCHEZ: This would have been in the early '70s.

FEINSTEIN: After you published *We a BaddDDD People*?

SANCHEZ: Yes. By the time I got back to New York, I had two books: *Home Coming* and *We a BaddDDD People*.

So the plane was delayed. The plane circled and didn't have enough fuel to get back to New York, and finally the pilot said, "Well, I guess we'd better try to land now." I was due to read at eight. The students were told what had happened; they had gone out, eaten, and come back. It is now about ten-thirty and they're ushering me into this packed auditorium. With introductions and all that, I'm reading at eleven o'clock at night. So I said, "I'll give you a good reading."

I did about an hour and a half from eleven to twelve-thirty—because they had waited, and they were so appreciative. And then someone said, "Would you entertain a couple of questions, Professor Sanchez?" I'm thinking, *I'm whipped, and I've got to teach a class tomorrow*, but I said, "Yes. A couple." And this young African American man said, "Would you read your Coltrane poem?" I said, "I've never read that poem out loud. I've read it silently, and I read it out loud as I was writing it, but I've never read it out loud." He said, "Yeah, I know—but we waited for you for two-and-a-half hours," and I thought, *Whoa! Okay*, and said, "Give me a minute to look it over."

I had always stretched words out, but that's as far as I would go with the music. I would go, "*Ahhhhhhhhh*"—merely stretching out the words, in spite of the music that I was hearing, because I didn't trust myself. "I'm not a singer. How can I do this?" In New York, we sometimes would read with musicians and drummers, so my voice was always there, but I had never done a piece like that by myself and made my voice assume all of the instruments, all of the sounds, all of the screams that the [Coltrane] poem encompasses. And when I would read with musicians, I would always be aware that *this* was the poem and *that* was the music.

Well, thank goodness for the Ancestors. And thank goodness for an appreciative audience. When I got to it, I *did* the music. I did Coltrane. The voice did everything. [Sings a brief, rising tone.] It just came to me. And from that point on, I was literally released to do whatever I wanted to do with a poem, with music, with sound. I began to investigate different languages as a consequence. I began to notate more—what should be done, what should not be done. I began the whole process of [thinking about] the poem and the music as one.

FEINSTEIN: You've performed with Archie Shepp. What was that like?

SANCHEZ: I started teaching at Amherst in 1973, and Max Roach and Archie Shepp were there, as well as the brother who teaches music—Horace Boyer—and I began to do things with them. We did a gig at Boston University [in 1974] that's on the Black Box series. (Someone recorded it and, afterwards, sold it without our permission.) Anyway, Max said, "Why don't we do something together, Sonia?" I said, "Yeah. You want to rehearse?" (I'll never forget that.) And he said, "Oh, no! Just read a little poem. Something short." I thought, "Oh my God . . ." Not that I hadn't done anything with musicians, but we're talking a huge audience: 1,000 people! They said, "You go on stage and start reading. We'll come and join you."

Well, I go out there, and, man, all of a sudden, Archie comes out and starts blowing: *Wooooooooo! Do do do-do do!* And you cannot continue to read as you were reading before. Of course I had to stop, because the audience clapped, and then I had to fit my voice and these lines over that music so they complemented each other. I truly appreciated jazz singers then; I really understood what they did on that stage. You go to a jazz place and you listen to people, and you think, "Okay. She's singing. She stops. He comes in. Simple." But they made me become a jazz singer on that stage—with poetry—and they also made me direct: "Now I'm gonna do it again as he plays"—whatever. I found myself repeating lines, also, in the same fashion that I remembered the jazz singers did. Then I'd let him play. Then I'd dip right back in. So we were doing that, and then all of a sudden, the pianist came in. Archie changed up with him, and I *couldn't* be left out, so I had to change up with the two of them. Then Max came out and started beating. It was an amazing moment.

When I finished, I left and let them play, and when they finished, Max said, "See? I told you it would work," and he threw me up in the air. And you know what it reminded me of? "Papa" Jo Jones. He would come to our house in Alabama for Sunday dinner—he'd come in chewing gum, with that kind of rhythm that he had—and he'd come for us: My sister and I would try to run away. But he'd grab me while talking to my father, throw me in the air, and, at the last minute, he caught me. I just knew he would not catch me, 'cause he was not looking at me. He'd say, "Okay, Sonia! And you know what I think—" and then he caught me. Your heart would be on the floor someplace, and your stomach . . . [Feinstein laughs.] And all the time he was talking, he had his foot moving.

It's only been in the last two years that I've stopped doing that, too—tapping my foot. People would say, "Why don't you stop?" My foot was always moving with a fast beat. When I'd walk with my children outside, I used to walk like my father and "Papa" Jo: *fast.* My children would say, "Ma! Why don't you slow down?" I would say, "Well, keep up!" [Chuckles.] It was always some kind of rhythm that was going on, some kind of beat that I kept with me.

The students at Amherst were so interested in jazz, and I did a lot with the students. They would play and I would read. As a consequence, they began to make the connections between music and poetry, that there was really no separation at all. The college had promised them more professors, and one of the things the students wanted was their own music person there because U Mass had Max and Archie. So I contacted Yusef Lateef and asked if he wanted to teach, and he said yes. The people in the music department didn't care who we got—until they found out who Yusef Lateef *was.* Then the music department started saying, "Well, a man like him should be in the music department." I said, "No! He should be in the Afro American Studies department," because we had different disciplines that made up the Afro American Studies department. Do you know they fought me for that? And Yusef didn't want to get caught in the middle. That's not his aura, you know? I had said to him, "It's not a controversy. Just say that you want to be in our department." But the music department *made* this a controversy, so he didn't come.

At Amherst, the more I listened to this music, the more music would infiltrate the lines of poetry. Now I find myself always, always, always—in each poem—making the music happen. But then I sometimes had a run-in with the music: I would want to be lyrical as opposed to musical. There was a battle that went on. Sometimes the lyrical would take hold. The music came out, however, when I spoke/wrote in Wolof. My brother, as he moved towards death, began to speak Wolof because the Ancestors spoke Wolof to him. So I would write "to be sung." I allowed the music to come out in that kind of history, as opposed to interfering with the lyricism of the poem. Because the poem took rhyme royal form, the lines that I had that were infused with music weren't working as well. I had to come in and cut—do you know what I'm saying?—cut the music from them.

I usually do two books at one time because when one's working, the other one's not working. I was doing *Wounded in the House of a Friend* and *Does Your House Have Lions?* I had started *Does Your House* first, but in the middle of this book, there were voices that I heard which were similar to the music. When I say "music"—I would hear music in a different language, and I would call my friends who are African and say, "What is this?" and they would say, "Oh—that's Wolof." I said, "I must have heard someone singing it someplace and picked it up. Tell me how to say this properly. Does this mean what I think it means?" It was a real joy.

When I did a piece for Gerald Penny—one of the young students who drowned at Amherst—I relied a lot on the music. That piece not only had African qualities but Native American qualities as well. I said to someone as I was doing this piece, "In this place it's like *massacres* have been here, so the sounds that I hear I know cannot be African— I know they're Native American," and someone told me about that whole area: "There was a massacre on this spot," and I said, "I know." I mean, I didn't *know*, but I could feel it, feel the chanting.

I believe all of our chants or chanting are the same, anyway. You cannot have people invade—the way the Moors did, get into France, and Italy, and as far away as Ireland—without leaving something behind (part of a language, and music, too). The *cante jondo*—the deep song—is in each one of our cultures. One of the *cante jondo* is the blues. The *cante jondo* that became urban—more modern—is jazz, in my head. At some point, when you hear that wail, that song, that fusion, that movement off the ground into the sky—then you know this is ancient and modern at the same time.

That's what I try to capture when I chant: a combination of what is ancient and what is modern. Sometimes I do the ancient part by incorporating the African language into it, and then the sound. I've done "Middle Passage" [published in *Wounded in the House of a Friend* as "Improvisation"] in the Midwest, my brother, and I have broken down because I have heard the Native American voices. And I've had Native Americans come up to me and give me something, like a piece of jewelry. They'll say, "I heard our voice in there," and I say, "Yes, because it's the same voice." When you travel and you hear the different cultures, then you know this is indeed the same voice. People have just separated our voices and said, "This one belongs over here—in Ireland. This one belongs in Scotland. This one belongs in the Middle East—and it's only a Middle Eastern sound"—and you know that's not true. These people have moved back and forth and have left their chants, their smells, their sounds, and new people have been born and picked up those old sounds and said, "Oh, look—a new sound." But we know it's the same *old* sound. That's why I'm so amazed when I hear flamenco. I stop—because it's an old sound, but a new sound. It's in the mountains, but it's also in a bare, urban apartment in Harlem.

That's what I try to do when I use music: I try to make people hear that which they ignore. I try to make people hear that which they would rather not sing. They'd rather *say* it and get it over with, and I'll say, "No—this is a poem that is to be sung. It is to be hummed. It is to be turned over on its side so you can see the juices inside. Sometimes I dry it off and then give it back to you in a dry fashion, but it is still the song and the poem—at the same time."

FEINSTEIN: Is it okay to talk about Etheridge Knight? [Sanchez and Knight were married 1968–1970.]

SANCHEZ: Sure.

FEINSTEIN: We were friends, and whenever we were on panels discussing jazz-related literature, Etheridge always mentioned your writing: "Sonia's work *drips* with jazz." How do you think jazz influenced his work?

SANCHEZ: I think jazz influenced his work in a different way from mine.

FEINSTEIN: Your poems *sound* different.

SANCHEZ: Yes. Very different. I think the jazz poems Etheridge did were always in *homage* to someone, you know what I'm saying? He made the line become jazz, but I would never say that Etheridge was a Jazz Poet the way that some of us are. Or let me put it this way: To me, his poems oozed of blues, which is very close to jazz but never makes that turn. There is so much pain in Etheridge's work that his poems are always infused with the blues life, the blues style, the blues way of looking at the world. If you do jazz, my brother, you see a win. That's why I love jazz. Jazz musicians, when they play, are saying, "I got it. I see a win."

When I do a blues, and I try to make it "smart" sometimes, I try to infuse an urban style blues, because Bessie [Smith], when she was talking about the rich man in her blues, there was a win there, there was a tartness there, there was a smartness there. And, as much as I loved Etheridge, I think he didn't see a win. He could *record* jazz, but he was not *of* jazz. He could admire all of those people, and listen to the music, but he couldn't *sing* it. Do you know what I'm saying? I don't know if I'm right or wrong on this. But if you listen to him read, he never could jazz it up from the voice. It was always like what I call "the old poetry," like Dudley Randall reading. It was just that kind of sing/song thing. There were times when he wrote lines and you wanted to say, "Whip it. Twist it, turn it. Send it up, and then send it back down." But he couldn't do it that way. That's what I meant [before]: He could write about jazz, and he did write about jazz—he wrote some exquisite poems, wonderful poems with the aroma of jazz—but when you opened it up, it wasn't jazz, it was blues.

FEINSTEIN: Who then—for you—would be among the true jazz poets?

SANCHEZ: I don't want to say that you have to be in an urban setting to do jazz. That's not necessarily true. But I do think that the people who really *touch* on a jazz motif not only make poems about jazz but create jazz riffs. In other words, the composition of the poem is jazz, the delivery of the poem is jazz, and the juice, infusing it, is jazz. Baraka does it well. Quincy [Troupe] does it well. Jayne [Cortez] does it well. A lot of the younger poets do it well. Ras Baraka is just like his father on so many levels. Sometimes I have to close my eyes to try to figure out the difference there. I think Eugene [Redmond] does it. Slightly.

FEINSTEIN: He thinks of himself much more as a blues poet.

SANCHEZ: That's what I'm saying—"slightly." He does more what Etheridge does, that is to say, he will write about a jazz person but he's not in it.

FEINSTEIN: I don't think Eugene would argue with that. He doesn't consider himself to be a jazz poet.

SANCHEZ: Some people think they *are,* and I don't want to give my opinion just to run over people. Some people think that if they're writing a poem about a jazz person, they are a jazz poet. I've been listening to Eugene. He will write a poem about a jazz person, but he's not really a jazz poet per se. I think you're right: He's more infused with the blues.

There were a lot of jazz poets in *Black Fire* [*An Anthology of Afro-American Writing* from 1968]. You don't see a lot of them now . . . That was an amazing collection: You saw what they were doing, how they were moving. And that anthology that you did [with Yusef Komunyakaa, *The Jazz Poetry Anthology*]: You can see that some of the poets in there are really jazz poets, because they got it. They not only have the composition of it but I've heard them deliver it, and they're *into* what a jazz poem is all about—from the riff on down to what I call the silences between the lines. That's what I try to do (though I'm not sure if it always works). When you're silent, you let the music resonate from your voice so people hear it, and then you come back in on it. That's when you don't have the music with you, so you do it. I try to make the silences. When I stop, I'm saying to an audience, "Come on. Hear it. Come back into it." That kind of thing.

I don't always know how one does it, but I know at some point that once you hear that music then it's all possible. But you have to hear that music back here, in the base of the skull. I used to ignore it because initially I kept saying, "I can't sing." I thought it had to do with singing, but it doesn't have to do with singing, you know what I'm saying? I was limiting myself. I was limiting myself to a jazz singer, as opposed to a jazz poet. So, when I said to that young man at Brown, "But, I've never read that. I don't sing" (and I had *written* "to be sung"), I was limiting myself. I had to leave that arena of limiting myself to being a jazz singer. As a poet performing with musicians, you sometimes have to go back to that arena because you have to do some of the things that a jazz singer would do. But when you're performing by yourself, you don't have to. You accomplish everything. You pull the horn with you. You pull the drums with you.

FEINSTEIN: What would you consider to be some of your representative jazz poems?

SANCHEZ: Well, obviously, the Coltrane poem. The first blues poem that I wrote is not a blues poem; it has the sensibility of the blues but it's

really, at its core, in its execution, it's a jazz poem. Another jazz piece
would be—and no one understands this, but I can hear Coltrane playing behind—"I have walked a long time / longer than death—." The
poem for Ella. The poem "Sequences" is a jazz poem; it's a jazz poem
with, like, Rahsaan Roland Kirk playing. It's a jazz suite, something
like what Langston [Hughes] did in *Ask Your Mama.* At the core of
that is the blues motif, but the execution is jazz.

FEINSTEIN: You got your book title *Does Your House Have Lions?* from
Kirk's CD set [*Rahsaan Roland Kirk Anthology*], right?

SANCHEZ: Yes. I was so stricken by the Kirk Anthology. I thought that
was an amazing question—"Does your house have lions?"—in many
contexts. And so typical of Rahsaan to pose that question that has so
many ramifications. ("You're building a house? Does your house have
lions?" "What do you mean?" "You know—*lions.*") All the important
buildings—libraries, banks—always used to have lions so you knew
you were entering a place that was mighty, that was fortified. But if
you go back to the continent of Africa and you talk about lions, you're
talking about something else, too—the lion as Juba—so that the lion
goes back beyond what we see here in the States. And that's why I
thought, "What a title!" and I put it in my journal.

As I was writing this book, which is about my brother [dying of
AIDS], I didn't have a title. All of a sudden, it hit me: This is what
I've been talking about—the idea of a family having lions, the kind
of protection that they should have at some particular point. About a
country, too, having that kind of protection. So I knew that was the
title.

We did this piece—[Sanchez taps the cover of *Does Your House Have
Lions?*]—with music, did you know that? Odean Pope, a percussionist,
Khan Jamal, and a dancer, Rennie Harris, who danced the part of my
brother. I read. We came on stage all dressed in white. It began with
the sister's voice, with the brother at seventeen (the dancer) coming
out in a green suit. By the time he was getting ready to die, of course,
he'd pulled off his layered clothes and was all in white, also. In many
societies, of course, people wear white when people die, or in celebration of life. Odean did all the music.

FEINSTEIN: He's a tremendous musician. There's a reason Max Roach
played with him for years.

SANCHEZ: He *is* amazing. He did the music for that. We were supposed to
have a director there at the theater, but he was away in California and
came back only two days before. Odean looked at me and I looked at

him, and we said to each other, "We'd better do this ourselves and plan this ourselves, 'cause this guy's going to come in and do lighting, but we're going to have to do the actual work." [Chuckles.] So we ended up directing ourselves.

FEINSTEIN: That's smart—to make sure that it's done the way that you want it to be done.

SANCHEZ: We had a chance to try it out before we did it on stage. I had a gig someplace up in Pennsylvania, and I told the people, "You have to send a big car for me," and we had this limo where we could put all the instruments in. So, lo and behold, I came into this place with "my posse" (like I told you yesterday, those students were "my posse" last night), and we heard what was not working, what was working, on stage. That was really very good for us, and when we did it again at the theater, it really came together. It was what music and theater could be, what poetry and dance could be.

FEINSTEIN: What was it like to be one of the relatively few female voices to represent the Black Arts Movement of the late 1960s?

SANCHEZ: [Laughs.] It was amazing. People complain and say that Black Arts was sexist. I say to people, "*America* was sexist." All the political organizations were sexist, so that was not just part of Black Arts. But: They weren't sexist on stage. Baraka, Ed Bullins, Marvin X, Larry Neal—I was the only woman on stage with them, and they did not treat me differently. They didn't make me go first, for example, which would have been the completely sexist thing to do.

I always tell this story about Baraka and myself: When we went out to California [in 1965], we thought we were some *baaad* people, know what I mean? And we did our first reading at San Francisco State— just the two of us, right? We did this reading where he read something and I read something—we did like a jazz thing. He did something and I answered him; he looked at me, and I answer him with a poem. He said, "Ta doo da doo doo," and I was, "Ta doo da dee dee," and he said, "Ra tuh ta ta," and I was "Dada tatata"—I mean, you loved what you were doing on stage and you understood what the stage was about. And then someone raised a hand and said, "Could you do that again?"—I remember being so taken aback—"You did it so fast. We didn't understand it." Whoa! (I think about the rappers today—talk about *fast* fast.) And we went, "Okay." And so he read, and then I read, but we were self-conscious.

That was an amazing moment for me. It was the first time I understood the difference between the East Coast and the West Coast, the first time I understood that when you're in different places you have to read things in a different fashion. And it got to be tricky, sometimes, because you always hear the rhythm. You know how you're going to read something, and all of a sudden I heard myself slowing it down 'cause I looked at the audience. "Where are you? Where are you off to?" You had to slow down the beat, just a little bit.

I remember a concert called ToBu—Towards a Black University— down at Howard University, where we honored Sterling Brown in a big gym. I'm trying to remember if there was another woman poet on that program; I don't think so. It was Baraka, Haki [Madhubuti], Larry [Neal], some other poets, and then Sterling at the end. I read right before Baraka. [Sanchez chuckles.] I *always* read right before Baraka—and then Sterling came on and the place exploded. And Sterling said [Sanchez deepens her voice to sound more formal]: "These young poets right here used to scare me."

He was like Dr. Arthur P. Davis—remember that seminal essay where he called us "The Poets of Hate"? (This is an aside but I think it's important because I think that people can change.) I had gone to Howard to do a reading, years later, and there, with his hand up, is Dr. Davis. And I said, "Oops . . ." [Laughs.] "How you doing, Sir?" He said [Sanchez imitates an exceedingly self-conscious tone]: "My name is Arthur P. Davis. I was here at Howard for forty-odd years, and I wrote an essay called 'The Poets of Hate.'" Then he said, "I was wrong." It was an amazing moment. We became very dear friends. During the time when he was ill, I used to take the train and read to him once a week. In fact—[Sanchez taps the cover of *Does Your House Have Lions?*]—I started that book during the time when he was ill, and I would read to him, and he said to me, "That is a great book." He said, "The thing that I realize is that you have exemplified people starting at one point and continuing to evolve and grow. What I said about all those poets . . . What they were saying, they *had* to say in that way."

No one would have heard us if we had said, "I am a poet. I am here to read you a poem." You had to come out and go, "*Ahhh ah ah!*" because *then* everyone looked up. There was no ready-made audience for poetry. Young people think, "Oh, I wish I had been back there with you." We had to *make* the audience. And you make an audience by learning how to walk a stage: If I came out and stayed right in the middle of the stage, people would look and then look away, but if I came out and moved on that stage, they followed you. People would wonder, "What is she doing?" And if you used a curse word, people would go, "*Oh . . .*" [Feinstein laughs.] But you'd never use another curse word, because you'd grabbed them, you'd brought them in. You needed all sorts of techniques to bring people into that arena because people were not interested in poetry.

Baraka probably won't tell this story, but Ed Bullins organized a program for us, and there were, at most, twenty people there. We got on stage and started to read, and someone leaned over and said, "What they doing?" Some guy says, "They reading poetry." "I thought they were gonna sing—let's go!" [Laughs.] The whole first row got up and left. But all they did was make us hone our skills, more and more. Hone the music. Made us appreciate what we were doing. And it also made us, initially, change to make it slower and then speed it up again. We brought them back with us. We said, "Okay. I gave you a chance to hear it, now come on—ride this way." And then, it made them do what we did: They came at it at another level, at our level. It was an infusion of the East Coast on the West Coast. We were privileged to be a part of the Black Arts on the East Coast, and then the Black Arts West in San Francisco. We were there with the Black House when Eldridge Cleaver came out of jail—but I *never, ever* liked that man. I went on record from the very beginning. I mean, the Panthers came to talk to me because I said, "He's not a revolutionary," and a lot of people said, "Well, you don't understand." *That's* when a lot of the sexism came out: "Well, you know, Sonia, you don't understand. You just a woman," and I said, "No. No no. I might be just a woman, but he is no revolutionary." Haki [Madhubuti] brought me *Soul on Ice* [to review for *Negro Digest*], and—I'll never forget—I stayed up and read that book. The next day, I got up and said, "Haki, when I write this review, the first line will be, 'Eldridge Cleaver is not a revolutionary. He's a hustler.' I come from New York. I've seen many a hustler." I don't know where that review is; back then, you'd send stuff off with no copies 'cause you just knew they were going to print it. But they never printed it.

Many of us were so political that they banned us from teaching in New York. We challenged the universities with the stuff we were teaching in African American Studies. I taught [W. E. B.] Du Bois and [Marcus] Garvey and [Paul] Robeson out at San Francisco State, and the FBI knocked on my door with my landlord and said, "You should put her out. She's out there teaching Du *Bwah*." [Feinstein laughs.]

This was 1966 or '67. People can teach Du Bois and Robeson now, but they were on the banned list then. America said they were communists; that was what that was all about. But we were such innocents. Young people think of Black Arts and say, "Oh, you knew everything." No! I was a real *inocente.*

FEINSTEIN: Certain qualities to your work have carried over throughout the years, but your poetry, of course, has changed, and your politics seem to have changed as well. I mean, I don't see you writing "a/coltrane/poem" at this point in your life.

SANCHEZ: You're right, but I use Coltrane in my music. That's the difference. Let me put it this way: When you truly are a jazz poet, you don't have to mention Coltrane; people will hear it. I carry the improvisational part of him into what I do. Coltrane is very much a part of "Middle Passage," but it's done in a different way. The music is in the beat, in the repetition.

FEINSTEIN: What about the very conscious fusion of Coltrane and politics, which was a common element of many Coltrane poems from the late 1960s?

SANCHEZ: This music *is* political. Although Coltrane never came out and said, "I am a political man," he did some music that was political by the very nature of the time and the nature of what he said.

FEINSTEIN: In titles—

SANCHEZ: In titles. But even when the titles aren't there, the music is still political, because all music, like poetry, is political; it either maintains the status quo or it talks about change. You see, when I first started to write, we had just found out that we'd been enslaved and no one had told us. So coming out of that we had to say something about being black. If we hadn't done that, we would not have understood our motion and movement. So you had to say, "Wow! I'm a black woman!" "Whoa! They didn't tell us we'd been enslaved!" "Oh my God! These people *did* this to us!" You had to come out slamming everybody and their mama. You had to do it. You had to exorcize that. But in the 1970s, if I happen to still be doing that, there was something wrong.

You meet people. You travel in the world. You read different poets. You get up on stages with people. One of the most important people I met in the late '60s was Paul Blackburn. He was a dear friend. I used to call Paul when he was ill with cancer, and we would talk and hug over the phone. Paul also had that great jazz sensibility—

FEINSTEIN: "Listening to Sonny Rollins at the Five-Spot"—

SANCHEZ: Oh, yes. Paul loved that [kind of] poetry. And I looked up to him. And he once said, "I know you're not talking to me when you're calling people 'honkies'—" [Feinstein laughs.] I said, "But you have to give voice to these people—you gotta call them *something*," and he said, "But you limited it in your poetry." And I did—it was in, like, two poems that I did, and they were mean poems. So we were laughing about that. But some people came with preconceived notions and they were surprised if you didn't take crap. I would say to some poets, "I come to you as an equal. I'm no flunky. Don't treat me like a flunky." That was the difference, and sometimes people didn't like that. But Paul treated me as an equal, and as a friend, and I read Paul's poetry in my classes. No one's heard of him.

FEINSTEIN: He's just not taught.

SANCHEZ: I suggested to a couple of students [at Bucknell] that they should really read him. I teach him in every class that I teach because I think he's such a fine poet and fine human being. That's a case of the good ones being taken early, you know what I mean?

FEINSTEIN: There's a long list for that.

SANCHEZ: A *long,* mighty list for that.

FEINSTEIN: Can you talk a little about your poem for Ella Fitzgerald?

SANCHEZ: Oh, yes. You know, I was going to perform that last night, but something happened to me last night: Every time I got ready to read something, the page flew open to something [else]. I'm serious. It happened three times, and you have to play that; something was happening.

I've done that Ella Fitzgerald piece on the Academy of Music stage—not with any musicians. I chose that piece because it was a celebration of Ella, and I love that piece because I try to make my voice at the end—[Sanchez sings three notes, the last rising until it's out of her vocal range]. The Philadelphia musicians who were there were like, "Whoa! We would have come out there with you if we had known you were going to do that," and I said, "Well, I never know how I'm going to do that with her." I just thought it was so important to celebrate that woman.

And I've got to do a Sarah [Vaughan] poem. (I don't have it yet; I've done parts.) Ella was very much of this earth. She never left this earth. She was given a voice like no other voice; her voice could travel but, as high as it got, it always stayed earthbound. The beauty of it was that it went *inside* the earth, then came up and out, and then came back down. But *Sarah* left the universe sometimes. Sarah sang so that you would close your eyes and move out of this world into another world. Sometimes she sounded ancient: She went back—really went back—back to Africa, back to India, back to the Middle East, back to Spain. Ella couldn't do that.

FEINSTEIN: Do you have a preference for early or late [recordings of] Sarah?

SANCHEZ: Well, I told you I grew up with music, and I remember when I heard Sarah for the first time, my father said, "She does too much with her voice. It's too rich," and then he said, "When she gets older it'll get better." I remember that. Sarah didn't know what to do with what she had in her early years. She'd go: [Sanchez scats briefly]. And when she got older—my God. The richness. The layers. So many layers. See, she was just an American voice in her early years. Then she became an international voice. She became a universal voice. She became Indian, African, Spanish, Mexican. She became Jewish; she became Palestinian. She went down in *there*—beyond her gut to her womb. Amazing. Much later, I said to my father, "You were right," and he said, "I know." He didn't ask what I was talking about. [Feinstein laughs.] My father always had something to say about something. But he was right.

I was working one night, and [the radio station] WRTI started playing this Brazilian album that she made. Actually, there are three [*I Love Brazil, Brazilian Romance,* and *Copacabana*], but there's one [tune, "Empty Faces/Vera Cruz," from *I Love Brazil*] where she starts doing this chant that's African/Jewish/Indian/Native American . . . I sobbed. I just sobbed. Then I bought the album. It is *amazing*. It does what every artist attempts to do.

I studied [at New York University] with a woman named Louise Bogan—

FEINSTEIN: Sure—

SANCHEZ: Bogan was right about the poet being a universal person, and I began to understand what that was about. I didn't have to change my skin to become universal. The moment you pull out and you give out this sound, this lyricism, these lines that might be talking about my experience in Harlem, or my experience—wherever—someone will pick it up and say, "Oh, yeah. I had a similar experience."

That's what happened when we went out to San Francisco: We left in search of our selves—our history and herstory in the black studies—and we found everybody else, hidden. I mean, I'd be in a classroom and someone would pass by and say, "Sonia, here is a picture. We think this is of a concentration camp for Japanese. You have a couple of Japanese students; bring it up in class." That was how we were teaching. And the students got *mad* at me: "*I don't know anything about that, Sonia!*" They really got pissed. But I said, "At least ask your parents about this." My brother, these eighteen year olds came back to class that Tuesday with tears in their eyes. Their parents had told them that they had been *in* the concentration camps, but they had kept it a secret. That's what happened to us: We went searching for our selves and we discovered other people hidden, too. Japanese. Chinese. Motion and movement. You couldn't teach this and stay in one place. You had to go out.

Bogan was an interesting woman. [Chuckles.] Very aristocratic woman, right? There were a couple of things she said that were amazing, that have held true. She's the reason I'm so strict in class. A lot of students don't understand that. The other day, I walked in when some students were throwing candy across the table, and I turned and said, "Stop it . . . You wouldn't do that in another class." I was saying to them, "This is creative writing. This is holy to me. Come make it holy." Some of the students are really privileged and spoiled; they're not accustomed to anyone saying anything like that, being strict. In a history class, or a science class, they wouldn't behave that way. But in a creative writing class, they're like, "Hey . . ." They *say* they want to write, but, my brother, they really don't. It's too casual. It's not what it means to you, or to me, or to Yusef [Komunyakaa] or someone else. I'm serious about that. In the classroom, I'll kid around—but you can't demean the atmosphere. Sometimes in private schools, creative writing is just like, "Oh, yeah, yeah. One credit—I'll get it. Whatever. I'm gone."

Bogan was strict, too, and I know that that's how I teach because she was my teacher on many levels. I'll never forget asking her, "Do I have any talent?" She said [Sanchez imitates a slow, haughty delivery]: "*Many* people have talent, Sonia." [Feinstein laughs.] I said, "Well, yeah—but I'm not talking about many people. I'm talking about *me*." I wanted to know, should I invest something in this? And she said, "It depends. What do you want to do with it?" And I said, "Well, you just informed me about this, and I don't think I know what to do with it—" and she said, "Yes, you doooo." As I look back on that question that she posed, it might have been a double-layered question because she's looking at me, and I was the only black in that class, right? But in that class, I was the first poet who got published because Bogan would make you send your work out. And I do the same thing. (I started doing it with this class at Bucknell but they weren't interested.) I'm always coming to my classrooms saying, "There's an anthology . . ." And I've always had students get into anthologies. I say, "Send stuff out. Mention that you're in my class—whatever." So I've had students included in books such as *Confirmation* [*An Anthology of African-American Women*] on down to *Bum Rush the Page* [*A Def Poetry Jam*]. I tell my students, "Send stuff in," and they're *in* there, you know? Because this is what this business is about, at some point.

But I'm also amazed by the people who don't have that kind of energy toward this thing that we do called poetry. I teach people who have such egos at such a young age. I say to those people in my class, "You will never, ever *move* with that ego. You've got to drop it." One way to do that is to work with musicians, 'cause you will drop your ego real fast—[Feinstein laughs]—if you're in there for about thirty minutes. They say, "Okay. Show me what you got," and you say, "Oh my God." You're going to get out in front of a whole bunch of people, 200 people, and you're thinking, "What am I *doing*?"

At the Painted Bride in Philadelphia, where they have readings and music and dance, we did an evening of poetry and music—[vibraphonist] Khan Jamal, Odean, and a bass player [Tyrone Brown], and it was really nice. I had given them the poem, and we played with it a great deal and had a lot of fun on stage. When we finished, the people said, "No. You can't get off the stage." We were tired. We had done about an hour. (An hour by yourself is tiring, but an hour with music—you're very much aware of whom you're dealing with.) But musicians are amazing people, let me tell you. Khan and Odean said, "Come on back, Sonia. Let's do something," and they started playing. [Sanchez sings musical lines in the spirit of Odean Pope.] And then Odean came and stood there right next to me. And you can't look at an audience and say, "I don't have anything written. . ." It got to be funny, so that's when I started with the laughter: [Sanchez laughs with a staccato sound]—and Odean went—[Sanchez sings with a similar rhythm]. That's why when I read "Middle Passage"—I start off with laughter. [Sanchez laughs again, then reads very quickly from "Improvisation" in *Wounded in the House of a Friend*]: "It was It was It was It was / It was the coming that was bad." I hear nothing but music in that.

The Ancestors. Thank God for the Ancestors. The Ancestors came in and helped me out. That's what they put in my mouth. "It was / it was the coming that was bad." Of course, I added stuff later on, and that's when we started moving on the stage. And Odean really pushed me. He pushed me to such a point that on stage I actually got down to my knees.

I did this piece down in Atlanta with—what's his name?—the jazz singer out of Chicago—Brown—

FEINSTEIN: Oscar?

SANCHEZ: Oscar Brown. We did a set together. He sang, and then he went off stage, and I read some blues pieces and then "Middle Passage" with some of his musicians. And these brothers were so subtle at first, so quiet, and then they started pushing me until I almost had to give up. Again, I literally got down on my knees to do that piece.

But Odean has pushed me to a place deeper than I have ever been. I have done the piece in other ways, but every time I do it, I hear Odean. That's what I meant about Coltrane, and what musicians will do: They cause you to make the word respond to the music until it becomes the music.

FEINSTEIN: I appreciate what you're saying about the poet and musician inspiring each other, but, in general, don't you think musicians tend to inspire writing more than writing inspires music? I mean, I've published a lot of pieces by writers on music, but very few by musicians on literature. It seems to be predominantly in one direction.

SANCHEZ: That's so true.

FEINSTEIN: Why do you think that is?

SANCHEZ: I don't know. I think that they probably don't see themselves necessarily as writers, or, if they are writers, they don't feel the need to talk about it. I think if you're a musician, and people can't write what you want, you probably have to write what you need to play, or to hear played, or you have to write what you're feeling at some particular point. Nobody else is going to do that for you. I think that is what you see—that writing became an extension of the music. And I think it takes a little genius to do that—a little extra genius to do that: "Now let me sit down and write this, too."

FEINSTEIN: I think music will always have the edge on literature. There are things that I can feel and understand through poetry that I do not understand so absolutely, perhaps, through music—either as a listener or a player—but there's an immediacy to music that literature can only aspire towards.

SANCHEZ: That is so true. I mean, that *is* so true. Sometimes you try to make the poem *do* all that, and when I read from *Does Your House Have Lions?* I repeat, I go back, like a musician would do. I'll do it three times. There's a section where I break the form in *Does Your House Have Lions?* where my brother talks about being touched. (I had gone down to take care of my brother and whenever I touched him, he said it hurt. You know, with AIDS patients every time you touch them it hurts, right?) Although I had written the passage three times, I had never read it three times:

> hold me with air
> breathe me with air
> sponge me with air
> whisper me with air
> comb me with air
> brush me with air
> rinse me with air.

And I didn't realize until I read with Odean that it needed that repetition. Isn't that something? I mean, that subconscious is a mutha, you know what I mean? [Both laugh.] It is a *mutha* . . .

I changed to sound like Odean, like his horn. I broke it up and repeated the lines. People hear the sweet lines, and all of a sudden you don't *want* people to hear the sweet lines. You want them to know how horrific it is, on many levels.

The first time I performed the piece, I tried to stay true to the line, because that's what you do if you're a writer: You don't want to change that line. But if you're working with musicians, you *have* to change it. That's why collaboration with musicians is something else: It changes the poetry so much. But also, the poem can change the music. I would say to Odean, "I hear how you're playing it, but that's not how I hear it." I'd read it, and he would hear what I meant. We both came with an idea of what that book was about, and then we collided—in a nice fashion—and we listened—in a most wonderful fashion—and then it became something else, something completely different. That's what's so wonderful about working with musicians.

John Sinclair. *Photo by Michael P. Smith.*

18

Ask Me Now
John Sinclair

The year prior to this interview, I'd come to New Orleans for the Tennessee Williams Festival, an annual event that paid its participants beignets but provided airfare, housing, and parties. Chaired by the scholar Henry Lacey, my panel on jazz and literature included Al Young, the conference professional, and John Sinclair, the supposed wild card. (Sinclair's history as a noncomformist terrified the administrators.) During that visit, I interviewed Lee Grue, and, for a number of uninteresting reasons, I could not piece together enough time to interview someone else. But a year later, when I returned to New Orleans, I made sure to book a date with Sinclair. From our experience on the panel, I knew he'd be gritty, forthcoming, and completely engaging.

John asked to meet at the Café de la Course, a coffeehouse in the French Quarter, and I obliged, especially since he said it would be quiet. It wasn't. Stereo speakers above the table played a range of tunes, and although we chose a table at the very back, our waitress and various customers buzzed by us with irritating consistency. Then someone opened the front doors of the coffeehouse, and a few moments later the street filled with a pre–St. Patrick's Day parade. Car horns, hollers, whistling—hey, it was New Orleans. John seemed completely undistracted, and I loved hearing his dark, gristly rasp, but I also knew transcribing the tape would be a bear. I was right.

Toward the end of the interview, he received a call from his daughter, and I took the opportunity to buy another cup of coffee, as well as an almond pastry. I returned to our table when I saw him hang up.

"Would you like me to get you one of these?" I asked, pointing to the dessert.

"No," he said. "I'd love it, but my doctor says this stuff'll kill me." Then he picked up his fork, cut and speared a considerable hunk, and added, "But I *have* to try it."

John Sinclair might be best known for his work on radio, but he is also a poet, blues performer, and music journalist. Previously, he was a professor of blues history at Wayne State University, the chairman of the White Panther Party, the manager of the radical rock 'n' roll group MC-5, and the producer of many cultural events, including the Ann Arbor Blues & Jazz Festival. His volumes of poetry include *This Is Our Music, Meditations: A Suite for John Coltrane, We Just Change the Beat: Selected Poems,* and his "elongated blues work in verse," *Fattening Frogs for Snakes: Delta Sound Suite.* A long-time resident of New Orleans, he now lives in Amsterdam.

The following four poems, discussed in our conversation, are from *thelonious: a book of monk.* The interview took place in New Orleans on March 9, 2002.

#11
in walked bud
for les reid & john petrie
john sinclair

first there was monk
before the war
& then from further up-
town, in harlem,

from the neighborhood
of coleman hawkins, sonny
rollins, & jackie mclean,
there was bud powell

or earl alfred "bud" powell
on piano, strict interpreter
of dizzy & bird
for the keyboard, fleet

of the single line & fast
to abandon
the heaviness in the left hand,
to make room for the bass & drums

& the harmonic
implications
of the melody, the farther
reaches

of the chords, the dizzy
atmosphere
which resulted
from the compression of experience

& the deep urban intelligence
of african-americans
born in manhattan
or brought to harlem as children,

coming up on the streets,
standing outside of bars
& after-hours joints with the whores
& the dope peddlers, straining

to listen
or to hear from the bandstand
or to see the musicians inside
with such aspirations, to get up there

themselves, with they little horns,
behind the drums, or at the piano,
hands on the keyboard
& a room full of people

looking up
from the depths of their lives
to flood the bandstand
with huge waves of love

& warmth, then back out
to the streets, & the ugly
stares, the cold
bitter hatred

of the white people,
the nightstick
across the head
in philadelphia, the loss

of consistent memory,
the shock treatments
inside the several nut houses,
a phony dope beef in new york city

& no more cabaret card,
loss of license to work
in the nightclubs of manhattan
or even brooklyn, iced

out
of everything
but the will to make music
out of the guts of a piano,

the amazing bud powell,
the blazing bud powell,
now faltering
& lost, now lucid, now

gone
again, in toronto
with bird & dizzy
& mingus & max roach,

fresh out of creedmore
& more shocks to the head,
may, 1953, on the same night
rocky marciano

knocked out jersey joe walcott,
drunk & crazy bud powell
back in manhattan, a night
at birdland with bird

in the first week of march,
1955, gone all the way out
of his motherfucking mind,
bud powell,

bud powell,
bud powell,
bird's voice ringing in his ears,
mingus pointing his finger

from the bandstand,
"these are sick men,"
he said, "ladies &
gentlemen, please

don't associate me
with this madness," & in
walked monk that night
to catch some music, with his head

set straight on his shoulders
& his feet
firmly on the ground, in control
of his faculties

like few men of any time,
1955, just a week before bird
would leave us here
& bud would stagger on,

the scene changes,
time waits,
exile in paris
from 1959 to the end

of his life, but on this night
at birdland there they are,
bird at the microphone
intoning his name & bud

staring off into space, & monk
taking it all in,
crazy
too, like a fox

to say to bird & bud, "i
told you guys
to *act* crazy, but i
didn't

tell you
to fall in love
with the act. You're *really*
crazy now. . . ."

louisville, ky
october 12, 1985 / detroit
december 7–14, 1985

#14
'round about midnight
for linda jones
john sinclair

there is a point
between night & day
where it all comes clear
& bright, a new beginning

where yesterday
can be left behind
& a new day is there
to greet us, clean

with promise
& a clear path
thru the hours before dawn
when the mind kicks in,

the squares all tucked in bed
& the people of the night
in charge of the scene—players,
musicians, whores,

countermen at diners & cats
delivering the morning papers,
garbage men & cops & drunks
in the rhythms of midnight

& the small hours after,
a different sphere completely
from daytime, traffic
& the peculiar world of commerce—

this is when the music is made,
in nightclubs until two
or four a.m., & then in after-
hours joints & people's cribs,

or in the recording studios
after the gig, with everyone nice
& relaxed, half-
juiced or hazy,

lazy, a little crazy maybe
but ready to put down some tunes
onto recording discs or tape
for the rest of the world to hear—

'round midnight & after, the end
of a day, or in the meta-
phorical mode, it's the last sigh
of an era, like around 1939

thru '44, with the war
going on abroad, & the nation
finally tearing itself loose
from the last dying grip

of pre-modern america,
all its young men at war
& only the rejects, mis-
fits & draft dodgers left

to shape some new form
from the ruins of the past,
some measure of their alienation
from the day before,

their allegiance to the flag
of tomorrow, like whatever
it might bring would be better
than what's happening right now,

the high discovery
of risk, or the existential premise
that something new & brilliant can be made
from the existing materials,

the intention
"to create & invent
on little jobs" that monk
spoke of in 1948, with no reward

but the beauty of the thing itself,
the challenge of invention
with no idea of what might come next,
no pattern to fall back on,

nothing but the driving force inside your self, & the long roots of culture
stretching back to west africa
& the southern united states,

the utter & absolute beauty
of making a bridge
across the years, to link the past
in a whole new way

with what would come next,
round about midnight
of a dying world, & round about 3 a.m.
of a brand new day,

monk at the piano
composing the future
& bud powell taking the piece
to cootie williams to record,

1944, a standard of modern music
even before its composer could record it,
the loveliest work in modern jazz
at just over three minutes long

yet longer than tomorrow,
longer than the 45 years
since monk eased it out of his head
& his gargantuan heart

& gave it to us,
"round about midnight," as a sign
that something was coming
that had never been here before

detroit
july 14/december 27–30, 1985

#38
carolina moon
      for thelonious monk
john sinclair

just so each day
dawns again
& everything is new
all over—

were it not for you,
o great monk
& your magic
ilk, it would

stay the same way
all the time, that
big fat stinky moon
just rotting in the sky

renaissance center bus stop
detroit
september 27, 1982

#76
i surrender, dear
      for penny
john sinclair

no matter what
i might do
to get you off my mind
you just won't leave the premises

& i don't know how to make it
any clearer, you been
gone so long
that i should be done got

over you by now
but no, there you are
in every motherfucking song
that enters my brain, every day

i want to call you
on the phone & tell you
i love you
in so many words like that,

i can't live without you,
let's get back together,
i want to marry you
& stay with you

for the rest of my life,
let's move to new orleans
& leave this place behind,
i'll be true to you

like i was so long
when we were together,
i don't want no one else
as long as i have you,

these are the words
i wish i could say, but my pride
& the hard times we had
make me hold my tongue,

when you put me
out i swore
there'd be no more going back
& i been trying to make it

without you so long
that it's driving me crazy,
no buts & no maybes—
do you want me back,

can you live without me,
shouldn't we be together,
can't we just swallow our foolish pride
& stop questioning everything

& face the facts for real—
you & me together,
baby, all ways
you & me

i surrender, dear

harmonic park
detroit
may 21, 1988

SASCHA FEINSTEIN: I want to focus on the series of Monk poems that you've been working on for the last twenty years, but let's set some groundwork. How did you get turned on to jazz?

JOHN SINCLAIR: I grew up in a little-bitty town in Michigan, about sixty miles from Detroit, ten miles from Flint (the Vehicle City), and I used to listen to blues and rhythm and blues on the radio. This was a time [early '50s] when television first came in, and radio was changing from television-type entertainment—serials, dramas—to all music. I was a radio fanatic; radio gave me my whole life, and that's why I'm on the radio even today. The first song I can remember is "One Mint Julip" by the Clovers. But then Chuck Berry, Little Richard, and Bo Diddley came out, and Fats Domino crossed over (I call them the Mount Rushmore of popular music).

In high school, I was a teenage disk jockey. I was modeled after a guy called Frantic Ernie—Ernie Durham of Flint, Michigan, later big in Detroit where he single-handedly broke Motown records on WJLB radio. But before that he was on a little station in Flint, and he was my idol. I just loved this guy, and he *rhymed* everything that he said. He was incredibly dynamic, and he played the *best* records in the world. So I used to steal 45s—I could steal any 45 that wasn't nailed down behind the cash register—

FEINSTEIN: John . . .

SINCLAIR: Oh yeah. I didn't have any money, and I loved these records, and I *had* to have them. [Laughs.] The statute of limitations has run out. [Both laugh.] I had a fantastic collection of 45s, and I wanted to be a disk jockey, so when I went to college—Albion College, a tiny college in Michigan—a guy I knew who had a show on the dorm radio station gave his show to me. It was from seven to eight in the morning; that's when I started staying up all night so I could make the show—a pattern I've continued for forty years. [Both laugh.]

I did a few of these shows (my theme song was "School Day" by Chuck Berry). I'd play an hour of Jimmy Reed and Muddy Waters and Chuck Berry and the Flamingos. And at our very straight Methodist college there was one beatnik, a guy named Rodney Coates. He wore sandals. One day he showed up at my dormitory, inquiring whether I was the guy doing the radio program: "Where did you get those records?" So I said, "They're my records." He said, "Oh, *man!* Can I come in?" So we sat and talked about records for about three hours, missing dinner and everything, and finally at one point he said, "Are you hip to jazz?" and I said, "No, I'm not," and he said, "Oh, man!" He grabbed me by the arm: "Come with me!" We went upstairs (I can remember this like it was yesterday) and he put on *Dig* [the Miles Davis recording, featuring Jackie McLean and Sonny Rollins].

FEINSTEIN: Fabulous.

SINCLAIR: So Jackie McLean was the first thing I ever heard. In about thirty seconds I'm saying, "Yeah, yeah, *yeah.*" [Laughs.] And that opened the floodgate.

In those days you could go to the record shop, take the records in the booth and play them, and I would take about ten albums. I would play one while I read [the liner notes on] the backs of the others, making the acquaintance of the great Ira Gitler, Orrin Keepnews, Leonard Feather, Nat Hentoff. Those guys left an indelible impression on my mind. Already being a fiendish collector of records, I just switched my allegiance to jazz.

I started college in '59, and the first records I got were [Miles Davis's] *Kind of Blue*—the greatest record ever made—and then I just developed my taste. "Jackie McLean—I wonder if he has any records of his own?" You know how it goes. And I devoured everything [in print as well]. *Down Beat. Jazz Review* and *Metronome* were still coming out. It was a very rich period from 1960 to '64 or '65. I was immersed in jazz, and I gravitated toward [the pioneers of free jazz, such as] John Coltrane, Cecil Taylor, Archie Shepp, Sun Ra, Pharoah [Sanders]. I got into the more advanced parts. That's where I started with jazz.

FEINSTEIN: And did it immediately influence your work?

SINCLAIR: When I started writing poetry, I wanted to deal with the jazz idiom. Baraka, or LeRoi Jones as they called him then, had become my principal influence because he was into both poetry and jazz, and I wanted to write about jazz as a critic, reviewer, whatever—prose. (I read the things that I wrote at that time, and I realize I was a slavish follower of Baraka. I look at it and say, "Jeez, I just stole that whole thing!" [Laughs.] Not so much exactly, but the approach to it.) He was my role model. When Baraka performs with music—or not—he is the most musical performer out there. I've seen Baraka, and it's like seeing Trane: He lifts the shit up off the ground just through the passion of his belief.

FEINSTEIN: Like Baraka, you not only fused music and poetry, but music, poetry, and politics.

SINCLAIR: Well, yeah. That was just life. I was a follower of Malcolm X. In fact, I was a follower of Elijah Muhammad.

FEINSTEIN: That helps to explain why you were one of the very few white poets to write about John Coltrane during his lifetime.

SINCLAIR: I know. Believe me, I know. [Laughs.] There were only about four people who had good things to say about [Coltrane's 1965 recording] *Ascension:* Hentoff, kind of . . . but Baraka, A. B. [Spellman], Frank Kofsky, and myself—we were the four who had something positive to say, while John Tynan was calling it "anti-jazz." These musicians were under attack from everywhere. So I have a lot of pride about that.

　I became the *Down Beat* correspondent from Detroit [in the fall of 1964]. A great Detroit pianist named Harold McKinney got a petition going to get me in because they thought the guy they had was too square. They thought I'd give the Detroit jazz players good coverage. And I started writing reviews for *Jazz* magazine: *Coltrane Live at Birdland, A Love Supreme*—I reviewed those when they first came out, and I was right on the money! [Laughs.]

FEINSTEIN: With these reviews, or your political writings, did you get flack from the black community?

SINCLAIR: No. I never had trouble with black people. I've only had trouble with white people. [Laughs.] I was what they used to call a "race man." Still am. One thing you have to say about black people: They have the most open minds of anybody in America, and they don't give a fuck what color you are. The Rap Browns and the Stokely Carmichaels and those guys—I supported them, too. They were right, too. These white college students come in and tell them how they should do this shit . . . it was backwards, man. I was a race man. I was brought up intellectually by black people, and also in the streets. Drugs—the whole thing. So I had a good grounding.

I thought Elijah Muhammad was on the right track, because the things he said about white people were all true—but he didn't know the half of it! [Laughs.] He didn't know how bad they were, really. But I thought looking to white people for a solution for black people meant they were looking in the wrong direction. As Elijah Muhammad pointed out, "These are the people who put you in the trick in the first place. They did this on purpose, to their benefit. It wasn't some kind of thing where it's a moral lapse and you've got to call it to their attention."

In my world, there was never any contradiction between being race-oriented politics, left-wing politics, libertarian politics, getting high, and jazz. Everyone I knew got high and listened to these records, and they all felt the same way about the government. It was never contradictory in my life; it was all part of a fabric that I enthusiastically grasped and clung to.

FEINSTEIN: So when Ornette Coleman titled his album *This Is Our Music*—a title you then used for your first book of poems—you don't think he was directing the "Our" to the black community?

SINCLAIR: No. He was talking about the four guys [in his group], which included a white bass player, Scott LaFaro—

FEINSTEIN: Charlie Haden.

SINCLAIR: Yeah, Charlie Haden. "This is *our* music"—and it had a picture of the four of them [on the cover].

FEINSTEIN: Some people feel differently.

SINCLAIR: Well, a lot of people are defensive. I never identified with white people. I didn't want no part of it. I still don't. I'm a radical. To me, the problem with America *is* white people. We had affirmative action for white people for 300 and some years. That's why they hate affirmative action—because it worked so well for them for so long. [Laughs.] So I didn't identify with that, and by the time I was nineteen I got used to being the only white guy on the set.

I remember the first time I got called "nigger," and I was so happy. [Laughs.] It was in Sweetie's Barbershop, listening to Gene Ammons playing "Canadian Sunset" or "Hittin' the Jug" on the jukebox. I'm sitting back with the rest of the cats, high on sleeping pills and cough syrup, while Sweetie and Junebug are doing hair. Then somebody asked after me, and somebody said, "Oh, that nigger back there." I was really happy to be accepted, you know what I mean?

When I became a political/cultural activist—around 1967—I was fully immersed in activism, and I didn't write poetry for about fifteen years. I was in prison for six months in 1966, but the second time—I did two and a half years from '69 to the end of '71—that was after the White Panther Party, and I was a hero to the black cons, 'cause I was always working for them, standing up for them, organizing, agitating. I was getting my ass kicked by the administration. So no black prisoner would have ever let anything happen to me.

FEINSTEIN: You did the time for dope?

SINCLAIR: For drug possession, then challenging the marijuana laws. I was a political activist. And then I got into rock 'n' roll. I was managing the MC-5—they were huge in Detroit—and we were turning all these kids on to rock 'n' roll. "Rock & Roll, Dope & Fucking in the Streets" was our motto. [Laughs.] So there was all of these things, plus the fact that I was challenging the constitutionality of the marijuana laws. They didn't like me. Another point of honor. [Laughs.]

I first read about this whole [racial] conflict in [Kerouac's] *On the Road* and then in [Mezz Mezzrow's] *Really the Blues*. I was sixteen then. *Really the Blues* is the template for people like myself who wanted to cross over. Mezz Mezzrow, when he went to jail, identified himself as a Negro so he wouldn't be put in with the white prisoners! [Laughs.] Before I got with black people, I got all my stuff from their records—and from Jack Kerouac, Lawrence Ferlinghetti . . . I remember discovering the Pocket Poets. You had to write away to get them, you know? I remember my first poetry readings, before I even wrote poetry: We'd be sitting on top of a ladder, with Chianti bottles, [reading poems from] *Pictures from the Gone World*. It was crazy. [Laughs.]

[Charles] Olson was God to me in poetry. From Baraka I got my subject: music. But Olson said at Berkeley, where I studied with him in '65: "I'm the last white man. I've never been arrested. I don't listen to jazz." [Laughs.] He was acknowledging Ginsberg.

FEINSTEIN: And Creeley, who tried so hard to get Olson interested in jazz, though he couldn't do it.

SINCLAIR: Yeah. Creeley was a mentor of mine and sponsored me at the Berkeley Poetry Conference. I think he liked my earliest poems not because they were so well written but because I was trying to deal with jazz, and he told me he was a jazz fanatic. [Shaking his head:] Oh, Creeley. [Sinclair places his fingertips to his lips and blows a kiss to the sky.]

·   ·   ·   ·

FEINSTEIN: You've been working on a book of Thelonious Monk poems for about twenty years.

SINCLAIR: Since 1982. As I told you, *nobody*'s asked me about it.

FEINSTEIN: Well, to work off a Monk title, let me ask you now. How did you begin the series?

SINCLAIR: One of the first poems was "carolina moon," which I didn't really do justice to. It's one of the great arrangements in contemporary music: Monk's version of "Carolina Moon" [*Genius of Modern Music, Volume 2*]. I was standing at a bus stop to take me to the East Side of Detroit, and there was this moon, and I thought of "Carolina Moon," and how Monk grew up in North Carolina. I wrote this small poem that ends with the premise of "were it not for you, / o great monk, / & your magic / ilk, it would / stay the same way / all the time."

FEINSTEIN: What time of year was this?

SINCLAIR: Spring, I think.

FEINSTEIN: Monk had just died [on February 17, 1982].

SINCLAIR: Yeah, that was the other thing. See, I wasn't a big listener to Monk [initially], because when I got into jazz, Monk's creative period as a composer was pretty much over. He was with Columbia by the time I started in the early '60s, and we thought of those records as being kind of lame. We got so we thought Miles Davis was lame by '65, you know? [In a self-mocking tone:] "That shit with Wayne Shorter. . ." We wanted *HooooWow!* [Laughs.] Now, of course, I'm able to enjoy it. "I was so much older then." [Laughs.]

When Monk died, it was like when Allen Ginsberg died: I never thought of Allen Ginsberg leaving. He was such a central part of my world that I just thought he was an eternal verity, and all of a sudden, wow, Ginsberg died. And Monk—you believed in Monk. You knew his music. Even when his creative period ended, he was still playing his ass off with that great quartet, and the orchestral projects. Again, I grew to understand this through study. Nobody was anything like him, and he created all these *great* original compositions. Even when he'd do a standard, he would fuck it up so much. He was such a genius, such a *sui generis* individual, and I thought, "I need to really study his music."

By '82, I was not in the trenches like I had been in the '60s, so I could go back and appreciate the early Blue Note stuff. I had the records, but I never *really* listened. And at the same time, like I said, I had just started writing poetry again after about fifteen years, and I felt very expressive. (If I could write all that stuff today, I would be so happy! They're much harder to come by now.) But I was generating a lot of work.

I usually get my ideas from listening to a song. (Why I do this, I couldn't tell you. I've just done it for thirty-five years or more. I also always date my poems or else I'd never remember when I wrote them.) But I had about four or five little [Monk] poems, and then the *Complete Blue Note Recordings* came out—when was that?

FEINSTEIN: Mosaic put out the LP set in 1983, I believe.

SINCLAIR: It had either just come out, or I was just able to afford one, but I acquired a set, and it had a discography. Well, I'm a freak for discographies, and *that* was what gave me the idea for the structure of a book: I decided I wanted to write a poem for every piece that Monk ever recorded—not the multiple times, just the first time. (In some cases, there were three or four, where the second time had a special edge to it.) So then I got the [complete recordings on] Riverside, Prestige—I just collected all the stuff.

At that time in my life, I was into making comprehensive tapes: The Complete Charlie Parker—live sets and studio sets—in order of recording.

FEINSTEIN: Wow . . .

SINCLAIR: You start with the discographies—follow the development— and you can hear the impact of how they made them, and the influence on the other musicians of the time. I did the same thing with Coltrane. I had, like, 100 cassettes. [Laughs.] Quite an undertaking.

So when I saw the Monk discography on Blue Note, I thought, "Yeah. This is it. This is my form: a discography in verse." I'd already written four poems from the first session, so they're a little out of sequence. (I don't think he cut "Thelonious" first, but my book starts with "thelonious.") "Humphf." "Suburban Eyes." "Evonce." [Chuckles.] Yeah.

Then I got the other discographies and divided the project into four books—Blue Notes, Prestiges, Riversides, Columbias—and I eliminated all the ones that were played several times. So there were 150 tunes. 150 poems that I was going to write.

The beautiful thing about using the discography is that your struc-

ture problem is solved. The tunes are numbered, and they can be re-
combined in any way, but the basic thing is the sequence of the order
in which they were recorded the first time. There's a balance. All these
formal things are built into this outline, which is a good thing. I know
what they're going to be called, and I know where they go, and I know
the tempo, and I know they have to go with the music—I just have to
write them. As we know: not as easy as it sounds.

Some are based on historical anecdotes, some are told by Monk,
some are told by Art Blakey, Budd Johnson, and other musicians. Some
of them deal with my love life. They can be about anything; I don't
have any limits on what they can be *about*. I got all that from Olson.
This isn't no endless "Song of I." I try to do what Olson says: Avoid
"the lyrical interference of the ego." I thought Olson gave you the license to write about *anything* under this roof. When you read *The
Maximus Poems,* anything could be in there, but it's all part of his central concern.

FEINSTEIN: Or, I suppose, Pound's *Cantos.*

SINCLAIR: I was a big follower of Pound as an organizer and publisher,
and I like his poetry, but it wasn't, for me, like Olson—not even Williams's *Paterson.* I guess if I were twenty years older they would probably be the shit. I got to Williams and Pound because they were the
masters, and Pound really excited me when I was young. He inspired
me to become a cultural organizer. *The ABC of Reading. Blast* magazine. The concept of a vortex. God, I admired that motherfucker.

FEINSTEIN: I was thinking of Pound's collage-like sensibility, coupled
with his interest in taking on a larger sense of history.

SINCLAIR: Obviously, that's where Olson got it, though he made it his
own. That's where we, the individual, come in, as in a jazz performance: We can say whatever we want about the things that are on our
minds.

FEINSTEIN: You mentioned Olson's "central concern." What's your central
concern with the Monk project?

SINCLAIR: The mind of Monk is the central organizer. The Monkian
Mind.

FEINSTEIN: And how do you go about approaching and exploring the
Monkian Mind?

SINCLAIR: He was a specific individual. I've got a few sources. I thought
that unfinished biography [by Peter Keepnews] would be good. I've
got a couple of very inferior ones. But you get the anecdotes. You get
anything you can.

FEINSTEIN: Why do you think no one has published a great Monk biography?

SINCLAIR: He's a hard guy to understand, unless you're out of your mind yourself. Monk was unique. The Unique Thelonious Monk. He lived with his mother and his wife all his life. He was an individual in every way. And you have to grasp that. You can't just take the standard approach ("He was born, he did this, he did that. . ."). Even Miles Davis was a fairly straightforward guy compared to Thelonious Monk. Even Coltrane. Cecil Taylor would be closer to Monk.

FEINSTEIN: Or Lester Young.

SINCLAIR: Lester was a very different type of guy, but, yeah, he had completely his own way of dealing with stuff. And Monk was more together than Lester. Monk didn't give a fuck! He did not care. He would go home, and there would be [his wife] Nellie, and there would be his mom. He had his piano in his kitchen. And he didn't have to go out if he didn't want to. He didn't have to work. In his most creative period, he hardly worked, and if it hadn't been for [the Blue Note producer] Alfred Lion, he wouldn't have even been documented. (Fortunately, Alfred realized this guy was a genius—*The Genius of Modern Music*— though it was probably thirty years before it really paid off.)

FEINSTEIN: I never knew Monk, so I can't judge from personal experience, but the biographies have been so disappointing. Leslie Gourse's book [*Straight, No Chaser*] is ridiculous.

SINCLAIR: Horrible.

FEINSTEIN: [Thomas] Fitterling [in *Thelonious Monk*] is mainly of interest because of the discography. The third one [Laurent de Wilde's *Monk*] is a bit better, as I recall. *The Thelonious Monk Reader* [edited by Rob van der Bliek] is mixed but includes some fine reprinted essays. You can present anecdotes, but they won't necessarily produce character.

SINCLAIR: When I get done with this [Monk project], my idea is that you'll get the feeling for who Monk was, not just as a composer but as a singular individual, "a man of whom it can be said / there's never been another / even to remotely resemble him." [Chuckles.]

Even in weak biographies, you get facts. I just read Francis Paudras's biography on Bud Powell [*Dance of the Infidels*]. It gives you a whole different idea of Bud Powell. A lot of them are just awful, but you get details that you can use. So I read them all.

I'll tell you a really good jazz book that I read. Now what the hell's the name of it . . . It's by an English guy, stories inspired by jazz . . .

FEINSTEIN: Geoff Dyer's *But Beautiful*?

SINCLAIR: Yeah! Now that's some good shit.

FEINSTEIN: Al [Young] was a little down on it. He felt that Dyer was appropriating the lives in a way that wasn't cool.

SINCLAIR [referring to Dyer:] Well, he's English. [Both laugh.] They're the biggest exploiters in the history of civilization! I say that as a person of British extraction. They're the worst people who were ever invented on earth. [Both laugh.] They're like Led Zeppelin making millions of dollars off of Willie Dixon tunes and not wanting to *pay* him.

The book was a lot better than I thought it was going to be, and there were some anecdotal things that I thought were really good.

FEINSTEIN: And there's solid prose, and genuinely imaginative explorations.

SINCLAIR: But how about Al Young's musical memoirs [collected in *Drowning in the Sea of Love*]? When I write my memoirs, I want to hijack his form. We've had the same kind of experience, where you relate everything to a song. When I think of my youth, I think of the songs that remind me what was happening, and when I read Al's things I think, "Man, what a beautiful way to do it."

FEINSTEIN: Was the Monk project the entire reason why you started writing again in '82?

SINCLAIR: What really brought me back to writing poetry in 1982 was reading Robert Palmer's great work, *Deep Blues*, which my friend Harry Duncans sent me one day, and I was reading the words of Muddy Waters, Robert Lockwood, Johnny Shines, Sunnyland Slim, and other bluesmen when I realized that the way they *talked* was powerfully poetic—maybe even more so than the songs, because their actual speech didn't have to be "rhymed up," as they say. I was writing down quotes from these artists in my notebook when their speech started falling into verse patterns on my page. Then I wrote some commentaries in the notebook, and those fell into verse patterns. So I had a new way to work. It was like what Charlie Parker said about feeling the higher reaches of the chords: "I came alive!" So that led to my work in blues called *Fattening Frogs for Snakes*, contemporaneous with *thelonious: a book of monk*, both started twenty years ago, and I had my poetry hand back—now two hands, actually: blues *and* jazz.

The other thing that got me back to poetry was reading Ed Sand-

ers's great little work called *Investigative Poetry*. And one of the reasons why I didn't write was because I was writing propaganda. I was
an activist. I wanted people to do things, *today*. And I felt my poetry wasn't like that. Sometimes I didn't understand them. (I have
poems that I wrote thirty-five years ago, and I don't know what they
mean. I like the way they sound, but I don't know what they mean.)
And I used to hate when people [giving readings] would explain, in
a lengthy introduction, what the poem was going to be about. And I
realized from Sanders that you could put everything—including all
the research—right in the poem. In fact, I could take the words these
guys said and put them into verse. And that got me writing again, because my concerns were historical, discographical, musical, analytical,
biographical—all those kinds of things.

But I'm still talking a lot about me, because this is who I am: I'm
the guy who stays up all night trying to figure out the order of the
Little Walter discography on Chess. This is what I do. This is me.

FEINSTEIN: Did you like what The Fugs did with Sanders's poetry?

SINCLAIR: I loved The Fugs—"the underground Rolling Stones." And I
love Sanders's *America: A History in Verse*. Sanders is one of my favorite living Americans. He's not my favorite poet, but the historical
stuff—I love that. Just that he's doing it. He's a guy who's rooted in
Greek, and in the rhythms of Sappho. And I'm an anti-European if
ever there was one, but I respect that that's him. Me, I'm going to
swing. When I put words down, the poem's going to swing or else I'm
going to throw it out. Or I'll beat it up until it swings. [Sinclair quotes
from his poem "bloomdido" and beats the table with each accent:] "In
the be**gin**ning / of the **mod**ern / **era** / in **Har**lem / in the **ear**ly days /
of the **new** / **mu**sic." Yeah.

FEINSTEIN: I know "carolina moon" got you started. Were there other
poems that helped open up the series?

SINCLAIR: Well, just like a record collector, you think of the ones you
don't have yet. "Criss Cross" is one I've been trying to write for fifteen
years. The music is so heavy, and then the concept: criss cross, across
the years, across space, criss cross. I haven't got that one. I've got several starts, but I haven't sustained that one.

I finally wrote a poem called "brilliant corners." I finally *got* "brilliant corners." I got a half-assed commission from the Cannabis Cup
in '99—when they inducted Kerouac, Ginsberg, Burroughs, and Neal
Cassady—so I wrote this piece and I got to deliver it at the Ginsberg induction ceremony. It posits Charlie Parker, Dizzy Gillespie,

Thelonious Monk, and Kenny Clarke as the brilliant corners of modern civilization, with Kerouac, Ginsberg, Burroughs, and Cassady as the literary counterparts. The corners of the foundation.

FEINSTEIN: You say you "finally got 'brilliant corners,'" so you must have struggled with that one.

SINCLAIR: Well, man—"Brilliant Corners": You can't be half-steppin' on that. It's one of the greatest pieces of music in the twentieth century! And after worrying about it for fifteen years, all of a sudden, *Bam*, it's there. [Sinclair quotes from the poem:] "out of the darkness / of american life." [Laughs.] The last thing I could ever do is tell you how I write a poem. I never have the same experience. I just feel I'm lucky I got it. Once in a while they give it to you, and sometimes you have to take it. Sometimes I have to work at something over and over and over, and sometimes it just flows.

"in walked bud" was an epiphany; I thought I got that.

FEINSTEIN: Have you heard Baraka read his poem "In Walked Bud"?

SINCLAIR: I don't think I know that one.

FEINSTEIN: It's one of my singular favorite poetry and jazz performances. When you hear it, you won't stop smiling.

SINCLAIR: That's generally the case when I hear my idol.

FEINSTEIN: What made you so pleased with your "in walked bud" poem?

SINCLAIR: The best part for me about writing anything is that you learn things. You start out with a premise, and then you find out how much you don't know about it, and then you do some research, plug it in, and then, when you tie it all together in the end, you learn something that you didn't know when you started.

I have a poem called "i surrender dear" in the Monk series. My wife and I, before we were married, were estranged (one of the five times that we were estranged!) and I started writing this poem. In the course of it, I learned that I wanted to marry her. It was really a powerful experience for me, because I didn't realize that when I started writing the poem. So you learn things, really important things about your real life.

FEINSTEIN: And what did you learn during the making of "in walked bud"?

SINCLAIR: With the song "In Walked Bud," you have all those anecdotes: the night at Birdland with Bud, and Bird was calling his name over the sound system. What put it together for me was I found out that Monk was there that night, and it gave me the ending to the poem, where he says to Bird and Bud, "I told you guys to *act* crazy, but I didn't tell you to fall in love with the act. You're *really* crazy now." [Laughs.] When I got that I thought, "Man, I got this motherfucker. I got Bird intoning his name at the mike, and Bud staring off into space. I've got them in Toronto the night Rocky Marciano knocked out Jersey Joe Walcott for the heavyweight championship. I've all these historical things." And so I thought I got that.

"'round about midnight" is one of my favorite things I ever wrote. I think I got that. I had the benefit of being friends with Kenny "Pancho" Hagood, during his last years in Detroit, and he sang, "'Round Midnight." [Sinclair sings:] "It begins to tell, 'round midnight, 'round midnight."

I'm a huge scholar of Eddie Jefferson, and we became very close friends before he died. (I used to lay him out because I could sing all his songs to him. That used to blow his mind. [Laughs, then sings:] "I just got back in town. . .") I started years ago on a major piece [on Jefferson] that I'm afraid to finish, it's so huge and I have to sing his songs (and I'm not a singer); it would be a half-hour/forty-five minute performance.

It's hard to do. I did something similar for Louis Armstrong and Mezz Mezzrow when they were inducted into the Cannabis Cup in '98—into the Cannabis Hall of Fame in Amsterdam. I was the High Priest, and I got to take my band from New Orleans. So I wrote this piece, using words from their writings woven in—just trying to tell their story.

I set all my poems to music. That's what I do. That's my bedrock. I've been doing that since '64. With the Monk poems, I'd get the guys to play something Monkish.

FEINSTEIN: For a performance of the Monk poems, though, you wouldn't be able to read 150 poems with music.

SINCLAIR: No, you don't have to do them all. And, again, the Monk poems are divided into four different books.

Eddie Jefferson taught me that his operating thesis was that when he wrote lyrics to a solo, they had to be at the tempo of the song, that was the governing fact. What I'm doing with Monk is like an abstracted extension of what Eddie was doing, though what he did was so incredible. I don't know if you've ever tried to write lyrics to a solo.

FEINSTEIN: No.

SINCLAIR: I have. And it's very daunting. I can't do it. But I can write a piece that goes with the tempo, and the music, and also the title. The poems don't rhyme—they're in projective verse—but I'm paying homage to these great guys.

FEINSTEIN: I really respect Eddie Jefferson, so what I'm about to say should not be taken as a slam. But one of the reasons why I haven't written lyrics is because I'm not interested in defining jazz solos with an absolute narrative.

SINCLAIR: Well, I hear what you're saying.

FEINSTEIN: I'm more interested in poems—like yours—that try to become their own expression.

SINCLAIR: But don't get too far away. I mean, I can read my poems without music; they're pretty musical, when I do it right. But everything I do I hear with music. Since I was a little kid, music was the only thing that really meant anything.

FEINSTEIN: So you'd rather have these Monk poems on a CD than in a book?

SINCLAIR: Yeah. Generally, I'd rather have my work recorded. I wanted to perform these [Monk poems] with the music, where they fit, and I wanted them to be played at the tempo of the original. I would make a cassette with a loop; I would record the tune over and over again for thirty minutes and then play the tape over and over again so I would be in the right tempo to give me the right musical information. And I do that now.

FEINSTEIN: And you're covering not only Monk's original compositions but also the standards?

SINCLAIR: Absolutely. Every title he recorded. I love what he does with standards, completely making them his own.

FEINSTEIN: Last year, when you and Al Young and I got together to talk about jazz and literature [at the 2001 Tennessee Williams Festival], you both read a poem titled "April in Paris," and they were so wildly different.

SINCLAIR: Exactly. I love that. I used to perform in Detroit in the '80s with a guy named Ron Allen, a black poet in Detroit who's a fucking monster. He's probably never published anything (he is a Vietnam vet, and a former dope fiend, and a cook; now he's a playwright, they tell me) but he played with music, and we would use the same ensemble at the same show. We would use the same musicians—and it would be completely different.

FEINSTEIN: Of the 150 Monk poems, about how many have you completed?

SINCLAIR: About eighty. I've got some people who have offered to publish it if I finish it, so I might try to finish it this year, if my economic system's in order. If I can get stabilized to support my Beatnik lifestyle. Rent is still the big fucker in my world.

I stopped working on the project about ten years ago 'cause I got fucked. The first record I made in '91 was a duet record with a great pianist from Cincinnati named Ed Moss. He knew quite a number of Monk pieces and learned the rest. I did fourteen Monk pieces and two instrumentals—sixteen pieces in all. But I couldn't get [producer] Don Sickler or Tootie [Monk's son, T. S. Monk] to give me permission to put it out. They wouldn't say no, but they wouldn't say yes. I'm still trying to find some little record company with enough nerve to put it out and send them the mechanicals. I offered them the publishing on my whole Monk work. I'm not doing this for money; I'm doing this 'cause I love the guy. [As though addressing T. S. Monk:] "Your *dad!*" That discouraged the shit out of me, and I just made a decision to stop writing the poems. It was kind of like cutting my own throat.

I finished the first half of the first book—the first twenty poems— in '85, and I had a deal, a commission, but I couldn't put this record out. So I recorded them without music in order to honor my obligation to the record company. But it really discouraged me. And then there was the difficulty of finding people who knew anything beyond [Monk's best known compositions, such as] "Straight, No Chaser," "Blue Monk," and "'Round Midnight." The more I performed, the less opportunity I had to do the Monk stuff.

FEINSTEIN: I'd like to hear about the times you actually heard Thelonious Monk.

SINCLAIR: They were inconsequential.

FEINSTEIN: "Inconsequential" because Monk wasn't playing well, or—

SINCLAIR: It was just a gig. I went to see the great Thelonious Monk, with Charlie Rouse and Larry Gales, Ben Riley, and it was pretty tame. But I saw him in '67 in Detroit at a big George Wein show at Cobo Hall. 12,000 seats, of which maybe 3,000 were filled. *Maybe.* He was billed with Coltrane, but there was a terrible snow storm on the East Coast, and Coltrane's band couldn't fly in. So Coltrane and [his wife] Alice took the train from Philadelphia, and when they got there, Coltrane and Monk played together.

FEINSTEIN: You're kidding?

SINCLAIR: Serendipity because of the weather. It was totally unexpected.

Of course, I was pissed off because there was no Rashid Ali and Jimmy Garrison and Pharoah [Sanders]. I really wanted to hear Coltrane with Pharoah, and Ali thrashing away!

FEINSTEIN: This is where our tastes diverge: I would much rather have heard Coltrane with Monk.

SINCLAIR: Well, I was on acid. [Both laugh.] What can I say? January, '67? You can pick just about any day in that month and assume that I was totally fried.

We used to take acid and listen to Coltrane's *Meditations*. When they'd do "The Father and the Son and the Holy Ghost," you'd feel it in your whole body. I'd put on [Sun Ra's] *The Magic City* about fifteen times in a row. [Sinclair rolls his eyes and leans his head back:] *Oooeeehh*. [Laughs.] When I hear *The Magic City* or "The Father and the Son and the Holy Ghost," I get flashbacks.

I used to hear Coltrane all the time. He was all music. There were no other parts of him. I remember how he would play for an hour and a half, and the last forty-five minutes would be just him and Elvin [Jones]. They would just be out there, sailing. I have one phrase [in "Blues to You"] where I say, "or get up from your chair / & walk smack into a pole / after 45 minutes of Elvin Jones." I did that. After they finished the set, I jumped up and ran straight into a pole. I had been totally transformed.

I would get some wine and smoke a joint outside with Jimmy Garrison, and we'd come back in and hear Coltrane practicing. Between sets! That was such a beautiful example for me, as a young man, to see someone so committed to his art.

FEINSTEIN: Although one might argue, too, that his incredible intensity was one reason for his death at age forty.

SINCLAIR: Oh yeah. There's only so much you can take. The biggest surprise for me in life is to be sixty years old. If someone had told me that I would live this long, that I would have grandchildren ... shit. But the beautiful thing is, it makes life a constant surprise because I never pictured any of this. I never expected to make thirty-five. So I've got twenty-five years of free play. [Laughs.]

I didn't care before; it didn't matter if you died young. When I started smoking—I was thirteen—you put a quarter in a cigarette machine and got a pack of Luckys with three pennies taped to the side as change. That's when I started smoking. Ha! That's several hundred thousand dollars in cigarettes. If I had all the money I've spent on cigarettes, coffee, and drugs, I'd be a rich man, but I wouldn't be anywhere near as happy as I am now. [Both laugh.] Wouldn't have had as much fun, in my way. What mattered was *saying* something. But I can't *believe* I made sixty!

FEINSTEIN: Did you come to New Orleans from Detroit because of the music?

SINCLAIR: Pretty much, and the Wild Indians. That's my passion: the Mardi Gras Indians and the music of New Orleans. That's the shit. I just love it here. This is the last outpost of civilization in the United States. If they can figure out how to Americanize this place, I'm gone, but as long as it exists, I'll stay here.

FEINSTEIN: And the kitsch doesn't get to you?

SINCLAIR: That's the fuel. It's like the automobile industry in Detroit. I live on the edge of the French Quarter, the cusp between the French Quarter and Tremé, the nation's oldest urban African American neighborhood, the birthplace of jazz. New Orleans is like a big set: The set stays the same but the people change all the time. If the same tourists were here all the time, it would be unbearable. But as it is, we're so full of suckers. [Feinstein laughs.] Basically, it's a carnival for suckers who are "moving on," going on to Ur-civilization.

FEINSTEIN: Of the souvenirs, what do you suggest I bring home for my nine-year-old son and five-year-old daughter?

SINCLAIR: Man . . . some records. Some Professor Longhair records. Blues. Muddy Waters.

FEINSTEIN: Lee Grue said to me about a year ago that your blues poems are among her favorite. Do you think blues poems tend to work well in part because of the history of spoken blues performances?

SINCLAIR: Yeah, and more people listen to blues. It's easier for them. The problem with jazz is that our society has been dumbing down. They don't have the intelligence. Fewer and fewer people in America have the ability to understand what Charlie Parker was talking about, and yet they don't hear anything that wasn't touched by Charlie Parker. They don't know who he *is*. They don't know who Monk is. Part of my mission is to get up there and say, "Thelonious Monk." They don't know who the fuck you're talking about. Muddy Waters! From a mission standpoint, I want to tell them about these people, because they're everything to me. In my cosmology, they come before God or the Devil. If I was in charge here, you'd hear Charlie Parker every morning before class for at least fifteen minutes, every day.

FEINSTEIN: I'm frequently asked, after readings, what a person should do if he or she doesn't know about the music being addressed, and I tell them they should get the music.

SINCLAIR: That's right: "You're in trouble. I suggest you get the records *now*—irrespective of anything that I'm doing—for your own mental health." [Feinstein laughs.] "I'm doing you a hell of a favor telling you about Muddy Waters, man. Get some Muddy Waters, you'll have something that's going to carry you through *life*." Period! Case closed.

Al Young. *Photo by Carolyn Clebsch.*

19

Makes Me Feel Like I Got Some Money
Al Young

Al Young and I have gotten together in tropical settings and major cities—speaking on panels and reading poems across the country, eating in lovely bistros and in my own home—but this interview took place in an antiseptic hotel room in Indiana. (Al was a featured workshop leader for the Indiana University Writers' Conference, and I had been asked to speak about *Brilliant Corners*.) Did the sterile setting diminish the conversation? Not at all. As the title of this interview suggests, Al Young has the ability to transform commonplace locations; as he travels with his stories, you travel with him.

One of my earliest encounters with jazz-related poetry was Al's "Dear Old Stockholm," a charming piece that brought me to his other jazz poems, especially those in *The Blues Don't Change*—"Billie," "Jungle Strut," "Lester Leaps In," and others. It would have been completely appropriate and interesting to focus our discussion exclusively on his jazz-related poems, but the first three interviews for *Brilliant Corners* had featured conversations with poets (William Matthews, Paul Zimmer, and Yusef Komunyakaa), and, for the sake of the journal's breadth, I wanted to break that trend. More important, however, I wanted to highlight his essays in *Drowning in the Sea of Love,* one of my favorite contributions to jazz literature—in any genre.

Two years after this interview, Al visited our college as an artist-in-residence. I remember the year in part because my students, completely independent of anything I orchestrated, made tee-shirts—"Al Young / Lyco 1999"—which they wore like giddy groupies. After he left, I asked my workshop if there was another writer they'd like to have on campus for a similar week-long residency. They paused, and then someone said, "Bring back Al." As he writes in "Gifts and Messages": "The crowd went berserk."

Al Young is a poet, fiction writer, and essayist who has published many books, including *Heaven: Collected Poems, 1956–1990; Mingus/Mingus: Two Memoirs* (written with Janet Coleman); and *Drowning in the Sea of Love: Musical Memoirs,* which won the PEN/USA Award for nonfiction. In addition, he is editor of *African American Literature: A Brief Introduction and Anthology.* A longtime writer of liner notes, his work regularly appears in Verve's *For Lovers* series. His many honors include fellowships from the National Endowment for the Arts and the Guggenheim Foundation. He travels widely, often performing his poetry to jazz accompaniment, and is currently poet laureate of California.

This conversation focused on the essays in *Drowning in the Sea of Love,* and excerpted passages precede the discussion. The interview took place at the Indiana Memorial Union at Indiana University, Bloomington, on June 22, 1997.

Introduction
(excerpt)
Al Young

All readers need to know is that it's crucial to recall, as you read along or skip around in these tender pages, that music can become a powerful way of remembering. Sometimes the remembering takes the form of a story or personal myth. At other times, the interplay between the author and the reader and the song shapes itself as reverie, prose poem, essay, solo, a take, a break, a fantasy, soliloquy, a solo.

Little did I know when I began this book that I would be opening up within myself a region so vast that it could never be fully explored or even charted.

If I stray a bit from the melody at times and vary the beat, it's because I'm learning what you already know so well about the meaning and sense of it all. Lean in and listen: "The Nearness of You" touched poet Carolyn Kizer so deeply that she lifted it whole right out of Hoagy Carmichael's song to name a powerful book of her own. The idea that there should even be such concepts as nearness, distance, here-and-nowness first began to strike me as strange when I listened to music in childhood. The song, indeed, has always been you, and it will forever be turning back into itself; drowning, as it were, in itself. "No wave can exist," Paramahansa Yogananda reminds us in *The Divine Romance,* "without the ocean behind it."

May you sooner or later find yourself adrift in an open sea of sound, or, as singer Joe Simon put it so lastingly in his soulful 1972 gospel-washed rhythm and blues hit: "Drowning in the Sea of Love."

Pennies from Heaven
(excerpt)
Frank Rosolino, 1959
Al Young

You never quite know what kind of pain anyone is suffering from when they pass through your life, smiling and wishing you well, yet leaving entire fields of themselves closed to you as if they sensed the explosive kinds of mines that might lie hidden there. What can I say? . . . Somewhere along the way, that very rain he played in so dauntlessly must have given way to a raging, private storm that demolished his umbrella and blew his whole house away.

Nostalgia in Times Square
(excerpt)
Charles Mingus, 1958
Al Young

In this Charles Mingus version of urban renewal, you can hear trucks rumbling and traffic moaning and somebody's heart that seems to have gotten run over in the scramble. For me it's all so clear, not unlike the way life is when you've just turned draft age in a world laid out for one-way wandering.

No wonder I respond to the power of this music by letting my shoulders shake ever so vibrantly, and by letting my boodie move while my ears pick up the huffy he-bump and the shadowy she-bump that's busy dislodging itself in there. And like that crazy feeling my ears are picking up, I too refuse to grind to any halt that a city runner of red lights wouldn't. This means: There comes a time to sit down and recall in slow motion all this one-wayness, a process that seems to see each moment as one of a kind.

Gifts and Messages
Rahsaan Roland Kirk, 1965
Al Young

Rahsaan's music is about as predictable as the rhythms of thunder breaking on a warm August night, or the evanescent shapes of falling snowflakes. It is solidly rooted in what he called Black Classical American tradition, and yet it is always attractively new.

Consider the evening, years ago, when his quartet opened a set at San Francisco's defunct Jazz Workshop with what was then a fresh, bossa-nova-flavored ballad called "The Shadow of Your Smile."

Soloing, Rahsaan descended from the stand and ambled through the audience, pausing at tables to permit one patron after another, just for the fun of it, to press a key on his tenor saxophone while he continued to blow. Working his way back toward the bar situated near the club's entrance, he lingered to slap hands with some latecomer and then—to the slow turning of heads—disappeared out the door. It didn't take long for most of us to realize that Rahsaan, with all of those exotic-looking instruments slung round his neck, had stepped out to stroll along Broadway, the avenue outside.

The rhythm section continued to cook and smoulder, taking, by turns, some memorable solos before Rahsaan re-entered the Workshop, still playing beautifully and trailed by a queue of strung-out listeners picked up during his brief Pied Piper excursion. Head bobbing, horn cocked at the jauntiest of angles, he meandered right back up to the bandstand, never missing a beat, and topped things off with an unforgettable finale sounded simultaneously on manzello, strich, and tenor sax.

The crowd went berserk.

Ruby My Dear
Thelonious Monk, 1959
Al Young

You are back again, re-entering the central train of trails: the quintessential U.S.A. of drowsy fields and sleepy fast-food chains; the U.S.A. of nipped buds and layaways negotiated in harsh, flatland cracker accents. Surrounded by them, hemmed in, you sometimes feel a little like one of those brainy slicksters over at the Federal Penitentiary in Milan, Michigan, for, like them, you're locked up and keyed down.

"Ruby My Dear" comes drifting down Lake Huron in the saline marshlands of an eternal summer. The midwestern night is steamy hot with mosquitoes, the air knotted and thick with gnats like Monk's gracefully gnarled chordal clusters; notes and spiraling nodes, encoded, glistening like Milky Way–encrusted swirls and specks of darkness.

You know what you're hearing is human yearning and rushes of the Divine calling you home to all the Africanized galaxies in this shimmering island universe.

SASCHA FEINSTEIN: I want to talk about your essays in *Drowning in the Sea of Love,* but perhaps we could start by discussing your jazz and poetry performances at the Monterey Jazz Festival. What makes such performances work well?

AL YOUNG: When it works well it's sublime because what happens is that you get practitioners of these oral idioms meshing in ways that are practically undiscussible. Musicians, like actors and actresses, really do listen for spaces—paying attention to see if they should lay out or lay in. I've always loved Herbie Hancock's story, recorded in "The Miles Davis Radio Project," that when they were playing "Nefertiti" he told Miles he couldn't think of what to play, and Miles came over and told him, "Well, if you can't think of nothin' to play, Herbie, then don't play nothin'!" [Laughs.] So he lays out. And that's what musicians will do. If they see that their contribution will be useless, they just lay back and let you go.

Sometimes, though, they will do things that will make you work. I will actually abandon text or alter it on the spot to conform with what's happening on stage. And when it works, it works beautifully.

I performed [in 1995] with Adlai Alexander, a guitarist and singer with a multi-ethnic heritage that he's trying to embody. (His father is African American and his mother is Japanese, and he accepts both traditions.) We can get together for about twenty minutes and work out a show. And we played with Jeff Saxton, another wonderful musician.

FEINSTEIN: Do you remember any prose pieces that you read from?

YOUNG: Yeah, we did "I Got Rhythm," which opened with Jeff playing solo bass line—[Young scats, very quickly and in tune, a walking bass line]—for about two choruses. Then I would read selections from that piece, because I've found what works best is brevity and vividness. (I'll edit the thing down where it will happen in three or four minutes.) You don't get any melody until the very end, and I actually sang the head.

FEINSTEIN: The crowd must've loved it.

YOUNG: Oh, they went absolutely crazy! [Laughs.] What's beautiful is that it re-energizes your work. You look at it again and you say, "Next edition of that I'm cutting this out and I'm cutting that out."

Now some people don't like it. One woman told me, "I just love it when you read your own poetry; I don't like it when you jazz it up and all that because you do things that seem unnatural." And I said, "Well, they're very different. One is a performance and the other is just a reading—which is also a performance but with a different audience." Sometimes [reading to jazz] you'll prolong syllables. You'll actually pitch your voice to the tonality of the music. So it's fun.

FEINSTEIN: Many of your essays move the way your poems move, like improvisations where one statement leads naturally to the next but by the end of the piece you find yourself somewhere you didn't quite expect to be.

YOUNG: That's why I loved writing the musical memories, because I never knew what was going to happen. In fact, it took me a long time to get the nerve up to do just that, because I would sit and I'd try to get these things all rounded up, structured beforehand. But when I was writing these, I understood that discoveries are engaged in working out anything. The only difference between this kind of stuff and formal essays is that they can stay "semi-finished." I discovered that when I was reading some of it to music. If you round them off too much then they get boxed in and nothing can happen. It was a form that allowed me to collect all of the odds and ends that I'm interested in. There's an open-endedness to them.

FEINSTEIN: You establish that immediately: The introduction to the book begins with the death of your brother but doesn't return to that event in any direct way. Like most of the other pieces, it uses events and images as a springboard for others—like poetry.

YOUNG: Yeah. This is why the cadenza is still one of my favorite parts of jazz—when the rhythm section comes to a halt, the whole band stops, and the soloist steps forward and blows for a few minutes before they come back in. It's a form of free association that is fascinating because it does go a lot of places. You get on a little phrase and then you explore that, turn it inside out, do all kinds of things with it, bridge into something else, come back at it as a reference point. And that's the spirit of these essays—they're like cadenzas.

FEINSTEIN: They don't all, of course, have that form.

YOUNG: No. Some are very tight.

FEINSTEIN: Some of the shorter pieces in *Drowning in the Sea of Love*—such as your first piece on Monk ["Ruby My Dear"] or the essay on Rahsaan Roland Kirk ["Gifts and Messages"]—read to me a bit like prose poems.

YOUNG: That was what I was striving for. The Rahsaan piece was written for jacket notes to his album *Gifts and Messages*. I forget the label—

FEINSTEIN: I think it was Mercury. Your essay has a marvelous surge to it.

YOUNG: I was trying at that time to see if I could bring poetry and prose together. The other, "Ruby My Dear," is very special to me because I wrote that on the BART train—Bay Area Rapid Transit—during a very tough period in the '80s. My wife had cancer and our marriage was breaking up; my mother had just died of cancer; my brother had been very troubled and committed suicide. Everything was going on at that time. So I was on a train, commuting from Fremont to UC Berkeley, and, as usual, I had my tape player on. I was listening to [Monk's] "Ruby, My Dear" and there was a bunch of school kids who were retarded. One was steadfastly reading a book and the other kids were messing with him: "Hey, what you readin' now?" and he said, "I'm readin' this book."

"What's the name of it?"

"*In Dubious Battle.*"

"*In Dubious Battle*? Who wrote it?"

"John Steinbeck."

"Never heard of him! What's it about?"

"Well, it's about these people, you know? They're tryin' to keep their jobs, like they're out pickin' fruit and all this kind of stuff, you know, and these other people are *fuckin'* with 'em. It's about what happens when they get tired of it."

"Who you say wrote it?"

"John Steinbeck."

"Well, I ain't never heard of him."

"Don't worry. You will."

So I was listening to that, and "Ruby, My Dear" was playing, and I opened up my notebook and I wrote that piece precisely the way that you see it. It just flowed—all of this business about accents and this stuff floating around you just seemed to me quintessentially American.

FEINSTEIN: Like your poems about musicians, most of these essays celebrate the pleasures of music rather than dwell on biographical tragedies. Even your piece on Frank Rosolino does not address the pathos of his suicide until the very close.

YOUNG: Rosolino has long fascinated me. I used to stand outside and listen to him. There was a window where you could see the musicians, and Rosolino would play for the people on the sidewalk. He'd always wave at me and do all sorts of funny things. Years later, as I explain in the essay, I used to see him in clubs. His manner of speaking was basically African American, and he was just such an upbeat guy—you can hear it in his music. He had this incredible power and joy. So I always associated him with happy times.

FEINSTEIN: And yet it's so unusual to find a writer who consistently emphasizes the positive.

YOUNG: Have you read that English writer—he's getting a lot of attention—

FEINSTEIN: Geoff Dyer?

YOUNG: Yeah, his book *But Beautiful.* What annoyed me ultimately about that book is that he works the tragic, dark stories—and distorts them—so that everybody is warped in some way. But the *New York Times* loved it.

FEINSTEIN: Every reviewer, it seemed, loved it—

YOUNG: And I could recognize the rich veins of writing, and the beauty of his imagination, but I felt it was unfair, that these players were deeper than that. I'd *known* some of them. Mingus was *fun* to be around, believe it or not, because he was always messin' with you! [Laughs.] Even when it was dark it wasn't as you might have imagined it was dark, novelistically.

FEINSTEIN: I love how your essays speak to musicians, even after they're gone, the way you do, say, in your letter to Charlie Parker ["Perhaps"] or in this passage from "What a Little Moonlight Can Do": "Billie, if you're out there listening somewhere, I just want you to know about one lovely night in Australia, of all places, when the sound of you at the back of my heart rose to the surface and helped the moonlight do what moonlight does so simply and gloriously." Why do you think it's so important for writers to reach out this way?

YOUNG: There's a theory on this, and then there's my belief. The theory's best proposed by Kennell Jackson's book *America Is Me.* It's one of those books where you pose a question and answer it, like, "Why aren't there many black scientists?" "Glad you asked that—" [Laughs.] That kind of thing. But he talks about how personal it can be. He says, "You guys seem to think it's like when you get up to Heaven that Saint Peter and Gabriel are going to ask, 'What's the word?' and somebody'll say, 'Billie Holiday,' and somebody else will say, 'Charlie Parker'—that you have to be an initiate." That's one view of it—that people who are involved with jazz get on a first name basis with people they like to listen to, whether they've met them or not.

I literally believe, in the same way that physics tells us that energy is neither created nor destroyed, that spirits pass out of visual range but don't really go away. And of course in art, when you write a poem or make a painting or perform music, what really informs that is your spirit. It is inexplicably the main ingredient, and it connects with the spirit of the listener (or the person who's reading or seeing it). So it has a *life* that is prolonged by a spectator or co-participant. In that sense, it has a life that gives you license to address the creator in familiar terms, because you live with that stuff.

I remember talking to Janine Pommy Vega at a gathering in San Francisco for the book *Women of the Beat Generation.* They got Diane di Prima, Anne Waldman, Hettie Jones, Bob Kaufman's wife Eileen. And Janine [talking about Bob Kaufman] said, "You know what I always liked about Bomkauf? He doesn't fuck with you when you're out there on the page and really need something." (She used to be shooting smack and all that kind of stuff.) She said, "I would read Bob and I would cry because he would give me hope and everything, and I would see that he was *tellin'* me something. I would hug that book, you know, and look at it. I got *straight* from reading Bob Kaufman." So there's something going on there that doesn't get transmitted in most literature classes. How *can* you transmit it? You're dealing with something that is apparently visible, and touchable, and analyzable, and all of that. But there's that sacred element you can only point to—"This is *you* talkin' to *you*."

So that's what I believe, and when I address Bird or I address Bud or any of them, as far as I'm concerned, they're right there. Now Janet— you know, Janet Coleman, [co-author of] *Mingus/Mingus*—she goes even further. We often call each other because something will happen and we know that Mingus made that incident possible. [Laughs.] If you believe that these people are still in your lives, they'll lead you.

I interviewed Joyana Brookmeyer, Bob Brookmeyer's ex-wife, be- cause I was going to do this Charlie Parker movie, and she said I had to interview her because she used to be the babysitter for Chan and Bird when they moved to the Village. One of the things she talked about was how she started playing saxophone in her late forties. She always wanted to play but she didn't think she had it. Then she had a dream where Bird appeared and said, "You get the horn and I will help you with it." Within two years she was playing saxophone in the Marin Symphony. She picked up the rudiments about ten times as quickly as people normally do, and as a middle-aged woman.

FEINSTEIN: It reminds me of Walter Davis, Jr.'s recording, *In Walked Thelonious*. The liner notes tell us that, one week before recording these Monk tunes, Davis had a vision of Monk—being in the room, physically. Months later, Dwike Mitchell heard the tapes and, without knowing the history, said, "I've been listening to Walter all my life and I know exactly how he plays. What's on this tape is not Walter; it's Monk playing through Walter's hands."

YOUNG: Frank Lacy, the trombonist for the Mingus Big Band, was play- ing Mingus's bass one night and he said that something happened that was totally mysterious to him. He was doing things that Mingus would: telling the people to be quiet, threatening the bartender, play- ing things he wouldn't ordinarily play. "I swear, man," he said, "that bass—that bass was possessing me." All the musicians agreed they hadn't heard him play that way before. He thinks Mingus inhabits that bass.

FEINSTEIN: We were talking earlier about childhood influences . . .

YOUNG: I was baptized at age seven in Mississippi—a literal baptism where they take you down to the river and dunk you in the water— and had been living that year with my aunt Doris and her husband

Cleve, who were running The Blind Pig on the weekends, selling whiskey and beer illegally. They were staunch Christians and would take
me to church on Sundays, and one of the things I used to love in
church was the band. The band was absolutely incredible: They had
trombones and saxophones and trumpets—the whole thing. That experience blurred the separations between music and poetry for me,
because what the minister was doing and what the musicians were doing meshed so completely. If you're a kid you just think, "These go together."

Years later, in Detroit [during the early 1950s], my high school
asked me to write for this magazine called *Idioms,* and I started hanging out at the New Music Society where they had these weekly jam sessions. All of the top Detroiters and visiting artists performed in them.
So there I was, sixteen years old, hanging around with these people
who were in their late twenties and thirties, and we loved painting
and music and books. Everything went together. It was a whole generation that came out of the bebop movement. Most of these people
were southern transplants—their parents had made an early migration from the South—but they were fairly squared away in a scuffling middle-class lifestyle, totally devoted to art and what we called
"progressive ideas": They hated racism and all things that segregated
people from one another.

You know, much is made about jazz's disreputable origins, but
the black middle class has always been a force in marshaling black
culture. (Ishmael Reed and I talk about this in Ortiz Walton's book
Music: Black White & Blue, a book really worth reading.) If you look
at the bebop musicians, you find that most did not come from down-
and-out, working-class backgrounds; they really do come from shaky
middle-class families. Mingus used to say, "We worked this music out
in people's homes—and we didn't call them *cribs,* either." [Laughs.]
There's a whole lot of darkness that's been put around the music,
largely by commentators who didn't know where these guys went
when they went home or where they came from. So they created a kind
of hothouse vocabulary that we're still dealing with now.

Bebop really was an expression of what was about to come. Seventy
percent of Americans who lived on the farm before the war came to
work in the plants—that whole displacement, and the pace at which
things were moving. I theorize that one of the reasons Charlie Parker
was so instrumental in shaping it was that he came from Kansas City
where they'd been doing that for years. (To grow up in New York was

no big thing; just let the honky tonk rule on.) Bebop was an expression of so many things that wouldn't blink into the common American consciousness until twenty years after the war, when you had middle-class, white kids saying, "Wait a minute—there's something wrong with this picture."

But I'd go over to [the painter] Harold Neal's house—a nice, comfortable two-story house—and lots of musicians would come by. Yusef Lateef. Barry Harris would come over there and sit up and pontificate. (Barry *loves* to be professorial.) Charles McPherson, who was a kid at that time. And I would just sit there and meet people. They would introduce me as a poet, which flattered me, because then I was writing *terrible* stuff. [Laughs.] But they would say, "His chops are getting stronger all the time"—they'd use language like that because the parlance was interchangeable. It was a very vibrant, multi-arts setting, and that was always for me the paradigm for what you did.

FEINSTEIN: Mingus seemed to believe in that, too.

YOUNG: Mingus was of a generation that didn't set up barriers between different kinds of art. He could actually quote poems to you. Almost all of the musicians of that generation could quote Omar Khayyam. They could hold forth for fifteen or twenty minutes quoting that stuff. Mingus could quote Langston Hughes to you. He could quote Kenneth Patchen to you. Anybody he worked with he read their stuff and absorbed it. He read literary magazines and the *Village Voice.* All the poets knew him when he walked down the street—[Paul] Blackburn, all of them.

What I loved about the New York scene that I walked into as a kid, meaning in my early twenties, was that it was a paint-driven scene: The painters were the ones who were really doing it and getting all the attention. But the painters were getting their cues from musicians, and they were all into jazz. And the musicians were also checking out the painters and the poets. So there was a synthesis going on that was very exciting.

FEINSTEIN: So many of the anthologies of African American poetry from the '60s offer political manifestos, and the jazz poems of the time also reflect intense political agendas, but I don't hear that kind of voice in your work, then or now.

YOUNG: At that time, political poetry was practically underfoot, so much so that it was devalued. I had gone through my most vitriolic political stage from, say, age seventeen through twenty-five. I was kicked out of the NAACP at the University of Michigan because I was considered too radical. [Chuckles.] I didn't want them to show *Birth of a Nation.* This was at the heart of the McCarthy era, and I was running around spouting Marxism and Leninism. "No compromise"—all of that stuff. And because of that early immersion thinking about political issues and problems, and being on picket lines, and having myself photographed by agents in trench coats, I'd come out the other side of something. I realized that culture was the most powerful weapon you could have, and I thought it was more advanced (or more evolved, as they say in California) to have your political opinions implicit in what you said. So you could be writing about something that did not identify itself as a social protest poem—which is what African American artists have long done—but if you look at it closely it says, "Tear it down!"

I've never forgotten sitting in the Astor Theater on Twelfth Street in Detroit for a matinee [of *Samson and Delilah*]: black kids filled the movie theater, running around, throwing the popcorn—until that scene when Victor Mature as Samson is about to get his revenge. They've done all these awful things to him and now he's back inside the Colosseum, and when he got his hands on those columns everyone in the theater stopped whatever they were doing, looked up at that screen, and yelled, "Tear it down, Samson! Tear that motherfucker down!" [Both laugh.] They realized what had to be done.

I did not like the way that socially active people separated politics and art. And I wasn't crazy; I saw what was going on in Soviet countries, and I saw how people were handcuffed and straitjacketed in official Left Wing camps, and I didn't want to be like that. In fact, I'd reached a point where I saw them as corny. I'd heard an interview with Big Bill Broonzy talking with Studs Terkel. Broonzy sings, "When will I get to be a man? Stop calling me boy," and when he finishes, Studs says, "Well, I guess you could call that some kind of an underground railroad song of 1958, huh?" and Broonzy just kind of laughs and says, "You can call it whatever you want to." [Both laugh.] But he adds, "I'll tell you something. The blues is kind of like a knife. You can peel an apple with it. You can cut up some food. You can cut rope. You can take it and *stab* somebody." [Laughs.] Broonzy was sharp enough to know, "Ah hah! You ain't gonna set *me* up for any McCarthy committee stuff!"

So, I thought, "Okay. Let's do this a different way." By that time, when I started to get published, I had gone through all of that.

FEINSTEIN: Of the many people writing about jazz [in the 1960s], who were some of the people you admired?

YOUNG: I used to love A. B. Spellman, those pieces he used to write for *Kulchur* magazine. I was interested, too, in LeRoi Jones's early approach to bebop. Baraka is an interesting example of that middle-class phenomenon, bringing a lot of myth that the general society's brought to jazz, but because he was an artist he was able to do things with it that were surprising. In that period leading up to the appearance of *Blues People*, his first book, he was saying some things from another angle that were fresh to hear. I love Orrin Keepnews's writing because he writes eloquently and always with passion. I'm aware that Orrin wants you to know that he was responsible for a lot of stuff happening, but he also has an overview that I think is quite charming. I'm always listening for something idiosyncratic, kind of strange, that hasn't been processed and passed on, the same data. And, of course, I couldn't help but admire Whitney Balliett's prose.

I particularly like first-person accounts by musicians, and one of the ones that had a profound effect on me was Alan Lomax's rendering of Jelly Roll Morton's memoirs, *Mister Jelly Roll*. I practically memorized that book—that's why it's quoted in *Snakes* as an epigraph. Jazz musicians have a way with words that's very witty.

FEINSTEIN: They're almost always captivating—

YOUNG: A few weeks ago I heard a show about Milt Jackson with concluding remarks about his contributions. Finally they came to Bobby Hutcherson, who said, "Well, what I like about Bags is that when I listen to Bags I feel around in my pockets—I feel like I got two or three hundred dollars that I'd forgotten about. Bags makes me feel like I got some *money*." I thought, "What better way to put it?" That's absolutely true about him. You feel this joy coming out.

Every time I read poems about jazz I'm fascinated how a conversation is taking place. That seems to be elementary to us, but you have to remind kids about this. It's not that they don't know it, because they *do* it, but when they take a lit class or study other arts more formally, they segregate it—they put it on this little island, separated from everything else. That's been happening so rapidly in our time: The data is replacing everything else as the measure of learning. It's happening in jazz, too.

FEINSTEIN: But it's not happening in your writing. This book alone [*Drowning in the Sea of Love*] is absolutely filled with prose that keeps you thinking. Here's one sentence [from the essay "Body and Soul"] among hundreds: "Essence in this instance is private song"—[Young speaks simultaneously]—"is you hearing your secret sorrow and joy blown back through Coleman Hawkins, invisibly connected to you and played back through countless bodies, each one an embodiment of the same soul force."

YOUNG: I know that one by heart. Mingus used to talk about the days when musicians would memorize their solos, and Illinois Jacquet talks about his famous solo on "Flying Home," how he realized that was a hit—better memorize that! [Laughs.] There are certain things that come through you, and all you can do is just respond and say, "My God, where did that come from? That was not me. Thank you, who-ever sent that." The proof of it is every time you recite it again you get that same feeling.

I really think the writer is something of a secretary. What you really do when you write a book is sit down and act like someone who's writ-ing a book. You set things up and so on. Then things start to come to you because you're in that mode, you're on that channel, that fre-quency. To me it's magic. Sometimes I'll wake up at three o'clock in the morning and, since I have a clip board right next to me, I say, "Okay, go," and when I read it the next day I'm just knocked out by the craziness that I've taken down and how you can make sense of it.

Do you have this situation where there's a voice that you can hear before you can even know what it's saying?

FEINSTEIN: Sure, like someone singing, or humming.

YOUNG: You get closer and you can hear the cadences, the rhythms, the tonalities. I can walk around all day, not knowing exactly what the words are, but I've got the whole sound of it. And I think that's an-other point of departure where writing and music meet. I just love it when I'm in that state.

Paul Zimmer. *Photo by Justine Zimmer.*

20

Something to Believe In
Paul Zimmer

Years before this interview, I contacted Paul Zimmer, with whom I'd corresponded but never met, and asked if we could have lunch in Iowa City. (At that time, he still directed the University of Iowa Press, and I had plans to pass through town.) At his suggestion, we agreed to meet at an Indian restaurant, not far from Prairie Lights bookstore. Just before the call ended, he said, a little hesitantly, "I assume we'll know how to recognize each other." I replied, "Well, I'm bald and bearded." Paul chuckled and said, "I look like a drunken Irishman." We've been pals ever since.

Conversations with Paul approximate his descriptions of listening to Count Basie—they're fun and uplifting—and his letters, always written with the rhythms of his voice and the honesty of someone who genuinely wants to speak with you, swing with the same pleasure. Here's a representative paragraph from a recent note:

One fine thing we did in France was go to a jazz festival called "Swing à Mirepoix." There were big French bands with names like Big Band Roquette and Poupon Swing and Hericot Rouge and a terrific swinging Latin band from Spain called Batucada. It was entrancing to hear those intense European musicians cooking hard on the old Ellington and Basie books, and the beautiful French chanteuses singing "Misty," "Here's That Rainy Day," and "Sophisticated Lady" in their enchanting French-intoned English. There was a group which vocalized Charlie Parker and Lester Young riffs with a lot of snap. It made me realize even more than ever how jazz is *the* great artistic gift that America has given to the world.

When he sent back the proofs for *Brilliant Corners,* he mentioned reading an interview with Jorie Graham: "She sounds so brilliant and articulate—and she's really saying something. . . . [I]t makes mine sound like some wino doing psycho-babble."
Nonsense. Give me Zimmer any day.

Paul Zimmer has published numerous books of poetry, among them *The Great Bird of Love, Big Blue Train,* and *Crossing to Sunlight: Selected Poems.* He is also the author of two prose collections, *After the Fire: A Writer Finds His Place* and *Trains in the Distance.* He has received many honors, including two fellowships from the National Endowment for the Arts, the *Yankee* Prize, a Borestone Mountain Award, and three Pushcart Prizes. Now retired from the publishing business, he lives on a farm in Wisconsin and, for part of each year, in the South of France.

This conversation focused on the following four poems: "Zimmer's Last Gig," "The Duke Ellington Dream," "Sitting with Lester Young," and "But Bird." The interview took place in my office at Lycoming College in Williamsport, Pennsylvania, on October 23, 1996.

Sitting with Lester Young
for Michael S. Harper
Paul Zimmer

Dusk must become your light
If you want to see Lester Young.
So Zimmer sits beside him at
His window in the Alvin Hotel.
Pres is blue beyond redemption.
His tenor idle on the table,
He looks down at the street,

Drinking his gin and port.
Buildings slice the last light
From the day. If Pres could
Shuffle into a club again like
A wounded animal, he would
Blow his ultimate melancholy,
But nights belong to others now.
Zimmer can only watch Pres
In the half-light of his sadness,
Old whispers slipping around,
Words into melodies,
As holy silence means the most.

The Duke Ellington Dream
Paul Zimmer

Of course Zimmer was late for the gig.
Duke was pissed and growling at the piano,
But Jeep, Brute, Rex, Cat and Cootie
All moved down on the chairs
As Zimmer walked in with his tenor.
Everyone knew that the boss had arrived.

Duke slammed out the downbeat for Caravan
And Zimmer stood up to take his solo.
The whole joint suddenly started jiving,
Chicks came up to the bandstand
To hang their lovelies over the rail.
Duke was sweating but wouldn't smile
Through chorus after chorus after chorus.

It was the same with Satin Doll,
Do Nothing Till You Hear from Me,
Warm Valley, In a Sentimental Mood;
Zimmer blew them so they would stay played.

After the final set he packed
His horn and was heading out

When Duke came up and collared him.
"Zimmer," he said. "You most astonishing ofay!
You have shat upon my charts,
But I love you madly."

Zimmer's Last Gig
Paul Zimmer

Listening to hard bop,
I stayed up all night
Just like good times.
I broke the old waxes
After I'd played them:
Out of Nowhere, Mohawk,
Star Eyes, Salt Peanuts,
Confirmation, one-by-one;
Bird, Monk, Bud, Klook, Diz,
All dead, all dead anyway,
As clay around my feet.

Years ago I wanted to
Take Wanda to Birdland,
Certain that the music
Would make her desire me,
That after a few sets
She would give in to
Rhythm and sophistication.
Then we could slip off
Into the wee hours with
Gin, chase, and maryjane,
Check into a downtown pad,
Do some fancy jitterbugging
Between the lilywhites.

But Wanda was no quail.
Bud could have passed
Out over the keys,
Bird could have shot
Up right on stage,

Wanda would have missed
The legends. The band
Could have riffed
All night right by
Her ear, she never
Would have bounced.

But Bird
Paul Zimmer

Some things you should forget,
But Bird was something to believe in.
Autumn '54, twenty, drafted,
Stationed near New York en route
To atomic tests in Nevada.
I taught myself to take
A train to Pennsylvania Station,
Walk up Seventh to 52nd Street,
Looking for music and legends.
One night I found the one
I wanted. Bird.

Five months later no one was brave
When the numbers ran out.
All equal—privates and colonels—
Down on our knees in the slits
As the voice counted backward
In the dark turning to light.

But "Charlie Parker" it said
On the Birdland marquee,
And I dug for the cover charge,
Sat down in the cheap seats.
He slumped in from the kitchen,
Powder blue serge and suedes.
No jive Bird, he blew crisp and clean,
Bringing each face in the crowd
Gleaming to the bell of his horn.
No fluffing, no wavering,

But soaring like on my old
Verve waxes back in Ohio.

Months later, down in the sand,
The bones in our fingers were
Suddenly x-rayed by the flash.
We moaned together in light
That entered everything,
Tried to become the earth itself
As the shock rolled toward us.

But Bird. I sat through three sets,
Missed the last train out,
Had to bunk in a roach pad,
Sleep in my uniform, almost AWOL.
But Bird was giving it all away,
One of his last great gifts,
And I was there with my
Rosy cheeks and swan neck,
Looking for something to believe in.

When the trench caved in it felt
Like death, but we clawed out,
Walked beneath the roiling, brutal cloud
To see the flattened houses,
Sheep and pigs blasted,
Ravens and rabbits blind,
Scrabbling in the grit and yucca.

But Bird. Remember Bird.
Five months later he was dead,
While I was down on my knees,
Wretched with fear in
The cinders of the desert.

⸱ ⸱ ⸱ ⸱ ⸱ ⸱ ⸱ ⸱ ⸱ ⸱ ⸱ ⸱ ⸱ ⸱ ⸱ ⸱ ⸱ ⸱

SASCHA FEINSTEIN: Your earliest published jazz poems [from the late
'60s] include "Blues for Charlie Christian" and "Mordecai Dying to
Jazz," but my favorite poems were written much later: "Zimmer's Last
Gig," "The Duke Ellington Dream," "Sitting with Lester Young," and
"But Bird." Since jazz was one of your greatest influences at the time

when you were developing as a poet, why did you make these poems, which are among your most ambitious, many years later?

PAUL ZIMMER: I think most of my ambitious poems come later. I like to think that I'm getting better as I grow older. When people ask me what is my favorite poem in my own work, I always say it was the last one I wrote. I hope it's a natural development and will go on to the end of my life. All poets hope for that—that they're getting better.

FEINSTEIN: Absolutely. But many young poets immediately turn to the most memorable episodes in their lives, and I think most writers, had they experienced at the age of twenty the genius of Charlie Parker and the terror of atomic bomb tests, would have written about such things in their first book. You waited almost forty years.

ZIMMER: Perhaps I was saving those things up and practicing in some ways to use them later. I'm glad that I didn't do it right away because I don't think I would have done it nearly as well as I did later. I've saved other things, too. For instance, I think I'm writing the best love poems I've ever written. After an enduring forty years of love, I'm writing the best ones now. I like to think that maybe I'm wiser than I was then. Maybe it was a natural thing for me to save those experiences.

FEINSTEIN: Bill Matthews has spoken a little bit about how some jazz figures were so large that they were hard to digest at a young age.

ZIMMER: Yes. That's true. You know, I've done a lot more listening since then, too, though I've been listening since I was fourteen. I used to special order records from a little shop in Canton, Ohio, and I've been listening ever since. But I think I'm a better listener now. I understand and experience the music more completely than I did when I was younger. When I was a teenager it was more of a sexual thing, I think. That's always there—but now there are other things. I realize more fully that it is an art form and not just some music that excited and titillated me.

FEINSTEIN: You must have been somewhat of an oddity, buying those records in Canton.

ZIMMER: I was, yeah. It was very strange! [Laughs.] But I had a bunch of buddies. We all liked each other, and they took to my records, too. It was a wonderful thing. I went away from Canton forty years ago and went back only for visits with my parents (and then they were gone—ten years ago). These were just brief visits. But I was invited back to read in Canton just recently, so I called ahead and asked one of my old buddies to gather the troops together, and amazingly we are all alive—in various states of physical decrepitude. One guy works in a factory;

one guy is a carpenter; one guy has a bread route. But we all got together and discovered that the one thing that had remained constant
in all our lives was jazz. They still collect jazz and listen to it, too. It
was a wonderful renewal—to know that it could happen after all these
years.

FEINSTEIN: That's actually the first time I've heard you talk about people
sharing your interest. I had this image of little Zimmer, by himself,
spinning 78s.

ZIMMER: [Chuckles.] I used to like different styles of jazz than I like
now. I've always loved the boppers, but I liked also [Stan] Kenton and
those big brass sounds. That used to electrify me when I was a kid,
but I can't bear to listen to them anymore. I was, of course, aware of
the Basie and Ellington bands; I used to buy their records and listen to
them very carefully. But I've gotten to be a more mature listener now,
and Basie is basic to my life. I can't live without him. Those great rolling sounds—they make me happy.

FEINSTEIN: Given time, too, one realizes the humanity of these artists,
the depth of feeling we often don't absorb at age twenty or so.

ZIMMER: Sure. I didn't understand it. I knew Pres and Bird were troubled,
for example. I saw Bud Powell in 1954 when Mingus brought him to
the stage and almost laid him out across the keyboard. Powell sat up
and played, and rather brilliantly—as well as he could at the time. But
it was a romantic thing, too—the notion that they were all troubled
and were having difficult lives with the drugs, which were so mysterious to me. I had no way of understanding it; that was another world.

   You think of the poets of that generation, too, starting with Dylan
Thomas, who thought they had to be drunks in order to be poets. And
I took that up when I was a very young poet. I thought if I didn't arrive on the scene half lit up, why, I wasn't really doing my job. I played
that role. So I look at things very differently now, and maybe with a
deeper understanding.

FEINSTEIN: You mentioned Lester Young's troubles. I find the gesture in
"Sitting with Lester Young" very moving, very touching—this reaching out in whatever way that you can to someone who's gone. The
poem actually transcends what would have been possible.

ZIMMER: Yes.

FEINSTEIN: Do you think that's one of the functions of poetry?

ZIMMER: Sure—that kind of vision: Put yourself in a room with Lester
Young, create that impossible world. It's not even a tension; it's a kind
of dream that you can make with a poem that's exciting to me. I could

actually do that in a poem—be in a room with him—and just sit with him. We could watch the people going into Birdland out the window of the Alvin Hotel.

I like the idea of creating unlikely scenes in my poems, the way I do in the poem "Zimmer Imagines Heaven." The poem's not about jazz, really, but I have my All-Star band with all the dead, wonderful players, and the poem includes the line, "Mozart chats with Ellington in the roses." Can you imagine such a thing? Wouldn't that be—wouldn't it have been—? I mean, what would they have said to each other? I'm sure they would have just locked in.

FEINSTEIN: They were both brilliant improvisers, for one thing.

ZIMMER: Yeah. Maybe I'll try to do a poem about that sometime. Wow!

FEINSTEIN: That would be a very different "Duke Ellington Dream."

ZIMMER: Yes! [Laughs.]

FEINSTEIN: The poem "The Duke Ellington Dream" reads as though it came to you quickly. Is that true or did you have to work a long time to achieve that tone?

ZIMMER: No, it came so fast that I was suspicious of it. I made that poem, and I sent it with a bunch of other poems (which I thought were much better) to a friend of mine, and he was just all over that poem. "This is it. Click this one in." I was surprised by that. But then I read it at a reading and everyone went nuts over it, so I realized that it was pretty good. Sometimes I like to tell jokes and happy stories in my poems, but I'm always suspicious when the poems come so easy. American poetry is *serious,* man! If you don't say "dark" at least twice in a poem you worry that you will be taken for granted.

FEINSTEIN: I know what you mean. But even last night, at your reading here at the college, the audience cheered after that poem—in the middle of the reading—and that kind of spontaneous applause rarely happens at poetry readings.

ZIMMER: [Laughs.] I guess the poem is fun to listen to. Here's this "ofay" dreaming that he's sitting in with the Ellington band and blowing these guys away—I mean, it's totally impossible. And that's funny, I think. It's preposterous to imagine that Ellington would come up to me afterwards and say, "You have shat upon my charts, / But I love you madly."

That was actually the last line I wrote—I remember that—"I love you madly." It was fun to write that poem. I enjoyed it. They're not all fun. They're all exciting and challenging and exhilarating, but they're not always fun.

* * * *

FEINSTEIN: Who else did you hear during that time [in the early 1950s]?

ZIMMER: Oh, those were golden years for me. I heard Lester Young, Bud Powell, Ben Webster, Gerry Mulligan, Chet Baker, Coleman Hawkins, Teddy Wilson, Roy Eldridge, Dave Brubeck, Erroll Garner, young Oscar Peterson, J. J. Johnson, Hank Jones, Gene Ammons, Stan Getz, and Thelonious Monk, as well as more obscure figures—Terry Gibbs, Hank Mobley, Johnny Smith, early Carmen McRae. Even that crazy tenor man who used to fall on the ground and wiggle around—Big Jay McNeely. He was a kick! [Laughs.] He used to lie down on his back. It was the beginning of rhythm and blues. They had him in Birdland and it was bizarre! I mean, at one point he acted like he wanted to throw his horn into the crowd because they weren't diggin' it. [Laughs.]

FEINSTEIN: Of the musicians you just mentioned, only Lester [Young] has appeared in your poetry. Why?

ZIMMER: I started very early loving Lester's work. I couldn't believe how beautiful his "Embraceable You" was at the Jazz at the Philharmonic [from 1949]. I lost out with a girlfriend and Pres helped me get through the pain. That was my first meeting with Lester Young, and I've been listening ever since. The records are spotty—some are good and some are bad—but when he was on the money he was somethin'.

Lester was a poet, a very poetic person. He invented his own lingo and what I know of that language makes it seem perfectly right. You know, "No eyes, man." [Laughs.] If he didn't like something, he had "no eyes for it." That kind of thing. Wonderful!

FEINSTEIN: Do you think that you will write about some of those other players?

ZIMMER: Well, I did see Ellington in those days, and I did write about him. And Diz . . . I don't know. I don't want to push the jazz poems too much. I suspect I will write more about jazz, but I want to do it when it feels right.

FEINSTEIN: Sure.

ZIMMER: They're kind of scattered in my work over the years. The jazz poems haven't come in clusters. And I think the last couple that I've done are kind of imitative of earlier things. I did one recently where Zimmer is touched by a jazz musician: Carmen McRae once said something to me in the hallway going into Birdland, and I made a little poem about that (you haven't seen it yet). But it seems imitative: The musicians touch me and then something happens. I've got to figure out another way to write about jazz. And I will.

FEINSTEIN: But what if they're telling you new things?

ZIMMER: If I can create some kind of tension and make something happen out of it all then that's fine. But I don't want to just make them amusements.

FEINSTEIN: Of course. I imagine this is a central issue for any artist—poet, musician, painter: After decades of work, you want to remain fresh. And this is related to the controversies surrounding the young contemporary jazz musicians. Whitney Balliett, for example, has called them the "neos" because they're polishing hard bop. [Zimmer smiles.] Now, I have no problem with that as long as the music's alive and moving.

ZIMMER: Yeah, that's right.

FEINSTEIN: I think there are some tremendous young players out there. What are your thoughts?

ZIMMER: Yes, and I don't mind at all that some of them are playing older styles of jazz. I'd be very sad indeed if I thought that great tradition was passing. Unlike some other people, I also think there are new things that can be done in the tradition. I know this is a big question, a great national debate. There are insults flying and all of that. But I adore the traditional forms of jazz.

I like music I can put on when I come home and am tired. You can't do that with free jazz. You really need to have a little time to sit down and groove with it, and I don't have that kind of time right now. I get the [free jazz] records but I don't tend to put them on; I want something that I can dig with my glass of beer. In a few years, when I retire and have time, I'll get serious with free jazz.

But I love the fact that some of the youngest musicians are working with the traditions. It would be a very melancholy business if that wasn't going on.

FEINSTEIN: Isn't that related, though, to writing what you call "imitative" poems? They may be imitative in some way, but as long as you have a beautiful piece I don't see why that should be a problem with the poem.

ZIMMER: Sure.

FEINSTEIN: So stick with that McRae poem and send it to me for this journal [*Brilliant Corners*]!

ZIMMER: [Laughs.] Okay, okay.

FEINSTEIN: Writing fresh jazz poems is indeed a challenge. Of the many poets who have written about jazz, whom do you admire?

ZIMMER: I admire Bill Matthews immensely, and Michael Harper—for different reasons. I think Michael can riff in ways that a lot of other poets simply can't. He takes off like a tenor player and, when he's really got his chops, plays whatever's in his head. Matthews is so elegant, and so damn intelligent, and he works from a different angle. Baraka is excited by the music, its traditions, its exclusiveness, and so forth. He's fun to read, too; I enjoy him.

I don't much like Ferlinghetti's stuff. I think he's a nice, wonderful icon, but he's not much of a poet, and I don't like those poems about jazz. I used to get my laughs listening to those jazz and poetry records [by Lawrence Ferlinghetti, Kenneth Rexroth, Kenneth Patchen, Jack Kerouac, and others from the late 1950s]. They strike me as funny— but the poets were so damn serious about it! [Laughs.]

FEINSTEIN: I do like Bob Dorough's version of Ferlinghetti's "Dog" from the LP *Jazz Canto,* and in some ways it was much more successful than Ferlinghetti's own recordings with Rexroth at The Cellar.

ZIMMER: Yes. I was in San Francisco toward the end of the '50s and early '60s. I caught some of that stuff. You know—I'd get stuck in the middle of a row and couldn't get out! [Laughs.] I just thought it was goofy. Jazz and poetry didn't marry. The tenor player was trying to figure out what the hell he could do . . . Occasionally something would happen—they would kind of come together for a while—but it was show time. Poetry's not show time.

I had some experiences doing poetry with jazz. Once on the West Coast, after Watts had exploded, I made some poems about the social tumult because I was so anguished over it. Someone showed those poems to Hampton Hawes and he got up a gig with Teddy Edwards on tenor and Ralph Peña on bass, and I read them with those guys. It was a thrill for me. All of us were troubled by what had happened in Watts. But there was more to tell than show in those performances. Fortunately there was never a recording made . . .

I also went on the road with the American Wind Symphony for a couple of years on their tours around the South and around the Coast, and the director asked me to write some poems that could be set to music by Robert Russell Bennett. But I didn't much like doing it and I don't think he did either. Here was his music, and there were my poems. I hope my poems have their own music. I think they do. You can write lyrics or you can write poems, and I don't much like writing lyrics, I guess.

FEINSTEIN: I've been a part of some truly dreadful poetry and jazz performances, so I know what you mean. And Rexroth did, too. He changed his mind radically about the validity of poetry-read-to-jazz.

ZIMMER: He was honest enough to be able to say that. He was a good poet, a generous poet.

FEINSTEIN: You mentioned Michael Harper as another poet you admired, and I know you dedicated your Lester poem to him. As associate director of the University of Pittsburgh Press, you published his first book, *Dear John, Dear Coltrane,* and I think it remains one of the best collections of jazz and poetry. Can you talk some more about the strengths of that book?

ZIMMER: I mentioned some earlier. He can riff almost like a saxophonist. You let yourself ride with him when he's doing it right and he takes you home. He's achieved that in other books, though I think *Dear John, Dear Coltrane* was one of his strongest. He works with his mind like a horn player, hopping from one idea to another, and if you can let yourself go with him it's quite wonderful.

Of course, he got the excitement and the inspiration from Coltrane's work, and he even quotes from the music. He's pretty skillful at doing that and was one of the very first. This wasn't labeling things; he was trying to get into the music. And he did it very well.

FEINSTEIN: It's also a political book, but one where the political statements aren't gratuitous—like the best work of his mentor, Sterling Brown. I admire that very much. There's a toughness to the lines.

ZIMMER: Yes, yes. A tension.

FEINSTEIN: And Harper knits the abstractions in that book with wonderful collage-like narratives.

ZIMMER: Yes, the skill—the skill of the playing.

FEINSTEIN: You've mentioned skill and craft several times, and the writing which you criticize obviously has less of that for you. I think you'll agree that one of the great misconceptions about jazz is that improvisation is not based on skill, that it emerges only from the gut. Furthermore, writing, no matter how spontaneous, is finally a very different craft. I think Kerouac, for example, could have been a much tougher poet had he gone back to his work. The lack of revision shows.

ZIMMER: Boy, it sure does! Yeah. In *Mexico City Blues,* he just put everything down. Parts of it are wonderful; parts of it are ridiculous.

With horn players, or any good jazz players, their creativity is right there (this has been said before, it's no revelation). It's right there, and what comes out is immediate. Whereas we, as poets, can tinker and fuss and take years, sometimes, to go over it. I remember listening to Charlie Rouse laughing about playing with Monk. Monk would be saying, "That's it, man," and Rouse would say, "Let's try it again," but Monk would insist, "No, that's it." And that was the end of it. Rouse said you had to get it right [on the first take] because it was going to be there for the rest of your life, for history! [Laughs.] You have to be a very brave person in many ways to do that. And Rouse was such a wonderful player. I really admired what he did with Monk, and beyond that, too.

FEINSTEIN: Yes, and he was good enough so that the first take was almost always terrific.

ZIMMER: It was wonderful.

FEINSTEIN: And Rouse could do that because of years of experience: knowing the tunes, knowing Monk, for that matter.

ZIMMER: Yes. Again it's a matter of skill and experience and talent.

FEINSTEIN: For years I've admired Hayden Carruth's book *Sitting In* [*Selected Writings on Jazz, Blues, and Related Topics*], which you published. It's a lovely collection of both poetry and prose. Did he propose that idea for the book?

ZIMMER: No, I proposed it to him. I said, "Why don't you bring your jazz stuff all together?"

FEINSTEIN: That was a great idea! There's really nothing else quite like it.

ZIMMER: He listens so carefully.

FEINSTEIN: Yes. Jazz has clearly been a salvation for him, too. And in his essay "Influences," he says, "Some people can hear jazz, and others, by far the greater number, cannot." That statement reminds me of your wonderful poem "Zimmer's Last Gig."

ZIMMER: Yeah. A lot of the material in that poem was true. I was in New York City during this golden period for myself [the 1950s] and I'd met this girl from Yonkers. I used to date her; we'd go to dances and stuff. I kept talking to her about jazz. She'd never been down to Manhattan. So I talked her into coming to town, met her at Grand Central, and we walked down to Birdland. I'd been talking to her about jazz for a long time and I thought this was going to be really groovy, that she'd be so taken up by the romance of the tunes, that she'd be all over me. [Laughs.] And she sat there like she didn't know what the hell was going on. She almost seemed threatened. She thought it was too loud and was really appalled by some of it. She didn't groove at all—not one tiny bit. What a disappointment, you know? Get this girl home and forget it. No eyes! [Laughs.]

FEINSTEIN: Some of your stories remind me of those told by my good friend Bob Gross, who's almost exactly your age. He's often told me that when he was quite young and hearing Bird live he didn't know what, exactly, he was hearing. That is, he knew this was important, that this was probably genius, but all he really knew at the time was that the music was irresistible. Was that the feeling you had in the early 1950s?

ZIMMER: Oh, it was such pristine, marvelous playing. Bird was so different from the other alto players—you know, Willie Smith or Jeep [Johnny Hodges] or Benny Carter or the others. He was *Bird,* with those dips and turns and changes. I didn't know what I was hearing, either, except I knew it was damn important and exciting. It was easy to feel that I was in the presence of greatness. I didn't know how great he was, I guess. But I still turn his recordings on and find they sound as fresh as they ever did. It pops.

FEINSTEIN: I love the way your poem "But Bird" offers a call-and-response of memory, and how even the title keeps the poem moving forward, like a refrain.

ZIMMER: Thank you.

FEINSTEIN: When in the process of making the poem did you know that Bird's magnificent playing and the experience at the Nevada atomic testing grounds needed or deserved to come together?

ZIMMER: I was working with the memory of hearing Bird and then naturally started thinking about the other significant thing that happened to me at that time in my life. I was really working with them separately and then I thought, "Hey—I should put these together," in order to make them play off each other, to create a tension off each other.

I was so lost as a young man. I was not a good student and teachers never paid any attention to me because I was kind of a dopey kid who was always dreaming and couldn't get the grades. I was terrified by this experience [of witnessing the atomic tests] and, of course, didn't really know what I was getting into. I needed something to truly believe in, and at that time I didn't know I could be a poet. I was trying a little bit but I was so far away from knowing what poetry really was.

Jazz was the art that I really knew (I didn't know painting or anything else) and it meant so much to me. It was something I could believe in at a time when I was totally unsure of myself and very frightened. It was the Eisenhower years, and the next thing that happened was nothing, and then nothing happened after that—no social movements. Not much to believe in. So I got lost in jazz and always went back to it. Always have. It's saved my life sometimes. It can heal you, you know that? You know that.

FEINSTEIN: It relates to what you said earlier: that without Count Basie in your life you'd be miserable.

ZIMMER: Absolutely. The first time I heard Basie was in a movie theater in the late '40s. We went and saw some croupy movie—some silly, B movie. This was in Canton, Ohio. Basie had traveled with his orchestra and they passed through town. We watched the movie, and then the orchestra started playing behind the screen. Then they lifted the screen—and there was Count Basie's orchestra.

What a revelation that was! I had some of his records and had listened carefully to them, but there he was, right in front of me. He had that marvelous smile, and he really drove that band. He also had beautiful chorus girls who'd come out and dance. We dug that, too! They'd be all jammed up on that little stage, bumping into each other, kicking and laughing. It was terribly exciting.

Then one time a few years later he came to the Civic Arena. He booked it for a concert/dance, and they played—but practically no one came. Oh, it was terrible. And I was so embarrassed because I was from Canton and there were about twenty people to hear Basie.

When they took a break, I got a beer and went up to their drummer, Gus Johnson. I said, "Hey, I want to apologize for this community. It's terrible. You guys come in here and you've got twenty people." But he said, "Man, don't worry about that. It's okay. We love to play. We're having a good time tonight."

ACKNOWLEDGMENTS

At a local jam session a couple of years ago, the drummer, Steve Mitchell, asked during the break why I hadn't come up to play. I told him I was having a good time just sitting and talking with my wife. "Oh, man," Steve said, putting his hand on my shoulder. "I'd rather sit and talk to Marleni than play with *Coltrane!*"

My favorite conversations take place at home, and I'm sure Marleni and our children, Kiran and Divia, know that I dedicate all my projects to them.

It has been a different kind of pleasure, and a genuine honor, to speak with the remarkable artists in this collection. Their names should be on the cover; in many respects, it is more their book than mine.

All the interviews, and the essay by Philip Levine, first appeared in *Brilliant Corners: A Journal of Jazz & Literature* (www.lycoming.edu/ BrilliantCorners). Founded in 1996, the journal has been sustained largely because of David Rife and Gary Hafer, my friends and colleagues; their editorial work continues to be invaluable. I would like to acknowledge other supporters of *Brilliant Corners,* especially our loyal subscription base, as well as Lycoming College, the Archipelago Foundation, the Pennsylvania Council on the Arts, and the National Endowment for the Arts. During the final stages of this project, I had outstanding assistance from Garrett Williams. And I also want to thank several friends who, in different ways, provided guidance and encouragement: Thorpe Feidt, G. W. Hawkes, Karen and Jack Humphrey, Kathy and Bob Klein, Bev and Bill McCauley, Patricia Walker, and JoAnn Hughes and Charlie Weiner.

The interview with William Matthews was reprinted in his posthumous collection, *The Poetry Blues: Essays and Interviews* (edited by Sebastian Matthews and Stanley Plumly; University of Michigan Press). The interviews with Jayne Cortez and Sonia Sanchez were reprinted in *Innovative Women Poets: An Anthology of Contemporary Poetry and Interviews* (edited by Cynthia Hogue and Elisabeth A. Frost; University of Iowa Press). The interview with Sonia Sanchez also appeared in *Conversations with Sonia Sanchez* (edited by Joyce A. Joyce; University Press of Mississippi). Most of the introduction first appeared in *Asheville Poetry Review*.

The reprinted texts preceding the interviews add enormous substance to these conversations, and I am extremely grateful to the authors and publishers who granted permission to reprint these works:

Amiri Baraka. "Black Art," the excerpt from "Duke Ellington: The Music's 'Great Spirit'," the excerpt from *Dutchman*, and the excerpt from "Jazz Writing: Survival in the Eighties." Copyright © by Amiri Baraka. Reprinted by permission of the author.

Hayden Carruth. "In That Session" (also known as "105" from *The Sleeping Beauty*) and "Paragraphs 26, 27 & 28" from *Collected Longer Poems* by Hayden Carruth. Copyright © 1994 by Hayden Carruth. Reprinted by permission of Copper Canyon Press. "What a Wonder Among Instruments Is the Walloping Tramboone!" from *Collected Shorter Poems* by Hayden Carruth. Copyright © 1992 by Hayden Carruth. Reprinted by permission of Copper Canyon Press. "Mort aux Belges!" from *Scrambled Eggs & Whiskey* by Hayden Carruth. (First printed with its final stanza in *Green Mountains Review* and *Brilliant Corners*.) Copyright © 1996 by Hayden Carruth. Reprinted by permission of Copper Canyon Press. Excerpt from "Freedom and Discipline" from *Toward the Distant Islands: New & Selected Poems* by Hayden Carruth. Copyright © 2006 by Hayden Carruth. Reprinted by permission of Copper Canyon Press.

Jayne Cortez. "About Flyin' Home," "Bumblebee, You Saw Big Mama," and "States of Motion" from *Somewhere in Advance of Nowhere* by Jayne Cortez. Copyright © 2006 by Jayne Cortez. Reprinted by permission of the author.

Bill Crow. Excerpt from "The Bass in Jazz" (*The Oxford Companion to Jazz,* edited by Bill Kirchner) and excerpts from "Charlie's," "The Gerry Mulligan Quartet," and "Stan the Man" (*From Birdland to Broadway* by Bill Crow). Copyright © by Bill Crow. Reprinted by permission of the author.

Cornelius Eady. Excerpt from *Running Man* by Cornelius Eady. First published in *Brilliant Corners* (Summer 2000, vol. 4, no. 2). Copyright © by Cornelius Eady. Reprinted by permission of the author.

Gary Giddins. Excerpts from *Bing Crosby, Celebrating Bird, Satchmo,* and *Visions of Jazz* (all by Gary Giddins). Copyright © by Gary Giddins. Reprinted by permission of the author.

Lee Meitzen Grue. "Babe Stovall on a Bare Stage," "In the Garden," "Lundi Gras," and "Tuesday Night on Frenchmen Street" by Lee Meitzen Grue. Copyright © by Lee Meitzen Grue. Reprinted by permission of the author.

David Jauss. "Black Orchid" and "Hymn of Fire" from *Improvising Rivers* by David Jauss (Cleveland State University Press). Copyright © by David Jauss. Reprinted with permission of Cleveland State University Press. "Brutes" and "Traps" from *You Are Not Here* by David Jauss. Copyright © by David Jauss. Reprinted by permission of the author and Fleur de Lis Press.

Yusef Komunyakaa. "Testimony" and the excerpts from "Safe Subjects" from *Pleasure Dome: New and Collected Poems* © 1993 by Yusef Komunyakaa. Reprinted with permission of Wesleyan University Press.

Philip Levine. "Detroit Jazz in the Late Forties & Early Fifties: Reflections in Poetry & Prose" (including the excerpt from "It Gets to You" and the poems "One Word" and "The Wrong Turn") first appeared in *Brilliant Corners* and is copyright © 1997 by Philip Levine. Reprinted by permission of the author. "Above Jazz," "I Remember Clifford," and "Songs" from *Unselected Poems* (Greenhouse Review Press) by Philip Levine. Copyright © 1997 by Philip Levine. Reprinted by permission of the author. "On the Corner" from *New Selected Poems* by Philip Levine. Copyright 1991 © by Philip Levine. Used by permission of Alfred A. Knopf, a division of Random House.

Haki R. Madhubuti. Excerpt from "Are Black Musicians Serious?" from *From Plan to Planet* by Haki R. Madhubuti, and "Don't Cry, Scream" from *GroundWork* by Haki R. Madhubuti. "Amiri" first appeared in *Brilliant Corners*. Copyright © by Haki R. Madhubuti and Third World Press. Reprinted by permission of Third World Press, Inc.

William Matthews. "Mingus at The Half Note," "Mingus at The Showplace," "Mingus in Diaspora," and "Mingus in Shadow" from *Search Party: The Collected Poems of William Matthews*. Copyright © 2004 by Sebastian Matthews and Stanley Plumly. Reprinted by permission of Houghton Mifflin Company. All rights reserved. Excerpt from "Unrelenting Flood" from *Flood* by William Matthews. Copyright © by William Matthews. Reprinted by permission of Sebastian Matthews.

Dan Morgenstern. Excerpts from "Bill Evans," "Breakfast with Champions," "Lester Young: The Pres/Pres," and "Paul Desmond" from *Living with Jazz* by Dan Morgenstern. Copyright © by Dan Morgenstern. Reprinted by permission of the author.

Hank O'Neal. Liner notes by Hank O'Neal for *The Dave McKenna Quartet Featuring Zoot Sims.* Copyright © by Hank O'Neal. Reprinted by permission of the author.

Eugene B. Redmond. Excerpts from *Drumvoices* and the introduction to Henry Dumas's *Knees of a Natural Man,* as well as the excerpt from the poem "We're Tight, Soul-Tight—Like Lincolnites" (all by Eugene B. Redmond). Copyright © by Eugene B. Redmond. Reprinted by permission of the author.

Sonia Sanchez. "a/coltrane/poem" from *We a BaddDDD People,* "Blues" from *Shake Loose My Skin,* "A Poem for Ella Fitzgerald" from *Like the Singing Coming Off the Drums,* and "Sister's Voice" from *Does Your House Have Lions?* (all by Sonia Sanchez). Copyright © Sonia Sanchez. Reprinted by permission of the author.

John Sinclair. "carolina moon," "in walked bud," "i surrender dear," and "'round about midnight," as well as excerpts from "bloomdido" and "brilliant corners," from *thelonious: a book of monk* by John Sinclair. Copyright © 2006 by John Sinclair. Reprinted by permission of the author. Excerpt from "Blues to You" from *Song of Praise: Homage to John Coltrane* by John Sinclair. Copyright © 2007 by John Sinclair. Reprinted by permission of the author.

Al Young. Excerpts from "Gifts and Messages," "Introduction," "Nostalgia in Times Square," "Pennies from Heaven," and "Ruby My Dear" from *Drowning in the Sea of Love* by Al Young. Copyright © by Al Young. Reprinted by permission of the author.

Paul Zimmer. "But Bird," "The Duke Ellington Dream," "Sitting with Lester Young, " and "Zimmer's Last Gig" from *Crossing to Sunlight* by Paul Zimmer. Copyright © by Paul Zimmer. Reprinted by permission of the author.

INDEX

Bold type indicates chapter on individual; italicized type indicates illustration.

Abbott, Berenice, 304–305, 306, 308, 309
The ABC of Reading, 388
Adams, George, 46
Adams, John, 158
Adams, Pepper, 223, 225–227
Adderley, Cannonball, 68
Adderley, Nat, 313
Adzinya, Abraham, 53
Ain't Nothin' but the Blues, 95
akLaff, Pheeroan, 9
Albany, Joe, 270
Albee, Edward, 12–13, 97–98
Albino Red, 322
Alexander, Adlai, 406
Alexander, Elizabeth, 335
Alexander, Margaret Walker. *See* Walker, Margaret
Ali, Rashid, 396
Allen, Henry "Red," 118
Allen, Ron, 394
Allen, Samuel, 243, 335
America: A History in Verse, 391
America Is Me, 409
American Jazz Orchestra, 109–110
Amiri, Johari, 239
Ammons, Albert, 27–28
Ammons, Gene, 222, 384, 426
Anderson, Cat, 419
Anderson, Coco, 47
Appel, Alfred, 125
Apronti, Elena and Jawa, 47
Archey, Jimmy, 30
Ark of Bones, 317, 319–320, 330
Armstrong, Louis, 7, 35, 102–103, 106–107, 110, 111, 113, 114, 115, 120, 123, 127, 205, 238, 239, 243, 246, 285, 287, 303, 304, 309, 310, 326, 393
Ashcraft, Edwin M. "Squirrel," III, 300–301, 302
Asher, Don, 121–122
Ask Your Mama, 14, 359
Asmussen, Svend, 276
Aubert, Alvin, 333, 335
Auden, W. H., 264
Austin, Lyn, 85

The Autobiography of a Jukebox, 93
Avakian, George, 300, 301, 302, 303
Ayler, Albert, 10, 11, 241, 287
Ayler, Donald, 10, 287

Babbit, Milton, 158
Bach, Johann Sebastian, 106
Bacon, Paul, 295–296
Baez, Joan, 160
Bailey, Dave, 75
Baker, Chet, 156, 164, 426
Baker, Houston, 243–244
Baldwin, James, 322, 328
Balitsaris, Matt, 165
Balliett, Whitney, xiii–xiv, 124, 166, 306, 414, 427
Baraka, Amina, 9
Baraka, Amiri, *xviii,* **1–22,** 38, 55, 81, 90–91, 124, 155, 209, 237, 239, 242, 243, 249–250, 282, 309, 318–319, 331, 333–334, 335, 357, 360, 361, 362, 383, 385, 392, 414, 428; on Edward Albee, 12–13; on Albert Ayler, 10, 11; "Black Art," 3–4, 10–11; on Black Nationalism, 12, 22; on Sterling Brown, 7–8; on *Bullworth,* 20–21; on Stanley Crouch, 16–17; *Dutchman,* 2–3, 12–13; on Duke Ellington, 5–6, 8, 9–10; on jazz and poetry in performance, 8, 9–11, 14–16; on jazz and theater, 12–14, 17; on Jazz at Lincoln Center, 8; on jazz criticism, 4–5, 6–7, 8, 16–18; on *Kulchur* magazine, 18; *The Life of Willie "The Lion" Smith,* 17–18; on Sunny Murray, 10–11; *A Recent Killing,* 13; *Skin Trouble,* 12; on the superficiality of New York City, 18–19
Baraka, Kimako, 46
Baraka, Ras, 357
Barker, Danny, 144
The Baron in the Trees, 163
Barron, Kenny, 167, 264
Barrow, George, 71
Basheer, Ahmed, 200
Basie, Count, 71, 75, 259, 273–274, 286, 417–418, 424, 432

Bearden, Romare, 46, 205, 231
The Beatles, 108, 177, 235
Beatty, Warren, 20–21
Be-Bop, Re-Bop, 335
Bechet, Sidney, 28, 29, 31, 32, 34–35, 258
Beckett, Samuel, 107
Beethoven, Ludvig van, 14, 36, 157
Beiderbecke, Bix, 154, 282, 302, 310
Beneath the Underdog, xiv, 71, 108, 122–123,
    183, 262–263
Bennett, Robert Russell, 428
Bennett, Tony, 105
Berigan, Bunny, 28
Bernstein, Peter, 313
Berry, Chu, 218
Berry, Chuck, 177, 381–382
Bess, Tamu, 47
*The Best of Jazz: Noted Writers on Great Jazz
    Records,* 306–307
Betty Shabazz International Charter School,
    241
Bey, Andy, 164
*Beyond Category: The Life and Genius of Duke
    Ellington,* 111
Bhumibol, King, 185
Bing Crosby: The Early Years 1903–1940, 104,
    110, 111–117
Bird: The Legend of Charlie Parker, xiv, 205
*Bird Lives! The High Life and Hard Times of
    Charlie (Yardbird) Parker,* 183, 205
Birth of a Nation, 413
Bishop, Elizabeth, 163
Black Artists Group (BAG), 325
The Black Arts Movement, 43, 238–239, 243,
    333, 339, 360–363
*Black Fire: An Anthology of Afro-American
    Writing,* 358
Black House, 362
Black Mass, 10
Black Music, 155, 243
Black Spirits, 15
Black Women Writers, 334
Blackburn, Paul, 363–364, 412
Blackwell, Ed, 46, 52–53
Blakey, Art, 17, 46, 174, 263, 388
Blast, 388
Blesh, Rudy, 311
Bley, Paul, 167, 259
Bliek, Rob van der, 389
The Blues Don't Change, 401
Blues for an African Princess, 330
Blues People, 243, 282, 414
Bluiett, Hamiet, 322
Blumenthal, Bob, 124
Bogan, Louise, 365–367
Bonier, Bess, 223–224
Book of Life, 244

Bostic, Earl, 336
Boyd, Melba, 335
Boyer, Horace, 353
Brackett, David, 125
Bradley's, xii, xiv, xvi
Braff, Ruby, 311
Breaux, Quo Vadis Gex. *See* Gex, Quo Vadis
Bresnick, Paul, 111, 113, 116
Brilliant Corners: A Journal of Jazz & Literature,
    xi, xii, xvi, 6, 49, 59, 60, 102, 181, 191–192,
    213, 296, 307, 317–318, 401, 418, 427
Brinks, Dave, 140
Brookmeyer, Bob, 64, 69, 410
Brookmeyer, Joyana, 410
Brooks, Gwendolyn, 231, 245, 247, 249
Broonzy, Big Bill, 413
Brothers, I Loved You All, 33
Brother's Keeper, 146
Brown, Arthur, 331
Brown, Boyce, 302
Brown, Clifford, 214–215, 310
Brown, James, 234
Brown, Kysha, 140
Brown, Marie, 325, 333
Brown, Oscar, Jr., 368
Brown, Rap, 383
Brown, Ray, 177
Brown, Sterling, 7–8, 52, 328, 329, 331, 332, 361
Brown, Tyrone, 367
Brown, Vernon, 30
Browne, Vivian, 46
Broyard, Anatole, 196, 209
Brubeck, Dave, 65, 122, 177, 271, 310, 426
Bruce, Lenny, 196, 282
Büchmann-Møller, Frank, 114
Buckley, William F., 308
Bukowski, Charles, 137
Bullins, Ed, 360, 362
Bullworth, 20–22
Bum Rush the Page: A Def Poetry Jam, 367
Bunick, Nico, 259
Burnett, T-Bone, 304
Burns, Ken, 102, 106
Burrell, Kenny, 223, 224–227
Burroughs, Charlie, and Margaret Burroughs,
    242, 245, 247
Burroughs, William, 282, 308, 391–392
Burt, Eluard, 136, 137, 140, 143–144, 146–
    147, 148
Burt, Kichea, 147
But Beautiful, 183, 390, 408
Byard, Jaki, 156, 167, 259, 289
Byas, Don, 27

Call and Response, 335
Callender, Red, 204
Calloway, Cab, 321

Calvino, Italo, 163
The Cannabis Cup, 391–392, 393
The Cantos of Ezra Pound, 388
Carmichael, Hoagy, 403
Carmichael, Stokely, 383
Carradine, John, 160
Carruth, Hayden, *24,* **25–40,** 308–309, 310, 430;
  on advantages of music over poetry, 33, 37;
  on contemporary poetry, 40; "Freedom and
  Discipline," 32–33; "In That Session," 28–29,
  35–36; introduction to jazz, 31–32; on Miff
  Mole, 37–38; "Mort aux Belges!," 29, 34–35;
  "Paragraphs," 26–28, 33–34; on poetry and
  jazz in performance, 38; on poets of his gen-
  eration, 39; *Sitting In,* 26, 38–39; "What a
  Wonder Among the Instruments Is the Wal-
  loping Tramboone!," 25, 30–31, 36–37
Carruth, Jo-Anne, 26
Carter, Benny, 127, 431
Carter, Elliot, 158
Carter, John, 47
Cartey, Wilfred, 46
Cartiér, Xam Wilson, 335
Cassady, Neal, 391–392
Cassin, Maxine, 141
Castro, Michael, 331, 335
Catlett, Big Sid, 27–28, 349
Cavett, Dick, 121
Celebrating Bird, 103, 110–111, 205
Chambers, Paul, 227
Charles, Ray, 304
Charles, Teddy, 69
Charters, Samuel, 311
Cherry, Don, 184
Chiaroscuro Records, 295–298, 311, 312, 314
Chilton, John, 118–119
Christensen, Tom, 164
Christgau, Bob, 109
Clarke, John Henrik, 331
Clarke, Kenny "Klook," 70, 392, 420
Claudel, Alice Moser, and Calvin Claudel, 143
Claxton, William, 206
Clayton, Buck, 29, 34–35, 308
Cleaver, Eldridge, 362
Clifton, Lucille, 242
Clooney, Rosemary, 301
The Clovers, 381
The Coasters, 323
Cocteau, Jean, 304
Codrescu, Andrei, 140, 141
Cohn, Al, 73, 76
Cole, Bill, 53
Cole, Cozy, 288
Cole, Nat King, 321
Coleman, Denardo, 53, 54
Coleman, George, 108
Coleman, Janet, 243, 261, 410

Coleman, Ornette, 54, 154, 166, 179, 184, 189,
  275, 288, 301, 303, 384
The Collected Poems of Langston Hughes, 91
Collected Shorter Poems (Carruth), 37
Collins, Kathy, 46
Coltrane: A Biography, 183, 243
Coltrane, Alice, 241, 395
Coltrane, John, xiv, 6, 11, 17, 18, 92, 93, 97, 108,
  114, 125, 155, 176, 179–180, 183, 186, 232–
  236, 237, 240–241, 242, 243, 248, 249, 258,
  265–266, 283, 286–287, 340–344, 352–353,
  358–359, 363, 368, 382, 383, 387, 395–396
Condon, Eddie, 68, 297, 304, 313
Condon, Phyllis, 297
A Coney Island of the Mind, 137
*Confirmation: An Anthology of African-
  American Women,* 367
Conover, Willis, 286
The Cookery, 51–52
Corea, Chick, 154, 155, 167
Cortez, Jayne, 16, *42,* **43–56,** 147, 242, 243,
  331, 334, 335, 357; "About Flyin' Home," 44–
  45, 49–50, 51; on the abuse of the blues, 54;
  on African American literature antholo-
  gies, 56; on Black Nationalism, 56; on Ed
  Blackwell, 52–53; "Bumblebee, You Saw Big
  Mama," 47–49, 51; on jazz poets, 52, 55; on
  poetry and jazz in performance, 53–55, 56;
  on rhythm and repetition in poetry, 50–
  51, 53; "States of Motion," 46–47, 50; on Big
  Mama Thornton, 51–52
Crane, Hart, 145
Crazeology, 68
Creeley, Robert, 385–386
Crichton, Sarah, 113–114, 116
Crosby, Bing, 104, 110, 111–117, 119
Crosby, Edward, 324
Crosby, Gary, 112, 117
Crosby, Howard, 115–116
Crosby, Israel, 27, 34
Crouch, Stanley, xiii, 15, 16–17, 111, 114, 124
Crow, Aileen, 59, 63
Crow, Bill, *58,* **59–78,** 183; on Bob Brookmeyer,
  64; on Charlie's Tavern, 61, 74; on Paul Des-
  mond, 65; on drugs and jazz musicians, 62,
  72–73; on Duke Ellington, 71–72; on Art
  Farmer, 63, 75; on Bud Freeman, 68–69; on
  the function of the bass, 60–61, 77; on Stan
  Getz, 62, 65–66, 73; introduction to litera-
  ture, 63–64; *Jazz Anecdotes,* 59, 60, 71, 76; on
  jazz criticism, 66–68, 71, 72, 73–74, 76–77;
  on Charles Mingus, 69–71; on Thelonious
  Monk, 77–78; on Gerry Mulligan, 62–63,
  72–73, 74–75, 77; on Jimmy Raney, 64–65;
  on Jimmy Rowles, 75–76; *What Is There to
  Say?,* 74–75
Cruz, Victor Hernandez, 335

Cuccia, Ron, 146–147
Cullen, Countee, 352
cummings, e. e., 324
Curtis, King, 273

Daáood, Kamau, 16, 335
Damas, Leon, 46
Damas, Marietta, 46
Dance, Stanley, 280, 283
Dance of the Infidels, 389
Dancing, 92–93
Datcher, Michael, 335
Davern, Kenny, 287
Davis, Angela, 324
Davis, Dr. Arthur P., 361
Davis, Eddie "Lockjaw," 322
Davis, Francis, 125
Davis, Frank Marshall, 328
Davis, Miles, xv, 17, 46, 93, 97, 108, 109, 119,
    120, 155, 156, 168, 173–175, 180–181, 183,
    184, 186, 216, 238, 239, 241, 243, 302, 322,
    382, 386, 389, 405
Davis, Rebecca Parker. See Parker, Rebecca
Davis, Sammy, Jr., 119
Davis, Stuart, 307
Davis, Walter, Jr., 410
de Koenigswarter, Baroness Pannonica "Nica,"
    202, 204
De Paris, Wilbur, 30
De Wilde, Laurent, 123, 389
Dear John, Dear Coltrane, 97, 429
Dearie, Blossom, 164
The Death of Bessie Smith, 97–98
The Death of Rhythm and Blues, 243
Deep Blues, 390
DeMicheal, Don, 287, 288
Dent, Tom, 133–134, 140, 141–142
Derricote, Toi, 98
Desmond, Paul, xiv, 65, 271–272, 274, 307
DeVeaux, Scott, 125
DeVries, John, 297
di Prima, Diane, 409
Dickenson, Vic, 25, 27, 28, 29, 30–31, 33, 34–
    38, 40
Dickinson, Emily, 162, 188
Diddley, Bo, 327, 381
The Divine Romance, 403
Dix, Otto, 205
Dixon, Willie, 390
Dobyns, Stephen, 39
Dodds, Johnny, 310
Dodson, Owen, 335
Does Your House Have Lions?, 355, 359, 361, 369
Dolphy, Eric, 11, 186, 265–266, 329
Domino, Fats, 381
Don't Cry, Scream, 240, 248
Dorough, Bob, 428

Dos Passos, John, 323
Dove, Rita, 335
Down Beat, 104, 107, 108, 279, 280, 281, 284–
    285, 286, 287, 288, 289, 290, 291, 306, 311,
    382, 383
Drew, Kenny, 259
Drowning in the Sea of Love, 390, 402–410,
    414–415
Drumvoices, 318–319, 320, 321, 325–330,
    333–336
Du Bois, W. E. B., 20, 115, 119, 125, 351,
    362–363
Duckworth, Bill, 39
Dufty, William, 281
The Duke Ellington Reader, 123
Dumas, Henry, 317, 319–320, 324, 325, 328,
    330–331, 335
Dumas, Loretta, 317–318, 325
Dunbar, Paul Laurence, 330, 352
Duncans, Harry, 390
Dunham, Katherine, 324, 325, 326–327
Dunn, Stephen, 178
Durham, Frantic Ernie, 381
Dutchman, 2–3, 12–13, 81, 209
Dutry, Honore, 30
Dyer, Geoff, 183, 390, 408
Dylan, Bob, 177

Eady, Cornelius, 80, 81–98, 322, 335; on
    Edward Albee, 97–98; on art and personal
    exposure, 87–88; on Amiri Baraka, 90–91;
    on collaboration and compromise, 86–87;
    as drummer, 94; on Michael Harper, 97; on
    Langston Hughes, 87, 91–92, 95; on integrat-
    ing jazz and theater, 85–89, 95; on jazz as
    common ground, 98; on own jazz poems, 87,
    92–94, 97, 98; on the label "Jazz Poet," 95–
    96; on Hank Mobley, 93–94; on Thelonious
    Monk, 94, 97, 98; on Diedre Murray, 85–88,
    95; on Side Man, 89–90; on August Wilson,
    90; on Al Young, 92–93
Early, Gerald, 322, 324
Eckstine, Billy, 321
Eddie Condon's Scrapbook of Jazz, 304, 305, 313
Edwards, Melvin, 50
Edwards, Teddy, 428
Ehrlich, Marty, 156
Eldridge, Roy "Little Jazz," 75, 118, 223, 275,
    280, 426
Elemental Blues, 333
Eliot, T. S., 106, 118, 332
Elling, Kurt, 158, 160–161, 164
Ellington, Duke, 5–6, 8, 9–10, 17, 71–72, 103–
    104, 111, 114, 115, 120, 122–123, 127, 155,
    189, 237, 243, 258, 273, 285, 303, 309, 336,
    350, 418, 419–420, 424, 425, 426
Ellington, Mercer, 111

Ellison, Ralph, 94–95, 124, 267, 279, 328, 330
Ellmann, Richard, 118
El-Shabazz, El-Hajj. *See* X, Malcolm
El'Zabar, Kahil, 240
Emerson, Ralph Waldo, 188
The Encyclopedia of Jazz, 306, 310
Ernst, Jimmy, 307
Ertegun, Ahmet, 300, 302, 304, 308
Ertegun, Nesuhi, 300, 302, 303, 307
Esquire Jazz Book, 311
Essays cited: "Are Black Musicians Serious?"
    (Madhubuti), 236–237, 244; "The Bass in
    Jazz" (Crow), 60–61, 76; "Bill Evans" (Mor-
    genstern), 270–271; "The Blues: Black and
    White America" (Baraka), 282; "Body and
    Soul" (Young), 414–415; "Breakfast with
    Champions" (Morgenstern), 273–274, 286;
    "Caught in the Act" (Morgenstern), 286;
    "Charlie's" (Crow), 61; "Contemporary
    American Poetry and All That Jazz" (Jauss),
    171–172; "Controversies" (Morgenstern),
    286; "Duke Ellington: The Music's 'Great
    Spirit' " (Baraka), 5–6; "Festivals and Events"
    (Morgenstern), 286; "The Gerry Mulligan
    Quartet" (Crow), 62–63; "Gifts and Mes-
    sages" (Young), 402, 404; "In Defense of
    'Commercialism' " (Morgenstern), 286; "Jazz
    Writing: Survival in the Eighties" (Baraka),
    4–5; "Lester Leaps In" (Morgenstern), 286;
    "Lester Young: The Pres/Pres" (Morgen-
    stern), 272–273; "One Night in Birdland"
    (Morgenstern), 286; "The Outreach of Jazz"
    (Morgenstern), 286; "Nostalgia in Times
    Square" (Young), 403–404; "Paul Desmond"
    (Morgenstern), 271–272; "Pennies from
    Heaven" (Young), 403; "Perhaps" (Young),
    409; "The Poets of Hate" (Davis), 361; "Ruby
    My Dear" (Young), 405, 407–408; "Stan
    the Man" (Crow), 62; "Tintoretto" (Sartre),
    110–111; "Titans of the Tenor" (Morgen-
    stern), 286–287; "What a Little Moonlight
    Can Do" (Young), 409; "The White Negro"
    (Mailer), 260
Eubanks, Robin, 187
Evans, Bill, 68, 109, 167, 270–271, 274
Evans, Gil, 126
Evans, Mari, 240, 334, 335
Evans, Sandy, 203–204
Evergreen Review, 107
Experiment in Higher Education (E.H.E.),
    324, 325

Fairchild, Sherman, 296
Farmer, Art, 63, 75, 288
Farrell, Joe, 155
Fattening Frogs for Snakes, 390
Faulkner, William, 323

Feather, Leonard, 277, 290, 291, 306, 310, 382
Feni, Dumile, 47
Ferguson, Maynard, 289
Ferguson, Otis, 305–306
Ferlinghetti, Lawrence, 137, 385, 428
Fields, Julia, 243
Fisher, Diane, 109
Fisher, Eddie, "The Third Cup," 322
Fitterling, Thomas, 389
Fitzgerald, Ella, 243, 346–349, 359, 364–365
Fitzgerald, F. Scott, 105, 223
The Five Spot, 8, 281, 363
Flanagan, Tommy, xii–xiv, xv, xvi, 167, 223,
    224, 226, 259, 264
Fleming, Renée, 164
Fomento, Dennis, 140
Forbes, Calvin, 335
Forrest, Jimmy, 322
Foster, Frank, 216
Fragments, 50
Francis, Panama, 38
Franklin, Aretha, 148
Fraser, Al, 122
Fraser, George, 307
Freeman, Bud, 68–69
French Quarter Poems, 137
Friedwald, Will, 124
From Birdland to Broadway, 59, 60
From Plan to Planet, 244
The Fugs, 391
Fuller, Hoyt W., 239, 245, 247, 249
Fulsom, Lowell, 327
Futterman, Steve, 124

Gabbard, Krin, 286
Gabler, Milt, 27–28, 304
Gage, Stan, 11
Gaillard, Slim, 8
Gales, Larry, 395
Gardner, Goon, 193
Garfein, Herschel, 157–158, 161
Garner, Erroll, 204, 220, 221, 297–298, 426
Garrison, Jimmy, 241, 396
Garvey, Marcus, 362
Gates, Henry Louis, Jr., 243, 329
The Gathering of My Name, 92–94
Gaye, Marvin, 155
George, Nelson, 243
Gershwin, George, 17–18, 88
Getz, Stan, 59, 62, 65–66, 73, 155, 224, 265–266,
    278, 279, 426
Gex, Quo Vadis, 140, 141
The Ghosts of Harlem, 312
Gibbs, Terry, 426
Gibson, Dick, 291
Giddins, Gary, xiii, 16, 67, *100,* **101–127,** 205,
    285, 306; on Louis Armstrong, 102–103,

106–107, 110, 111, 113, 114, 121, 127; on becoming a critic, 105–106, 108–109; on Bob
Blumenthal, 124; *Celebrating Bird,* 103, 110;
on John Chilton, 118–119; on Bing Crosby as
innovator, 104, 112–113; on Stanley Crouch,
124; on Duke Ellington, 104–105, 114, 119,
120, 123, 127; introduction to music, 105,
111; on jazz autobiographies, 120, 121–123;
on jazz criticism, 107–108, 114–115, 117–
121, 123–125, 127; on Dan Morgenstern,
107, 108, 123–124; on Gerry Mulligan, 125–
126; studying music, 109–110; on Martin
Williams, 107, 124; on writing the Bing
Crosby biography, 110–117, 119
Gillespie, Dizzy, 8, 46, 71, 75, 108, 122, 127,
183, 188–189, 222–223, 239, 373–374, 391,
420, 426
Ginsberg, Allen, 152, 282, 295, 307–308, 385,
386, 391–392
Gitler, Ira, 124, 292, 382
Giuffre, Jimmy, 69–70
Gleason, Ralph, 121
Golijov, Osvaldo, 163
Golson, Benny, 215
Gonsalves, Paul, 108, 155
Gonzalez, Babs, 8
Good Morning Blues, 71
Goodbye, Sweetwater, 317
Goodman, Benny, 31, 185, 218, 278
Gordon, Dexter, 93, 288–289
Gordon, Max, 69
Gordon, Ricky Ian, 160
Gottlieb, Robert, 285–286, 288
Gourse, Leslie, 389
Gowans, Brad, 30
Grace, C. M. "Sweet Daddy," 15
Graham, Jorie, 418
Granz, Norman, 303
Grauer, Bill, 311
Gray, Wardell, 174, 216, 227
Greco, Juliette, 173–175, 181
Green, Grant, 322
Greenlee, Sam, 328, 330, 334–335
Greenwell, Freddie, 72
Greger, Max, 278
Grey, Sonny, 278
Gross, Bob, 431
Grue, Lee Meitzen, *128,* **129–149,** 371, 397;
"Babe Stoval on a Bare Stage," 130–131; on
Tom Dent, 140, 141–142; on fiction, 139; "In
the Garden," 133–134, 141; "Lundi Gras,"
134–136; on Brenda Marie Osbey, 138–139;
on poetry and jazz in performance, 136–
138, 139–140, 143–144, 146–148; on poetry
and politics, 142, 145; on John Sinclair, 138,
140; on the spirit of New Orleans, 130, 136,
137–138, 149; "Tuesday Night on French-

men Street," 131–133; upbringing of, 136; on
Eudora Welty, 139; on writing jazz poetry,
137, 140, 143
Guettel, Adam, 160
Guevara, Che, 325
Guide to Jazz, 310
Guillén Nicolás, 47
Guralnick, Peter, 114
Gushee, Larry, 6
Guy, Buddy, 327
Gwaltney, Tom, 300

Hackett, Bobby, 300, 304
Haden, Charlie, 184, 384
Hadlock, Dick, 6–7
Haggart, Bob, 104
Hagood, Kenny "Pancho," 393
Hajdu, David, 183
Haley, Bill, 304
Hall, Jim, 70
Hamill, Pete, 281
Hamilton, Scott, 305
Hammond, John, 295, 300, 302, 306, 307
Hampton, Lionel, 49, 51
Hancock, Herbie, 155, 167, 405
The Hanging Judge, 17
Hanna, Sir Roland, 259
Harper, Michael, 38, 187, 228, 242, 328, 330,
331, 335, 418, 428, 429
Harris, Barry, 223–224, 412
Harris, Jerome, 156, 322
Harris, Peter, 335
Harris, Rennie, 359
Harrison, Jim, 30
Harrison, Max, 124
Hartman, Johnny, 321
Hasse, John, 111
Hawes, Hampton, 121, 428
Hawkins, Coleman, 28, 118, 177, 182, 258, 280,
286–287, 290, 311, 372, 415, 426
Hawkins, Yusef, 85
Hawthorne, Nathaniel, 105, 188
Hayden, Robert, 52, 319, 328–329, 332, 335
Haynes, Roy, 70, 313
*Hear Me Talkin' to Ya: The Story of Jazz by the
Men Who Made It,* xiv, 312
Heckman, Don, 124
Hemingway, Ernest, 103, 105, 106, 323
Hemphill, Julius, 38, 124
Henderson, Joe, 157
Henderson, Stephen, xv, 321, 331, 334
Hentoff, Nat, 67, 68, 258, 259, 280, 281, 290–
291, 306, 312, 382, 383
Herbert, Lyon, 325
Herman, Shael, 146
Herman, Woody, 73, 224
Hersch, Fred, *150,* **151–169;** on composing,

157–159, 160–161, 165–166; on contemporary singers, 163–164, 168; education of, 152–157, 168; on encountering Whitman's poetry, 156–157; on Joe Henderson, 157; on Earl Hines, 154; influences on, 167; on instrumental responses to poetry, 164–165; on integrating poetry and music, 157–159, 160–163; on Oscar Peterson, 154; on Luciana Souza, 163; on Oscar Treadwell, 153–154
Herskovitz, Melville, 326
Higgenbotham, J. C., 30
Hill, Phil, 216
Hindemith, Paul, 160
Hines, Earl, 107, 154, 167, 313
Hipp, Jutta, 278
Hodges, Johnny "Jeep," 28, 419, 431
Hogue, Cynthia, 339–340
Holiday, Billie "Lady Day," 17, 28, 34, 179–180, 218–219, 233, 238, 243, 281, 304, 310, 409
Holland, Dave, 154, 187
Holley, Eugene, 125
Holley, Major, 297
Holroyd, Michael, 118, 119
Home Coming, 352
Horace, 260–261
Hornback, Vernon, 324
Hornick, Lita, and Morton "Morty" Hornick, 18
Hot Chocolates, 286
Howlin' Wolf, 323, 327
Hubbard, Freddie, 148, 155, 240
Hudson, George, 322
Hughes, Langston, 8, 14, 38, 54–55, 81, 87, 91–92, 95, 246–247, 261, 319, 320, 324, 328, 332, 352, 359, 412
Hull, Lynda, 173, 181
Hunter, Alberta, 52
Hurston, Zora Neale, 326, 331, 351
Hutcherson, Bobby, 414
Hutson, Jean, 350–352

I Put a Spell on You, 243
Improvising Rivers, 184
Institute of Jazz Studies, 269–270, 285
Institute of Positive Education/New Concept School, 241, 242
Investigative Poetry, 391
Invisible Man, 94–95, 279

Jackson, Angela, 243
Jackson, Cliff, 297
Jackson, D. D., 9, 90
Jackson, Kennell, 409
Jackson, Milt "Bags," 227, 414
Jackson, Oliver, 324
Jacquet, Illinois, 49, 221, 415
Jamal, Ahmad, 156, 167
Jamal, Khan, 359, 367

James, Elmore, 323, 327
Jamison, Eddie, 215
Jarrell, Randall, 39
Jarrett, Keith, 154
Jauss, David, 170, **171–189**; "Black Orchid," 173–175, 180, 184; "Brutes," 175, 182; on Ornette Coleman, 184–185, 189; on cultural ignorance of jazz, 180, 188–189; on fiction, 179; on Lynda Hull, 181; "Hymn of Fire," 176, 186; on integrating jazz history into poetry, 179, 180–181, 183–187; introduction to jazz, 177–178, 189; on jazz as greatest cultural contribution, 188; on jazz literature, 183; on poetic form, 181–182, 186; on Art Porter, Jr., 185; "Traps," 172–173, 177, 187–188
"Jazz" (Matisse), 205
Jazz (PBS series), 102, 106
Jazz albums cited: *Africa/Brass* (Coltrane), 283; *Albert Ammons and the Rhythm Kings,* 33; *Ascension* (Coltrane), 383; *Bob Wilber and the Scott Hamilton Quartet,* 305; *Brazilian Romance* (Vaughan), 365; *Buddy Tate and His Buddies,* 305; *The Clown* (Mingus), 261; *Coleman Hawkins Encounters Ben Webster,* 182; *Coltrane Live at Birdland,* 383; *The Complete Blue Note Recordings of Thelonious Monk,* 387; *The Complete Candid Recordings of Charles Mingus,* 259; *The Complete Charlie Parker on Verve,* 205; *The Complete 1959 Columbia Recordings of Charles Mingus,* 69; *The Complete Pacific Jazz and Capitol Recordings of the Original Gerry Mulligan Quartet and Tentette with Chet Baker,* 126; *A Conference of the Birds* (Holland), 154; *Copacabana* (Vaughan), 365; *Crescent* (Coltrane), 179; *Crystal Silence* (Corea), 154; *Dancing in Your Head* (Coleman), 184; *The Dave McKenna Quartet Featuring Zoot Sims,* 296–298; *Dig* (M. Davis), 382; *Ellington at Newport,* 155, 303; *Facing You* (Jarrett), 154; *First Blues* (Ginsberg), 295, 307; *The Fred Hersch Trio + 2,* 165; *The Genius of Coleman Hawkins,* 177; *Genius of Modern Music, Volume 1 & 2* (Monk), 386, 389; *Gifts and Messages* (Kirk), 407; *Heavy Love* (Cohn), 76; *I Like Jazz,* 301, 310; *I Love Brazil* (Vaughan), 365; *In Walked Thelonious* (W. Davis), 410; *Jazz Canto,* 160, 428; *Jazz of Two Decades,* 301, 310; *Kind of Blue* (M. Davis), 382; *Leaves of Grass* (Hersch), 151–152, 160, 164–166, 169; *Light as a Feather* (Corea), 154; *Live! On Frenchmen Street* (Grue), 136; *Live at the Cookery* (M. L. Williams), 305; *Live at the Floating Jazz Festival* (N. Adderley), 313; *Louis Armstrong and Earl Hines,* 107; *A Love Supreme* (Coltrane),

xiv–xv, 97, 248, 341, 343, 383; *The Magic City* (Sun Ra), 396; *Meditations* (Coltrane), 396; *Midnight at Eddie Condon's,* 310; *Mulligan Meets Monk,* 77; *Neruda* (Souza), 163; *New York School* (Christensen), 164; *Night Life* (M. L. Williams), 305; *Nights at the Village Vanguard* (Flanagan), xiii; *North and South* (Souza), 163; *Odetta Sings the Blues,* 38; *The Poems of Elizabeth Bishop & Other Songs* (Souza), 163; *Recorded in Concert at the Brussels Fair, 1958* (Bechet), 34; *Sound Museum: Hidden Man* (Coleman), 184; *Sound Museum: Three Women* (Coleman), 184; *Stompin' at the Savoy* (Goodman), 31; *Sun Ship* (Coltrane), 242, 248; *Sunset and the Mockingbird* (Flanagan), xiii; *Taking the Blues Back Home* (Cortez), 51, 54; *There It Is* (Cortez), 54, 147; *This Is Our Music* (Coleman), 384; *Transition* (Coltrane), 242, 248; *Weary Blues* (Hughes), 38, 261; *What Is There to Say?* (Mulligan), 59, 74–75; *Workout* (Mobley), 93

Jazz and Pop, 284

Jazz Anecdotes, 59, 60, 71, 76, 183

Jazz at the Philharmonic, 278, 426

Jazz compositions and standards cited: "Air-Conditioned Jungle," 10; "Alice in Blue," 194–195; "April in Paris," 94, 173, 181; "Autumn Leaves," 155, 156; "Better Get It in Your Soul," 255; "Bird in Paradise," 203; "Black Bottom Stomp," 302; "Blood Count," 9, 10; "Blue Monk," 395; "Body and Soul," 199, 273; "Bottom Blues," 28; "Brilliant Corners," 392; "A Caddy for Daddy," 93; "Canadian Sunset," 384; "Caravan," 419; "Carolina Moon," 386; "Cherokee," 193–194, 208; "Criss Cross," 391; "'Deed I Do," 298; "Denardo's Dribbles," 53; "Diminuendo and Crescendo in Blue," 155, 303; "Do Nothing Till You Hear from Me," 419; "Don't Get Around Much Anymore," 9; "Drowning in the Sea of Love," 403; "Easy Living," 218, 219; "Embraceable You," 426; "Empty Faces/Vera Cruz," 365; "Endless Stars," 166; "Erroll," 298; "Evonce," 387; "The Father and the Son and the Holy Ghost," 396; "Flyin' Home," 44–45, 415; "Foolin' Myself," 218; "Grooveyard," 297; "Heebie Jeebies," 121; "Hello Dolly," 103; "Here's that Rainy Day," 418; "Hittin' the Jug," 384; "Honeysuckle Rose," 193; "How Deep Is the Ocean," 296, 298; "How High the Moon," 221; "Humph," 387; "I Got It Bad and That Ain't Good," 9; "I Got Rhythm," 406; "I Must Have That Man," 218; "I'm Coming, Virginia," 282; "In a Sentimental Mood," 9, 185, 419; "In Defense of 'Commercialism,'" 286; "In Walked

Bud," 392; "In Your Own Sweet Way," 65; "Lady Be Good," 348–349; "The Lady in Red," 195; "Lester Leaps In," 273; "Lester's Blues No. 1," 273; "Lester's Blues No. 2," 273; "Limehouse Blues," 298; "Linger Awhile," 297; "Lonely Woman," 184–185, 189; "Lotus Blossom," 9; "Lover Come Back to Me," 143–144; "Lover Man," xiv, 219; "Mack the Knife," 303; "The Man I Love," xv, 18; "Mean to Me," 218; "Miss Brown to You," 219; "Misty," 418; "Mood Indigo," 9; "Muggles," 107, 110; "Muscrat Ramble," 104, 301; "My Favorite Things," 186, 235, 248, 287, 340, 343; "My Funny Valentine," 222; "The Nearness of You," 403; "Neenah," 273; "Nefertiti," 405; "News from Blueport," 63; "Night Train," 9; "On Moonlight Bay," 126; "One Bass Hit," 222–223; "One Good Turn," 297–298; "Paris Nights," 305; "Perdido," 347; "Prisoner of Love," 171, 175, 182; "A Riddle Song," 161, 165, 166; "'Round Midnight," 344–346, 376–379, 393, 395; "Ruby, My Dear," 405, 407–408; "Satin Doll," 419; "The Shadow of Your Smile," 404; "Slice of the Top," 93; "Society Blues," 34; "Song of Myself," 160–161; "Sonnymoon for Two," 287; "Sophisticated Lady," 418; "Splanky," 274; "St. James Infirmary," 107; "Straight, No Chaser," 395; "Strange Fruit," 218, 248; "Suburban Eyes," 387; "Summertime," 18; "Sunday," 273; "Tea for Two," 94; "Thelonious," 387; "There'll Be Some Changes Made," 297; "These Foolish Things," 94; "This Old House," 301; "Tight Like That," 107; "A Tisket, A Tasket," 347; "Un Poco Loco," 9; "Warm Valley," 419; "West End Blues," 107, 110, 309; "What Price Love," 195; "Wherever There's Love," 297

Jazz Journal, 280–281, 288

Jazz magazine, 283–284, 383

Jazz Masters of the Thirties, 72

Jazz Modernism, 125

Jazz People, 285

Jazz People: As Serious as Your Life, 243

Jazz Poet, xiii

The Jazz Poetry Anthology, 140, 295, 358

The Jazz Record Book, 277

The Jazz Review, 67, 382

Jazz Set, 14

JazzSpeak, 311–314

JazzTimes, 8

Jefferson, Eddie, 393–394

Joans, Ted, 55, 200

Johnson, Blind Willie, 304, 311

Johnson, Brian, 112

Johnson, Budd, 193, 388

Johnson, Fenton, 319

Johnson, Gus, 432
Johnson, J. J., 243, 426
Johnson, James P., 14, 17, 91–92
Johnson, James Weldon, 326
Johnson, Pauline, 46
Johnson, Sy, 259
Jones, Elvin, 70–71, 176, 223–227, 241, 396
Jones, Hank, 426
Jones, Hettie, 409
Jones, "Papa" Jo, 70, 199, 349, 354
Jones, LeRoi. *See* Baraka, Amiri
Jones, Linda, 376
Jones, Quincy, 243
Jones, Sarah, 331
Jones, Taylor, 325
Jones, Thad, 215, 216
Jones, Willie, 281
Jordan, Clifford, 46
Jordan, Steve, 300
Joyce, James, 13, 118, 262, 304

Kain, Gylan, 15
Katz, Dick, 70
Kaufman, Bob, 140, 207, 328–329, 331, 334, 335, 409
Kaufman, Eileen, 409
Keepnews, Orrin, 311, 382, 414
Keepnews, Peter, 123, 388
Kent, George, 249
Kenton, Stan, 424
Kerouac, Jack, 206, 282, 385, 391–392, 428, 429
Kerry, Bob, 309
Kgositsile, "Willie" Keorapetse, 141, 239
Khayyam, Omar, 203, 412
King, Albert, 327
King, B. B., 327
King, Martin Luther, Jr., 137, 262
King, Nancy, 164
King, Nel, 108, 122
King, Woodie, 15
Kirchner, Bill, 76, 286
Kirk, Rahsaan Roland, 359, 404, 407
Kirstein, Jean, 152–153
Kizer, Carolyn, 403
Klee, Paul, 65
Klinkowitz, Jerome, 73, 126
Knees of a Natural Man, 317, 319–320
Knepper, Jimmy, 262,
Knight, Etheridge, 356–357
Kofsky, Frank, 284, 383
Koller, Hans, 278
Komunyakaa, Yusef, 39, 144, *190,* **191–211,** 295, 330, 335, 358, 366, 401; artistic breakthroughs of, 208–209, 210; on *Dutchman,* 209; on Sandy Evans, 203–204; on jazz and color, 205–206; on Bob Kaufman, 207–208; on Jack Kerouac, 206; on Charlie Parker:

dual nature of, 205, 208, and the Midwest, 206, 211, misinformation about, 204, in photographs, 204–205, 206, and race, 209, telegrams sent by, 209, as trickster figure, 207; "Testimony": 192–203, inspiration for, 203–205, 207–208, 209, structure of, 204, 210, voices in, 206, 209
Konitz, Lee, 278
Kral, Irene, 164
Kulchur magazine, 18, 414

Lacy, Frank, 410
Lacy, Henry C., 371
Ladner, Joyce, 324
LaFaro, Scott, 384
Lambert, Dave, 286
Lande, Art, 167
The Last Poets, 15
Lateef, Yusef, 227, 287, 354–355, 412
Leaves of Grass (Whitman), 151–152, 157–161
LeChiusa, Michael John, 90
Led Zeppelin, 390
Lee, Don L. *See* Madhubuti, Haki R.
The Legend of Charlie Parker, 205, 209
Levine, Philip, *212,* **213–229;** "Above Jazz," 228–229; on Pepper Adams, 223–227; on The Bluebird, 215–216, 227; on Bess Bonier, 223–224; on Clifford Brown, 214–215; on Kenny Burrell, 223–227; on Tommy Flanagan, 223–226; on Erroll Garner, 220–221; on Dizzy Gillespie, 222–223; on Barry Harris, 223–224; on Billie Holiday, 218–219; "I Remember Clifford," 214–215; "It Gets to You," 222; on Milt Jackson, 227; on Elvin Jones, 223–227; "On the Corner," 220–221; "One Word," 217–218; on Charlie Parker, 222; on Bud Powell, 227; "Songs," 218–219; on Sonny Stitt, 222–223; on Art Tatum, 220–221, 227; on Lester Young, 216, 217
Lewis, David, 115, 118, 119
Lewis, George, 32
Lewis, John, 109, 127, 223
Lewis, Mel, 110, 127
Lewis, Norman, 46
Lewis, R. W. B., 119
Lieberman, M. M., 105–106
Lieberson, Lorraine Hunt, 164
Liebler, M. L., 331
The Life of Willie "The Lion" Smith, 17
Ligeti, György, 158
Lincoln Center, 8, 11, 90, 124, 168, 246
Lindsay, Vachel, 55
Lion, Alfred, 389
Listen: Gerry Mulligan, 73, 126
Litweiler, John, 125, 183
Living with Jazz, 123–124, 270–274, 285–288
Locke, Alain, 329

Lockwood, Robert, 390
Lomax, Alan, 310, 414
Longhair, Professor, 397
Lorca, Federico García, 188
Lorde, Audre, 46
Lovano, Joe, 187
Lubitsch, Ernst, 120
Luciano, Felipe, 15
Lugg, George, 30
Lunceford, Jimmy, 312
Lush Life, 183
Lutcher, Nellie, 51
Lyle, Curtis, 335
Lytle, Cecil, 155

MacDonald, Julie, 205
Machito, 197–198, 280
Madden, Gail, 72
Madgett, Naomi Long, 243
Madhubuti, Haki R., 230, 231–250, 333, 334, 335, 361, 362; on African American poetry anthologies, 243–244; "Amiri," 237; "Are Black Musicians Serious?," 236–237, 244; and aspirations as trumpeter, 238–240, 246, 250; on Houston Baker, 243–244; on Amiri Baraka, 237, 249–250; on the Black Arts Movement, 238–239, 243, 249; on John Coltrane, 240–242, 248–249; "Don't Cry, Scream," 232–236, 240, 244, 248–249; on family, 244–245; as founder of schools, 241, 242, 244; on jazz literature, 243; on jazz poets, 239–240, 242–243; on mentors: Gwendolyn Brooks, 245, 247, 249, Charles Burroughs and Margaret Burroughs, 242, 245, Hoyt W. Fuller, 245, Dudley Randall, 245–247, Malcolm X, 245; on racism, 236, 238, 241; on Third World Press, 239, 241, 244–246; upbringing of, 238–239
Madhubuti, Dr. Safisha, 244
Mafia, Kesuku, 147–148
Maggin, Donald, 66
Mailer, Norman, 260, 322
Major, Clarence, 242
Majors, Bill, 47
Makatini, Johnny, 46
Makiadi, Franco L., 47
Mardigan, Art, 216
Marie Christine, 90
Marks, Peter, 89
Marley, Bob, 47
Marsalis, Branford, 149
Marsalis, Delfeayo, 149
Marsalis, Ellis, 137
Marsalis, Jason, 137, 149
Marsalis, Wynton, 8, 124, 149, 243, 246
Matisse, Henri, 205

Matthews, William, xiii, xv–xvi, 44, 55, *252*, **253–267**, 401, 423, 428; on *Beneath the Underdog*, 262; on John Coltrane, 265–266; on Eric Dolphy, 265–266; on Duke Ellington, 258; on Stan Getz, 265–266; on Norman Mailer, 260; on Charles Mingus: as band leader, 258–260, 262–263, dual nature of, 262, 265, as mythic figure, 264–265, and pianists in his band, 258–259, 264, and poetry, 261, as tutelary figure, 260, 266–267; "Mingus at The Half Note," 255–256, 263; "Mingus at The Showplace," 254–255, 261, 263; "Mingus in Diaspora," 256–257, 264–265; "Mingus in Shadow," 257, 264; on Dannie Richmond, 259; on translating Horace, 260–261; on writing poetry, 263–264, 267; on Al Young, 261; on Lester Young, 266–267
The Maximus Poems, 388
Maybelle, Big, 52
Mayfield, Irvin, 149
Mays, Walter, 153
McBain, Fiona, 303–304
McBride, Christian, 77
McDonald, Audra, 90, 164
MC-5, 385
McGarity, Lou, 30
McGarry, Kate, 158
McGary, Jimmy, 155
The McGuire Sisters, 301
McKay, Nellie, 329
McKenna, Dave, 296–298
McKinney, Harold, 383
McLean, Jackie, 372, 382
McNeely, Big Jay, 426
McPartland, Jimmy, 300
McPartland, Marian, 70, 300
McPherson, Charles, 412
McRae, Carmen, 426, 427
McShann, Jay "Hootie," 194, 195
McTell, Blind Willie, 304
Medea, 90
Medina, Tony, 331
Melville, Herman, 188
Mendieta, Ana, 47
Metronome, 4–5, 281–282, 291, 382
Mexico City Blues, 206, 429
Meyer, Sheldon, 76, 285–286, 288
Mezzrow, Mezz, 385, 393
Micheline, Jack, 8
Miles: The Autobiography, 180, 183, 243
Milkowski, Bill, 125
Miller, Eddie, 104
Miller, Ethelbert, 335
Miller, Fred, 297
Miller, Glenn, 307
Miller, Henry, 282

The Mills Brothers, 276
Milner, Ron, 14
Mingus, Charles, xiv, xv–xvi, 8, 14, 69–71, 89, 108, 122–123, 154, 183, 254–267, 289–290, 310, 374–375, 403–404, 408, 410, 411, 412, 415, 424
Mingus/Mingus: Two Memoirs, 243, 261, 410
Mister Jelly Roll, 310, 414
Mitchell, Billy, 216
Mitchell, Dwike, 410
Mobley, Hank, 93–94, 426
Modern Jazz Quartet, 259, 303
Mole, Miff, 30, 37–38
Monk, 123, 389
Monk, Nellie, 389
Monk, Thelonious, xv, 8, 44, 46, 77–78, 94, 97, 98, 114, 119, 123, 166, 179, 183, 237, 295, 296, 310, 372–381, 386–396, 397, 405, 407, 420, 426, 430
Monk, T. S. "Tootie," 395
Moody, James, 223
Moore, Dick, 94
Moore, Michael, 156
Mor, Amus, 15, 16
Morello, Joe, 70, 177
Morgan, Herbie, 9
Morgan, Lee, 240
Morgenstern, Dan, xiii, 6, 16, 107, 108, 122, 123, *268,* **269–292**; on Louis Armstrong, 286, 287; on army years, 277–279; on Albert Ayler and Donald Ayler, 287; on Count Basie, 273–274, 286; on Lenny Bruce, 282; on Ornette Coleman, 275; on John Coltrane, 283, 286–287; on Stanley Dance, 280, 283; on Paul Desmond, 271–272, 274; on Duke Ellington, 273, 285; on Bill Evans, 270–271, 274; on Leonard Feather, 277; on Tommy Flanagan, xiii; on Nat Hentoff, 280–281, 290–291; introduction to jazz, 276; on jazz critics, 277, 285, 286, 289–292; on Frank Kofsky, 284; *Living with Jazz,* 270–282, 285–287; on Art Tatum, 279–280; on Bob Thiele, 283–284; upbringing of, 275–277; on Fats Waller, 276; as writer and editor of journals: *Down Beat,* 284–291, *Jazz Journal,* 280–281, 288, *Metronome,* 281–283, 291; on Lester Young, 272–273, 281–282, 286
Morris, Tracie, 331
Morris, Wilber, 9
Morrison, Toni, 325, 331
Morrow, Brad, 308
Morton, Jelly Roll, 310, 414
Mosaic Records, 126, 387
Mosca, Ray, 297
Moss, Ed, 395
Mostel, Zero, 217

Mraz, George, 77
Muhammad, Elijah, 383, 384
Mulligan, Gerry, 59, 62–63, 67, 72–75, 77, 125–126, 426
Murphy, Rose, 51
Murphy, Turk, 303
Murray, Albert, 117–118, 124
Murray, David, 9
Murray, Diedre, 81, 85–88, 95
Murray, Sunny, 10–11
Music: Black White & Blue, 411
Music Is My Mistress, 71–72, 120
Music on My Mind, 17

Naked Lunch, 282
Native Son, 209
Navarro, Fats, 123, 174, 181
Naylor, Genevieve, 304–305
Neal, Harold, 412
Neal, Larry, 15, 46, 242–243, 332, 360, 361
Neal, Mark Anthony, 243
Nelson, David, 15
Nelson, Steve, 187
Neruda, Pablo, 163
The Neville Brothers, 146
New Laurel Review, 143
Newport Jazz Festival, 68, 168, 284, 286, 287, 288
Newton, Huey, 324
Nix, Bern, 51
Nolan, James, 138
The Norton Anthology of African American Literature, 243, 329, 335
Nothing for Tigers, 32
Nuez, Gilberto de La, 47
Nwapa, Flora, 47

Oates, Joyce Carol, 322
O'Brien, Floyd, 30
O'Brien, Father Peter, 305
Odetta, 38
O'Farrell, Marty, 149
O'Hara, Frank, 18, 164, 180
Oliver, Joe "King," 121
Olson, Charles, 385, 388
On the Road, 385
Onassis, Jackie, 306, 308
O'Neal, Hank, *294,* **295–314**; on Berenice Abbott, 304–305, 306, 308–309; on Louis Armstrong, 303; on Whitney Balliett, 306; *The Best of Jazz: Noted Writers on Great Jazz Records,* 306–307; on Hayden Carruth, 308–309; on Chiaroscuro Records, 298, 311–314; and CIA experience, 296, 299–300, 309; *Eddie Condon's Scrapbook of Jazz,* 304–305, 313; on Otis Ferguson, 305–306; on

Allen Ginsberg, 307–308; introduction to jazz, 298–302; on jazz as common ground, 302; on jazz critics, 305–307; on jazz literature, 308–312; on JazzSpeak and oral traditions, 311–314; on "Mack the Knife," 303; on Dave McKenna, 296–298; on record producers: George Avakian, 300, 301, 302–303, Ahmet Ertegun, 300, 304, Nesuhi Ertegun, 300, 302–303, 307, John Hammond, 300, 306, Bob Thiele, 302, George Wein, 302; on Zoot Sims, 296–298, 312–313
O'Neal, Shelly, 302
The Organizer, 14, 81, 91–92
Ornette Coleman: A Harmolodic Life, 183
Ortiz, Simon, 331
Ory, Kid, 30
Osbey, Brenda Marie, 138–139
The Other America, 324
Otis, Johnny, 51
Otis Ferguson Reader, 306
The Oxford Companion to Jazz, 76–77, 286

Page, Hot Lips, 27
Palmer, Robert, 390
Panassié, Hugues, 310
Parker, Chan, 200, 202, 209, 410
Parker, Charlie "Bird," xiv, 2, 8, 16, 18, 70, 72, 103, 110–111, 114, 124, 173, 174, 191–211, 215, 221, 227, 243, 280, 286, 313–314, 329, 336, 373–376, 387, 390, 391–393, 397, 409, 410, 411, 418, 420, 421–422, 423, 424, 431
Parker, John "Ikey," 196–197, 209
Parker, Rebecca, 111
Parlan, Horace, 259
Patchen, Kenneth, 14–15, 137, 412, 428
Paterson, 388
Patterson, Raymond R., 55, 317, 331–333
Paudras, Francis, 389
Payne, Cecil, 223
Payton, Walter, 135
p'Bitek, Okot, 46
Peebles, Melvin Von, 247
Peña, Ralph, 428
Penny, Gerald, 355
Pepper, Art, xiv, 72, 122, 183
Perkins, Bill, 297
Peterson, Oscar, 154, 156, 426
Pettiford, Oscar, 69, 77
Pfister, Professor Arturo, 140
Phillips, Little Esther, 46, 52
Piazza, Tom, 307
Picasso, Pablo, 13, 65, 157, 205
The Pictorial History of Jazz, 311
Pictures from the Gone World, 385
Pissstained Stairs and the Monkey Man's Wares, 50
Play Ebony, Play Ivory, 317

Plumpp, Sterling, 55, 239, 243, 328, 329, 332, 333
Poche, Rodger, 147
Poems cited: "About Flyin' Home" (Cortez), 44–45, 49–50, 51; "Above Jazz" (Harper), 228–229; "After the Dazzle of Day" (Whitman), 158, 161; "After the End of the World" (Jauss), 180; "Amiri" (Madhubuti), 237; "The Angels of Detroit" (Levine), 215; "April in Paris" (Sinclair), 394; "April in Paris" (Young), 394; "Asylum" (Carruth), 33; "At the Close of Day" (Whitman), 164, 165, 166; "Babe Stoval on a Bare Stage" (Grue), 130–131, 137; "Being Colored" (Baraka), 9; "Billie" (Young), 401; "Black Art" (Baraka), 3–4, 10; "Black Orchid" (Jauss), 173–175, 180–181, 184; "bloomdido" (Sinclair), 391; "Blues" (Sanchez), 344, 358–359; "Blues for Charlie Christian" (Zimmer), 422; "Blues to You" (Sinclair), 396; "brilliant corners" (Sinclair), 391–392; "Brutes" (Jauss), 171, 175, 182; "Bud Powell, Paris, 1959" (Matthews), 55; "Bumblebee, You Saw Big Mama" (Cortez), 47–49, 51; "But Bird" (Zimmer), 421–422, 431; "carolina moon" (Sinclair), 379, 386, 391; "Chazz" (Baraka), 9; "a/coltrane/poem" (Sanchez), 340–344, 352–353, 358; "The Coming of John" (Mor), 15; "Contra Mortem" (Carruth), 33; "The Day Lady Died" (O'Hara), 180; "Dear John, Dear Coltrane" (Harper), 242; "Dear Old Stockholm" (Young), 401; "Diminuendo and Crescendo in Blue" (Jauss), 182, 183–184; "Dog" (Ferlinghetti), 428; "Don't Cry, Scream" (Madhubuti), 232–236, 240, 244, 248–249; "The Duke Ellington Dream" (Zimmer), 419–420, 422, 425; "Ellingtonia" (Baraka), 9; "The Empress of the Blues" (Hayden), 52; "The Evening News: A Letter to Nina Simone" (Osbey), 138–139; "Everywhere Drums" (Cortez), 53; "Freedom and Discipline" (Carruth), 32–33; "Gratitude" (Eady), 92; "The Guitars I Used to Know" (Cortez), 51; "Hank Mobley's" (Eady), 93–94; "The Hatchet" (Jauss), 183; "Hymn of Fire" (Jauss), 176, 186; "I Remember Clifford" (Levine), 214–215; "I See Chano Pozo" (Cortez), 53; "i surrender, dear" (Sinclair), 379–381, 392; "If the Drum Is a Woman" (Cortez), 53; "Improvisation," see "Middle Passage"; "In That Session" (Carruth), 28–29, 35; "In the Garden" (Grue), 133–134, 141; "In Walked Bud" (Baraka), 392; "in walked bud" (Sinclair), 372–376, 392–393; "It Gets to You" (Levine), 222; "I've Got Your Picture" (Salter), 162–163; "Jungle Strut" (Young), 401; "King" (Grue), 137; "Lang-

ston Blues" (Randall), 246; "Lester Leaps In" (Young), 401; "Listening to Sonny Rollins at the Five-Spot" (Blackburn), 363; "Lundi Gras" (Grue), 134–136; "Ma Rainey" (Brown), 52, 222; "Magic Johnson" (Troupe), 322; "The Master Musicians of Joujouka" (Jauss), 179, 184; "Middle Passage" (Sanchez), 356, 363, 367, 368; "A Miles Davis Trumpet" (Cortez), 49; "Mingus at The Half Note" (Matthews), 255–256, 263; "Mingus at The Showplace" (Matthews), 254–255, 261, 263; "Mingus in Diaspora" (Matthews), 256–257, 264–265; "Mingus in Shadow" (Matthews), xv–xvi, 257, 263–264; "Mordecai Dying to Jazz" (Zimmer), 422; "Mort aux Belges!" (Carruth), 29, 34, 35; "The Mystic Trumpeter" (Whitman), 160–161; "A Negro Love Song" (Dunbar), 352; "Now and Then" (Levine), 213; "O Captain, My Captain" (Whitman), 159; "On the Beach at Night Alone" (Whitman), 161, 165; "On the Corner" (Levine), 220–221; "One Word" (Levine), 217–218; "Ornithology" (Hull), 181; "Paragraphs" (Carruth), 26–28, 33, 34; "Photo of Dexter Gordon, About to Solo, 1965" (Eady), 93; "Photo of Max Roach Solo, 1964" (Eady), 93; "Photo of Miles Davis at Lennies-on-the-Turnpike, 1968" (Eady), 93; "A Poem for Ella Fitzgerald" (Sanchez), 346–349, 359, 364; "Requiem" (Jauss), 181; "'round about midnight" (Sinclair), 376–379, 393; "Safe Subjects" (Komunyakaa), 208–209; "Sequences" (Sanchez), 359; "The Sheets of Sound" (Eady), 92, 97; "Sister's Voice (read to ''Round Midnight')" (Sanchez), 344–346; "Sitting with Lester Young" (Zimmer), 418–419, 422, 424–425, 429; "The Sleepers" (Whitman), 161; "Snapshots" (Salter), 160; "Song of Myself" (Whitman), 152, 159, 160–161; "Songs" (Levine), 218–219; "Spirit That Form'd This Scene" (Whitman), 161, 165; "States of Motion" (Cortez), 46–47, 50, 51; "Street Life Meditation" (Grue), 143; "Suburban Eyes" (Sinclair), 387; "A Supermarket in California" (Ginsberg), 152; "Terminal" (Grue), 143; "Testimony" (Komunyakaa), 191–211; "Thelonious" (Eady), 94; "Thou Shalt Not Kill" (Rexroth), 15; "Traps" (Jauss), 172–173, 177, 187–188; "Tuesday Night on Frenchmen Street" (Grue), 131–133; "239th Chorus" (Kerouac), 206; "Unrelenting Flood" (Matthews), 254; "We're Tight, Soul-Tight—Like Lincolnites" (Redman), 323; "What a Wonder Among the Instruments Is the Walloping Tramboone!" (Carruth), 25, 30–31, 36–37; "What I Heard at the Close of the Day" (Whitman), 156–

157; "When Lilacs Last in the Dooryard Bloom'd" (Whitman), 159; "The Wrong Turn" (Levine), 225–227; "Yardbird's Skull" (Dodson), 335; "Zimmer Imagines Heaven" (Zimmer), 425; "Zimmer's Last Gig" (Zimmer), 420–421, 422, 430–431

The Poetry Blues, xvi
Pop magazine, 284
Pope, Odean, 359–360, 367–369
Porter, Art, Jr., 185
Porter, Lewis, 125
Potter, Chris, 187
Pound, Ezra, 329, 332, 388
Powell, Bud, 8, 9, 70–71, 167, 173, 223, 227, 258, 372–376, 378, 389, 392–393, 410, 420, 424, 426
"Powerhouse," 139
Price, Robert Earl, 335
Price, Sammy, 52
Priestly, Brian, 264

Raeburn, Ben, 306–307
Rainey, Gertrude "Ma," 52, 222
Raise Up Off Me, 121–122
Randall, Dudley, 242, 245, 246, 247, 357
Raney, Jimmy, 64–65
Ratliff, Ben, 124–125
Ravelli, Pauline, 283–284
Ray, Shreela, 92
Really the Blues, 385
A Recent Killing, 13
The Record Changer, 6
Redman, Dewey, 301
Redmond, Eugene B., 242, 243, *316,* **317–336**, 357–358; advice to scholars, 318–319, 328; on African American literature anthologies, 329, 335; on Amiri Baraka, 318–319, 333–334; on the Black Arts Movement, 333; on the blues, meanings of, 319, 327–328; on blues and jazz poets, 328–333; on Sterling Brown, 328; on Jayne Cortez, 334; *Drumvoices,* 318–319, 320, 325–330, 333–336; on Henry Dumas, 319–320, 325, 330–331; on Katherine Dunham, 326–327; on Cornelius Eady, 322; education and upbringing of, 321–325; on Sam Greenlee, 328, 330, 334–335; on Robert Hayden, 319, 328–329; on Bob Kaufman, 328–329; on Yusef Komunyakaa, 330; on Haki Madhubuti, 333–334; on Raymond Patterson, 331–333; on Sterling Plumpp, 329; on Ishmael Reed, 334; on Leon Thomas, 323; on Emmett Till, 323; on Quincy Troupe, 322, 331
Reed, Ishmael, 242, 334, 411
Reed, Jimmy, 382
Reinhardt, Django, 276, 302
Reisner, Robert, 205, 209

Reluctantly, 37
Rexroth, Kenneth, 14–15, 38, 137, 428, 429
Rich, Buddy, 70, 172–173, 177, 178, 187–188,
    273–274
Richard, Little, 177, 235, 381
Richmond, Dannie, 71, 255 [as "Danny"], 259
Riley, Ben, 395
Rivers, Larry, 18
Rivers, Sam, 53
Roach, Max, 93, 196, 349, 353–354, 359, 374
Robeson, Paul, 362–363
Rodgers, Carolyn, 239
Rodney, Red, 183
The Rolling Stones, 177, 188, 304
Rollins, Sonny, 105, 286–287, 372, 382
Rose, Wally, 310
Rosolino, Frank, 227, 403, 408
Rouse, Charlie, 395, 430
Rowles, Jimmy, 75–76, 164
Roy, Darlene, 335
Ruffins, Kermit, 134–135, 138
Rugolo, Pete, 310
Running Man, 81, 82–84, 86, 87–89, 92, 94–96
Rushton, Joe, 302
Russell, George, 75
Russell, Pee Wee, 28, 68
Russell, Ross, 183, 205

Sahl, Mort, 307
Salaam, Kalamu ya, 140, 239, 242, 243, 333–334
Salter, Mary Jo, 160, 162–163, 168
Samson and Delilah, 301, 413
Sanchez, Mungu, 339–340
Sanchez, Sonia, 239, 242, 331, *338,* **339–369**;
    on African American literature antholo-
    gies, 358; on Amiri Baraka, 357, 360–361;
    on the Black Arts Movement, 360–363; on
    Paul Blackburn, 363–364; "blues," 344; on
    the *cante jondo,* 355–356; "a/coltrane/poem,"
    340–344, 352–353; *Does Your House Have Li-
    ons?,* 355, 359, 361, 369; education and up-
    bringing of, 349–352, 365–366; on Etheridge
    Knight, 356–357; on Yusef Lateef, 354–355;
    on performing, 352–354, 358, 360–362, 367–
    369; "A Poem for Ella Fitzgerald," 346–349,
    364; on Odean Pope, 359–360, 367–369; on
    racism, 350–351; on Max Roach, 353–354;
    on Archie Shepp, 353–354; "Sister's Voice,"
    344–346; on teaching, 362, 365–367; on
    Sarah Vaughan, 364–365; *Wounded in the
    House of a Friend,* 355, 359, 367; on writ-
    ing, 355
Sanders, Ed, 390–391
Sanders, Pharoah, 10, 11, 155, 242, 287,
    382, 396
Santoro, Gene, 124
Sartre, Jean Paul, 110–111, 174

Satchmo, 102–103, 110–111
Saxton, Jeff, 406
Schaap, Phil, 205
The Schomburg Center for Research in Black
    Culture, 350–352
Schuller, Gunther, 124, 156
Schwartz, Delmore, 39
Scott, Tony, 68
Scott-Heron, Gil, 240
Scrambled Eggs & Whiskey, 35
The Second Set, 317
*Setting the Tempo: Fifty Years of Great Liner
    Notes,* 307
Seven Guitars, 90
Seymour, Gene, 124
Shahn, Ben, 307
Shange, Ntozake, 242, 331
Shapiro, Nat, 312
Shaw, Artie, 117, 301
Sheed, Wilfrid, xii
Shepp, Archie, 242, 243, 282, 287, 353–354, 382
Shines, Johnny, 390
Shining Trumpets, 311
Shorter, Wayne, 166
Sickler, Don, 395
Side Man, 89–90
Simon, Joe, 403
Simone, Nina, 138–139, 243
Simpkins, C. O., 183, 243
Sims, Louise, 298, 312–313
Sims, Zoot, 59, 65, 73, 76, 286, 296–298,
    312–313
Sinatra, Frank, 105, 321
Sinclair, John, 138, 140, *370,* **371–398**; on Amiri
    Baraka, 383, 385, 392; "carolina moon," 379,
    386, 391; on Ornette Coleman, 382; on John
    Coltrane, 382, 383, 395–396; on drugs, 385,
    391, 393, 396; education and upbringing
    of, 381–382; on Allen Ginsberg, 386; "i sur-
    render, dear," 379–381, 392; "in walked bud,"
    372–376, 392–393; on Eddie Jefferson, 393–
    394; literary influences on, 383, 385–386,
    388, 390–392; on literary jazz sources, 389–
    391; on the necessity of music, 397–398; on
    racial politics, 383–385; "'round about mid-
    night," 376–379, 393; on Ed Sanders, 390–
    391; on writing, 386–393; on Al Young, 390
*Sitting In: Selected Writings on Jazz, Blues, and
    Related Topics,* 26, 38–39, 308, 430
The Skin Game, 17
Skin Trouble, 12
The Sleeping Beauty, 33
Slim, Lightnin', 235
Slim, Sunnyland, 390
Smith, Bessie, 3, 52, 97–98, 328, 357
Smith, Charles Edward, 277
Smith, Henry "Buster," 199

Smith, Johnny, 426
Smith, Michael, 47
Smith, Willie, 431
Smith, Willie "The Lion," 17
Snakes, 414
Snitzer, Herb, 282
The Snowflakes, 126
So What: The Life of Miles Davis, 119
Solomon, Dave, 282–283
Somewhere in Advance of Nowhere, 49
Sondheim, Stephen, 160
Sordoni, Andrew, 296, 312
Soul on Ice, 362
Souls of Black Folk, 351
Southern Road, 7
Souza, Luciana, 163
Spellman, A. B., 7, 242, 282, 383, 414
The Spook Who Sat By the Door, 328
St. John, Primus, 335
Stan Getz: A Life in Jazz, 66
Stearns, Marshall, 310
Steele, Shelby, 324
Steinbeck, John, 305, 407–408
Stewart, Rex, 72, 419
Stitt, Sonny, 70, 174, 222, 289
The Story of Jazz, 310
Straight, No Chaser, 389
Straight Life: The Story of Art Pepper, xiv, 72,
  122, 183
Straub, Peter, xiii
Stravinsky, Igor, 14, 157
Strayhorn, Billy, 9, 10, 183, 258
Strouse, Jean, 115
Sun Ra, 10, 46, 50, 180, 382, 396
Sundiata, Sekou, 15–16, 331
Sunny's Time Now!, 10–11
A Superb Obituary, 324
Swann, Roberta, 109
Szwed, John, 119

Taking the Blues Back Home, 51, 54
Tate, Buddy, 305
Tatum, Art, 105, 193, 208, 220–221, 223, 227,
  254, 279–280, 349
Taylor, Cecil, 11, 126, 155, 382, 389
Taylor, Creed, 283
Taylor, J. R., 124
Taylor, John, 167
Teagarden, Jack, 30
Tennessee Williams Festival, 371, 394
Terkel, Studs, 413
Terry, Clark, 310, 312, 313
Terry, Sonny, 327
Tesh, John, 167
Un Théâtre de Situations, 110
Their Eyes Were Watching God, 351
thelonious: a book of monk, 390–393

Thelonious Monk: His Life and Music, 389
The Thelonious Monk Reader, 389
Thiam, Mor, 325
Thiele, Bob, 283–284, 302
Thieves of Paradise, 210
Thigpen, Ben, 322
Third World Press, 231, 239, 241, 242, 244, 245
Thomas, Amos Leon, 323
Thomas, Dylan, 15, 223, 424
Thomas, Lorenzo, 335
Thoreau, Henry David, 188
Thornhill, Claude, 126
Thornton, Clifford, 53
Thornton, Willie Mae "Big Mama," 46, 47–49,
  51–52, 323
Threadgill, Henry, 88
Till, Emmett, 323
Time & Money, 263–264
Tizol, Juan, 71, 258
To Be or Not to Bop, 71, 122
Tolson, Melvin, 327, 332, 334
Tosh, Peter, 47
Touré, Askia, 15, 242–243, 335
Traill, Sinclair, 281
Trains and Other Intrusions, 137
Treadwell, Oscar, 153–154
Tristano, Lennie, 310
Troupe, Quincy, 242, 243, 322, 328, 331, 332,
  334, 335, 357
Tucker, Mark, 123
Turner, Darwin T., 249
Tyler, Charles, 46
Tynan, John, 383
Tyner, McCoy, 167, 241

Ulanov, Barry, 112
Understanding the New Black Poetry, xv, 321
Up from Slavery, 351
Upshaw, Dawn, 164
U'Tamsi, Tchikaya, 46

Varese, Edgard, 201
Vaughan, Sarah, 17, 47, 127, 156, 310, 364–365
Vechten, Carl Van, 39
Vega, Janine Pommy, 409
Vesey, Paul. *See* Allen, Samuel
Victims of the Latest Dance Craze, 92
The Village Vanguard, 69, 108, 162, 168
Visions of Jazz, 103–104, 285

Wadud, Abdul, 38
Waits, Nasheet, 165
Waldman, Anne, 409
Walker, Evan, 47
Walker, Margaret, 319, 328, 330
Waller, Thomas "Fats," 17, 276, 318
Wallington, George, 287

Walter, Little, 391
Walton, Ortiz, 411
Ward, Geoffrey, 118
Ware, Wilbur, 53, 68
Washington, Booker T., 351
Waters, Muddy, 323, 327, 382, 390, 397, 398
W. E. B. Du Bois, 115, 119
We a BaddDDD People, 352
We Walk the Way of the New World, 244
Weathersby, Carl, 51
Webb, Chick, 31
Webster, Ben "Brute," 171, 175, 182, 195, 258,
    419, 426
Wein, George, 279, 302, 395
Wein, Joyce, 302
Wells, Dickie, 30
Welty, Eudora, 139
Werner, Craig, 334
West, Cornell, 244
West, Dwight, 9
West, Harold Doc, 204
Wettling, George, 68, 279
What the Music Said, 243
Wheeler, Kenny, 166
White, Dr. Michael, 144
Whitman, Walt, 151–152, 156–161, 164–
    166, 188
Wilber, Bob, 305
Wilder, Joe, 291
Williams, Chris, 203–204, 206, 208
Williams, Cootie, 378, 419
Williams, Joe, 321
Williams, Kelvyn, 124
Williams, Martin, 6, 16, 67, 107, 124, 286
Williams, Mary Lou, 28, 51, 305, 313
Williams, Saul, 331
Williams, Sherley Anne, 242–243
Williams, William Carlos, 39, 388
Willis, Chuck, 140
Wilmer, Valerie, 243
Wilson, August, 14, 81, 90
Wilson, Edmund, 106, 118
Wilson, John S., 108, 289–290
Wilson, Nancy, 243
Wilson, Teddy, 218, 426
Winstone, Norma, 158
W;t, 89
Wolpe, Stefan, 201
Women of the Beat Generation, 409
Wonder, Stevie, 155
Wondisford, Diane, 85
Woodly, Abe, 216
Woods, Phil, 314
World Saxophone Quartet, 325

Wounded in the House of a Friend, 355, 367
Wright, Jay, 319, 335
Wright, Richard, 209, 267

X, Malcolm, 10, 245, 247, 262, 325, 383
X, Marvin, 360

Yeats, William Butler, 264, 329
Yevtuschenko, Yevgeny, 240
Yogananda, Paramahansa, 403
You Don't Look Like a Musician, 68
You Don't Miss Your Water: play, 81, 85, 86,
    87, 88, 89; poetry collection, 81, 85, 87,
    88, 93
You Just Fight for Your Life, 114
Young, Al, 55, 92–93, 96, 242, 243, 261,
    328, 334, 335, 371, 394, *400,* **401–415**;
    on Amiri Baraka, 414; on Big Bill Broonzy,
    413; *Drowning in the Sea of Love,* 402–410,
    414–415; education and upbringing of, 410–
    413; on the eternal spirits of jazz musicians,
    409–410, 415; "Gifts and Messages," 404;
    on Bob Kaufman, 409; on Rahsaan Roland
    Kirk, 404; on Charles Mingus, 403–404, 408,
    411–412, 415; on Thelonious Monk, 405,
    407; on the New York art scene, 411–412,
    414; "Nostalgia in Times Square," 403; "Pen-
    nies from Heaven," 403; on poetry and jazz
    in performance, 405–406; on racial politics,
    411, 412–413; on Frank Rosolino, 403, 408;
    "Ruby My Dear," 405, 407–408; on writing,
    406–410, 414–415
Young, Lester "Prez," 65, 119, 120, 199, 216–
    218, 227, 258, 266–267, 272–273, 280, 281–
    282, 286, 290, 310, 389, 390, 418–419, 424–
    425, 426
Young, Trummy, 30

Zimmer, Paul, 39, 401, *416,* **417–432**; on Count
    Basie, 432; "But Bird," 421–422, 431; on
    Hayden Carruth, 430; "The Duke Ellington
    Dream," 419–420, 425; on Michael Harper,
    428–429; introduction to jazz, 423–424; on
    jazz as healing source, 431–432; on jazz po-
    ets, 428–429; on Thelonious Monk, 430; on
    Charlie Parker, 431; on poetry and jazz in
    performance, 428–429; "Sitting with Lester
    Young," 418–419, 424–425; on writing jazz
    poems, 423, 426–427; on Lester Young, 418–
    419, 424–425, 426; "Zimmer's Last Gig,"
    420–421, 430–431
Zoo Story, 12–13
Zubena, Sister, 325
Zu-Bolten, Ahmos, 135, 141–142, 331

Sascha Feinstein won the Hayden Carruth Award for his poetry collection, *Misterioso*. His other books include *Jazz Poetry: From the 1920s to the Present*. He is Professor of English at Lycoming College, where he co-directs the Creative Writing Program and edits *Brilliant Corners: A Journal of Jazz & Literature*.

Milton Keynes UK
Ingram Content Group UK Ltd.
UKHW020945110724
445408UK00005B/199